THE PSYCHOLOGY

OF

STALKING

*This book is
dedicated
to my family.*

THE PSYCHOLOGY
OF
STALKING

Clinical and Forensic Perspectives

Edited by

J. Reid Meloy

ACADEMIC PRESS

An Imprint of Elsevier

Amsterdam   Boston   Heidelberg   London   New York   Oxford   Paris   San Diego
San Francisco   Singapore   Sydney   Tokyo

Front cover: Edvard Munch, *Moonlight*, 1893.
Photo by J. Lathion.
© Nasjonalgalleriet

This book is printed on acid-free paper.

Academic Press
An imprint of Elsevier
525 B Street, Suite 1900, San Diego, California 92101-4495, USA
http://www.academicpress.com

Academic Press
84 Theobalds Road, London WC1X 8RR, UK
http://www.academicpress.com

Library of Congress Catalog Card Number: 98-84369

International Standard Book Number: 0-12-490560-9 (casebound)
International Standard Book Number: 0-12-490561-7 (paperback)

PRINTED IN THE UNITED STATES OF AMERICA
04   05   06   07   MM   9   8   7   6

"*The Psychology of Stalking* is a comprehensive, up to date, scholarly review that includes everything from Shakespeare's stalking sonnets to cyberstalking. It provides a wealth of useful information. The book is must reading for law enforcement and mental health professionals that deal with stalkers."

Phillip J. Resnick, M.D.
Director of Forensic Psychiatry
Case Western Reserve University

"J. Reid Meloy and his colleagues have blended clinical insight, scientific rigor, and legal precision to produce the one indispensable book on stalking. Encyclopedic in coverage and gracefully written, this work will have enormous influence on practice, policy, and research. With the publication of *The Psychology of Stalking: Clinical and Forensic Perspectives,* the study of stalking has come of age."

John Monahan, Ph.D.
University of Virginia School of Law

It is the cause, it is the cause, my
  soul,—
Let me not name it to you, you chaste
  stars!—
It is the cause.—Yet I'll not shed her blood;
Nor scar that whiter skin of hers than snow,
And smooth as monumental alabaster.
Yet she must die, else she'll betray more
  men.
Put out the light, and then put out the light:
If I quench thee, thou flaming minister,
I can again thy former light restore,
Should I repent me:—but once put out thy light,
Thou cunning'st pattern of excelling nature,
I know not where is that Promethean heat
That can thy light relume. When I have
  pluck'd thy rose,
I cannot give it vital growth again,
It needs must wither:—I'll smell it on the
  tree.—
O balmy breath, that dost almost persuade
Justice to break her sword!—One more, one
  more.—
Be thus when thou art dead, and I will kill thee,
And love thee after.—One more, and that's
  the last:
So sweet was ne'er so fatal. I must weep,
But they are cruel tears: this sorrow's heavenly;
It strikes where it doth love.
        Othello, Act V, Scene II

CONTENTS

CHAPTER 3
Developmental and Social Antecedents of Stalking
Kristine K. Kienlen

CHAPTER 4
Psychiatric Diagnosis and the Offender–Victim Typology of Stalking
Michael A. Zona, Russell E. Palarea, and John C. Lane, Jr.

CHAPTER 7
Stalking and Domestic Violence
Lenore E. Walker and J. Reid Meloy

CHAPTER 8
The Stalking of Clinicians by Their Patients
John R. Lion and Jeremy A. Herschler

CHAPTER 9

Preventing Attacks on Public Officials and Public Figures: A Secret Service Perspective

Robert A. Fein and Bryan Vossekuil

CHAPTER 10

De Clérambault On-Line: A Survey of Erotomania and Stalking from the Old World to the World Wide Web

Robert Lloyd-Goldstein

CHAPTER 11

Cultural Factors in Erotomania and Obsessional Following

Judith Meyers

CHAPTER 12

False Victimization Syndromes in Stalking

Kris Mohandie, Chris Hatcher, and Douglas Raymond

CHAPTER 13

Stalking, Erotomania, and the Tarasoff Cases

Glenn S. Lipson and Mark J. Mills

CHAPTER 14

Applying Functional Analysis to Stalking Behavior

Darrah Westrup

CHAPTER 15
Threat Management of Stalking Cases
Stephen G. White and James S. Cawood

CONTRIBUTORS

The numbers in parentheses indicate the pages on which the authors' contributions begin.

James Cawood, CPP (295), Principal, Protective Solutions, Inc., and Factor One, Inc.

Robert A. Fein, Ph.D. (175), consulting psychologist to the United States Secret Service and Visiting Fellow (1992–1996), National Institute of Justice

Doris M. Hall, Ph.D. (113), Assistant Professor, Department of Criminal Justice, California State University, Bakersfield

Chris Hatcher, Ph.D. (225), President, National Assessment Services, and Clinical Professor of Psychology, University of California, San Francisco

Jeremy H. Herschler, M.D. (163), Addictions Fellow, University of Maryland School of Medicine

Kristine K. Kienlen, Psy.D. (51), Clinical and Forensic Psychologist, Minnesota Security Hospital, St. Peter, Minnesota

John C. Lane, Jr., M.P.A. (69), Principal, Omega Threat Management Group, Inc.

John R. Lion, M.D. (163), Clinical Professor of Psychiatry, University of Maryland School of Medicine

Glenn S. Lipson, Ph.D. (257), Principal, Lipson & Berlin, Inc., and Diplomate in Forensic Psychology, American Board of Professional Psychology

Robert Lloyd-Goldstein, M.D., J.D. (193), Director, Legal Issues in the Practice of Psychiatry Program, Department of Psychiatry, College of Physicians and Surgeons, Columbia University

J. Reid Meloy, Ph.D. (1,139), Associate Clinical Professor of Psychiatry, University of California, San Diego, and Adjunct Professor, University of San Diego School of Law

Judith Meyers, Psy.D. (213), Assistant Clinical Professor of Psychiatry, University of California, San Diego

Mark J. Mills, J.D., M.D. (257), Clinical Professor of Psychiatry, Departments of Psychiatry at UCLA, Georgetown University, and New York Medical College, St. Vincent's Hospital, and Principal, Forensic Sciences Medical Group, Washington, D.C.

Kris Mohandie, Ph.D. (225), Police Psychologist, Los Angeles Police Department, and Senior Risk Assessment Professional, National Assessment Services

Russell Palarea, M.A. (69), clinical psychology doctoral candidate, University of Nebraska-Lincoln

Douglas Raymond (225), Detective, Threat Management Unit, Los Angeles Police Department

Rhonda Saunders, J.D. (25), Deputy District Attorney and Head, Stalking and Threat Assessment Team

Glen D. Skoler, Ph.D. (85), Clinical and Forensic Psychologist, Washington, D.C., metropolitan area

Bryan Vossekuil (175), Assistant Special Agent in Charge, United States Secret Service

Lenore Walker, Ed.D. (139), Executive Director of the Domestic Violence Institute, Denver, Colorado

Darrah Westrup, M.A. (275), clinical psychology doctoral candidate, West Virginia University

Stephen G. White, Ph.D. (295), President, Work Trauma Services, Inc., and Assistant Clinical Professor, Department of Psychiatry, University of California, San Francisco

Michael A. Zona, M.D. (69), Diplomate of the American Board of Psychiatry and Neurology, and Principal, Omega Threat Management Group, Inc.

PREFACE

Stalking is an old behavior, but a new crime. Shakespeare captured certain aspects of it in the obsessive and murderous thoughts of Othello. Louisa May Alcott, an ardent believer in women's rights, wrote a novel about stalking in 1866, *A Long Fatal Love Chase,* which remained undiscovered and unpublished for over a century. And our American cinema has produced a plethora of stalking films following the artistic benchmark "Play Misty for Me," acted and directed by a young man named Clint Eastwood.

Public fascination and dramatic portrayal of stalking have far outstripped our scientific understanding of this behavior—until now. *The Psychology of Stalking: Clinical and Forensic Perspectives* is, to my knowledge, the first scholarly book on the subject, a compilation of the writings of the best minds that I could find. Each of the contributors has chosen to investigate this dark and compelling aspect of human psychopathology and has produced clear and, in some cases, remarkable results.

This book is organized in such a manner that all facets of stalking are addressed: who stalks, why they stalk, what they do when they stalk, how dangerous they are, and the successful risk management of stalking cases. Although the book is filled with empirical data, I also asked each contributor to write a *thinking* chapter. In this context, they have made masterful attempts to address difficult technical problems—weapons use, threat assessment, psychodynamics, restraining orders, third parties, prosecutorial discretion, and situational triggers, to name a few—and have innovatively explored new ideas and findings. These latter writings represent some of the most exciting material in the book: early attachment disruption and recent losses that may precipitate stalking, false victimization syndrome, acculturation problems and stalking, threats and attacks on public officials, the myths and archetypes of stalking, functional (behavioral) analysis and stalking case management, and cyberstalking.

I hope this scholarly endeavor accomplishes what I set out to do: to clarify and refine what we currently know about stalking and to point directions for future research in this most intriguing area of abnormal psychology. Perhaps then we can navigate an objective, safe, and wise course through the hidden and shifting shoals of this Cape Fear.

J. Reid Meloy

CHAPTER 1

The Psychology of Stalking

J. Reid Meloy, Ph.D.

When Diana, Princess of Wales, was killed in an automobile accident on August 31, 1997, I mourned her death. But I was not alone. Millions of others grieved at the loss of what they felt to be a personal relationship with a woman they had never met. They had cherished her in fantasy, and perhaps identified with both her gifts—her capacity to openly express affection, her beauty, and her ability to confront injustice and human suffering—and her vulnerabilities—her failed relationships with men, her bouts with depression and bulimia, and her loneliness. They became a part of her life by bearing witness to her death. But they did not know her personally, and she did not know them.

Recognizing the force of fantasy as a central component of intense emotion and inexplicable behavior (Person, 1995) is the first step in understanding the psychology of stalking. Moreover, the photographers who were pursuing Princess Diana at the time of her death, and who continued to take photographs of her and her fatally injured companions in the severely damaged Mercedes Benz S280, have been referred to as *stalkerazzi:* tenacious pursuers seeking proximity to a person who has no desire, at least some of the time, to be photographed. But to what end? To sell images for a high price to the tabloid media for the purpose of visually communicating to the public the private moments of a celebrity life that can only be linked to in fantasy: "If I can see her privately, perhaps I can come to know her intimately, to be with her in fantasy, and to perhaps be more like her. Then she may know me." The narcissistic link is forged in the mind of the follower and admirer.

The Psychology of Stalking: Clinical and Forensic Perspectives

Princess Diana had, in fact, been stalked by others for different reasons. Several years ago a British physician who evidenced symptoms of erotomania stalked her incessantly, wishing only to save her from the nefarious motives of the Royal Family. When I spoke in London to an audience of mental health and law enforcement professionals at the Tavistock Clinic in 1996, one of Scotland Yard's finest said to me that there wasn't much they could do to "nick that bloke." The situation was rectified the next year when Britain legislated its first stalking law, the Protection from Harassment Act (s.3[9]; the Act received Royal Assent on March 21, 1997).

DEFINITIONS

Stalking is a crime involving acts of pursuit of an individual over time that are threatening and potentially dangerous. To stalk, in Webster's (1990) definition, is "to progress in an ominous, silent manner." Legal definitions of stalking vary from state to state, but generally have three elements to them: (1) a pattern (course of conduct) of behavioral intrusion upon another person that is unwanted; (2) an implicit or explicit threat that is evidenced in the pattern of behavioral intrusion; and (3) as a result of these behavioral intrusions, the person who is threatened experiences reasonable fear.[1] In other words, stalking is "the willful, malicious, and repeated following and harassing of another person that threatens his or her safety" (Meloy & Gothard, 1995, p. 258). The most common prohibited specific act in stalking statutes is to pursue or follow (National Institute of Justice, 1996), and generally the victim has to know she is being stalked in order for someone stalking to be criminally prosecuted. There are now explicit stalking laws in all 50 states and the District of Columbia; and at the federal level, the crime of stalking was signed into law in 1996 as part of the Violence Against Women Act (Title IV of the Violent Crime Control and Law Enforcement Act of 1994, Public Law 103-322). Stalking laws in the United States have survived most constitutional challenges (National Institute of Justice, 1996);[2] and Canada has a federal stalking law, which it labels criminal harassment (Section 264 of the Criminal Code of Canada, proclaimed August 1, 1993).

Clinical definitions of stalking likewise vary, but tend to be more easily operationalized and measurable than legal definitions. We coined the term *obsessional following* as a clinical corollary of stalking and drew from Zona, Sharma, and Lane (1993) to define it as, "an abnormal or long term pattern of threat or

[1]In most states, the stalker must display a criminal intent to cause fear in the victim. In other states, the intent element of the crime is met if the victim is in reasonable fear.

[2]Defendants who challenge stalking laws usually argue that they are "void for vagueness" under due process principles, or are overly broad and therefore infringe upon constitutionally protected speech or activity (National Institute of Justice, 1996).

harassment directed toward a specific individual" (Meloy & Gothard, 1995, p. 259). A pattern of threat or harassment was defined as "more than one overt act of unwanted pursuit of the victim that was perceived by the victim as being harassing" (p. 259). The purposes of these definitions are different. Legal elements are set forth to define and prosecute criminal behavior in a constitutionally acceptable manner. Behavioral definitions are set forth to further scientific investigation and clinical understanding.

INCIDENCE AND PREVALENCE OF STALKING

Until recently there have been no data on the incidence or prevalence of stalking. In July 1997 the Center for Policy Research in Denver, funded by a grant from the National Institute of Justice and the Centers for Disease Control and Prevention, published a study that reported the results of a telephone survey (a national probability sample) of 8000 men and 8000 women concerning their experiences with stalking (Tjaden & Thoennes, 1997). The report indicated that 8% of adult American women and 2% of adult American men have been stalked sometime in their lives (lifetime risk); and an estimated 1 million adult women and 0.4 million adult men are stalked annually in the United States. Half of all stalking victims report their stalking to the police, and one-quarter of these result in an arrest. About 12% of all stalking cases result in criminal prosecution.

These findings indicate that stalking is a substantial criminal justice and public health concern, although there are no prevalence data available, as yet, from other countries. These data also indicate that most cases of stalking do not result in criminal justice intervention, and very few result in criminal prosecution. For example, in San Diego County, California, with an adult female population of 1 million, there were 45 cases of stalking prosecuted by the District Attorney in 1996. If we apply the national prevalence data that indicate that 1% of adult women have been stalked in the preceding 12 months, then of the 10,000 women stalked in San Diego County in 1996, only 0.45% of the perpetrators were arrested and prosecuted for the crime of stalking (I am assuming that most of the victims of stalking were women, and not considering other related crimes).

THIS BOOK

When I was approached by Academic Press to develop this book, I was delighted. Their position, with my full agreement, was that this new topic of behavioral science had ripened to the extent that a scholarly book was warranted. As plans unfolded, I invited everyone who had made what I considered a substantial research contribution to write a chapter, and virtually everyone accepted. Some of the authors will be recognized because of their standing as major psychiatric and psychological researchers in this topic and related areas. Other authors will not be recognized because of their relative youth and limited scholarly contributions, but they will not disappoint. They hold promise as the next generation of clinical and forensic researchers. I have also organized the book in such a way that most areas of clinical and forensic interest are covered. Before we delve into this wealth of data and complexity of thought, however, I would like to do two things: provide an overview of general findings concerning stalking; and discuss some new areas that will likely receive future clinical and forensic research attention.

CURRENT FINDINGS

What do we currently know about stalking and the victims and perpetrators who are marked by this criminal behavior? The extant research provides some answers and directions for further work.

• Stalking is an old behavior, but a new crime. The first stalking law was passed in California in 1990.

• The majority of stalkers are males, and the majority of victims are females.

• Both victims and perpetrators of stalking are older than most criminals and crime victims, the criminal behavior likely occurring in the fourth decade of life.

• Stalkers are likely to have prior criminal, psychiatric, and drug abuse histories.

• Immigration is a risk factor in some cases of stalking.

• Axis I mental disorders are evident in the majority of stalkers, and likely include drug and alcohol diagnoses, mood disorder, or schizophrenia.

• Delusional disorder, erotomanic subtype, is an unlikely primary diagnosis among stalkers, contrary to early research assumptions.

• Axis II personality disorders are also evident in a majority of stalkers, particularly Cluster B, although both Cluster A (paranoid personality disorder) and Cluster C (dependent personality disorder) are evident in some cases.

• Most individuals who stalk are not psychotic at the time of their stalking.

• Empirical research is beginning to support the theoretical hypothesis that stalking is a pathology of attachment, evident in the subject's early childhood attachment disruptions and a recent, major loss in adulthood prior to the advent of the stalking (see Kienlen, Chapter 3).

• There is suggestive research that stalkers are more intelligent than other criminals, perhaps accounting for their manipulative skills.

• There are no data that indicate that stalking is disproportionately more prevalent in a particular racial or ethnic group, although Native American/Alaskan Native women appear to be at greater risk of being stalked than women of other racial backgrounds (Tjaden & Thoennes, 1997).

- Most stalkers are unemployed or underemployed at the time of the stalking; time is necessary to carry on this protracted crime.
- There is some evidence to consider stalking, at least for some individuals, a courtship disorder (Freund, Scher, & Hucker, 1983). There is usually a history of failed intimate relationships, and usually the stalker is not in a sexual pair bond at the time of the criminal behavior. Stalking for some individuals is a maladaptive response to social incompetence, social isolation, and loneliness (Meloy, 1996).
- The most useful perpetrator typology appears to be the one developed by Zona et al. (1993), which identified three groups—simple obsessionals, love obsessionals, and erotomanics.
- A useful relational typology identifies three groups of victims—prior sexual intimates, prior acquaintances, and strangers (Meloy, 1996).
- The most common form of stalking involves simple obsessional males stalking prior sexually intimate females.
- The length of pursuit by stalkers is measured in months or years; this is not a brief encounter.
- Stalking marks the far end of a continuum that begins with "obsessive relational intrusions" (Spitzberg & Cupach, 1994), which are not, per se, criminal acts.
- Pursuit patterns by stalkers are multiple and varied and most commonly include physical approach behavior and telephoning. New methods of stalking, such as the use of e-mail, are evolving as technological innovation in communication continues.
- Although most victims of stalking are women, men are most likely to be stalked by other male acquaintances or strangers (Tjaden & Thoennes, 1997).
- At least one-half of stalkers explicitly threaten their victims, and even though most threats are not carried out, the risk of violence likely increases when there is an articulated threat.[3]
- Most stalkers are not physically violent, but if they are, it is usually directed toward the object of their stalking rather than toward property or a third party.
- If stalkers are physically violent toward their object, the violence is usually committed without a weapon and serious physical injury does not usually result.
- The frequency of violence among stalkers toward their objects averages in the 25–35% range, suggesting a quite high rate for violence when compared to other criminally violent groups. The most likely group of stalkers to be violent are the simple obsessionals, those individuals who have had a prior sexually intimate relationship with the victim.
- The homicide rate among victims of stalking is less than 2%.

[3]Several studies have found exceptions to this finding, usually dependent upon the behavior subsequent to the threat that was being measured and the "stalking" population sampled. I will discuss this later in the chapter.

• There are no scientific data, as yet, on the prediction of violence among stalkers, although certain factors appear to correlate with stalkers who are violent. Many of these factors are similar to correlates of criminal violence in general, such as male gender, prior felony convictions, weapons involvement, prior drug abuse (including alcohol), and psychiatric history.

• The primary motivation for stalking is not sexual, but is, instead, conscious anger or hostility toward the victim (Meloy, 1996); the most commonly *perceived* motivation for stalking by victims of stalking is control (Tjaden & Thoennes, 1997).

• Typical psychological defenses exhibited by stalkers include denial, minimization, and projection of blame onto the victim.

• One psychodynamic theory put forth to explain stalking postulates that such individuals form a narcissistic linking fantasy with their victims, which is then met with rejection when acted upon. The rejection stimulates shame, which is defended against with rage, and thus fuels the pursuit of the victim. If the victim is sufficiently devalued, the narcissistic linking fantasy, which idealizes the victim, can be restored (Meloy, 1989, 1992, 1996).[4] This psychodynamic theory is receiving some empirical support, but other theories, both within and outside psychoanalytic thought, may also be valid (see Westrup, Chapter 14).

• Most victims of stalking suffer major life disruptions and serious psychological effects, including anxiety, depression, and symptoms of trauma. These conditions may be diagnosable, but are expectable, intense reactions to an abnormal and continuously intrusive behavior by another (see Hall, Chapter 6; Pathé & Mullen, 1997).

• New research suggests that "obsessive relational intrusions," in some cases arising to the level of criminal stalking, are a significant social problem among adolescents and warrant further research (Fremouw, Westrup, & Pennypacker, 1997; Spitzberg & Cupach, 1994; Romans, Hays, & White, 1996).

• "False victimization syndrome" (Zona, Lane, & Palarea, 1997) describes a small group of victims, probably 2%, who claim they are being stalked and are not.

• Although the majority of research studies indicate that protection (restraining) orders are effective (Meloy et al., 1997; Keilitz et al., 1997) in suppressing the defendant's behavior toward the victim, most studies have drawn their samples from domestic violence populations and are nonrandom survey studies of relatively short duration. Victims of stalking, however, report that most of their stalkers violated a protection (restraining) order, if served (Tjaden & Thoennes, 1997; see

---

[4]The restoration of the idealized relationship in fantasy is sometimes evident in the dreams of the perpetrator subsequent to his violence toward the victim (see Meloy, 1992). A recent case example of this is a dream reported by O. J. Simpson after the death of his ex-wife, Nicole Brown Simpson, by stabbing and subdecapitation: She "comes to me from time to time in my dreams and it's always a positive dream. Occasionally I dream that I single-handedly solve the case." The defenses of denial, idealization, and grandiosity should be quite apparent in the manifest content of this dream (*Newsweek,* June 23, 1997, p. 43).

Hall, Chapter 6). This disparity is most easily explained by the obsessive and relentless quality of stalking when compared to other behaviors that violate restraining orders. Regardless of the outcome of such studies, in individual cases the most likely predictor of the stalker's reaction to an order of restraint is his prior reaction, if any, to an order of restraint.

• The American popular culture, including, but not limited to, movies, television, music, and advertising, tacitly sanctions obsessional pursuits[5] (See Skoler, Chapter 5).

NEW AND CONTROVERSIAL AREAS

THREATS

Although explicit threats of harm to the victim, or target, have historically warranted close attention in the risk management of stalking cases, current research suggests some caution for several reasons.

First, because only about half of stalkers explicitly threaten their victims, and instead induce fear through a course of conduct, it seems ill advised for stalking statutes to require an overt threat of violence for criminal prosecution. The judicious course would be to codify a threat as either explicit or implicit, the latter inferred by a course of conduct that would cause reasonable fear.

Second, there is no research, as yet, demonstrating that threats *predict* violent behavior; in other words, no predictive equations have been constructed demonstrating that threats account for any proportion of the explainable variance in cases where the stalker has become violent. There is evidence, however, that explicit threats are more frequent in cases where stalkers become violent, although most threats are not acted upon (Macdonald, 1968; Meloy, 1996; Zona et al., 1997).

Third, there are studies of small or unusual samples of individuals that found no relationship between explicit threats and violence (see, for example, Fein & Vossekuil, Chapter 9; Meloy & Gothard, 1995) and no relationship between explicit threats and approach behavior to Hollywood celebrities (Dietz et al., 1991a). There is one study, moreover, that found a negative association between explicit threats and approach behavior to U.S. Congressmen (Dietz et al., 1991b). Approach behavior in these latter two studies, however, was not synonymous with

---

[5]These stimuli are more subtle and pervasive counterpoints to the lurid and dramatic portrayals of stalking—*Play Misty for Me* and *Fatal Attraction* are two cinematic examples—that intermittently appear in the popular culture. The stimuli that sanction obsessional pursuits, or stalking, end with a positive outcome, or reinforcement, for the behavior: we sympathize with Carmen's murderer, we laugh at Charlie Brown's little sister, Sally, for tenaciously pursuing Linus, we splash on Calvin Klein's Obsession (Orion, 1997), and we repetitively sing songs of stalking, such as Sting's lyrics, "every breath you take, every move you make, I'll be watching you." Stalking is the dark heart of romantic pursuit.

violence and may have instead been a behavioral search for sexual affection or beneficence, respectively.

Fourth, nomothetic (group) studies on threats and their relationship to behavior are not necessarily helpful in idiographic (single case) research or risk management, beyond the making of risk probability statements if the stalker fits closely into the reference group. Such studies may overshadow the commonsense premise that threats have one of three relationships to subsequent violence in single stalking cases: they inhibit violence, they disinhibit violence, or they have no relationship to the individual's violence. Careful scrutiny of the subject's threat/violence history should be the investigative focus when this relationship is analyzed in an individual stalking case; and the importance, or weight, of threats in a risk management situation should be determined by searching for the presence of other factors that may aggravate or mitigate violence (Monahan & Steadman, 1994). The only discriminant function analysis of violence related to this topic found that "dangerousness" in a small, nonrandom sample of erotomanic individuals ($N = 29$) could be predicted with 88.9% accuracy using a combination of two variables: multiple delusional objects and serious antisocial behavior unrelated to the delusions (Menzies, Fedoroff, Green, & Isaacson, 1995). This second variable is probably related to an increased likelihood of antisocial personality disorder.

Findings suggest that future nomothetic research should focus on a careful definition of *threat* and the subsequent behavior that is being predicted;[6] the use of predictive equations (logistic regression, discriminant function analysis) to test the hypothesis that threats account for a proportion of the explainable variance in stalking cases that become violent; and should refine associational (correlational) studies between threats and subsequent behavior.

The analysis of threats in relationship to violent behavior in a case, however, is only half the story. The other half, which often consumes the risk manager's thought, but is often not systematic, is the relationship of the threat to the state of mind of the stalker. It is the usually complex answer to the simple question, Why did he threaten her?

Threats are either *instrumental* or *expressive*. Instrumental threats are motivated by a purpose or goal that may be conscious or unconscious for the stalker. The goals of the instrumental threat may be to control the victim, to frighten the victim, or coerce the victim into doing something, to dominate the victim, or to seduce the victim. Such threats may be spontaneous or carefully weighed to maximize impact. They also may be accompanied by emotion, but affective expression is a secondary product.

Expressive threats are motivated by emotion, and help the stalker regulate his own affect. They are not primarily object related, as instrumental threats are,

---

[6]For instance, Fein, Vossekuil, and Holden (1995) have made the important distinction between *making* a threat and *posing* a threat, the latter more relevant to risk management in individual cases.

but instead serve a more internal, homeostatic purpose (even though they may have a very disconcerting impact on the victim). Expressive threats are often used to espouse anger or hatred (Akhtar, Kramer, & Parens, 1995), to defend against grief due to a loss or perceived abandonment, to defend against fear or shame, or to defend against anxiety. The latter may be based on the perception of a real threat (e.g., police intervention), or an imagined one (e.g., a paranoid delusion).

Threats, whether instrumental or expressive (the motivation), are invariably framed or contextualized by a particular psychological defense that is not conscious (A. Freud, 1966; Vaillant, 1993). Table 1 lists commonly utilized defenses and the threatening verbalizations that infer their presence. These are actual threats from my case files.

Although the motivations and defenses related to threats are more difficult than overt behavior to assess in a stalking case, they give us insight into the mental state, emotional makeup, and personality of the stalker. They also provide a counterpoint to the threat > subsequent behavior analysis, which should also be done. Locating the articulated threat at the interface of the stalker's internal

Table 1

Psychological Defenses and Articulated Threats

1. Sexualization
   "I'm going to fuck you and fuck you up."

2. Displacement
   "Your new boyfriend is dead."

3. Devaluation
   "You deserve to die and you will."

4. Idealization
   "If I can't be with you forever and fulfill our perfect destiny, no one will be with you."

5. Grandiose elaboration
   "Anytime . . . anywhere."

6. Projection
   "Tell them I'll be waiting for them . . ."

7. Projective identification
   "I'm watching you all the time, and if you keep taunting me I'll hurt you."

8. Denial
   "I didn't threaten you."

9. Minimization
   "I was just kidding."

10. Rationalization
    "She deserves it—look what she did to me."

psychology and external behavior may substantially contribute to our growing knowledge of this little understood, but ubiquitous, phenomenon in violence risk assessment.

CYBERSTALKING

The neologism *cyberstalking* has entered the English lexicon, connotating a paranoid tinged world of malicious and intrusive activity on the Internet. The rather mundane reality is that every new technology can serve as a vehicle for criminal behavior, and the Internet is no exception (see Lloyd-Goldstein, Chapter 10). The extraordinary dimensions of this new technology, however, are its rapid growth and infinite capacity to make communication both universal and instantaneous. The planet, in a sense, becomes a replicant of the human cortex: billions of neurons synaptically firing at random or in concert, multitasking without interference—prefrontal websites, hemispheric chatrooms, temporal lobe flaming, occipital e-mail.

Although there is no research on cyberstalking at present, there are legal cases in which the Internet has been utilized as a means of unwanted communication to stalk someone; the most common method is leaving e-mail messages for the target that are perceived as malicious or harassing and induce fear. In one case, the young actress Jennie Kwan was sent the following quip by an anonymous stalker: "Everyone knows you haven't made it in show biz until you have your first obsessed fan" (Burt, Sulkowicz, & Wofrage, 1997).[7]

The Internet as a means of stalking can be used for two criminal functions: (1) to gather private information on the target to further a pursuit;[8] and (2) to communicate (in real time or not) with the target to implicitly or explicitly threaten or to induce fear. There are technical means that make both tasks difficult to trace to the perpetrator, such as sending e-mail through two or three sequential servers ("anonymous remailers," often located overseas, provide such a service).

[7]These authors also report the case of a 23-year-old single female college student who presented at an outpatient psychiatric clinic. She complained of depression and compulsive monitoring of a male relative on the Internet for 8 hours a day as he communicated with another woman. On admission her score on the Yale–Brown Obsessive–Compulsive Scale was 38 out of 40 points. They note that she did not meet criteria for OCD until she had on-line access.

[8]Websites such as Dig Dirt and SpyForU sell unlisted phone numbers and bank account numbers and trace beeper numbers to home addressses. DBT-Online matches a name with a Social Security Number, date of birth, and telephone number for a nominal fee. Civil judgments, property tax filings, and names and addresses of business associates and neighbors cost an additional fee. Unscrupulous private investigators can also secure otherwise private information by falsely representing themselves, via computer or telephone, as someone they are not. This is called "pretexting" in the business of information exchange. I call it deception and fraud (see the *New York Times,* Sept. 15, 1997, p. A20).

It is unlikely, however, that a criminal stalking case would be prosecuted solely on the basis of cyberstalking. The more reasonable fact pattern would have the Internet as one of several means of pursuit. In Wisconsin, for instance, stalking is partially defined as, "intentionally engaging in a course of conduct (repeatedly maintaining a visual or physical proximity to a person) . . ." (Wisconsin statute 940.32), and would, by definition, exclude seeking electronic or computer access to the target. Other pursuit behavior would be necessary for charging or filing. Only seven states have statutory language that addresses stalking by computer (Jenson, 1996).[9] Curmudgeons might also argue that so-called cyberstalking is akin to the person who listens to an obscene phone call for 30 minutes: Why doesn't the victim just disconnect her telephone or delete her e-mail? Anonymity of the offender, jurisdictional problems, and vagueness of statutory language are likely to trouble the enforcement of any cyberstalking laws (Branscomb, 1995; Carmody, 1994).

Cyberstalking, however, does have a certain psychodynamic appeal for the perpetrator. The Internet allows communication with another person unconstrained by social reality. Only written words are used, and other avenues of sensory perception are eliminated; one cannot see, hear, touch, smell, or emotionally sense the other person. There is also, if one wants, a suspension of real time. Messages can be sent and electronically stored, and their reception is no longer primarily dictated by the transport time of the medium, but instead, by the behavior of the receiver. Some individuals may always return their phone calls the day they receive them, while reviewing their e-mail at leisure.

These unusual circumstances provide opportunities for the stalker. First, the lack of social constraints means that social anxiety, particularly as an inhibitor of aggression, is nonexistent. Therefore certain emotions and desires endemic to stalkers—anger, jealousy, envy, possessiveness, control (Kienlen et al., 1997; Meloy, 1996, 1997b; Meloy & Gothard, 1995)—and the aggressive impulses they stimulate to devalue or injure can be coarsely and directly expressed toward the target.

Second, the absence of sensory-perceptual stimuli from a real person means that fantasy can play an even more expansive role as the genesis of behavior in the stalker. Targets become easily available containers for his projections, and narcissistic linking fantasies (Meloy, 1996) may set the stage for real world rejection, humiliation, and rage. In a sense transference, both positive and negative, abounds on the World Wide Web.

A hypothetical case: John, a 35-year-old recently divorced male, was just terminated from his computer design position with a publicly traded software firm whose last quarter earnings were abysmal. John has no children and has always been socially awkward. He is now desperately lonely. His IQ is in the very superior range, however, and he therefore retreats to what he does and knows best, surfing the Internet.

[9]They are Alaska, Delaware, Connecticut, Michigan, Montana, Oklahoma, and Wyoming.

His social life has now been transformed from accompanying his wife to her social functions to sedentary hours in front of a computer screen. But his unwanted solitude has abated because he has "met" a divorced woman about his age in a chatroom for computer professionals. He has never been with her, spoken to her, touched her, or gazed upon her, yet he feels intense pleasure and affection toward her, and in his fantasies has idealized her. She represents in his mind everything he has longed for: a passion and affection that were starkly absent in his marriage. His dreams of love and a fateful encounter have been realized (Person, 1988).

Over time, many e-mail messages, and "chats," the relationship appears to blossom. The problem is that it is fantasy based, and all fantasies are perfect (R. Hazelwood, personal communication, June 1997). John is told by Jane that she is quite beautiful and voluptuous, expressed modestly of course, and John, fearful of losing her, reciprocates with a similar description of himself as tall, dark, and handsome—although it is false.

They eventually arrange an actual meeting in a city equidistant from both of them, and the harshness of reality intrudes. Jane is as beautiful as he imagined, but she is shocked by his appearance and dismisses him with abruptness and anger because of his deception of her. John is humiliated—this event unfolds in a restaurant—but after returning home his shame, the vulnerable aspect of his narcissism, or felt pride, has become rage. In his mind he begins to devalue her, and on the Internet he begins to harass her; he belittles her with accusations and implicitly threatens her by sending her data on herself that she considers a violation of her privacy. A constellation of behaviors that may progress to criminal stalking has begun.

The third opportunity that the Internet presents to the stalker was alluded to in this case: truth-telling is just a prosocial option, and the wish to deceive is not attenuated by the usual social anxiety of being caught. In fact, deception could be a common phenomenon on the Internet because: (1) most people believe other people tell the truth even if they do not; (2) deception, along with the inclination to trust, in ordinary social communication is very common; and (3) there are very few ways to independently verify truthful statements in a medium that is currently limited to written words, electronically transferred.

The final opportunity that the Internet offers to stalkers is the element of surprise. Messages of any length can exist indefinitely in cyberspace, stumbled onto like a land mine by the victim at some point in time. Such surprise could magnify her fear and distress, particularly if her fantasy intensifies the sense of him being out there, somewhere—or perhaps everywhere. He may even become a projective identification for her: she attributes to him a characteristic of herself—fury at his behavior, for instance—and then feels all the more threatened by his intrusive messages (Ogden, 1982; Meloy, 1991).

My thoughts concerning cyberstalking are largely theoretical and speculative. Even a small sample of stalking cases in which the Internet was used has yet to be published. But theory directs empirical research, and empirical findings should inform clinical and forensic understanding and application. Cyberstalking remains a pristine area for study.

In Defense of Obsessional Thinking

The first use of the term *obsession* to describe a subgroup of stalkers, simple obsessionals (Zona et al., 1993), has been criticized for deviating from the commonly understood meaning of the term. Our use of the phrase *obsessional follower* (Meloy & Gothard, 1995) has likewise been criticized for adding definitional confusion to a term that is understood to mean, "persistent ideas, thoughts, impulses, or images that are experienced as intrusive and inappropriate and that cause marked anxiety or distress" (APA, 1994, *DSM-IV*, p. 418). The central argument of these criticisms is that obsessions are, by definition, unwanted, nonvolitional thoughts and should not be used to describe thoughts that are wanted and volitional. From a psychoanalytic perspective obsessions are ego–dystonic, not ego–syntonic, the former term being "the individual's sense that the content of the obsession is alien, not within his or her own control, and not the kind of thought that he or she would expect to have" (*DSM-IV*, p. 418).

I argue, to the contrary, that the term obsession, derived from the Latin *obsidere*, to beseige, is the most accurate word to be used to describe much of the object-related thinking of the stalker. Obsessional thoughts, when they appear in general clinical practice, are often initially welcomed by the patient because they serve some defensive purpose, such as warding off anxiety. It is only after they interfere with functioning, and perhaps are redefined as a symptom by the clinician and the patient, that they shift to a position of being unwanted and intrusive (ego-dystonic), and therefore warrant treatment. The current approaches that are most effective in alleviating obsessions appear to be pharmacological (potent SRIs) or behavioral (habituation) (Greist & Jefferson, 1995).

Obsessions are behaviorally maintained because they are positively reinforced (in stalking, for example, intermittent contact with the victim results from a relentless pursuit) or result in the removal of an aversive stimulus (negative reinforcement; in stalking, for example, anxiety is reduced when the obsessions concerning her behavior at the moment are decreased by making an unwanted phone call). Whether these thoughts are ego-dystonic or ego-syntonic, I contend, varies from moment to moment, and is dependent on other emotions, pleasant or unpleasant, that are felt before, during, or after the thoughts. The relationship of obsessional thoughts to the ego, or conscious sense of self, is temporally unstable and should not define the term. *DSM-IV* even hints at this position:

> Even in adults there is a broad range of insight into the reasonableness of the obsessions or compulsions . . . and any given individual's insight may vary across times and situations. . . . In the course of the disorder, after repeated failure to resist the obsessions and compulsions, the individual may give in to them, no longer experience a desire to resist them, and may incorporate the compulsions into his or her daily routines. (pp. 418–419)

At the risk of seeming presumptuous, I suggest that the central definition of an obsession be shifted to the degree of *preoccupation* with a thought: a term more easily understood by lay individuals, often used synonymously with the word obsession in the culture, more temporally stable, and easily behaviorally measured through frequency counts (how many times an hour does he think of her?) This conceptual shift would dissolve the criticism of our use of the term, and also unbridle *obsession* from less easily measurable and esoteric words such as syntonic, dystonic, and nonvolitional. Obsession becomes functionally defined as *the frequency of conscious preoccupation with an object*, the pathological threshold to be determined by the clinician, the patient, or both.

This definitional shift opens the door to consider treatments for obsessive–compulsive behavior in stalking cases and does not alter other, psychodynamic understandings of obsessions among stalkers. Obsessions may serve a variety of unconscious functions, including, most commonly, a means to defend against intense feelings of grief or humiliation, or to maintain grandiose delusions, in psychotic cases, of a narcissistic link to the object. Both motivations could also be accompanied by anger or rage subsequent to a real world rejection, although the emotions *not* felt and defended against are likely more vulnerable and less tolerable: loneliness, yearning, sadness, envy, desperation, shame, embarrassment, jealousy, or self loathing, to name a few. Deep analytic work with these individuals, however, is unlikely to be done due to patient resistance and limited economic resources. Behavioral approaches to modify either the stalker's or the target's habit patterns seem more parsimonious from a risk management perspective (see Westrup, Chapter 14).

THE NATURE OF STALKING VIOLENCE

I earlier mentioned the findings concerning the probability of violence among stalkers and the fact that frequency of violence toward the object is high enough to warrant serious concern. The rates of violence in any particular study covary with the type of stalkers, the relationships to the victims, the length of time the victims have been stalked, the efficiency and effectiveness of interventions by mental health and law enforcement, and the definition of violence that is applied to a particular stalking sample. These variables concerning the probability of violence in a group of stalkers may be quite distinct from risk factors that would predict violence in any single case.

But what is known about the nature of violence, should it occur? There is some suggestive data from our work and others' studies. Physical violence is most likely directed toward the object of stalking, and the second most likely target is a person who is perceived by the stalker to be interfering with his access to the victim (Meloy, 1996). Such a triangulation may increase the risk of violence since it implies the emergence of a paranoid (or real) interpersonal dynamic in the stalking behavior. For example, I consulted on a criminal case where a 40-year-old male developed a delusional disorder, persecutory subtype, over the course of 7 years, believing that he was being stalked by a counselor of his ex-wife. As his delusions worsened, and he began to abuse both alcohol and benzodiazepines, his behavior toward his neighbors escalated. He eventually was involved in a shootout with the local police at his home during which a police officer was killed and he was wounded. He had come to believe that the police were agents of the stalker, sent to his house to harass and intimidate him. This was an unusual example of false victimization syndrome caused by a paranoid delusional disorder that had no basis in reality (see Mohandie, Hatcher, & Raymond, Chapter 12). In stalking cases where the triangulation is based on paranoia, it usually signals the displacement of rage toward the rejecting object onto a third party (Meissner, 1978; Meloy, 1989).

On the other hand, system interventions can triangulate the stalking situation and increase violence risk in the absence of any paranoid condition. In another case in which I testified, a 60-year-old man began stalking his ex-girlfriend, which culminated in an auto pursuit and serious accident 1 month after it began. Following the service of a protection order 7 days after the accident, the stalking escalated over the course of the next year—she received insulting telephone calls, inappropriate letters and greetings, multiple violations of the permanent restraining order ensued, and her property (home and automobile) was damaged. The stalking ceased when the perpetrator was arrested for stalking, plea bargained to multiple contempt of court citations, and was placed under close probation supervision (*Earll v. Freeman,* 96 CV 796, State of Wisconsin Circuit Court, Winnebago County).

In a third case in which I consulted with the prosecution, Robert Hoskins, an itinerant, unemployed male, was eventually convicted of stalking the singer Madonna Ciccone. Although he evidenced both bizarre and inappropriate beliefs, his stalking escalated to violence toward her security guard (the third party) when he was refused access to her on the third occasion (Meloy, 1997a; see Saunders, Chapter 2). This real world triangulation complemented his chronic amphetamine abuse, which may have increased his propensity for paranoid ideation and heightened aggression: both reality-based and paranoid triangulation converged (*People v. Hoskins,* BA115862, California Superior Court, Los Angeles County).

Stalking violence is also likely to be an affective, rather than a predatory, mode of violence. These two modes of violence have received substantial research attention over the past 30 years and appear to represent two biologically distinctive modes of violence in mammals (Meloy, 1988, 1997c; Mirsky & Siegel, 1994). Affective violence is the common, garden-variety aggression we observe between people who are violent and is preceded by heightened autonomic arousal, accompanied by anger or fear, and is a reaction to an immediate perceived threat—in stalking cases, the threat is often perceived rejection. Predatory violence, by contrast, is planned, purposeful, and emotionless. It is not preceded by heightened autonomic arousal and its goals are numerous—in stalking cases in which predatory violence occurs, a relatively rare event, the goal is likely control, intimidation, or devaluation of the victim. As most cases of violence in stalking do not result in injury to the object and are characterized by punching, slapping, pushing, grabbing, hitting, or fondling, affective violence appears to be the rule. Because predatory violence in stalking cases does occur on occasion, evidence of it should prompt a careful evaluation of the personality or character pathology of the subject; predatory violence significantly and positively correlates with psychopathy (Meloy, 1988, 1995; Williamson, Hare, & Wong, 1987; Serin, 1991), and will likely be related to severity of antisocial traits from a *DSM-IV* perspective (see Meloy, 1988, pp. 281–286, for the case of a bipolar disordered and ASPD male who stalked a female judge over the course of 3 years).

Homicide in stalking cases occurs less than 2% of the time, as I noted earlier. The perpetrator is likely to be known to the victim, usually a prior sexual intimate, and the weapons of choice are a firearm or a knife. These instruments are expected, because their lethality risk, especially that of firearms, is higher than that of other available objects that could be used as a weapon. I have documented one stalking homicide case in detail where the weapons of choice were acid, gasoline, and fire (Meloy, 1992), and the criminal behavior was shaped by both myth and culture.

The study of weapons in cases of stalking has received a little, unsystematic attention. In Table 2, I list all the studies of stalkers where the sample size was ≥25 in which weapons were mentioned.

The aggregate results of these findings are useful. Although these samples are disparate, all subjects evidenced preoccupation with their objects; the behavioral expression of that preoccupation ranged from letter writing to murder. When the samples are combined ($N = 576$), only 12 subjects threatened with a weapon, and 11 subjects used a weapon at the time of their offense, if they committed one; 51 subjects mentioned or possessed a weapon (9%). These data, however, are only suggestive, and should lead to only one general finding: both threats with weapons and weapons use in cases of obsessional following or stalking are unusual.

We have attempted to shed further light on this area in a new sample of obsessional followers ($N = 65$) charged with stalking and other related crimes and

Table 2

Stalking and Weapons

Study	Subjects	N
Kienlen et al. (1997)	Incarcerated stalkers	25

Finding: 36% (9) had weapon at offense; firearms, knife, pipe; nonpsychotic more likely than psychotic to use weapon ($p < .10$).

Menzies et al. (1995)	Erotomanics	29

Finding: 2 cases—"offensive weapon," "weapon conviction"

Garrod et al. (1995)	Criminal harassment	100

Finding: 17% of subjects made a firearm threat if victim was a prior intimate; 12% entire sample.

Harmon et al. (1995)	Harassment/menacing	48

Finding: 2 charged with criminal possession of weapon; 10 subjects assaultive (7 had threatened); bottle, knife mentioned.

Zona et al. (1993)	Erotomanics/obsessionals	74

16% (5) love obsessionals, 9% (3) simple obsessionals, and no erotomanics mentioned or possessed a firearm; none used.

Dietz et al. (1991a)	Subjects/threat letters	214

13 subjects mentioned a weapon, usually a handgun, in letters; 9 of these subjects approached Hollywood celebrities.

Dietz et al. (1991b)	Subjects/threat letters	86

26 subjects mentioned a weapon in their letters to U.S. Congressmen.

clinically evaluated in the Forensic Evaluation Unit of the San Diego County Courthouse. These findings are part of a larger validation study we are conducting.

Weapons were used by 15% of the subjects ($N = 10$), and included automobiles ($N = 4$), knives ($N = 4$), and firearms ($N = 2$). Although 22% of the sample were psychotic at the time of offense ($N = 14$), only one of those who used a weapon was psychotic (10%), strengthening the finding of Kienlen et al. (1997) noted in Table 2. Most interestingly, in each case in which a weapon was used, it did not result in physical injury to the victim: the automobiles did not hit the victims, the knives did not cut the victims, and the firearms did not shoot the victims. Our analysis indicates that in all cases of stalking violence involving weapons, in this moderately sized sample, weapons were used to control and intimidate, rather than injure, the victim. The absence of physical injury to the victim, *when lethal means were readily available and literally in the hands of the perpetrator,* may also reflect the intense, ambivalent, and oscillating emotion that surrounds stalking (Meloy, 1989, 1992).

Automobiles take a beating in stalking cases. Not only were they used as weapons, but in cases where there was damage only to property ($N = 9$), cars were the targets 55% ($N = 5$) of the time. These findings have been validated in a larger, yet unpublished study of >300 cases followed by the Threat Management Unit of the Los Angeles Police Department (Russell Palarea, personal communication, August, 1997).

PSYCHODYNAMICS AND ATTACHMENT PATHOLOGY

The psychodynamics of stalking refer to the thoughts, emotions, and defenses in the mind of the stalker that are related to the object of pursuit. My psychodynamic theory to explain the continuous behavior of stalking is illustrated in Figure 1. The ovals indicate either external behaviors or internal states that are sequentially linked by arrows, the latter representing different points in time. The general psychodynamic begins with the individual forming in his mind a narcissistic linking fantasy to a particular object. Such fantasies are characterized by conscious thoughts of being loved by or loving, admired by or admiring (idealizing), being exactly like (mirroring) or complementing (twinship), or sharing a destiny with a particular object or person (merger). Such fantasies are not unusual in normal individuals (Person, 1995), are often characterized by idealization, and form the basis for romantic love and infatuation. There is also evidence that certain biochemicals, such as phenylethylamine, support these linking fantasies (Fisher, 1992). I refer to them as narcissistic, drawing on Rothstein's (1984, p. 4) simple and elegant definition of narcissism, "a felt quality of perfection"; emotions of contentment, elation, and excitement will bathe such thoughts, and facilitate sexual pair bonding and the differential biochemistry of attachment, recently focusing upon the neuropeptides oxytocin and vasopressin (Insel, 1997). Such narcissistic beliefs, and their accompa-

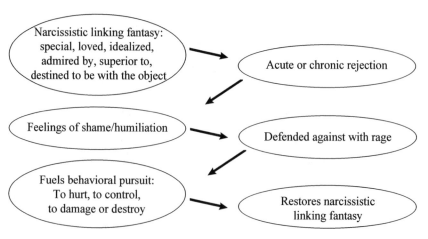

Figure 1   Stalking: The pursuit of the object (victim).

nying emotions, are normative, and should not be considered pathological. They often represent, as Samuel Johnson, the English essayist (1709–1784) once noted, the triumph of hope over experience. These narcissistic fantasies serve reality in actual relationships, and may facilitate ambition, rather than envy, when they are linked to public or celebrity figures. In normative behavior such conscious thoughts may motivate the pursuit of a sexual partner that eventuates in a long-term relationship, or the written request for a signed photo of a celebrity or political beneficence from a public figure.

An actual behavioral approach is represented by the second oval. In normative relationships, such an approach may eventually culminate in a sexual pair bond that is both temporally stable and loving. When seeking such contact with a celebrity or public figure, acknowledgment through a letter or photograph may instill in the subject a feeling of reciprocal closeness, even though in the latter case it remains mostly fantasy based and prone to emotional and cognitive distortion.

When acute or chronic rejection occurs, however, the object of pursuit (or attachment) becomes aversive, and normal individuals will withdraw: the suitor searches for another sexual pair bond after experiencing a range of emotions (hurt, anger, grief) depending on the history and depth of the attachment; the spouse leaves the marriage; or the pursuer of contact with a celebrity or public figure may devalue the object, or at least remove some idealizations, and perhaps rationalize or minimize the lack of response. All remains well in the course of human socialization, often dependent on the capacity of the subject to represent himself and other people as whole, real, and meaningful objects that have their own and separate internal lives. He will also experience emotions that necessitate such whole object relating: empathy, grief, sympathy, gratitude, and hope for the future with another.

In stalking cases, however, a different course of events unfolds. The subject, because of his pathological narcissism—a character structure that, in part, perceives others as self objects (Kohut, 1971) or part objects (Kernberg, 1975) primarily meant to gratify him—is extraordinarily sensitive to rejection and the feelings of shame or humiliation that accompany it.[10] To avoid these intolerable emotions, he defends against them with rage—not anger—and the heretofore idealized object is grossly devalued, an internal maneuver that infers the defense of splitting (Meloy & Gothard, 1995; Grotstein, 1981).[11]

---

[10]In an earlier work (Meloy, 1989), drawing on Kernberg (1975), I discussed stalking as a defensive attempt to stabilize the grandiose self structure through a fusion of the ideal self and ideal object representations; an example would be the conscious fantasy of sharing a perfect destiny with another person. Such adulthood behavior may also be a reparative attempt, through narcissistic mechanisms, to heal the wounds of abandoning or lost childhood objects (see Kienlen, Chapter 3).

[11]Hatred may also be present in stalking cases, but is a developmentally more advanced and complex emotion than narcissistic rage. As Freud wrote, "the ego hates, abhors, and pursues with intent to destroy all objects which are a source of unpleasurable feeling for it" (1915, 1957, p. 138). Bollas (1985) also described "loving hate" as a means of preserving an object tie, and Pao (1965) discussed the ego-syntonic use of hatred, such as forming a negative identity (e.g., "the Madonna stalker," see Saunders, Chapter 2). For a detailed explication of hatred, see Gabbard (1996), who wrote, "To hate is to hold on to an internal object in an unforgiving way" (p. 48).

I think that the rage (Kohut, 1972) is a central component in motivating the behavior of the stalker to then pursue the object. The intent is to dominate, devalue, and in some cases, destroy. Envy might also play a role, because if the object is sufficiently devalued, she was not worth having in the first place. Jealousy, a more complex emotion that infers competition for the "love" object, may also adhere, with the goal to possess her so that no one else can have her.

There are data accumulating that empirically support these motivational emotions in stalkers. Kienlen et al. (1997) found that 65% of their nonpsychotic stalkers were motivated by anger and 24% by jealousy. Fifty-three percent blamed the victim, a measure of projection. Tjaden and Thoennes (1997) found that many stalking victims (21%) perceived control as the primary motivator of the stalker. And we found in a new sample of stalkers ($N = 65$) that 55% were motivated by anger and hostility, 42% projected blame, and 26% were jealous. Minimization (52%), denial (46%), and projective identification (40%) were the most prominent defenses recognized during their clinical evaluations.

The most troubling and difficult concept to grasp in the psychodynamic understanding of stalking is the last oval in Figure 1: the restoration of the idealized narcissistic linking fantasy with the victim if the object is sufficiently devalued. Although this concept is supported only by anecdotal data at present, it is intellectually compelling. If the real object, which now has become an aversive stimulus, or negative reinforcement, due to its rejection of the stalker, can be removed, the linking fantasy can, once again, restore the narcissistic equilibrium of the stalker: in psychostructural terms, the conceptual refusion of the ideal self and ideal object in the grandiose self structure (Kernberg, 1975; Meloy, 1992).

There is probably no better example than the stalking of Jodie Foster by John Hinckley, Jr. Following his repeated and unsuccessful attempts to court her, he resorted to what rational minds would consider a "crazy" act: he would assassinate a public figure to win her affection. He finally settled on President Ronald Reagan, and attempted to kill him on March 30, 1981. Hinckley scripted a note to her just prior to the shooting: "Jodie, I would abandon this idea of getting Reagan in a second if I could only win your heart and live out the rest of my life with you" (Caplan, 1987, p. 21).

The assassination failed, and Hinckley was found not guilty by reason of insanity and continues to be confined at St. Elizabeth's Hospital in Washington, D.C. He was also most recently diagnosed with narcissistic personality disorder (*DSM-IV*) by the forensic clinicians who evaluated him during his attempt to be released on a weekend pass to his parents, a diagnosis suggested by my theory (*U.S. v. John W. Hinckley, Jr.*, U.S. District Court for the District of Columbia, No. 81-0306, June 9, 1997).

But a curious phenomenon has occurred. John Hinckley, Jr., did, in a sense, accomplish what he set out to do. The public will always link him with Jodie Foster; and most importantly, as a basis for gratification in Mr. Hinckley's mind,

Ms. Foster will likely never forget him. Her consciousness of him validates his narcissistic linking fantasy, one that perhaps remains a hidden preoccupation for him 17 years later. As he said to an interviewer 2 months after the assassination attempt, "To link myself with her for almost the rest of history, if you want to go that far" (Low, Jeffries, & Bonnie, 1986, p. 44). He did.

FINAL THOUGHTS

The criminal behavior of stalking as a focus of behavioral science is very new, and the preliminary findings are quite encouraging. Definitions are being refined, methodologies are being improved, and samples are becoming larger and more disparate—fundamental research markers that foreshadow the expansion of scientific knowledge in this dark area of human behavior. It seems fitting to close this chapter, moreover, by returning to my point of departure, the death of Princess Diana. All of us, particularly women, the most likely victims of stalking, can find resonance in the compelling eulogy by her brother, Charles Spencer:

> It is a point to remember that of all the ironies about Diana, perhaps the greatest is this: that a girl given the name of the ancient goddess of hunting was, in the end, the most hunted person of the modern age.
>
> Charles Spencer
> Westminster Abbey
> September 6, 1997

REFERENCES

Akhtar, S., Kramer, S., & Parens, H. (1995). *The birth of hatred*. Northvale, NJ: Jason Aronson.

American Psychiatric Association. (1994). *Diagnostic and statistical manual of mental disorders (4th ed.)*. Washington, DC: Author.

Bollas, C. (1985). Loving hate. *The Annual of Psychoanalysis, 12/13*, 221–237.

Branscomb, A. (1995). Anonymity, autonomy, and accountability: Challenges to the first amendment in cyberspaces. 104 *Yale Law Journal* 1639.

Burt, T., Sulkowicz, K., & Wofrage, K. (1997). Stalking and voyeurism over the internet: Psychiatric and forensic issues. *Proceedings of the American Academy of Forensic Sciences, 3*, 172.

Caplan, L. (1987). *The insanity defense and the trial of John W. Hinckley, Jr.* New York: Dell.

Carmody, C. (1994). Stalking by computer. 80 Sep. *American Bar Association Journal* 70.

Dietz, P., Matthews, D., Van Duyne, C., Martell, D., Parry, C., Stewart, T., Warren, J., & Crowder, J. (1991a). Threatening and otherwise inappropriate letters to Hollywood celebrities. *Journal of Forensic Sciences, 36*, 185–209.

Dietz, P., Matthews, D., Martell, D., Stewart, T., Hrouda, D., & Warren, J. (1991b). Threatening and otherwise inappropriate letters to members of the United States Congress. *Journal of Forensic Sciences, 36*, 1445–1468.

Fein, R., Vossekuil, B., & Holden, G. (1995). Threat assessment: An approach to prevent targeted violence. In *National Institute of Justice: Research in action*. Washington, DC: U.S. Department of Justice, Office of Justice Programs.

Fisher, H. (1992). *The anatomy of love*. New York: Norton.

Fremouw, W., Westrup, D., & Pennypacker, J. (1997). Stalking on campus: The prevalence and strategies for coping with stalking. *Journal of Forensic Sciences, 42*, 664–667.

Freud, A. (1966). *The ego and the mechanisms of defense* (Rev. ed.). New York: International Universities Press.

Freud, S. (1957). Instincts and their vicissitudes. In *The standard edition of the complete psychological works of Sigmund Freud* (Vol. 14, pp. 109–140). London: Hogarth Press. (Original work published 1915).

Freund, K., Scher, H., & Hucker, S. (1983). The courtship disorders. *Archives of Sexual Behavior, 12*, 369–379.

Gabbard, G. (1996). *Love and hate in the analytic setting*. Northvale, NJ: Aronson.

Garrod, A., Ewert, P., Field, G., & Warren, G. (1995). The nature and extent of criminal harassment in British Columbia. In *The report of the criminal harassment unit*. Vancouver, BC: Author.

Greist, J., & Jefferson, J. (1995). Obsessive–compulsive disorder. In G. Gabbard (Ed.), *Treatments of psychiatric disorders* (2nd ed. Vol. 2, pp. 1477–1498). Washington, DC: American Psychiatric Press.

Grotstein, J. (1981). *Splitting and projective identification*. New York: Jason Aronson.

Harmon, R., Rosner, R., & Owens, H. (1995). Obsessional harassment and erotomania in a criminal court population. *Journal of Forensic Sciences, 40*, 188–196.

Insel, T. (1997). A neurobiological basis of social attachment. *American Journal of Psychiatry, 154*, 726–735.

Jenson, B. (1996). Cyberstalking: Crime, enforcement and personal responsibility in the on-line world. UCLA Online Institute for Cyberspace Law and Policy. Available: http://www.law.ucla.edu/Classes/Archive/S96/340/cyberlaw.htm

Keilitz, S., Davis, C., Efkeman, H., Flango, C., & Hannaford, P. (1997, September). Civil protection orders: Victims' views of effectiveness. *National Institute of Justice*, p. 23.

Kernberg, O. (1975). *Borderline conditions and pathological narcissism*. New York: Jason Aronson.

Kienlen, K., Birmingham, D., Solberg, K., O'Regan, J., & Meloy, J. R. (1997). A comparative study of psychotic and nonpsychotic stalking. *Journal of the American Academy of Psychiatry and the Law, 25*, 317–334.

Kohut, H. (1971). *Analysis of the self*. New York: International Universities Press.

Kohut, H. (1972). Thoughts on narcissism and narcissistic rage. *Pyschoanalytic Study of the Child, 27*, 360–400.

Low, P., Jeffries, J., & Bonnie, R. (1986). *The trial of John W. Hinckley, Jr.: A case study in the insanity defense*. Westbury, NY: Foundation Press.

Macdonald, J. (1968). *Homicidal threats*. Springfield, IL: Charles C. Thomas.

Meissner, W. W. (1978). *The paranoid process*. New York: Jason Aronson.

Meloy, J. R. (1988). *The psychopathic mind: Origins, dynamics, and treatment*. Northvale, NJ: Jason Aronson.

Meloy, J. R. (1989). Unrequited love and the wish to kill: Diagnosis and treatment of borderline erotomania. *Bulletin Menninger Clinic, 53*, 477–492.

Meloy, J. R. (1991). The "blurring" of ego boundary in projective identification [Letter to the editor]. *American Journal of Psychiatry, 148*, 1761–62.

Meloy, J. R. (1992). *Violent attachments*. Northvale, NJ: Jason Aronson.

Meloy, J. R. (1995). Antisocial personality disorder. In G. Gabbard (ed.) *Treatments of psychiatric disorders* (2nd ed., Vol. 2, pp. 2273–2290). Washington, DC: American Psychiatric Press.

Meloy, J. R. (1996). Stalking (obsessional following): A review of some preliminary studies. *Aggression and Violent Behavior, 1*, 147–162.

Meloy, J. R. (1997a). The clinical risk management of stalking: "Someone is watching over me . . ." *American Journal of Psychotherapy, 51*, 174–184.

Meloy, J. R. (1997b). A Rorschach case study of stalking: "All I wanted was to love you . . ." In R. Meloy, M. Acklin, C. Gacono, J. Murray, & C. Peterson (Eds.), *Contemporary Rorschach interpretation* (pp. 177–190). Mahwah, NJ: Lawrence Erlbaum Associates.

Meloy, J. R. (1997c). Predatory violence during mass murder. *Journal of Forensic Sciences, 42*, 326–429.

Meloy, J. R., Cowett, P. Y., Parker, S., Hofland, B., & Friedland, A. (1997). Do restraining orders restrain? Finally some data. *Proceedings of the American Academy of Forensic Sciences, 3,* 173.

Meloy, J. R., & Gothard, S. (1995). A demographic and clinical comparison of obsessional followers and offenders with mental disorders. *American Journal of Psychiatry, 152,* 258–263.

Menzies, R., Fedoroff, J. P., Green, C., & Isaacson, K. (1995). Prediction of dangerous behavior in male erotomania. *British Journal of Psychiatry, 166,* 529–536.

Mirsky, A., & Siegel, A. (1994). The neurobiology of violence and aggression. In A. Reiss, K. Miczek, & J. Roth (Eds.), *Understanding and preventing violence: Vol. 2. Biobehavioral influences* (pp. 59–111). Washington, DC: National Academy Press.

Monahan, J., & Steadman, H. (Eds.). (1994). *Violence and mental disorder: Developments in risk assessment.* Chicago: University of Chicago Press.

National Institute of Justice. (1996). *Domestic violence, stalking, and antistalking legislation.* Washington, DC: U.S. Dept. of Justice, Office of Justice Programs.

Ogden, T. (1982). *Projective identification and psychotherapeutic technique.* New York: Aronson.

Orion, D. (1997). *I know you really love me.* New York: Macmillan.

Pao (1965). The role of hatred in the ego. *Psychoanalytic Quarterly, 34,* 257–264.

Pathé, M., & Mullen, P. (1997). The impact of stalkers on their victims. *British Journal of Psychiatry, 170,* 12–17.

Person, E. (1988). *Dreams of love and fateful encounters: The power of romantic passion.* New York: Norton.

Person, E. (1995). *By force of fantasy.* New York: Basic Books.

Rothstein, A. (1984). *The narcissistic pursuit of perfection.* New York: International Universities Press.

Romans, J., Hays, J., & White, T. (1996). Stalking and related behaviors experienced by counseling center staff members from current or former clients. *Professional Psychology: Research and Practice, 27,* 595–599.

Serin, R. (1991). Psychology and violence in criminals. *Journal of Interpersonal Violence, 6,* 423–431.

Spitzberg, B., & Cupach, W. (1994). *The dark side of close relationships.* Mahwah, NJ: Lawrence Erlbaum Associates.

Tjaden, P., & Thoennes, N. (1997). *Stalking in America: Findings from the National Violence against Women Survey.* Denver, CO: Center for Policy Research.

Vaillant, G. (1993). *The wisdom of the ego.* Cambridge, MA: Harvard University Press.

Webster's encyclopedic dictionary of the English language. (1990). New York: Lexicon Publications.

Williamson, S., Hare, R., & Wong, S. (1987). Violence: Criminal psychopaths and their victims. *Canadian Journal of Behavioral Sciences, 19,* 454–462.

Zona, M., Lane, J., & Palarea, R. (1997, August). *The psychodynamics of stalking.* Paper presented at the Seventh Annual Threat Management Conference, Los Angeles, CA.

Zona, M., Sharma, K., & Lane, J. (1993). A comparative study of erotomanic and obsessional subjects in a forensic sample. *Journal of Forensic Sciences, 38,* 894–903.

CHAPTER 2

The Legal Perspective on Stalking

Rhonda Saunders, J.D.

"I have an obsession with the unattainable. I have to eliminate what I cannot attain." These words were penned by Robert John Bardo to his sister shortly before he murdered actress Rebecca Schaeffer.

As a result of this crime, and the physical attack on actress Theresa Saldana by drifter Arthur Jackson several years earlier, in 1990 the California legislature passed the first anti-stalking law (Penal Code Section 646.9) in the United States, effective Janaury 1, 1991. By 1992, stalking or harassment laws were enacted in 30 other states: Alabama, Arizona, Colorado, Connecticut, Delaware, Florida, Hawaii, Kansas, Idaho, Illinois, Iowa, Kentucky, Louisiana, Massachusetts, Michigan, Mississippi, Nebraska, New York, North Carolina, Ohio, Oklahoma, Rhode Island, South Carolina, South Dakota, Tennessee, Utah, Virginia, Washington, West Virginia, and Wisconsin. The District of Columbia and all the remaining states, with the exception of Maine, passed stalking laws in 1993.

Stalking is a continuous crime, and all stalking statutes require at least two or more incidents to constitute the crime. In Illinois, the stalking statute requires a threat and relevant conduct in furtherance of the threat (*People v. Bailey,* 1995). Other states, including California, require a "continuity of purpose" (*Culbreath v. State,* 1995; *Bouters v. State,* 1995; *Luplow v. State,* 1995).

In most states, the crime of stalking requires a credible threat, direct or implied, that places the victim in reasonable fear. In *Long v. The State of Texas* (1996), Texas' stalking law (Texas Penal Code Section 42.07(a)(7)) was found to be unconstitutionally vague on its face. One of the grounds upon which the court found vagueness was that the statute did not incorporate a reasonable

The Psychology of Stalking: Clinical and Forensic Perspectives

person standard, so that it could clearly be understood whose sensitivities must be offended.

In most states, the stalker must have the specific intent (criminal intent) to place the victim in reasonable fear, and the course of conduct must be willful, purposeful, intentional or knowing. In *Long* (supra, p. 293) the court found that the statute lacked an element of specific intent, which was necessary because,

> (I)n addition to creating greater specificity, these kinds of limiting elements help to avoid a vagueness problem by taking the First Amendment out of the picture. Conduct which alone would constitute protected activities may be actionable if it is part of a common plan that includes activity that is clearly unprotected. And, while conduct does not lose First Amendment protection merely because the actor intends to annoy the recipient, such conduct is much less likely to enjoy protection where the actor intends to "frighten" the recipient, and such conduct is unlikely to enjoy any protection where the actor intends to place the recipient in fear of death or bodily injury.

For purposes of this chapter, California's stalking and stalking-related laws, unless otherwise noted, will be utilized to illustrate the range of protections that can be given to victims of stalking and harassment. California's stalking law has been constitutionally upheld in five different cases; *People v. Heilman* (1994), *People v. McClelland* (1996), *People v. Tran* (1996), *People v. Falck* (1997), and *People v. Halgren* (1996).

The seriousness of the crime of stalking is seen in the facts surrounding the Theresa Saldana and Rebecca Schaeffer cases. In 1982, Arthur Jackson, while living in Scotland, saw Theresa Saldana in the movie *Deliverance*. He was immediately attracted to her, but realized that they could never have a normal relationship, so he left Scotland and came to the United States specifically to kill her, get caught, receive the death penalty, and be with her forever in the afterlife. When he arrived in Los Angeles, he hired a private detective agency to locate Saldana. The agency obtained the information through the California Department of Motor Vehicle records. On March 18, 1982, Jackson went to Saldana's home address and waited for her as she left the house and walked to her car. Jackson approached, took out his knife, and stabbed her 10 times. Fortunately, Jeff Fenn, a water deliveryman, saw what was happening and intervened, thus saving Saldana's life.

Jackson was convicted of attempted murder and sentenced to prison for 12 years. While in prison, Jackson sent Saldana numerous threatening letters. In 1988, he was charged with and convicted of threatening Saldana. Jackson was sentenced to an additional 7 years in prison. Just prior to his release from prison in early 1996, Jackson was extradited to Great Britain, where he was prosecuted for a murder that occurred more than 30 years ago. On January 29, 1997, Jackson pled guilty to manslaughter due to "diminished responsibility" and was sentenced to an indefinite commitment at a criminal psychiatric hospital. Jackson's obsessive behavior was mirrored several years later by Robert Bardo.

The facts surrounding Robert Bardo's murderous obsession with actress Rebecca Schaeffer have been documented in numerous police and newspaper reports, prosecutors' files, and television profiles. Bardo first saw Rebecca Schaeffer on the television series *My Sister Sam* in 1986, while he was living in Tucson, Arizona. He was attracted to her youthful innocence and began writing fan letters to her. She sent him a handwritten card and autographed picture, which validated his delusion of their mutual attraction. Bardo took a bus to Los Angeles and attempted to contact Schaeffer on the set of her show, but was ejected from the lot by security guards. On his second trip to Los Angeles, he was again rebuffed by studio security guards. Bardo returned to Tucson, but immediately made plans to go to Los Angeles again. This time he carried a knife. In his diary Bardo wrote, "I don't lose. Period." Once again, he failed in his mission.

In 1988, Bardo went to see the movie *Scenes from the Class Struggle in Beverly Hills,* in which Schaeffer had a minor role. Bardo grew infuriated when, in one scene, Schaeffer was in bed with a male character. His fan letters took on a more threatening tone. In one letter he referred to Schaeffer as "Miss Nudity 2-Shoes", and he later told his court-appointed psychiatrist, "If she was a whore, God was going to appoint me to punish her." In a magazine, Bardo read about how Arthur Jackson had located Theresa Saldana's home address and decided to obtain Schaeffer's address in the same manner. The private detective agency that Bardo hired easily located Schaeffer's address through the Department of Motor Vehicles. Subsequent to this case, the California legislature enacted Vehicle Code Section 1808.21, which provides that stalking and threat victims may now request confidentiality regarding their DMV records.

Bardo bought a gun and hollow point ammunition. He drew a diagram of a body and filled it with Xs and Os where he planned to shoot Schaeffer. Bardo packed the card and autographed picture that Schaeffer had sent him 2 years previously, and left for Los Angeles.

When Bardo arrived in Los Angeles, he called his sister and told her that he was going to fulfill his mission to "stop Schaeffer from forsaking her innocent childlike image for that of an adult fornicating screen whore." He went to Schaeffer's apartment and rang the bell. Schaeffer answered the door. After a brief conversation in which Bardo proudly showed her the card and autographed picture that Schaeffer had sent to him, Schaeffer told him not to come to her front door anymore. He shook her hand and left. He went down the street, put a bullet into his gun, returned to her apartment building, and again rang the bell. When Schaeffer came to the door, she had what Bardo described as, "a cold look on her face." Bardo grabbed the door as he reached for his gun. He brought out the gun, which was concealed in the small of his back, and shot Schaeffer once in the chest. In a video-recorded confession following his arrest, Bardo described that as she died, Schaeffer screamed at him, "Why, why?" Rebecca Schaeffer was murdered at the age of 21.

EVOLUTION OF THE FIRST STALKING LAW

Ironically, California's stalking law, as it existed in 1991, would not have protected either Schaeffer or Saldana, even if it had been in effect at the time of their attacks. Between 1991 and 1993, California's stalking law required that a stalker make a "credible threat of death or great bodily injury" toward the victim, placing the victim in reasonable fear of the same. Neither Saldana nor Schaeffer was aware of the threats being made against her by her stalker. Even if they had known, the threats themselves were implied and not direct.

In 1994 major revisions were made to California Penal Code Section 646.9, enhancing the ability of law enforcement and prosecutors to intervene and protect stalking victims at the earliest time, before death or great bodily injury occurred. These changes were made in direct response to the following aggravated case in which stalking could not be charged due to the inadequacy of the stalking law at that time.

In 1992, I was given a truly bizarre case to prosecute. When I first read the police reports, it was apparent that the victim, "Jane," had been stalked by the suspect, "Laura," for at least a year. Jane had repeatedly gone to the police asking for help, but was told that nothing could be done because the suspect had not made any overt threats to physically hurt her.

Jane worked for Laura's father as a design consultant. Their initial contact consisted of polite small talk. She left that job and did not see Laura again for 3 to 4 years. Jane later discovered that after she left her job, Laura had tried, unsuccessfully, to obtain her address and phone number from other people at the company.

In November 1990, Jane encountered Laura and her father at a local cinema. Laura took Jane aside and told her that she needed to talk to her because she was distraught over the death of her stepsister who, ironically, had recently been stalked and brutally murdered by a security guard. Jane agreed to meet with Laura for lunch the following week. Shortly thereafter, Laura and Jane entered into a sexual relationship. Within a couple of weeks, Jane became frightened because Laura was becoming physically violent and demanding in their relationship. Jane tried to convince Laura that the relationship was not working, but that they could remain friends.

Laura began to exhibit obsessive behavior, calling Jane at all hours of the day and night. She left gifts, theater tickets, and numerous letters, begging Jane to resume their relationship. Laura wrote in one letter that Jane would never be able to get rid of her as she could always find her. These gifts and letters were left at Jane's house, at work, and on her car windshield. Laura began showing up at Jane's place of work and, in one instance, had to be escorted outside due to her explosive outburst of obscenities directed at Jane. Jane's boss asked her to look for another job, as he was afraid of the potential workplace violence that might occur.

In February 1991, Jane began to hear strange sounds coming from beneath her house. She would hear loud banging noises coming from the pipes in the crawl space, often so loud that she could not sleep at night. Jane called an exterminator who told her that a squirrel or possum had probably gotten under the house and was making the noise. The exterminator came to the house and threw some poisoned bait into the crawl space, but the noises did not stop.

In June 1991, Jane left town for the weekend. Her friend John was housesitting for her. John left the house one evening to get a package of cigarettes. When he returned, he saw a light on in one of the back rooms. When he put the key in the door, the light went out. Knowing that Laura had been following and harassing Jane, John entered and ordered Laura to come out of the back room. Laura appeared and had a brief conversation with John, in which he told her to leave Jane alone. John did not tell Jane about this incident when she returned from her trip because he did not want to alarm her.

Within a few weeks of this incident, Jane's friends, relatives and business associates began receiving long rambling letters from Laura, entitled, "The Saga of Jane and Laura." Most of these people had never met Laura and had no idea how she had obtained their names and addresses, as many of them were unlisted. When these people began to call Jane to inform her about the letters, Jane searched her house to see if anything was missing. She discovered that her Rolodex directory, containing the names, addresses, and phone numbers of her friends, business associates, and relatives, was missing. When John found out what happened, he told Jane about the night he found Laura in the house.

The number of phone calls and letters increased. The tone of these communications was becoming more ominous, but there were no specific threats to kill or physically harm Laura. The tenor of those messages and Laura's other conduct did make Jane fear for her life. One evening, as Jane was taking a shower, she heard the sound of breaking glass coming from her living room. Jane went into the living room and discovered that Laura had broken one of the glass panes in her French doors and was attempting to stick her head through the opening, all the while screaming obscenities at Jane. Jane called the police, but by the time they arrived, Laura was gone.

In October 1991, Jane heard about the Los Angeles Police Department's Threat Management Unit, which was founded in 1990 to investigate long-term harassment-type cases. Detective Doug Raymond determined that there was enough evidence to arrest Laura for burglary. An arrest warrant was issued, and when Raymond went to Laura's apartment to serve the warrant, he found her in the process of addressing a "saga" letter to the parents of Jane's new boyfriend. Raymond also found a makeshift altar dedicated to Jane.

Laura was arrested, but was bailed out of jail by her father the same day. She went to his house and located a loaded gun that he kept for protection. Laura then went directly to Jane's house with the gun.

Jane was in her dining room having lunch with two friends. For the first time in a year she felt free and had all her windows open. She got up to go to the restroom, and was confronted by Laura in her hallway. Laura was holding the gun to her own head, but as she started to point it toward Jane, Jane screamed and ran out of the house, leaving her two friends there with Laura. One of these friends tried to talk Laura into putting the gun down, but instead, Laura pointed the gun at the woman and threatened to kill her. The woman and Jane's other friend managed to run out of the house, leaving Laura alone with the gun.

The Los Angeles Police Department's SWAT Team was summoned and tried to negotiate with Laura to come out of the house. Laura came out of the house, but instead of surrendering, pointed the loaded gun at one of the SWAT Team officers. He did not shoot at her and she returned inside the house. The police put Jane on the phone to Laura to try to reason with her. Laura told Jane that she might not want to be with her now, but they would be together in heaven soon. Finally, 8 hours later, Laura surrendered to the police.

The next day, Jane hired a security company to put an alarm system in her house. While stringing a cable in the crawl space under the house, the installer found a pillow, a blanket, and a pair of red sneakers. Jane immediately recognized the red sneakers as belonging to Laura. There was dried food scattered near the makeshift bed. The telephone switch box had scratch marks on it that the installer, at trial, testified were consistent with someone tapping into the phone system.

Laura was convicted by a jury of threatening the SWAT Team officer and the luncheon guests with a gun. The jury hung 11 to 1 for guilty on the burglary count. She was sentenced to $7\frac{1}{2}$ years in state prison. The judge ordered the California Department of Corrections to place Laura in a prison that had psychiatric facilities and for her to receive treatment for her mental condition. Unfortunately, the court's order was not carried out, and Laura was not seen by a mental health professional until shortly before her release from prison, 5 years later.

In 1992, when the case was prosecuted, Laura's case presented numerous legal problems from a prosecutor's viewpoint. Stalking could not be charged for the following reasons:

• The law required a threat of death or great bodily injury directed toward the victim. Laura was very careful not to directly threaten Jane's life. In one phone message, Laura told Jane, "You know I'll never physically hurt you, but I'm going to torture you mentally." This message did not reassure Jane that she was not in danger and, coupled with Laura's other behavior, made Jane even more afraid.

• The term "credible threat" was not defined at that time, and many judges interpreted it to mean that the suspect had to be standing in front of the victim holding a weapon for the threat to be "credible."

• The law required that a restraining order be in effect at the time the stalking took place for the crime to be filed as a felony. Without a restraining order, the crime was a misdemeanor, punishable by 1 year or less in county jail. Even if the stalker received the maximum sentence of 1 year, with good-time/work-time credits, the stalker would be back on the street in less than 6 months. Jane had never sought a restraining order because she feared that it would anger Laura so much that she would carry out her implied violent threats.

In January 1996, Detective Raymond and I received a *Tarasoff* warning from Laura's prison psychiatrist. *Tarasoff* (1976) is the landmark case that establishes an affirmative duty on the part of psychiatrists, psychologists, and other mental health professionals to protect a potential victim if his or her client/patient has revealed an intent to seriously harm the victim. Laura's psychiatrist told us that based on her interviews with Laura, she believed that once Laura got out of prison, "someone could die."

Laura was released in May 1996 and placed on stringent terms of parole. She was not permitted to be in the Los Angeles area, had to attend psychotherapy sessions three times a week and take any prescribed medication, and had to report to her parole officer once a day. She continues to be focused on the "wrong" that was done to her by the people involved in her trial, despite the overwhelming evidence in the case. She claims that she only went over to Jane's house to kill herself, not to hurt anyone else. Of course, if this were true, she would have had plenty of time to do so when she was left alone in Jane's house with two loaded guns during the 8-hour SWAT Team standoff.

As soon as she was released from prison, Laura called the District Attorney's Office and demanded that criminal charges of perjury be filed against Detective Raymond, the victim, the SWAT Team officer (who did not shoot her), and the other witnesses who testified at the trial and who had "set her up." She also attempted to file complaints with the LAPD Internal Affairs Division against Raymond and the SWAT Team Officer for lying about her. At no time has Laura acknowledged any responsibility for her criminal conduct.

CALIFORNIA'S CURRENT STALKING LAW

As a direct result of the above case, California's stalking law was amended in 1994. The new law specifies:

> Any person who willfully, maliciously, and repeatedly follows or harasses another person and who makes a credible threat with the intent to place that person in reasonable fear for his or her safety, or the safety of his or her immediate family, is guilty of the crime of stalking.

To convict a defendant of the crime of stalking, the prosecutor must prove the following elements beyond a reasonable doubt:

1. A person willfully, maliciously, and repeatedly followed or harassed another person;
2. The person following or harassing made a credible threat; and
3. The person who made the threat did so with the specific intent to place the other person in reasonable fear for his or her safety or the safety of the immediate family of such person(s).

Several recent California Court of Appeal cases have defined the wording of the stalking statute. In *People v. Heilman* (1994) the court defined the term "repeatedly" as meaning "on more than one occasion." "Harassment" was defined in that case as "multiple acts, over a period of time, however short, evidencing a continuity of purpose." "Harasses" is defined in Penal Code Section 646.9(e) as, "a knowing and willful course of conduct directed at a specific person that seriously alarms, annoys, torments or terrorizes the person, and that serves no legitimate purpose. This course of conduct must be such as would cause a reasonable person to suffer substantial emotional distress, and must actually cause substantial emotional distress to such person." At trial and preliminary hearing, I have established the element of substantial emotional distress through actions taken by a victim, such as hiring a bodyguard, changing his or her daily routine, adding additional security measures around the home and at work, avoiding public appearances, or seeking psychological counseling.

In *People v. McClelland* (1996) the court held that the victim's state of mind and knowledge of the suspect's prior history is relevant and admissible at trial. Intent to actually carry out the threat is not required and the specific intent element is satisfied if the suspect intended to place the victim in fear (*People v. Carron*, 1995). During a recent trial, the defense attorney argued to the jury that his client's conduct was not egregious because the victim could not show them any scars. The obvious reply to that argument was, "(N)ot all scars are external."

"Course of conduct" is defined in Penal Code Section 646.9(f) as, "a pattern of conduct composed of a series of acts over a period of time, however short, evidencing a continuity of purpose." For example, a stranger follows the victim's car for several miles on the freeway. When the victim leaves the freeway, the suspect follows. The suspect then tries to run the victim off the road with his car. The crime would be assault with a deadly weapon (the car). If the suspect began to follow the victim on the freeway the next day, turned off the freeway when the victim did and followed her down different streets, but did not try to run her off the road that day, the crime would be stalking (and assault with a deadly weapon from the previous day). Stalking is a continuous crime, and there must be at least two or more incidents before charges can be filed.

Most importantly, the term "credible threat" has been redefined to include not only a verbal or written threat, but also "a threat implied by a pattern of conduct or a combination of verbal or written statements and conduct." The threat(s) does not need to be direct. Stalking is a crime of conduct and context, not necessarily words. For example, a stalker may send a note stating, "I love you" and enclose a bullet in the envelope. The credible threat made by the stalker must be against the safety of the victim or the victim's immediate family. There no longer needs to be a threat of "death or great bodily injury." The language of the statute was changed in 1994, from a "threat of death or great bodily injury" to a "threat against a person's safety" to incorporate threats of sexual assault and kidnapping into the statute. The current test of "credible threat" is whether a reasonable person would fear for his or her safety, or the safety of his or her immediate family; whether the victim believed the suspect would carry out the threat; and whether the threat actually caused substantial emotional distress to the victim. Thus, the victim must be aware of the threat, but it can be conveyed by third parties.

Penal Code Section 646.9(k) defines "immediate family" as "any spouse, parent, child, any person related by consanguinity or affinity within the second degree (grandparent, brother, sister), or any other person who regularly resides in the household, or who, within the prior six months, regularly resided in the household." Stalkers often try to frighten and intimidate their victims by directing their threats toward third parties who are close to the victim because the stalker perceives these persons as standing between him or her and the victim. A comprehensive study (Meloy, 1996) has indicated that intervention by third parties to help or protect the victim might increase the risk of violence because it can confirm the paranoid fantasies of the stalker.

One study (Pathé & Mullen, 1997) has shown that stalking takes a heavy psychological toll on its victims and those around them. After her stalker had been convicted and sentenced to jail, a stalking victim once stated to me, "I have given up all hopes of ever having a safe life. For the rest of my life, I will be looking over my shoulder, expecting to see him there."

Incarceration is not a defense to stalking. Many stalkers, such as Arthur Jackson, while in jail or prison, will continue to send letters or make phone calls to their victims. New charges of stalking can be filed against them, and telephone and mail privileges can be restricted. The inmate could also lose "good-time/work-time" credits toward an earlier release date.

In many states a first-time stalking crime can be prosecuted only as a misdemeanor, unless there are aggravating circumstances such as use of a weapon (Minnesota), violation of a restraining order (Oklahoma), conduct directed toward a victim under the age of 16 (Alaska), or commission of a prior stalking offense (New Hampshire). The New Hampshire statute (N.H. Rev.Stat.Ann.Section 633.3-a Supp. 1994) provides for misdemeanor warrantless arrests if a law enforcement officer has probable cause to believe that a stalking violation occurred within 6 hours preceding the arrest.

Under California's current law, a first-time convicted stalker can be sentenced to 3 years in state prison, even if there is no restraining order in effect. If there is a court or restraining order or if the defendant had previously been convicted of felony stalking against *any person,* he or she could be sentenced to 4 years in state prison.

In *People v. Kelley* (1997) the court held that Section 646.9 does not define the crime of stalking in terms of a restraining order. Section (b) merely creates a punishment enhancement. To prove aggravated stalking, the following three elements must also be established:

4. A court had previously issued a temporary restraining order, injunction, or any other order prohibiting such behavior against the same other person; and

5. The temporary restraining order, injunction, or other court order was in effect at the time of the conduct described in elements 1, 2 and 3; or

6. The suspect has previously been convicted of felony stalking against *any* person.

Other provisions of Penal Code Section 646.9 provide that the sentencing court may issue a restraining order valid for up to 10 years, require that the stalker participate in counseling, and, in certain cases, order the stalker to register as a sex offender. Failure to comply with these terms can result in new criminal charges being brought against the defendant. After reviewing the evidence in each case, the court can also make a recommendation to the California Department of Corrections that the stalker receive mental health treatment while incarcerated.

PROBATION AND PAROLE

When a defendant is about to be released from jail or prison following a conviction for stalking or a felony offense involving domestic violence, the victim, family members of the victim, and witnesses to the offense, upon their request, have the right to be notified by the California Department of Corrections, county sheriff, or director of the local department of corrections, "not less than 15 days prior to the release" (Penal Code Section 646.92). Stalking is a chronic behavior, and can continue for many months or years, and incarceration or restraining orders may not diminish the stalker's obsession (Meloy, 1996). However, he or she can be returned to prison for up to 1 year if the terms of parole are violated. This procedure can be repeated twice, for a maximum of up to 3 additional years in prison.

The notification form (CDC 707) that the victim, family member, or witness fills out contains a section in which they can request certain terms of parole or probation. In several stalking cases that I have prosecuted, I have recommended that the victim request terms such as:

• The defendant shall not follow, surveil, harass, or have contact, directly, indirectly, or through third persons, by letter, fax, e-mail, phone, in person, or by any other means of communication with the following persons (victim, victim's family, employer or employees, etc.)

• The defendant shall stay at least 500 yards away from the homes, workplaces, and schools of the above-named persons.

• The defendant shall be paroled to a location that is at least 35 miles away from the victim's residence, school, or place of employment.

• The defendant shall make restitution to the victim, through the probation department or parole board, for any property damage or reasonable medical or mental health counseling bills incurred by the victim or the victim's family as a result of the defendant's conduct.

• The defendant shall enter and remain at (psychiatric, or drug/alcohol abuse) live-in facility until further order of the court.

• Upon his/her release from the above facility, the defendant will continue to attend outpatient treatment sessions and take all prescribed medication, until further court order.

• The defendant will agree to submit to periodic laboratory testing to determine if he/she is properly taking all prescribed medication and have those reports released to either the court or his/her probation or parole officer.

• The defendant shall not own, possess, or have in his/her custody any firearm or deadly or dangerous weapons.

ASSOCIATED STALKING STATUTES

Several other California statutes relate specifically to stalking, although they are not contained within Penal Code Section 646.9. Penal Code Sections 12021(a)(1) and (c)(1) provide that it is a crime for any person who is convicted of stalking (felony or misdemeanor) to possess or have custody or control of a firearm. Civil Code Section 1708.7 establishes the tort of stalking, whereby a victim can sue the stalker for general, special, and punitive damages. The Code of Civil Procedure Section 527 allows victims of harassment or threats to obtain a civil restraining order at no cost to them, and Code of Civil Procedure Section 527.8 permits a stalking victim's employer to obtain a restraining order against someone who is stalking or harassing one of their employees.

THE FEDERAL STALKING LAW

On July 25, 1996, the United States Senate passed the Interstate Stalking Punishment and Prevention Act of 1996 (Title 18 USC Section 2261), making it a federal crime to cross state lines to injure or harass another person. It was signed by President Clinton two months later.

The victim must be in reasonable fear of the death of, or serious bodily injury to, that person or a member of their immediate family. The definition of "victim" includes any person who is stalked, not only domestic violence victims. Punishment includes up to 5 years in prison for stalking, up to 10 years in prison for stalking with a dangerous weapon or if serious bodily injury occurs, up to 20 years if permanent disfigurement or a life-threatening injury occurs, and life in prison if death results from the stalking. The act also makes a restraining order issued in one state enforceable in other states. The Act was signed into law on September 23, 1996, as part of a comprehensive bill addressing violence against women.

THE CRIME OF TERRORIST THREATS

In California the crime of making a terrorist threat, Penal Code Section 422, is often charged with or in lieu of stalking. It is defined as follows:

> Any person who willfully threatens to commit a crime which will result in death or great bodily injury to another person, with the specific intent that the statement is to be taken as a threat, even if there is no intent of actually carrying it out, which, on its face and under the circumstances in which it is made is so unequivocal, unconditional, immediate, and specific as to convey to the person threatened a gravity of purpose and an immediate prospect of execution of the threat, and thereby causes that person reasonably to be in sustained fear for his or her own safety or for his or her immediate family's safety.

The crime of making a terrorist threat differs from stalking in that it is truly a crime of words, not conduct. However, the context and the circumstances under which the statement was uttered are important. For example, in a workplace situation, an employee facetiously may say to another person, "I'm going to kill you," after the other person has bumped into him making him drop some files. The threat takes on a different meaning, of course, if it is said to a supervisor who has either just fired the worker or given him an unfavorable review.

The words themselves must be a direct, not implied, threat of death or great bodily injury. Section 422 does not require a "pattern of conduct." One threat is sufficient. The threat must place the victim in reasonably sustained fear. In *People v. Allen* (1995) the court held that 15 minutes of fear is more than sufficient to constitute "sustained fear."

Although the statute states that the threat must be "so unequivocal, unconditional, immediate and specific," case law has held that the language of the statute does not mean that the suspect must be standing in front of the victim with a weapon in his or her hand when he or she makes the threat. The crime does not require that the suspect had the intent to carry out the threat, only that the suspect intended the statement to be taken as a threat. *In Re David L.* (1991) was the first case to define the meaning of Penal Code Section 422. The Court held that there does not have to be a showing that the suspect has the immediate ability to carry out the threat, nor does the statute require a time or specific manner of execution. It only requires that the words used be of an immediately threatening nature and convey an immediate prospect of execution. In other words, was the victim frightened for his or her life when first made aware of the threat? The threat may be conveyed directly to the victim by the suspect, by letter, fax, e-mail, telephone, or through third parties.

A conditional threat (e.g., "Listen Chump! Resign or you'll get your brains blown out") can be a violation of Section 422 if its context and the surrounding circumstances reasonably convey to the victim that the threat is intended to be taken seriously by the victim. In *People v. Stanfield* (1995) the court held that "the use of the conditional word 'if' does not absolve a defendant from conviction under Penal Code Section 422." Both the *Stanfield* and *People v. Brooks* (1994) cases strongly disapprove a prior case, *People v. Brown* (1994), which held that threats must be unconditional.

Terrorist threats are often made in celebrity cases. It is not uncommon for the suspect to make threats against the celebrity's family, staff, agent, manager, or lawyer. These people are seen as obstacles who must be eliminated because they are standing between the stalker and the celebrity. Intervention by these third parties to help or protect the victim could increase the risk of violence toward themselves or the victim. This dynamic may change if the intervention is done by law enforcement or private professionals trained in the fields of stalking and threat assessment.

THE MADONNA STALKING CASE

The recent case of *People v. Hoskins* illustrates how California's stalking and terrorist threat laws work hand in hand to protect victims. In May 1995 Hoskins was arrested and charged with the following crimes:

- Stalking and making a terrorist threat against entertainer Madonna Ciccone;
- Making terrorist threats against Madonna's bodyguard, Basil Stephens, and personal assistant, Caresse Henry; and
- Assaulting Madonna's bodyguard.

In April 1995, Hoskins scaled a wall surrounding Madonna's Los Angeles home and proceeded to the courtyard adjacent to the living quarters. Basil Stephens, Madonna's bodyguard, observed him and scared Hoskins away. He returned the next day and was rebuffed by Caresse Henry, Madonna's personal assistant, who was alone in the house. Hoskins, who was at the gated entrance to the house, grew enraged and threatened to kill both Madonna and Henry. He left a note for Madonna in her intercom call box at the gate. The note was written over a printed religious tract named "DEFILED" (Figure 1). The word "Madonna" is written above the word "defiled" and "Louise Ciccone" (Madonna's middle and last names) is written under the title. The note reads, "I love you. Will you be my wife for keeps. Robert Dewey Hoskins." The other side of that page reads "I'm very sorry. Meet me somewhair (sic). Love for keeps. Robert Dewey Hoskins." On the side of that page, contained in a drawn circle were the words, "be mind (sic) and I'll be yours." Beneath this "love note," the printed religious tract describes how sinners who fornicate outside marriage should be killed and those who do not go around properly clothed should be punished.

Henry, who knew that Hoskins had scaled the wall the night before and gained access to the property, telephoned Stephens who responded by returning to the house and confronting Hoskins. Hoskins threatened to kill the bodyguard if he did not give Madonna the note he had left. Hoskins told Stephens that if

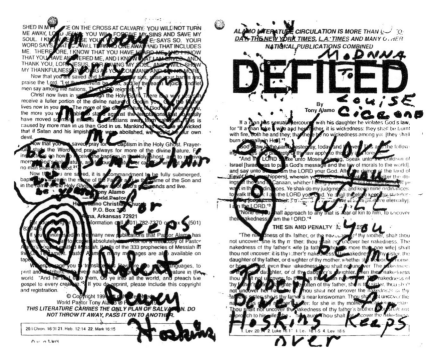

Figure 1

Madonna didn't marry Hoskins that evening, he would "slice her throat from ear to ear." Stephens chased Hoskins away, but as Hoskins walked down the road, he encountered Madonna pedaling up the road on her bicycle. Madonna testified that Hoskins stopped and gave her a look that "chilled" her, but then walked on, fortunately not recognizing her.

The threats were conveyed to Madonna by Stephens and Henry when she arrived at the house 3 minutes after Hoskins' departure. The police were called but could not locate him. Madonna testified at trial that when she was shown Hoskins' note, she "shivered."

Hoskins returned to the house 7 weeks later and again scaled the wall to gain entry onto the property. When he was confronted by Stephens, Hoskins threatened to kill him. Hoskins lunged for the bodyguard's holstered gun. A struggle ensued, and Stephens was able to regain control of the gun. Despite repeated commands to surrender, Hoskins again lunged and was shot twice in the abdomen with a .45 caliber semi-automatic pistol by the bodyguard. Madonna testified at the trial that she was still having nightmares about Hoskins 8 months after these incidents occurred, a not unusual symptom of psychological trauma (*DSM-IV*). She described that in one of these nightmares, she was sitting in her office at home and Hoskins came up the stairs and confronted her. She was paralyzed with fright and asked him "How did you get into my house?" Hoskins replied, "I've been hiding downstairs for quite a while and now seems like the time to come upstairs" (Reporter's Transcript on Appeal, Vol. I, p. 63). She also testified that she had other nightmares in which Hoskins was in her house, trying to kill her, and chasing after her (Reporter's Transcript on Appeal, Vol. I, p. 57).

THE MEDIA AND THE JURY

Prosecuting a case involving a world-famous personality, such as Madonna, presented some unique problems. From the day that Hoskins was arrested until after his sentencing, this case was scrutinized by the worldwide press, magazine and television reporters, and cameramen. At first, the press found the surrounding facts of the case amusing. One headline referred to Hoskins as "Mr. Madonna" and focused on how he told several people that he was Madonna's husband. He was portrayed as a harmless eccentric. These articles did not include how Hoskins had threatened to slice Madonna's throat from ear to ear. A reporter from a British newspaper called and asked how our office could prosecute this poor man who, after all, had been shot by Madonna's bodyguard. It was pointed out to the reporter that Hoskins was shot only after he had attacked and tried to kill Basil Stephens.

The danger of all this pretrial publicity was that a lot of misinformation was being given to the public from which the jury pool was to be selected. When a jury is first seated, they must be fair and impartial, and not tainted by things they may have previously seen or heard in the media, even if they are true. A prime example of this occurred when Madonna was reluctant to come to court and testify. The detective in this case had to surveil her home waiting for her to go jogging with her trainer. When she finally emerged from the house, the detective had to jog after her to personally serve her with a subpoena to be in court the next day. This was reported by the media, who had also staked out Madonna's house, hoping something would happen. The next day, as reporters surged around the courthouse, Madonna failed to appear in court despite the subpoena. Her lawyer went to court and argued that Madonna was not needed to testify at trial as she was not a material witness. The press had a field day with that argument. The prosecution argued that we could not go forward with the case without her, as we had to establish that Hoskins' actions subjectively put her in fear for her safety. We requested that a body attachment be issued for her arrest, to guarantee that she would be present at trial. A body attachment is similar to an arrest warrant, but it is issued for a witness who disobeys a court order (i.e., the subpoena) and fails to appear in court as ordered. The witness must then remain in custody until needed for trial, or guarantees an appearance by posting the equivalent of bail.

The judge issued a body attachment in the amount of 5 million dollars, but stated that it would not be released until the day of the actual trial, when Madonna would have to appear or be taken into custody. These proceedings were reported in newspapers and on television programs across the United States.

The trial began 2 weeks after the body attachment incident. The potential jury panel was specifically questioned as to what they had already seen or heard about the case. Almost everyone on the panel was aware of the incident that had taken place 2 weeks previously. Many of them stated that they had heard or seen other media reports regarding the case itself.

The judge asked individual jurors their opinion about cameras in the courtroom, as the court had just held a highly contested hearing in which the media argued that they had a First Amendment right to have cameras record the Hoskins trial. Both the prosecution and the defense, joined by Madonna's attorney, argued that the cameras should be kept outside the courtroom. The O. J. Simpson criminal trial had been held 2 months previously in the same courthouse, and many blamed the media for the circus-like atmosphere surrounding that trial. When asked by the judge, no one in the Hoskins jury pool wanted cameras in the courtroom because they believed that it would be too intrusive. The cameras were banned.

Madonna appeared in court, as ordered, and was called as the People's first witness. As most members of the jury were already aware that the prosecution had to force her to come to court, damage control was necessary. I asked Madonna on the stand how she felt about being in court with Hoskins across from her. She replied, "Sick to my stomach . . . I feel incredibly disturbed that the man who has repeatedly threatened my life is sitting across from me and we have somehow made his fantasies come true (in that) I am sitting in front of him and that is what he wants" (Reporter's Transcript on Appeal, Vol. I, p.p. 102-103). The look on her face said it all as she glanced at Hoskins. Hoskins just sat at the counsel table, humming a song to himself.

CONVICTION AND SENTENCING

The jury found Hoskins guilty of stalking, making terrorist threats, and assault on Madonna's bodyguard. After the trial, several of the jurors were interviewed by the media. One female juror was asked whether she would have been afraid of Hoskins if she was in Madonna's place. Her reply was, "Of course. Who wouldn't be?"

Between the time of his conviction and the time of his sentencing, Hoskins filled his cell walls with graffiti that read, "I Love Madonna" and "Madonna Love Me" and underneath his bed he wrote "The Madonna Stalker" (Figures 2 and 3). When a Sheriff's Deputy confronted him about the graffiti, Hoskins said Madonna wrote it and that when he got out of jail, he was "going to slice the lying bitch's throat from ear to ear." At the sentencing hearing, the Sheriff's Deputy was called as a witness to repeat Hoskins' statement. The judge sentenced Hoskins to the maximum term of 10 years in the state prison.

On July 11, 1997, Hoskins was brought back to court on a legal technicality in which the judge needed to indicate on the record that she knew that she had jurisdiction to ignore his prior burglary conviction but chose not to do so when

Figure 2

Figure 3

she had originally sentenced him. Hoskins appeared in court and seemed much calmer and lucid than he had been during the trial. The judge commented on the improvement in his appearance. After the judge made it clear that she believed that 10 years in prison was the appropriate sentence for Hoskins' crimes, she asked him if he had been receiving any type of mental health treatment while in prison. Hoskins became visibly upset and told the judge that he had not received any treatment because there was "nothing wrong with me." He then stated that he had been mistreated in prison, but that he had a friend on the outside who would help him take care of things. Hoskins then leaned toward the judge and told her that when he got out of prison, he was coming back to take care of everyone in the court.

CONCLUSION

Robert Hoskins, Robert Bardo, and Arthur Jackson are clear and dramatic examples of obsessed fans who were willing to commit acts of violence in order to narcissistically link (Meloy, 1996) their names forever with the names of their celebrity victims. In prison, Hoskins is now referred to as "the Material Guy" by his fellow inmates. However, despite his "fantasy fulfillment" of finally being linked with Madonna, Hoskins had to be prosecuted and incarcerated before someone was seriously injured or killed. His actions and statements, even after his conviction, illustrate the risk potential for violence that is posed by stalkers.

Stalkers do not simply "fade away." Their continued actions can, and in some cases do, lead to murder or serious injury. Strong state stalking laws, if properly utilized, could prevent tragedies from occurring. Legislators need to realize that by enacting tough stalking laws, they will enable law enforcement to intervene before these cases turn into homicides or serious bodily injury is inflicted on the victim or those surrounding the victim. Stronger sentencing, meaning longer terms of incarceration, and felony classification need to be implemented in states that view stalking as merely a low-grade misdemeanor. Prosecutors and law enforcement need the proper "tools" to protect the citizens of their states who depend on them. With strong stalking laws and the education of the public and law enforcement as to the seriousness of the crime of stalking, lives can be saved.

APPENDIX: RECENT CALIFORNIA CASE LAW

STALKING CASES

People v. Heilman 25 Cal.App.4th 391

1. Upholds validity of pre-1994 stalking law.
2. "Repeatedly" means "more than one time."
3. "Harassment" means "multiple acts"—course of conduct is a series of acts, over a period of time, *however short,* evidencing a continuity of purpose.

People v. Carron 37 Cal.App.4th 391

1. Pre-1994 law.
2. Penal code section 646.9 does not require the intent to carry out the threat.
3. Specific intent is that the suspect intended to place the victim in fear

People v. McClelland 42 Cal.App.4th 144

1. Upholds constitutionality of 1994 law.
2. Victim's state of mind (knowing that her husband had firebombed his ex-wife's house) is relevant. "A reasonable person, aware that defendant had been convicted of attempted murder in burning his former wife's house, would reasonably fear for her safety upon hearing such a remark." (See *People v. Garrett.*)

People v. Tran 47 Cal.App.4th 253

1. The term, "No legitimate purpose," is not constitutionally vague.
2. PC646.9 is sufficiently clear to give notice to suspect.

People v. Falck 52 Cal.App.4th 287

1. Defendant met and became obsessed with victim in 1982. He was arrested and convicted of trespass and ordered by the court to leave victim alone. In November 1994 he stopped taking his medication and continued his stalking because the planets told him the time was right to try to get together with the victim. He repeatedly phoned the victim and sent pornographic pictures cut from a magazine.

2. Although defendant stated he had no intention to cause fear in the victim, it could be inferred from the fact that he insisted on maintaining contact with her even though she clearly was attempting to avoid him, and he had been warned away by the police, the court, and the victim's husband.

3. Term "safety" as used in 646.9 has commonly accepted usage: (1) Condition of being safe; freedom from danger or hazard. (2) Quality of being devoid of whatever exposes one to danger or harm.

People v. Halgren 52 Cal.App.4th 1223

1. When victim told suspect over the phone to leave her alone, he stated, "Bitch, you don't know who you are F . . . ing with. I am going to call you whenever the F . . . I want to, and I'm going to do to you whatever the F . . . I want to."

2. Challenge to definition of "credible threat." Suspect argued that a mere harmless expression of anger or disappointment could subject a person to criminal charges.

3. It is clear that the perpetrator's intent, rather than the definition of the conduct engaged in, triggers the applicability of the statute.

4. 646.9 applies only when there has been a credible threat made with the intent to instill fear for personal safety.

5. Conduct consisted primarily of phone calls.

People v. Kelley 52 Cal.App.4th 568

1. Defendant was charged with and convicted of two counts of violating a restraining order. Two months after his release from jail, he was charged with stalking. The dates were alleged as April 1 through December 7, 1994, excluding the days that had been alleged in the violation complaint.

Issue: Does a conviction for violation of a restraining order bar prosecutors from later filing stalking charges when the stalking behavior continues?

2. Answer by the court: "Not so."

3. "Section 654 does not prohibit multiple prosecutions where, as here, at least some of the acts giving rise to the charge occurred after the prosecution for the related crime . . . under these circumstances, the prosecution was not precluded from filing felony charges when Kelley was not deterred the first time."

4. Section 646.9 does not define the crime of stalking in violation of a restraining order. [Section (b)] merely creates a punishment enhancement, so there is no double jeopardy issue.

People v. Gans 52 Cal.App.4th 147

1. Conviction of 646.9(b) challenged because victim resumed relationship with suspect after restraining order was in effect.

2. PC 13710—The terms and conditions of the protective order remain enforceable, notwithstanding the acts of the parties.

3. Court rejects due process argument that victim might use restraining order to entrap the suspect, if suspect believes he is acting in compliance with victim's desire.

4. Describes "learned helplessness" theory—a woman *or* man is conditioned to believe that she/he cannot control what happens, and perception becomes reality.

5. Endorses use of expert testimony per EC Section 1107.

6. Operative dates in the information reflected the time period when the victim finally broke off the relationship (even though the restraining order was in effect prior to this occurrence) to the time of suspect's arrest.

Terrorist Threat Cases

In Re David L. 234 Cal.App.3rd 1655

1. A terrorist threat may be communicated through a third party.

2. "PC422 does not in terms apply only to threats made by the threatener personally to the victim, nor is this limitation reasonably inferable from its language. The kind of threat contemplated by Section 422 may as readily be conveyed by the threatener through a third party as personally to the intended victim." at 1659

3. "Imminent conduct"—The statute does not require the showing of immediate ability to carry out the stated threat. at 1660

4. Section 422 requires only that the words used be of an immediately threatening nature and convey an immediate prospect of execution, even though the threatener may have no intent actually to engage in the threatened conduct. at 1660

5. Section 422 does not require a time or precise manner of execution. at 1660

People v. Fisher 12 Cal.App.4th 1556

1. Upholds constitutionality of PC 422.

2. Proof of specific intent to carry out threat is not mandated.

People v. Brown 26 Cal.App.4th 1251

1. PC 422 type threats must be unconditional.
2. Criticized in *Brooks, Stanfield, and Dias.*

People v. Brooks 26 Cal.App.4th 142

1. Criticizes *Brown.*
2. "A threat is not excluded from PC 422 merely because it is conditional. Conditional threats are true threats if their context reasonably conveys to the victim that they are intended." at 149
3. "Under *Brooks* approach, every threat that is conditional would go unpunished, no matter how much fear is reasonably felt by the victim. This would lead to such absurdity as excluding from the statute's prohibition the threat, 'If the sun rises tomorrow, I will kill you'." at 149
4. Cites two federal cases that "echo the notion that the conditional nature of a threat does not mean it is not a true threat, and thus punishable."
    A. *US v. Schneider* (7th Cir. 1990) 910 F.2d 1569, 1570: "Most threats are conditional; they are designed to accomplish something. The threatener hopes that they will accomplish it so he won't have to carry out the threat."
    B. *US v. Cox* (2d Cir. 1994) 957 F.2d 264, 266: "A threat is not to be construed as conditional if it has a reasonable tendency to create apprehension that its originator will act in accordance with its tenor."

People v. Stanfield 32 Cal.App.4th 1152

1. Criticizes *Brown.*
2. Defendant stated that if her lawyer did not join her in bringing her "Universal Reform Party" into power, she would hire gang members to kill him. The threats were made through the lawyer's seretary and another lawyer in the firm.
3. "The use of the conditional word "if" does not absolve a defendant from conviction under PC 422." at 1162
4. "A seemingly conditional threat contingent on an act highly unlikely to occur may convey to the victim a gravity of purpose and immediate prospect of execution." at 1158
5. A threat which may appear conditional on its face can be unconditional under the circumstances. at 1158
6. "The word 'so' indicates that unequivocal, unconditional, immediate and specific are not absolutely mandated, but must be sufficiently present in the threat and *surrounding circumstances* to convey a gravity of purpose and immediate prospect of execution to the victim" at 1157
7. *US v. Kelner* (2d Cir. 1976) 534 F.2d 1020 explained: The court did not intend "unconditionality" to prohibit punishment of threats including "if"

language. The constitution mandates only an inquiry as to whether the threat convincingly expressed an intention of being carried out. Kelner compares these types of threats to those made for extortion, blackmail and assault. at 1160–1161

People v. Allen 33 Cal.App.4th 1149

1. "Sustained fear"—15 minutes of fear is sufficient.
2. "Sustained" means a period of time that extends beyond what is momentary, fleeting or transitory. at 1156
3. The victim's knowledge of defendant's prior conduct is relevant in establishing that the victim was in sustained fear. (Cites to *Garrett* 30 CA4th 962) at 1156

People v. Gudger 29 Cal.App.4th 310 (PC 76)

1. Suspect made a phone call to presiding judge's secretary conditionally threatening to kill another judge.
2. A literal approach to the so-called conditional language used is not determinative . . . of the sufficiency of the evidence. It is necessary to review the language and *context* of the threat to determine if the speaker had the specific intent that the statement was to be taken as a threat. at 321–322

People v. Garrett 30 Cal.App.4th 962

1. Mental state of the victim is relevant.
2. 1101(b) evidence: "Nothing in this section prohibits the admission of evidence that a person committed a crime, civil wrong, or other act when relevant to prove some other fact . . . other than his disposition to commit such act."

People v. Dias 52 Cal.App.4th 46

1. Criticizes *Brown*.
2. A threat subject to an apparent condition may violate PC 422, depending on its context. A seemingly conditional threat contingent on an act highly unlikely to occur may convey to the victim a gravity of purpose and immediate prospect of execution.
3. Cites to: *Shackelford v. Shirley* (5th Cir. 1991) 948 F.2d 935, 937–938— "As speech strays further from the values of persuasion, dialogue, and free exchange of ideas the first amendment was designed to protect, and moves toward threats made with specific intent to perform illegal acts, the state has greater latitude to enact statutes that effectively neutralize verbal expression . . . Threats made with specific intent to injure and focused on a particular individual easily fall into that category of speech deserving of no first amendment protection."
4. The federal courts have concluded that not all threats to perform illegal acts are protected by the first amendment, and a conditional threat may be culpable depending upon its context.

5. Cites to *Stanfield, Brooks,* and *Gudger.*

In Re M.S. 10 Cal.App.4th 698

1. PC 422.6 (hate crime) case. Discusses criminalization of threats and definition of "apparent ability."

2. A threat is an expression of an intent to inflict evil, injury, or damage on another.

3. Conditional language: As long as the threat reasonably appears to be a serious expression of intention to inflict bodily harm, and its circumstances are such that there is a reasonable tendency to produce in the victim a fear that the threat will be carried out, the fact that the threat may be contingent on some future event does not cloak it in constitutional protection.

4. "Apparent ability"—The threat must be one that would reasonably tend to induce fear in the victim (context).

People v. Martinez 53 Cal.App.4th 1212

1. Defendant was convicted of two counts of 422. The convictions were based on statements in which he told his girlfriend's work supervisor, "I'm going to get you," and "I'll get back to you, I'll get you," and on statements in which he threatened to blow up his girlfriend's car and home.

2. Although the words to the supervisor, standing alone, may not have conveyed a threat to commit a crime that would result in death or great bodily injury, in light of the strong public policy behind 422 that every person has the right to be protected from fear and intimidation, and in light of the surrounding circumstances of the case (he later set fire to the building where the supervisor worked, and the fire was discovered shortly after the supervisor reported to work, and later attempted to set fire to his girlfriend's car), his words met the requirement that he make a grave threat to another's personal safety.

3. When making the threat, the defendant approached the supervisor quickly, he yelled and cursed at him, and he displayed very angry behavior. This type of situation can be very intimidating and can carry an aura of serious danger.

4. Held: The meaning of the threat must be gleaned from the words and all the surrounding circumstances.

5. Threat to blow up his girlfriend's car was made after they had argued and he hit her. She knew he had previously been convicted of 422 when he poured gasoline around her friend's house.

REFERENCES

Bouters v. State, 659 So.2d 235, 236 (Fla. 1995).
Culbreath v. State, 667 So.2d 156, 158 (Ala.Crim.App. 1995).

In Re David L., 234 Cal.App.3rd 1655 (1991).

In Re M.S., 10 Cal.App.4th 698 (1995).

Long v. The State of Texas 931 S.W.2nd 285 (1996).

Luplow v. State, 897 P.2d 463, 465 (Wyo. 1995).

Meloy, J. R. (1996). Stalking (obsessional following): A review of some preliminary studies. *Aggression and Violent Behavior, 1,* 147–162.

Pathé, M., & Mullen P. (1997). The impact of stalkers on their victims. *British Journal of Psychiatry, 170,* 12–17.

People v. Allen, 33 Cal.App.4th 1149 (1995).

People v. Bailey, 167 Ill.2d 210 (1995).

People v. Brooks, 26 Cal.App.4th 142 (1994).

People v. Brown, 26 Cal.App.4th 1251 (1994).

People v. Carron, 37 Cal.App.4th 391 (1995).

People v. Dias, 52 Cal.App.4th 46 (1997).

People v. Falck, 52 Cal.App.4th 287 (1997).

People v. Fisher, 12 Cal.App.4th 1556 (1993).

People v. Gans, 52 Cal.App.4th 147 (1997).

People v. Garrett, 30 Cal.App.4th 962 (1994).

People v. Gudger, 29 Cal.App.4th 310 (1994).

People v. Halgren, 52 Cal.App.4th 1223 (1996).

People v. Heilman, 25 Cal.App.4th 391 (1994).

People v. Hoskins, BA122741 (Los Angeles Superior Court, 1996).

People v. Kelley, 52 Cal.App.4th 568 (1997).

People v. Martinez, 53 Cal.App.4th 1212 (1997).

People v. McClelland, 42 Cal.App.4th 144 (1996).

People v. Stanfield, 32 Cal.App.4th 1152 (1995).

People v. Tran, 47 Cal.App.4th 253 (1996).

Tarasoff v. Regents of the University of California, 17 Cal.3d 425 (1976).

CHAPTER 3

Developmental and Social Antecedents of Stalking

Kristine K. Kienlen, Psy.D.

Stalking is generally defined as an individual's persistent unwanted pursuit or obsessional harassment of another person, causing him or her fear of bodily injury. Based on two precursory studies of this population (Meloy & Gothard, 1995; Zona, Sharma, & Lane, 1993), Meloy (1996) coined the clinical term "obsessional follower" to describe "a person who engages in an abnormal or long-term pattern of threat or harassment directed toward a specific individual" (p. 148).

While stalking behavior may be manifested by seemingly benign gestures (e.g., gifts, letters) meant to be symbols of the stalker's affection, the victim reacts in fear due to the stalker's inability or unwillingness to accept the reality that the victim is uninterested in a relationship. Even legal interventions, such as restraining orders prohibiting the stalker's contact with the victim, are often ineffective deterrents to the stalker's behavior. Repeated rejection by the victim may lead to escalation of the stalker's behavior to overt threats or violence (e.g., assault, rape, murder) toward the victim. Sometimes third parties such as friends and family members are perceived as impeding the stalker's relationship with the victim and may also be targets of violence.

Although stalkers often pursue a former intimate partner or casual acquaintance to seek an amorous relationship, other stalkers harass strangers or acquaintances for hostile, paranoid, or delusional reasons (Harmon, Rosner, & Owens, 1995; Kienlen, Birmingham, Solberg, O'Regan, & Meloy, 1997; Meloy & Gothard, 1995).

The Psychology of Stalking: Clinical and Forensic Perspectives

There is no single profile of a "stalker." Individuals who stalk exhibit a broad range of behaviors, motivations, and psychological traits. Some similarities emerge, however, from the research on stalking: Stalkers tend to be older, educated men with unsuccessful relationship and employment histories (Harmon et al., 1995; Kienlen et al., 1997; Meloy, 1996; Meloy & Gothard, 1995; Zona et al., 1993).

The stalker's absence or instability of relationships may be explained by Meloy's (1992, 1996) theory that obsessional following is a pathology of attachment. In the first empirical examination of the early relationships of stalkers, Kienlen et al. (1997) found that most stalkers experienced severe disruptions in childhood caretaking relationships. Disturbances in early attachments may contribute to unstable adult relationships and stalking behavior.

The following review of attachment research forms the framework for a theoretical perspective on how unstable attachment histories can developmentally contribute to the pathology of stalking. Social antecedents of stalking, including recent loss, are also examined.

ATTACHMENT THEORY

Although research on attachment theory has historically focused on early childhood bonds with caregivers, the literature maintains that attachment behavior persists throughout the life cycle (Ainsworth, 1989; Bowlby, 1969). "During the course of healthy development attachment behaviour leads to the development of affectional bonds or attachments, initially between child and parent and later between adult and adult" (Bowlby, 1980, p. 39). While stable early attachments contribute to an individual's healthy development, recent research has focused on the correlation between pathological attachment patterns and the development of various maladaptive personality traits and psychopathology (Dutton, Saunders, Starzomski, & Bartholomew, 1994; Fonagy, Leigh, Steele, Steele, Kennedy, Mattoon, Target, & Gerber, 1996; Rosenstein & Horowitz, 1996; West & Sheldon, 1988). Pathological attachment patterns have also been linked to criminal or violent behavior (Dutton, 1995b; Dutton & Golant, 1995; Meloy, 1992; Raine, 1993).

Attachment is generally defined as a strong affectional bond with a specific person. Ainsworth (1989) defined an affectional bond as "a relatively long-enduring tie in which the partner is important as a unique individual and is interchangeable with none other" (p. 711). Although a specific attachment figure cannot be replaced, an individual may have attachment bonds with various individuals. A secure attachment provides the sense of assurance, comfort, and confidence the child needs to explore the environment.

Bowlby (1980) explained that attachment behavior is "any form of behaviour that results in a person attaining or retaining proximity to some other differentiated and preferred individual" (p. 39). In the presence of the accessible and responsive attachment figure, a child's attachment behavior may simply consist of checking the whereabouts of the caregiver for reassurance. However, certain conditions (i.e., a strange or frightening situation, fatigue of the child, or unavailability of the caregiver) may elicit attachment behavior (i.e., following, clinging, or crying) meant to gain the attention of the caregiver. "Since the goal of attachment behaviour is to maintain the affectional bond, any situation that seems to be endangering the bond elicits action designed to preserve it; and the greater the danger of loss appears to be the more intense and varied are the actions elicited to prevent it" (Bowlby, 1980, p. 42). In addition to attention-seeking behavior such as crying and clinging, angry coercion may be used to maintain the affectional bond. Such attachment behavior dissipates with the ready availability and responsiveness of a caregiver (Bowlby, 1980).

Bowlby's explanation of attachment behavior may to some extent explain the variety of ardent behaviors utilized by stalkers who are pursuing a love object. When the stalker's phone calls, letters, or following of the victim prove ineffective, angry verbal abuse, threats, or even violence may be used in an attempt to coerce the victim into a relationship.

In describing parallels between infant-caregiver attachment and adult romantic love, Shaver and Hazan (1987) pointed out that the infant's joy and distress depend on the caregiver's perceived responsiveness, just as the adult's mood depends on perceptions of the love partner's reciprocation or rejection. Both infants and adults actively react to separation with intense distress, attention-consuming reunion efforts, and sadness when reunion is not accomplished (Shaver & Hazan, 1987).

Bowlby (1980) described the following intense emotions connected to attachment relationships: Love is associated with the formation and maintenance of an attachment bond; anxiety is aroused with the threat of loss, and sorrow occurs with actual loss of the attachment bond; anger or rage may also be elicited by loss and/or sorrow; and joy is experienced upon reunion with the attachment figure.

In addition to the above behavioral and emotional manifestations of attachment, Bowlby (1973) coined the term "working models" to explain the cognitive aspect of attachment. Bowlby (1973) explained that individuals build working models of the world and particularly about attachment figures (i.e., who they are, where they are, their expected response) and of themselves (i.e., perception of how acceptable or unacceptable one is to the attachment figure). Bretherton (1992) explained that if the attachment figure recognizes the child's need for comfort and protection while respecting the child's needs to independently explore the environment, the child will likely develop a working model of self as valued and self-reliant. To the contrary, if the caregiver frequently fails to meet the child's needs for comfort and exploration, the child will likely develop a working model of self as unworthy or incompetent. The child utilizes working models to predict the behavior of the attachment figure and to plan a response (Bretherton, 1992). Bowlby (1973) theorized that more than one working model of oneself and the attachment figure may exist and that primitive unconscious or semiconscious working models developed in the early years may sometimes dominate over more sophisticated, incompatible models.

OBJECT RELATIONS THEORY

The central theme of object relations theory is that early caretaking relationships, usually with the mother, are internalized and transformed into a sense of self. Melanie Klein, considered one of the founders of object relations theory, focused on the mother–child relationship because it is the foundation for the construction of the child's inner world and the prototype for all subsequent relationships (Cashdan, 1988). The relationship model that an individual constructs and internalizes as a child plays a role in the creation and maintenance of relationships throughout the life span. Abandonment or rejection threatens the sense of self.

Mahler, Pine, and Bergman (1975) referred to the "psychological birth of the individual" or the separation–individuation process in which the individual establishes a sense of separateness from the primary love object and the world (p. 3). Separation–individuation involves four subphases: differentiation, practicing, rapprochement, and libidinal object constancy. An individual's development during these four subphases determines the degree of separateness that is achieved and influences the individual's sense of self and relationships.

During the *differentiation* subphase (beginning at the fifth or sixth month and extending to the tenth month) the perceptual-conscious system develops (i.e., distal senses such as vision evolve) enabling the child to be more aware of the mother's separateness (Cashdan, 1988; Mahler et al., 1975).

During the *practicing* subphase (beginning at 10 or 11 months and extending to 15 to 16 months) the child gains locomotive skills, including walking, and is able to play a more active role in determining closeness and distance from the mother. Although the child has a sense of omnipotence, the mother continues to be the center of the child's world or the "home base" for "emotional refueling" through physical contact (Mahler et al., 1975, p. 71). While the child is able to gradually venture out and explore the environment, he continues to seek reassurance from the mother and checks for her presence. A brief period of increased separation anxiety is observed during this stage (Cashdan, 1988; Mahler et al., 1975).

The *rapprochement* subphase (beginning at 15 or 16 months and extending to 30 months) involves the child's rapid attainment of new skills and independence, but continued need for assistance, reassurance, and love (Cashdan, 1988; Mahler et al., 1975). The child remains concerned about the mother's whereabouts and exhibits exacerbated separation anxiety with increased fear of losing the object's love, rather than fear of object loss. With a greater awareness of separateness from the mother, the child comes to the realization that he and the mother may have conflicting wishes. Optimal emotional availability of the mother during this phase is important. While a child's "shadowing" of the mother is normal during this subphase, the more emotionally unavailable the mother, the more intense and desperate are the child's attempts to "woo" her; some children exhibit impulsive "darting away" behavior with the goal of motivating the mother to follow (Mahler et al., 1975, p. 80). During this third subphase, the child experiences a period of rapprochement crisis or ambivalence between desires to be separate from and united with the caregiver. Intense reactions upon separation, including temper tantrums and sadness, are exhibited. Children with developmental disturbances during this period may rapidly alternate among clinging, coercive, and negativistic behaviors. The child is splitting his object representational world into "good" and "bad." In order to successfully resolve this rapprochement crisis, the mother must be able to provide the child with a balance of emotional support and firmness while encouraging a healthy level of independent activity (Cashdan, 1988). As the rapprochement crisis diminishes, the child finds the "optimal distance" from the mother or "the distance at which he could function best" (Mahler et al., 1975, p. 101).

In the final subphase, the *libidinal object-constancy* phase (beginning at $2\frac{1}{2}$ years and extending to approximately 3 years), the principal task is the development of a stable inner representation of the mother so that the child is able to function independently in the mother's absence (Cashdan, 1988; Mahler et al., 1975). If this stage is not successfully accomplished, the child must have the presence of the actual mother for security and cannot develop an autonomous sense of self. The integration of positive and negative images of the mother into one whole representation is also necessary. If integration does not occur, the child will continue to use splitting as a predominant defense and will respond to others as either punitive and rejecting or unrealistically gratifying (Cashdan, 1988).

Dutton and Golant (1995) described the phenomenon of splitting—the extreme idealization and devaluation of women—among abusive men: "As tension and feelings of being unloved and unappreciated build, his rageful self (split off or hidden outside of consciousness) begins to emerge and his view of his wife becomes increasingly negative" (p. 104). After the man relieves tension through abusive behavior, he "idealizes his mate and devalues himself" (p. 104).

Dutton and Golant (1995) indicated that an incomplete rapprochement subphase is common in abusive men and results in difficulty in intimate relationships. Adults with developmental disturbances during the rapprochement subphase experience anxiety about both closeness and separation and are unable to tolerate being alone.

Meloy (1996) proposed that when considering the childhood attachment pathology of obsessional followers, specific consideration be given to developmental disturbances during the differentiation and practicing subphases of separation–individuation. However, the above research by Dutton and Golant (1995) suggests

that disturbances during the rapprochement subphase likely contribute to pathological attachment in stalking.

Attachment research (Ainsworth, Blehar, Waters, & Wall, 1978; Main, 1996)
has identified the following four categories of infant–mother attachment: (1) *secure*
(the child misses the parent on separation and actively greets the parent upon
return before resuming play); (2) *avoidant* (the child is unemotional, does not cry
upon separation from the parent, and actively avoids and ignores the parent upon
return); (3) *resistant–ambivalent* (the child is preoccupied with the parent, may seem
passive or angry, and alternatively seeks or resists the parent); and (4) *disorganized–
disoriented* (the child exhibits disorganized or disoriented behaviors in the parent's
presence and may exhibit ambivalent behaviors such as clinging to the parent while
leaning away).

STALKING AND ATTACHMENT

Bartholomew developed a corresponding four-type model of adult attachment based on positive or negative models of self and others (Bartholomew,
1990; Bartholomew & Horowitz, 1991; Dutton et al., 1994). While the following
categories represent four theoretical prototypes of attachment, individuals may
exhibit varying degrees of more than one attachment style.

The first category, *secure attachment,* involves both a positive self-model and
a positive other-model resulting in confidence and comfort in close adult relationships. Individuals with secure attachments had responsive caregivers during childhood. The second category, *preoccupied attachment,* involves a negative self-model
and positive other-model. Individuals with a preoccupied attachment style have a
poor self-image and actively seek approval and validation from others. During
childhood, these individuals concluded that they were unworthy of love because
their caregivers provided affectionate messages, but were inconsistent and insensi-
tive. The third category, *dismissing attachment,* involves a positive self-model and
a negative other-model. Individuals with a dismissing attachment style maintain a
positive self-image by remaining emotionally distant from others and viewing
relationships as unimportant. Finally, the fourth category, *fearful attachment,* involves
a negative self-model and negative other-model. Individuals with a fearful attachment style experience ambivalence between a desire for interpersonal relationships
and distrust of others and fear of rejection (Bartholomew, 1990). Anger is a
prominent feature of a fearful attachment and post-traumatic stress symptoms,
including depression, anxiety, dissociative states (sometimes accompanied by rageful
acting out), and sleep disturbances, are common (Dutton & Golant, 1995). Dutton
and Golant (1995) theorized that fearfully attached individuals were traumatized
by severe attachment disruptions and react with rage in subsequent intimate relationships. Bartholomew (1990) indicated that individuals with either fearful or

dismissing attachments exhibit avoidance in adult relationships due to childhood experiences of rejecting or emotionally unavailable caregivers.

Because both the preoccupied and fearful attachment styles are likely to experience chronic anxiety about rejection and abandonment in close relationships, individuals with these attachment styles are prone to intimacy anger, jealousy, and mood instability (Dutton et al., 1994). Anger, jealousy, and borderline personality organization (Kernberg, 1977), with central features of affective instability, anger, and projection of unacceptable impulses onto a devalued female object, are strongly associated with verbal and physical abuse in intimate relationships and attachment style (particularly fearful attachment, and to a lesser extent, preoccupied attachment) (Dutton, 1994; Dutton & Starzomski, 1993; Dutton et al., 1994).

EARLY ATTACHMENT DISRUPTION—A PREDISPOSING FACTOR OF STALKING

Meloy (1992, 1996) theorized that obsessional following or stalking is a pathology of attachment and suggested the need for clinical investigation of the childhood and adolescent attachment histories of individuals who engage in stalking behavior.

Kienlen et al. (1997) conducted the first empirical investigation of childhood relationship disturbances among individuals who exhibit adult criminal stalking behavior. Most stalkers (63%) experienced a change or loss of a primary caregiver during childhood ($N = 24$). Close to one-half of the subjects (42%) experienced disruption in caregiver relationships during early childhood (Age 6 or younger). Parental separation or divorce most often led to the disturbed relationship with the primary caregiver. Subsequent to the parental separation, most subjects had infrequent or no contact with the noncustodial parent. Other reasons for a change or loss of a primary caregiver were the caregiver's abandonment, death, or incarceration in prison. The parents of some subjects may have also been emotionally absent due to mental illness or substance use. Many of the subjects (55%) reported that they experienced childhood emotional, physical, or sexual abuse by primary caregivers, suggesting disturbed attachment relationsips ($N = 20$). Childhood history of abuse and family history of mental illness and substance abuse may have been underreported in the study. Kienlen et al. (1997) theorized that disturbed childhood experiences such as separation from a primary caregiver, abuse by a parent, or emotional absence of a parent due to mental illness or substance abuse might contribute to the development of a preoccupied attachment pattern in adulthood (Bartholomew, 1990) and ultimately to stalking behavior.

Pathological attachment patterns are also characteristic of personality disorders (West & Sheldon, 1988), which are common in individuals who stalk (Kienlen et al., 1997; Meloy, 1996; Meloy & Gothard, 1995; Zona et al., 1993). A prominent feature of both personality disorders and stalking behavior is a pattern of conflicted or impoverished relationships during adulthood. Recent studies (Harmon et al., 1995; Kienlen et al., 1997; Meloy & Gothard, 1995; Zona et al., 1993) indicate that most individuals who exhibit stalking behavior were historically unsuccessful at establishing or maintaining intimate relationships. Stalkers usually were not involved in an intimate relationship at the time of the stalking behavior, which may have contributed to their preoccupation with, and relentless pursuit of, the victim.

ADULT RECENT LOSS—A PRECIPITATING FACTOR OF STALKING

Kienlen et al. (1997) also investigated precipitating factors, including psycho-social stressors and recent losses, that might contribute to stalking behavior. Most stalkers (80%, $N = 20$) had significant stressors, usually losses, within 7 months of the onset of the stalking behavior. They experienced the breakup of an intimate relationship or marriage (48%), terminated employment (48%), potential loss of a child (i.e., custody battles, restricted visitation, questioned paternity) (28%), or potential loss of a parent who was seriously ill (8%). Many of the subjects (44%) experienced more than one of the above losses prior to the onset of their stalking. Kienlen et al. (1997) theorized that stalkers attempt to compensate for a recent loss through pursuit of the object or stalking victim. We further proposed that some angry stalkers might view the harassing or stalking behavior as a means of revenge toward the victim, whom they blame for the loss.

Preliminary clinical observations appear to support the above findings that an individual's stalking behavior is often precipitated by one or more significant stressors or losses that represent a blow to his identity and sense of self-worth. In addition to the losses described above, some stalkers have been observed to have physical health problems (i.e., a chronic illness or significant injury) that affects their perceived sense of worth. The stalker who is unable to effectively cope with such a loss may pursue the object as a means to alleviate grief, to fill a void in his life, or to vent anger.

PREOCCUPIED ATTACHMENT

Meloy (1996) also theorized that obsessional following or stalking is an abnormal attachment most similar to the preoccupied attachment pattern of Bartholomew's four-type model of adult attachment (Bartholomew, 1990; Bartholomew & Horowitz, 1991). Because individuals with a preoccupied attachment pattern have a poor self-image, but view others positively, they seek approval or validation from others. Meloy (1996) referenced Dutton's work on domestic abuse to point out that individuals with a preoccupied attachment style "actively seek to gain their attachment figure's approval in order to validate their tenuous sense of self worth. Their feelings of unworthiness and strong approach orientation are expected to be associated with high levels of intimacy-anger" (Dutton, 1995a, p. 153). Meloy (1996) indicated that the *preoccupied* attachment pattern is consistent with the stalker's unstable affect, borderline defenses, and obsessional thoughts regarding the stalking victim.

Dutton conducted several studies (Dutton, 1994; Dutton & Starzomski, 1993; Dutton et al., 1994) that highlighted the association among preoccupied attachment, intimacy-anger, jealousy, and borderline personality organization. Dutton (1995b) noted that men high in borderline personality organization as measured by Oldham et al. (1985) rely on intimate relationships to maintain their ego integrity. When the intimate relationships fails, "anger escalates because the very sense of self is threatened and because the use of projection as a defense results in an externalization of blame to his partner" (Dutton, 1995b, p. 578).

Consistent with Dutton's observations, we found (Kienlen et al., 1997) that most nonpsychotic stalkers exhibited extreme anger or hostility toward the vicitim and projected blame onto the victim. One subject in our study murdered his estranged girlfriend and blamed her for the incident because she angered him by obtaining a restraining order prohibiting his contact. Many stalkers were jealous of actual or perceived relationships the victim had with others.

One 25-year-old subject in our study (Kienlen et al., 1997) diagnosed with borderline personality disorder (DSM-IV) described an "intense emotional attraction" toward his first significant girlfriend. Prior to this relationship, he had not been involved in an intimate relationship for more than 2 weeks because he was "too shy." Shortly after he began dating this woman, he quit his job so that he could spend more time with her. He was preoccupied and infatuated with her. He stated that they were "soul mates . . . seemed to be made for each other." After his girlfriend terminated the relationship, he became extremely distraught and suicidal and he engaged in self-mutilation. He had obsessive thoughts or "lots of thoughts, daydreams and things of reuniting . . . some of teaching her a lesson." For a period of approximately 1 month after the breakup of their relationship, this subject contacted his estranged girlfriend on at least 30 occasions by visiting her home or workplace. He often watched the victim through the windows of her residence and sometimes knocked on the door, but fled. He contacted several of the victim's friends for information about her and threatened at least three of her male friends. On one occasion, he became enraged when he observed his estranged girlfriend having sexual intercourse with another man in her residence. The subject said he felt "destroyed . . . mad and furious beyond anything I could describe." After using methamphetamine, he returned to the residence and stabbed the man with a knife. This subject's infatuation with the victim and his need to be with her in order to validate his sense of self-worth suggest that he had a preoccupied attachment style. He clearly had disturbed early attachment relationships. When he was an infant, his mother separated from his father and the subject had minimal subsequent contact with her. Until age 7, the subject was raised by his father. He then lived with his grandparents while his father was incarcerated. After his father's release from prison, the subject lived with his father, with whom he had a "love–hate" relationship, and three different stepmothers. The subject reported that he was verbally abused by his father and stepmothers, physically abused by one stepmother, and sexually abused by an older male neighbor.

While individuals with preoccupied attachments may most closely resemble stalkers due to their active pursuit of the attachment figure's approval, stalkers are a diverse group and may exhibit a variety or combination of pathological attachment patterns, including preoccupied, fearful, and dismissing.

FEARFUL ATTACHMENT

Both the preoccupied and the fearful attachment patterns are associated with a negative sense of self-worth and chronic anxiety about rejection and abandonment, which contribute to intimacy-anger, jealousy, and affective instability (Dutton et al., 1994). The two categories of attachment differ, however, in their expectations of how trustworthy or supportive significant others will be (Bartholomew, 1990; Dutton et al., 1994). Preoccupied individuals have a positive representation of significant others and view others as trustworthy and supportive. To the contrary, fearful individuals have a negative model of significant others and view others as unreliable and unsupportive. Individuals with fearful attachments experience ambivalence between a desire for intimate relationships and pervasive distrust of others and fear of rejection (Bartholomew, 1990). Due to their hypersensitivity to rejection, the fearfully attached avoid close relationships resulting in chronic frustration of attachment needs. Bartholomew (1990) described a strong and unresolvable approach/avoidance pattern among fearfully attached individuals in which "perceived threats of abandonment lead to tendencies to approach the attachment figure who rejects physical contact, thus generating withdrawal accompanied by an even stronger need for attachment" (Dutton et al., 1994, p. 1369).

The approach/avoidance pattern of individuals with a fearful attachment may explain, at least to some extent, clinical observations that some stalkers exhibit contradictory combinations of avoidant and dependent personality traits/disorders on the Millon Clinical Multiaxial Inventory-II (Millon, 1989). These individuals vacillate between feelings of dependence upon and mistrust and fear of rejection by others (Meloy, 1997). When such individuals become involved in a supportive intimate relationship, they are particularly vulnerable to and infuriated by rejection. While avoidant and dependent personality disorders appear to have opposite features, substantial overlap has been found among the diagnoses; the underlying common feature among these groups is a fear of losing the attachment figure (Trull, Widiger, & Frances, 1987). Diverse behaviors are exhibited, however, in reaction to this fear. While individuals with dependent personality traits exhibit "compulsive care-seeking" behavior to meet their needs for security, individuals with avoidant personality traits engage in "compulsive self-reliance" due to their lack of confidence in the caregiver's responsiveness (West & Sheldon, 1988, p. 158).

One 31-year-old subject in our study (Kienlen et al., 1997) began a persistent unwanted pursuit of an early adolescent female acquaintance after his divorce from his wife. He attended most of the victim's extracurricular athletic practices and games. He sent a letter to the victim's brother indicating that he wanted to date the girl. After 4 years, his incessant contacts of the victim appeared more daring. He broke into her residence and left numerous notes in her bedroom. Unfortunately, this subject's obsessional harassment of the victim occurred before the state had an anti-stalking law. He was eventually arrested for burglary after he stole the victim's photo album and began returning individual pictures to her. This subject's seemingly incongruent dependent personality disorder with schizoid personality features appears consistent with a fearful attachment style. Although he depended on a few close relationships for security and support, he did not trust them and feared rejection. This subject had an emotionally distant relationship with his father who was described as "shy and quiet." Like his father, this subject was described as socially fearful and introverted. He said he was "always a loner" and had few close relationships. As a youth, he was bullied and teased by his peers because he was "quiet," and as an adult he lost opportunities for promotions in the military because he was "unassertive." Although the subject was married to a woman from a foreign country for 6 years, he described the relationship as unstable and conflictual due to his wife's infidelity. He had a history of domestic abuse toward his wife. Shortly after his divorce, he began stalking his unattainable adolescent love object.

DISMISSING ATTACHMENT

In contrast to the fearful attachment style, which involves an approach/avoidance pattern due to a negative sense of self-worth and fear of rejection, the dismissing attachment style involves maintaining emotional distance from others in order to preserve a positive self-image. Individuals with dismissing attachment styles "rely on an attachment strategy that minimizes distressing thoughts and affects associated with rejection by the attachment figure" (Rosenstein & Horowitz, 1996, p. 250). Consequently, such individuals engage in behaviors that will alleviate their internal distress, such as substance abuse and other behaviors associated with conduct disorder or antisocial personality disorder (Allen, Hauser, & Borman-Spurrell, 1996; Rosenstein & Horowitz, 1996). Dismissing attachment patterns and lack of resolution of previous trauma have also been associated with criminal behavior in young adults (Allen et al., 1996).

Recent studies (Kienlen et al., 1997; Meloy, 1996) have found that most obsessional followers or stalkers had a diagnosis other than antisocial personality disorder. Meloy and Gothard (1995) attributed these findings to the fact that while most personality disorders are considered disorders of attachment, antisocial personality disorder involves a chronic detachment from others, especially its most severe variant, psychopathy (Gacono & Meloy, 1994).

Because individuals with an antisocial personality disorder tend to avoid attachment to others, one might question why even a few stalkers carry this diagnosis if stalking involves a pattern of intense pathological attachment. The reasons are twofold: (1) Some individuals with antisocial personality disorders, depending on severity, do form attachments and do bond with others. (2) In comparison to other stalkers, individuals with antisocial personality disorders likely have different motivations for stalking. Instead of pursuing the object out of desperation and preoccupation, individuals with antisocial personality disorders are seeking retaliation against the rejecting and wounding object. As Meloy (1996) explained, "A real event, such as acute or chronic rejection, challenges the compensatory narcissistic fantasy that the obsessional follower is special, loved, idealized, admired, superior to, in some way linked, or destined to be with the object of pursuit. Disturbance of this narcissistic fantasy, imbued with both a sense of grandiosity and a feeling of pride, triggers feelings of shame or humiliation that are defended against with rage" (pp. 159–160). Rejection is perceived as a narcissistic injury or blow to the sense of self and the stalker experiences intense anger to defend against feelings of grief, shame, and humiliation (Meloy, 1996). The stalking behavior is a kind of talionic revenge toward the stalking victim, devalued and blamed for the narcissistic injury. Individuals with narcissistic and antisocial character pathology, particularly when accompanied by a history of aggressive and criminal behavior, are at increased risk of violence toward the victim.

The only two subjects in our study (Kienlen et al., 1997) who murdered their stalking victims had narcissistic and antisocial features; and based on their disturbed childhood experiences, they appeared to have severe attachment pathology. Both murdered estranged girlfriends. One 33-year-old subject indicated that he was "infatuated" and obsessed with his estranged girlfriend. Regarding his obsession, he stated, "I was letting this relationship run my life . . . she was like a drug for me." The day he murdered her, he planned to take her at gunpoint to the courthouse and force her to retract a court order for protection. This subject probably had a dismissing attachment style. His disturbed attachment relationships are indicated by his lack of relationships with his biological parents; he never knew his father and had very little contact with his mother, who abused substances. He was primarily raised by his aunt and uncle. When the subject was 12 years old, his uncle died and his aunt began abusing substances. She frequently became verbally abusive toward him when she was intoxicated. This subject described himself as a "loner" as a child with few friends. As a youth, he engaged in numerous antisocial behaviors, including frequent fire setting, truancy, and running away from home. As an adult, this subject began abusing illicit drugs. He described himself as controlling, dominating and physically abusive toward women. Although he lived with a woman for several years, the couple had an "open relationship" and agreed to date other people. He subsequently began prostituting both his live-in girlfriend and the woman whom he later dated, stalked, and murdered.

The other subject who murdered his estranged girlfriend, a 69 year old, was outraged and preoccupied with seeking revenge toward her for leaving him. After the breakup of the relationship, according to a witness, this subject drank alcohol daily and engaged in "never ending conversation" regarding his desire to kill the victim, burn her house down, or steal from her because he would "not be worth a shit" unless he got revenge. Childhood emotional and physical abuse by his father may have been at the root of this subject's dismissing attachment pathology. He claimed that his father tied him to a pole for 3 days after he was caught smoking. This incident, however, was based on self-report and may have been exaggerated. The subject subsequently ran away from home and lived independently for a period of time. He began abusing alcohol as an adolescent and had an extensive criminal history of violent felony offenses (nature unknown) as an adult.

ATTACHMENT AND PSYCHOPATHOLOGY

Rosenstein and Horowitz's (1996) study found that adolescents with dismissing attachment patterns attempted to deny or minimize emotional distress through behaviors such as substance abuse or antisocial behavior. Adolescents with dismissing attachments were more likely to have a conduct disorder, substance abuse disorder, and antisocial and narcissistic personality disorders. Adults with dismissing attachments have been associated with criminal behavior (Allen et al., 1996).

To the contrary, Rosenstein and Horowitz's (1996) study found that adolescents with preoccupied attachment patterns relied on behaviors that signal distress and elicit the attention of an inconsistent attachment figure. Consequently, adolescents with preoccupied attachment patterns tended to have affective or obsessive–compulsive disorders as well as histrionic, borderline, and schizotypal personality disorders. Adults with preoccupied attachments have been found to have features consistent with major mental illness, including higher levels of emotional distress, helplessness, anger, and mental confusion (Dozier, Stevenson, Lee, & Velligan, 1991; Pianta, Egeland, & Adam, 1996; Main, 1996).

Regardless of type of attachment style, research suggests an association between insecure attachment and various psychopathologies in adolescents and adults (Allen et al., 1996; Fonagy et al., 1996; Pianta et al., 1996; Rosenstein & Horowitz,

1996). Lack of familial and social support has been linked to insecure attachment patterns and may increase vulnerability to those with a predisposition for psychopathology (Allen et al., 1996; Cicchetti, Cummings, Greenberg, & Marvin, 1990). For example, one study (Walsh, 1978) indicated that offspring born within 2 years of a mother's loss of a family member are more likely than others in the family to develop schizophrenia. Adults with psychiatric disorders often have unresolved issues regarding difficult early relationships (Fonagy et al., 1996). Main (1996) identified the following five attachment risk factors that may contribute to the development of mental disorders: (1) unsuccessful attachment between ages 6 months and 3 years; (2) insecure attachment status; (3) separation from and permanent loss of attachment figures; (4) early maltreatment resulting in disorganized attachment; and (5) second-generation effect of the parent's trauma resulting in disorganized attachment. When considering the type of insecure attachment, Allen et al. (1996) found that lack of resolution of previous trauma, such as abuse or frightening behavior by an attachment figure, and to a lesser extent loss were associated with severe psychopathology.

PSYCHIATRIC FEATURES OF STALKERS

In addition to the predominance of attachment disturbances among criminal stalkers, most present with a variety of major Axis I psychiatric diagnoses and Axis II personality disorders (Harmon et al., 1995; Kienlen et al., 1997; Meloy, 1996; Meloy & Gothard, 1995; Zona et al., 1993). Two studies found that most stalkers have an Axis I diagnosis of mood disorder, adjustment disorder, or substance abuse and/or an Axis II Cluster B (i.e., borderline, narcissistic, and less frequently antisocial) or dependent personality disorder (Kienlen et al., 1997; Meloy & Gothard, 1995).

Additionally, we found that one-third of a small sample of incarcerated stalkers had a psychotic disorder (Kienlen et al., 1997). Although some stalkers appear to have a psychotic disorder, few have a diagnosis of erotomania, the delusional belief that one is loved by another person, usually of a higher social status (Kienlen et al., 1997; Meloy & Gothard, 1995; Zona et al., 1993). Stalking behavior of psychotic stalkers was found to be primarily motivated by delusional beliefs or disorganized behavior (Kienlen et al., 1997). Psychotic stalkers might also have attachment pathology that contributes to their delusional content and their stalking behavior.

One psychotic subject included in our study persistently pursued a woman because he believed that she was his wife and her children were his children. In fact, the victim had the same name as the subject's wife, who had left him approximately 1 month prior to the onset of the stalking behavior. The subject, who was unaware of the whereabouts of his actual wife and children, had delusional beliefs that explained their disappearance (i.e., the Mayor kidnapped them, the President was holding them in the White House). This subject had experienced physical abuse by his mother during childhood and the death of his father and depression of his mother as an adolescent, from which severe attachment difficulties can be inferred.

SUMMARY

Stalkers are a diverse group presenting with a complex array of disturbed attachment styles and a variety of mental disorders. Recent research on stalking, however, highlights two important similarities among this population. First, early attachment disturbance might be a predisposing factor to stalking behavior. Second, adult recent loss might precipitate stalking. It appears that stalkers are unable to cope with loss and therefore engage in an obsessive pattern of pursuit of another person as a means to alleviate grief or to vent anger. Preliminary research on stalking suggests that future research and treatment in this area should focus on issues surrounding coping with loss and grief. Additionally, further research on the relationship between disturbed childhood attachments and adult stalking pathology is needed, particularly utilizing structured attachment inventories or interviews. As Francois Mauriac indicated, "We are moulded and remoulded by those who have loved us; and though the love may pass, we are nevertheless their work, for good or ill" (cited in Bowlby, 1969, p. 331). Attachment research clearly links early attachment patterns, whether "good or ill," to adult relations.

REFERENCES

Ainsworth, M. D. S. (1989). Attachments beyond infancy. *American Psychologist, 44*(4), 709–716.

Ainsworth, M. D. S., Blehar, M. C., Waters, E., & Wall, S. (1978). *Patterns of attachment: A psychological study of the strange situation.* Hillsdale, NJ: Erlbaum.

Allen, J. P., Hauser, S. T., & Borman-Spurrell, E. (1996). Attachment theory as a framework for understanding sequelae of severe adolescent psychopathology: An 11-year follow-up study. *Journal of Consulting and Clinical Psychology, 64*(2), 254–263.

Bartholomew, K. (1990). Avoidance of intimacy: An attachment perspective. *Journal of Social and Personal Relationships, 7,* 147–178.

Bartholomew, K., & Horowitz, L. M. (1991). Attachment styles among young adults: A test of a four-category model. *Journal of Personality and Social Psychology, 61*(2), 226–244.

Bowlby, J. (1980). *Attachment and loss: Vol. III. Loss, sadness and depression.* New York: Basic Books.

Bowlby, J. (1973). *Attachment and loss: Vol. II. Separation, anxiety, and anger.* New York: Basic Books.

Bowlby, J. (1969). *Attachment and loss: Vol. I. Attachment.* New York: Basic Books.

Bretherton, I. (1992). The origins of attachment theory: John Bowlby and Mary Ainsworth. *Developmental Psychology, 28*(5), 759–775.

Cashdan, S. (1988). *Object relations therapy.* New York: W. W. Norton & Company.

Cicchetti, D., Cummings, E. M., Greenberg, M. T., & Marvin, R. S. (1990). An organizational perspective on attachment beyond infancy. In M. T. Greenberg, D. Cicchetti, & E. M. Cummings (Eds.), *Attachment in the preschool years* (pp. 3–49). Chicago: University of Chicago Press.

Dozier, M., Stevenson, A. L., Lee, S. W., & Velligan, D. I. (1991). Attachment organization and familial overinvolvement for adults with serious psychopathological disorders. *Development and Psychopathology, 3,* 475–489.

Dutton, D. G. (1994). Behavioral and affective correlates of borderline personality organization in wife assaulters. *International Journal of Criminal Justice and Behavior, 17*(3), 26–38.

Dutton, D. G. (1995a). *The domestic assault of women.* Vancouver: University of British Columbia Press.

Dutton, D. G. (1995b). Male abusiveness in intimate relationships. *Clinical Psychology Review, 15*(6), 567–581.

Dutton, D. G., & Golant, S. K. (1995). *The batterer.* New York: Basic Books.

Dutton, D. G., & Starzomski, A. (1993). Perpetrator characteristics associated with women's reports of psychological and physical abuse. *Violence and Victims, 8*(4), 326–335.

Dutton, D. G., Saunders, K., Starzomski, A., & Bartholomew, K. (1994). Intimacy-anger and insecure attachment as precursors of abuse in intimate relationships. *Journal of Applied Social Psychology, 24*(15), 1367–1386.

Fonagy, P., Leigh, T., Steele, M., Steele, H., Kennedy, R., Mattoon, G., Target, M., Gerber, A. (1996). The relation of attachment status, psychiatric classification, and response to psychotherapy. *Journal of Consulting and Clinical Psychology, 64*(1), 22–31.

Gacono, C. B., & Meloy, J. R. (1994). *The Rorschach assessment of aggressive and psychopathic personalities.* Hillsdale, NJ: Lawrence Erlbaum Associates.

Harmon, R. B., Rosner, R., & Owens, H. (1995). Obsessional harassment and erotomania in a criminal court population. *Journal of Forensic Sciences, 40*(2), 188–196.

Kernberg, O. (1977). The structural diagnosis of borderline personality organization. In P. Hartocollis (Ed.), *Borderline personality disorders: The concept, the syndrome, the patient* (pp. 87–121). New York: International Universities Press.

Kienlen, K. K. (1995). *An obsessive and potentially dangerous pursuit: A case study approach to the phenomenon of stalking.* Unpublished doctoral dissertation, Minnesota School of Professional Psychology, Minneapolis.

Kienlen, K. K., Birmingham, D. L., Solberg, K. B., O'Regan, J. T., & Meloy, J. R. (1997). A comparative study of psychotic and non-psychotic stalking. *Journal of the American Academy of Psychiatry & the Law, 25*(3), 317–334.

Mahler, M. S., Pine, F., & Bergman, A. (1975). *The psychological birth of the human infant: Symbiosis and individuation.* New York: Basic Books.

Main, M. (1996). Introduction to the special section on attachment and psychopathology: Overview of the field of attachment. *Journal of Consulting and Clinical Psychology, 64*(2), 237–243.

Meloy, J. R. (1992). *Violent attachments.* Northvale, NJ: Jason Aronson.

Meloy, J. R. (1996). Stalking (obsessional following): A review of some preliminary studies. *Aggression and Violent Behavior, 1*(2), 147–162.

Meloy, J. R. (1997). A Rorschach case study of stalking: "All I wanted was to love you . . ." In J. R. Meloy, M. Acklin, C. Gacono, J. Murray, & C. Peterson (Eds.), *Contemporary Rorschach Interpretation.* (pp. 177–190). Mahwah, NJ: Lawrence Erlbaum Associates.

Meloy, J. R., & Gothard, S. (1995). Demographic and clinical comparison of obsessional followers and offenders with mental disorders. *American Journal of Psychiatry, 152*(2), 258–263.

Millon, T. (1989). *Manual for the MCMI-II* (2nd ed.). Minneapolis: National Computer Systems.

Oldham, J., Clarkin, J., Appelbaum, A., Carr, A., Kernberg, P., Lotterman, A., & Haas, G. (1985). A self-report instrument for borderline personality organization. In T. H. McGlashan (Ed.), *The borderline: Current empirical research* (pp. 1–18) [Progress in Psychiatry Series]. Washington, DC: American Psychiatric Press.

Pianta, R. C., Egeland, B., & Adam, E. K. (1996). Adult attachment classification and self-reported psychiatric symptomatology as assessed by the Minnesota Multiphasic Personality Inventory-2. *Journal of Consulting and Clinical Psychology, 64*(2), 273–281.

Raine, A. (1993). *The psychopathology of crime: Criminal behavior as a clinical disorder.* San Diego: Academic Press.

Rosenstein, D. S., & Horowitz, H. A. (1996). Adolescent attachment and psychopathology. *Journal of Consulting and Clinical Psychology, 64*(2), 244–253.

Schoenewolf, G. (1990). *Turning points in analytic therapy.* Northvale, NJ: Jason Aronson.

Shaver, P., & Hazan, C. (1987). Being lonely, falling in love: Perspectives from attachment theory. In M. Hojat & R. Crandall (Eds.), Loneliness: Theory, research, and applications, [Special issue]. *Journal of Social Behavior and Personality, 2*(2, Pt. 2), 105–124.

Trull, T. J., Widiger, T. A., & Frances, A. (1987). Covariance of criteria sets for avoidant, schizoid, and dependent personality disorders. *American Journal of Psychiatry, 144,* 767–771.

Walsh, F. (1978). Concurrent grandparent death and birth of schizophrenic offspring: An intriguing finding. *Family Process, 17,* 457–463.

West, M., & Sheldon, A. E. R. (1988). Classification of pathological attachment patterns in adults. *Journal of Personality Disorders, 2*(2), 153–159.

Zona, M. A., Sharma, K. K., & Lane, J. (1993). A comparative study of erotomanic and obsessional subjects in a forensic sample. *Journal of Forensic Sciences, 38,* 894–903.

CHAPTER 4

Psychiatric Diagnosis and the Offender–Victim Typology of Stalking

**Michael A. Zona, M.D., Russell E. Palarea, M.A., and
John C. Lane, Jr., M.P.A.**

Until the early 1990s, knowledge concerning the psychology and behavior of stalkers was limited. Most people who were aware of this phenomenon probably viewed the issue in terms of the "obsessed fan": an individual who repeatedly attemped to make contact with a "celebrity" for a variety of purposes. The average citizen and the professional mental health community had minimal understanding of why people behaved in such a manner, nor did they understand the profound impact on the victim, or object, of a stalker's focus. Similarly, prior to 1990, there was limited insight within the law enforcement community that "stalking" could be criminal in nature; in fact, the term itself did not exist within the criminal justice vocabulary.

All this changed in 1990 when legislation that established the nation's first stalking law was passed in California (PC 646.9). This law recognized that stalking behavior was universally impacting the community at large. It defined criminal stalking as behavior wherein an individual initiates a pattern of annoying, harassing, or threatening action toward another person with the intent to cause the person to fear for his/her safety or the safety of his/her family.

There have been several attempts to characterize the various stalking behaviors and relationships that we describe in this chapter. Regardless of the stalking typology one chooses to use, the most fundamental aspect of these individuals is that they are portraying *a behavior*. These behaviors naturally result from the underlying psychiatric and psychological processes occurring in the stalker. First we review some of the more important diagnostic issues that involve stalking cognitions and behaviors. Then we address early attempts to understand stalker/

The Psychology of Stalking: Clinical and Forensic Perspectives

victim typologies. Several scenarios are highlighted to exemplify the various typologies. Finally, we review the newest work on understanding stalker psychology and behavior.

PSYCHIATRIC DIAGNOSIS OF STALKERS

Although it is not illegal for an obsessed individual to think about his object of desire, stalking or obsessional following arises when the individual couples a behavior to his cognition. Any understanding of a stalker's behavior must first be understood as a more fundamental psychiatric or psychological process.

In any disease process a pattern or constellation of symptoms is expressed. In psychiatric and psychological disease processes, many of these symptoms are expressed in cognitive and/or behavioral patterns. These patterns of behaviors and cognitions are described in the *Diagnostic and Statistical Manual of Mental Disorders, Fourth Edition (DSM-IV*, American Psychiatric Association, 1994). In the *DSM-IV*, a mental disorder is defined as a clinically significant behavioral or psychological syndrome or pattern associated with present distress or disability. A review of the *DSM-IV* does not reveal any syndrome or disorder that is pathognomonic of stalking or stalking behavior; thus, an understanding of stalking behavior must be put into the diagnostic framework that the *DSM-IV* provides. The *DSM-IV* uses a multiaxial system for the classification of psychiatric disorders. Axis I identifies the major mental disorders that afflict individuals. The three primary Axis I disorders afflicting many stalkers are thought disorders, mood disorders, and substance abuse disorders. There is also a proportion of stalkers who do not have an Axis I disorder. They are likely to fall into the Axis II category, which usually describes personality disorders. Individuals who stalk often suffer from a combination of disorders on both of these two axes.

One of the most prevalent Axis I problems afflicting stalkers is thought disorder. Individuals who suffer from thought disorders typically have problems discerning real from unreal. Symptoms of thought disorders include hallucinations, delusions, and disorganized thought. Almost all psychotic patients have one or more of these symptoms. A hallucination is a sensory perception that has the compelling sense of reality as a true perception, but that occurs without external stimulation. A delusion is a fixed, false belief, based on an incorrect inference about external reality. Disorganized thought occurs when an individual is unable to organize his thought processes with any cogent meaning, and is also referred to as formal thought disorder.

Stalkers who suffer from thought disorders typically have Axis I diagnoses of schizophrenia or one of the various types of delusional disorder. Schizophrenia is a disorder of thought in which symptoms such as delusions, hallucinations, and disorganized speech are often present. This familial disorder often first afflicts people in their early twenties. Their hallucinations are typically auditory in nature; that is, they "hear voices." Sometimes they act on these voices, especially when they are the command type. A command auditory hallucination occurs when a person hears a voice telling him to do something. Many times individuals believe that the voices they are hearing are from famous people and will specifically identify a famous individual as the author of the voices or hallucinations. Other times, individuals with schizophrenia may blame a particularly notable individual for putting the voices into their head.

These individuals often develop bizarre delusions. An example of a delusion that a person with schizophrenia implicated in stalking might exhibit would be to believe he is the spouse of a celebrity. No amount of psychotherapy or fact-based discussion will dissuade him from this false belief. Individuals suffering from these delusions will then couple them with behaviors, such as letter writing, physical following, and approaching the object of their delusion. They may also develop a campaign of retribution directed toward the individual they falsely believe is putting these voices into their head.

Individuals who are psychotically disorganized typically manifest their stalking behavior in writing and non-goal-directed activities aimed at their victims. Such individuals typically construct multipaged letters to celebrities. For example, a delusional stalker might try to convince a celebrity of impending chaos in the world based on the results from each Friday's *New York Times* crossword puzzle. Their writing typically displays loosening of associations and ideas of reference and is quite clearly disorganized and chaotic. Typically, stalking individuals with schizophrenia will suffer from the paranoid type, wherein they believe other people are out to get them or hurt them—evidence of persecutory and grandiose delusions.

Another thought disorder linked to stalking is the delusional disorder. Individuals with this diagnosis are similar to those who suffer from schizophrenia, but they do not typically suffer from hallucinations and/or disorganized thought. They do, however, manifest one circumscribed, often systematic delusion. There are several types of delusional disorder. The most prevalent in stalking cases are the erotomanic, jealous, or persecutory subtypes. Individuals with erotomania suffer from the delusion that another person, usually of a higher status, is in love with the individual. The vast number of individuals who suffer from erotomania fixate on their love object or object of desire and firmly hold that this individual is in love with them. They believe their love is one of a "pure union." The majority of these victims or love objects are of higher socioeconomic status or fame, which conveys a feeling of importance on the oftentimes lonely, socially isolated individual who suffers from erotomania (Segal, 1989; Meloy, 1990). The victim, or love object, is typically involved in the political, athletic, or entertainment industry.

The jealous type occurs when the suspect maintains the delusion that his spouse or lover is being unfaithful to him in the absence of any supporting data. This has historically been referred to as morbid or pathological jealousy. The persecutory type occurs when the suspect maintains the delusion that he is being mistreated in some way by another. These latter two types may be more prevalent in stalking than the erotomanic type, because erotomania is so rare. The *DSM-IV*, in fact, directly alludes to stalking in the jealous subtype when describing the disordered person's behavioral interventions with the imagined infidelity, "e.g., restricting the spouse's autonomy, secretly following the spouse, investigating the imagined lover, attacking the spouse" (*DSM-IV*, p. 298).

Another feature typically associated with delusional stalkers is the symptom called "ideas of reference." While not exclusive to the various types of delusional disorder, this symptom occurs when ordinary events are interpreted by the delusional person to have a special personal meaning. For example, a female TV newscaster wears a purple blouse and the delusional individual believes that this is a special message to approach her this weekend.

The next major category of Axis I psychiatric disorders often displayed by stalkers is the mood disorder. Simply speaking, mood disorders are disorders of the mind and brain that involve some form of depression or manic disorder. Mood is defined in the *DSM-IV* as a pervasive and sustained emotion that colors an individual's perception of the world. Symptoms of depression include sadness, dysphoria, inability to obtain pleasure, lack of concentration, sleep and appetite disturbances, and agitation. When individuals are suffering from a severe case of depression, they will often manifest psychotic symptoms, which may include hallucinations and delusions. People who suffer from depression have a tendency to color their life experiences and the future in an extremely negative frame of reference, impairing their ability to engage in meaningful relationships. Often, individuals who are depressed suffer relationship discord and schisms and seek to rectify or reestablish a relationship as a means of maintaining their self-esteem. Suicidality, and more uncommonly, homicidality, are also features of depression. Such depressed individuals may be involved in cases of stalking, especially those entailing workplace violence.

Another mood disorder related to stalking is called manic disorder, and its most common diagnosis, bipolar disorder, formerly known as manic-depression. These individuals suffer from symptoms that include heightened motor activity, extreme elation, inflated self-esteem, grandiosity, decreased need for sleep, pressured speech (incessant talking), flight of ideas, racing thoughts, and distractibility. They exhibit intense goal-directed activity and engage in excessive pleasurable activities. Many of these individuals stabilize and appear quite normal between their episodes of mania or depression, which vary greatly in cycle length. One of the most troublesome symptoms in these individuals is their grandiose beliefs, which often manifest in delusions of power, wealth, and special relationships.

The last Axis I category that commonly affects individuals engaged in stalking behavior is a substance use (abuse or dependence) disorder. Substance dependency, be it alcohol, amphetamines, cocaine, or any other of the myriad drugs available, is defined in the *DSM-IV* (p. 81) as, "A maladaptive pattern of substance use, leading to clinically significant impairment or distress, as manifested by three (or more) of the following, occurring at anytime in the same 12-month period: tolerance, withdrawal, taking a substance in larger amounts or over a longer period than was intended, persistent desire or unsuccessful efforts to cut down, spending increased time to obtain the substance, reducing social or occupational activities because of the substance, and continues use despite acknowledgement of its negative effects." Among stalkers, the most frequent drugs of abuse or dependence include alcohol, marijuana, cocaine, and amphetamines.

The other major types of psychiatric disorders that are important in understanding the cognitions and behavior of stalking are the Axis II personality disorders. The *DSM-IV* separates personality disorders into three groups: Cluster A personality disorders focus on odd, eccentric features; Cluster B personality disorders focus on dramatic, emotional, or erratic features; and Cluster C personality disorders focus on anxious or fearful features. The most pervasive cluster in stalking cases is the Cluster B, which includes the antisocial, borderline, histrionic, and narcissistic personality disorders (Meloy, 1996).

Individuals suffering from antisocial personality disorders (ASPD) display the following symptoms: failure to conform to social norms regarding behaviors, deceitfulness, lying, use of aliases, impulsivity, history of physical violence, reckless disregard for safety, irresponsibility, and lack of remorse.

Such a diagnosis among stalkers historically involves abusive domestic relationships. Perpetrators present a false image of themselves regarding their life history, experiences, and interest in the stalking victim. They have a unique sense of which women are vulnerable and prey on their weaknesses. Such female victims many times have a history of involvement with ASPD men. Domestic violence is a prominent theme during the relationship. When a break-up occurs, the stalker may attempt to intimidate the victim through telephonic and written threats, stalking, and physical confrontation of the victim. Many times these individuals are violent toward their victims. In one such case, a stalker threw a hammer through the bedroom window of the victim's bedroom while she was sleeping. Days later while she was at work, the stalker backed his truck into the front door of her apartment. These situations, in particular, must be aggressively managed by the victim with support from law enforcement and/or experienced professionals because of the potential for violence.

Central features of borderline personality disorder include frantic efforts to avoid real or imagined abandonment. These individuals demonstrate unstable and intense interpersonal relationships. In severe cases, they present with identity disturbances and recurrent suicidal gestures and threats. They are affectively unstable often with wildly vacillating moods. This is not apparent among the mood disorders, which generally change over weeks or months. Finally, individuals with borderline personality disorders have feelings of emptiness and intense anger and can develop stress-related paranoid ideation.

Much like the relationship portrayed in the movie *Fatal Attraction,* these individuals create a sense of importance or depth of relationship that is not consistent with their partner's attachment. Consider the example of a male attorney who briefly dated a woman. After a short dating period, she broke off the relationship. He could not accept the reality and began to obsessively attempt to reestablish what he believed to be a significant commitment on her part. He telephoned, followed her during her daily activities, and at one point was seen hiding in a tree outside her parents' home where she was visiting. Many such cases can result in the mind set, "If I can't have her, nobody can!"

Individuals suffering from histrionic personality disorder become uncomfortable if they are not the center of attention. They are inappropriately sexually seductive, with rapidly shifting shallow emotions, and often use their physical appearance, usually eroticized, to create attention. They consider relationships to be more intimate than they really are. They are often very dramatic in their emotional expression. An example of a histrionic personality disorder is presented in the False Victimization Syndrome section later in this chapter.

The final type under Cluster B is the narcissistic personality disorder (NPD). These individuals demonstrate a grandiose sense of self-importance and are preoccupied with fantasies of power, brilliance, beauty, and ideal love. They often think they should be treated "special." They require excessive amounts of admiration and are interpersonally exploitive; they lack empathy and are often envious of others. NPD is common among stalkers; narcissistic traits are pervasive (Meloy, 1992, 1996).

These four personality disorders—antisocial, borderline, histrionic, and narcissistic—are the most frequently involved in stalking. The essential feature of this cluster is that, at their core, individuals with these disorders lack their own identity, or sense of self, which prevents them from establishing an appropriate rapport with and attachment to others. It is important to note that some characteristics of these disorders are very similar. Many antisocial individuals are also highly narcissistic. A narcissistic individual who shows excessive attention-seeking behaviors may also be histrionic. These disorders may stand alone, but often blend together.

In addition to the Cluster B personality disorders, several other personality disorders also warrant attention. In the Cluster A disorders, stalking behaviors may be conducted by individuals with paranoid personality and schizoid personality disorders. Individuals with a paranoid personality disorder are distrustful and suspicious of others. They have great difficulty trusting other people, often read neutral situations as threatening or demeaning toward themselves, and may be suspicious of spousal infidelity. Their paranoia often makes them hypersensitive to input or reaction from others, and they may perceive being mistreated by another individual when no mistreatment really occurred. Schizoid personality disordered individuals are characterized by a detachment from social relationships and a restricted range of expressed emotions in interpersonal situations. Individuals with this disorder are socially isolative, and when they do form an intimate relationship, they may be unwilling to give it up. Their stalking may be a result of either a desire to continue it, or an act of vengeance toward one of the few individuals that they became interpersonally invested in and trusted. Additionally, these individuals have poor social skills and may not understand how their nonmalicious behaviors are perceived as harmful by the victim. In the Cluster C arena, the personality disorder most likely to display stalking behaviors is the dependent personality disorder (DPD). These individuals are marked by an excessive need to be taken care of that leads to active submissive and clinging behaviors and fears of separation. The DPD individual will most likely display stalking behaviors after the break-up of an intimate relationship. They may pursue their former partner in a nonmalicious but harassing manner with the theme of, "I can't live without you."

THE THREAT MANAGEMENT UNIT

A watershed event occurred in 1989 with the murder of actress Rebecca Schaeffer by a stalker named Robert Bardo. One outgrowth of this event was the challenge directed toward the Los Angeles Police Department to become more proactive in the intervention of such cases before they reached a tragic end. In July of 1990 the Department created the Threat Management Unit (TMU) as developed by Lieutenant John Lane. The TMU began with three detectives. Its mission was to understand the elements of stalking and implement a new organizational paradigm for the management of these cases by law enforcement officials. It would no longer be acceptable to respond only when reportable crimes were committed or when someone was physically assaulted. The TMU now consists of nine detectives. Its current mission is to investigate long-term, abnormal threat and harassment cases. It is not required that such behavior involve criminal activity, only that it create a threatening climate for the victim.

In the early stages of the TMU's development, Lt. Lane was introduced to Michael Zona, M.D., a psychiatric fellow at the University of Southern California Institute of Psychiatry, Law, and Behavioral Science. Dr. Zona trained the TMU on psychiatric disorders and developed a profile document to capture pertinent case information. This information became the framework for our research. Russell Palarea was later brought on as the Threat Management Unit's research assistant. He helped revise the Zona Profile and the Threat Management Unit database, collected the data over several years, and statistically analyzed the current database. He holds a Masters degree in Clinical Psychology, authoring his thesis on stalking in intimate relationships, and is earning his doctorate in forensic clinical psychology at the University of Nebraska–Lincoln. His contribution has been significant and instrumental in further refining our understanding of stalkers. The research from this database over the past 6 years has helped to crystallize conceptually useful and working typologies of the stalker/victim relationship and further clarify the assessment of dangerousness in stalking perpetrators.

During the early stages of the TMU's development, a gradual appreciation evolved for the multitude of stalking cases that impacted elements of society removed from the celebrity realm. This was a turning point in the Unit's history, as we realized that many of the commonly held beliefs about stalking were inaccurate. We discovered that a large population of stalking cases involved ordinary citizens. Because our existing intervention methods were geared toward celebrity and public dignitary cases, new intervention methods needed to be created

Understanding stalkers in terms of diagnostic categories in the *DSM-IV* is useful, but has several limitations. Many stalkers do not exclusively fit into one diagnostic category. Furthermore, our research has indicated that these cases are best understood in terms of the stalker/victim dyad. It is the relationship between the two parties, real or imagined, that best informs our understanding of stalkers and their motivations. From this frame of reference, the various stalker/victim types were developed.

The data collected on the TMU's cases provided an opportunity to define who was being victimized, who was committing these acts, and under what circumstances. The result was the first stalking article by Zona, Sharma, and Lane (1993). This study of 74 stalking cases handled by the TMU was the first comprehensive analysis of criminal stalking. The original types discussed in that article consisted of the simple obsessional, love obsessional, and erotomanic groups.

STALKER–VICTIM TYPES

SIMPLE OBSESSIONAL

These are cases wherein the victim and suspect (perpetrator) have some prior knowledge of one another. They are the most common cases, not only in the cited research, but also throughout the country in cities large and small. As we discuss in more detail later, these cases are also the most dangerous.

Although simple obsessional cases do not always involve an intimate relationship, a significant number are the outgrowth of these relationships, that is, ex-husband/wife or ex-dating partners. Many such cases are the postscript of a domestic violence situation where an individual breaks away from the relationship only to have his or her ex-partner initiate a campaign of harassment, intimidation, and mental terrorism. The stalker's motive may be to coerce the victim back into a relationship or simply to seek revenge by making the victim's life miserable.

In contrast to the domestic violence type case, many relationships involve nothing more than brief dating, with one of the two partners deciding not to continue the contact. Such breakups are not always the result of abusive behavior, simply two people who prove to be incompatible at the time. In certain situations, however, one partner may have an unrealistically high degree of emotional investment in the relationship and becomes angered as a result of a loss of control, an attack on his self-image, or a sense of mistreatment. Significant personality disorders typically exacerbate the reaction, manifested by excessive acts such as physical stalking (following) and direct threats to do harm.

The other major category of simple obsessional cases involves nonintimate situations that often occur in the work environment. They may overlap with the phenomenon of workplace violence. One such scenario typically involves the suspended or terminated employee who perceives that one particular supervisor is the direct cause of his troubles and initiates a pattern of stalking behavior designed to terrorize this person. Such cases, if left unchecked, may continue to escalate to the point of direct confrontation and violence.

Another common case within the workplace involves the employee, usually male, who attempts to establish a personal relationship with a co-worker and has his advances rejected. Similar to the dating relationship, these individuals continue to impose themselves on the victim to the point where, having not been successful, their adoration turns to anger and a pattern of stalking begins.

A variety of other nonintimate relationships exist within the simple obsessional type. The largest group involves people who had some prior form of professional relationship, such as physician–patient, psychotherapist–client, teacher–student, business partners, and other similar relations. Other nonintimate groups include neighbors, schoolmates, roommates, friends, individuals who dated the same person (e.g., former girlfriend stalks her ex-boyfriend's current girlfriend), and other acquaintances. As with the workplace violence cases, the perpetrator may be either pursuing an intimate relationship with the victim or seeking vengeance for some real or imagined act of mistreatment (Harmon, Rosner, & Owens, 1995).

LOVE OBSESSIONAL

These cases are characterized by the absence of an existing relationship between the perpetrator and victim. Many times, victims are only known via the media, including radio, television, and motion picture celebrities. There are other cases, however, that develop in which the victim is an ordinary citizen who simply falls prey to this type of stalker. Within this group, the most common type of suspect is one who focuses on a celebrity or public figure. A large number of these stalkers suffer from schizophrenia or bipolar disorder. Many are socially maladjusted and have seldom, if ever, been involved in a meaningful intimate relationship. A typical case may evolve when such an individual observes an attractive female newscaster. His attraction escalates to the point where he unrealistically believes that if he could make himself known, she would likewise be attracted to him. Subsequently he begins a pattern of correspondence wherein he expresses his adoration and desire to meet with her. Many times the very content of his letters is disturbing to the victim. As time elapses and the suspect receives no response, or no positive response, the tone of the letters may demonstrate increased frustration, anger, and intent to physically confront the victim. Such a scenario may continue to play out over an established period of time, requiring a long-term management approach.

There are also love obsessional cases that impact ordinary citizens. For example, a woman began receiving harassing phone calls for no apparent reason. The male caller would first discuss his interest in dating her, but would then become angry and threaten to harm her. The investigation ultimately revealed that the night prior to the first phone call, the woman was out at a dance club. After exiting the club, she verbally exchanged her phone number with another person. The perpetrator happened to be within earshot of the victim and, while eavesdropping on her conversation, memorized her phone number. He then began a campaign of harassment that lasted for many months. Although the exhibited behaviors can be very alarming, our research has demonstrated that when considered among the entire universe of cases, the love obsessional type is usually less dangerous than the simple obsessional.

EROTOMANIC

Such cases are distinct from the love obsessional cases since the suspect delusionally believes that he/she is loved by the victim. Although very rare in the general population, erotomania (primary or secondary) is not unusual within the stalking arena. The most unique feature of erotomanic stalking cases is that the majority of suspects are female. The victims are often older men of higher socioeconomic status. These cases are difficult to resolve due to the nature of the delusion.

For example, a partner in a law firm introduces himself to a young woman who has been hired as a temporary office secretary. Although the contact is brief and professional, the woman suddenly develops a delusional belief that the lawyer is in love with her. The next day, the secretary walks into the lawyer's office and initiates a conversation that is much too personal given their relationship. She begins leaving notes on his desk that express a belief that they are involved in a relationship. Ultimately the woman obtains the lawyer's home telephone number and attempts to reach him. When that occurs, the lawyer realizes that the situation has become serious. Although such stalkers can be very aggressive in their pursuit to contact, our research has shown that such cases are not likely to result in physical harm to the victim.

As the number of cases managed by the TMU continued to increase, statistics were generated for a population of 200 cases (this included the first 74 studied [Zona et al., 1993]). An outgrowth of these data was the identification of an additional group, the false victimization syndrome.

FALSE VICTIMIZATION SYNDROME

These cases develop when an individual constructs an elaborate scenario to falsely support the position that he or she is being stalked. In reality no such stalker exists. Case experience has demonstrated that the majority of these "victims" are female and are motivated by an attempt to resurrect what she perceives to be a failing relationship. These individuals often display features most consistent with the histrionic personality disorder (*DSM-IV*), including a demand to be the center of attention, the expression of shallow and rapidly shifting emotions, and cognitions that are excessively impressionistic and lacking in detail. They may actually resort to harming themselves in an attempt to validate their claims and increase their credibility. Such cases can be very difficult to investigate and drain valuable resources.

For example, a woman believed that her husband was having an affair with his secretary. She fabricated a police report, stating that a man forced his way into her home and attacked her with a knife, causing numerous lacerations. She provided a very detailed description of the perpetrator. As expected, this caused a good deal of alarm for her husband. This event was followed up by a series of threatening notes left on her front porch. One night when her husband was away she claimed to see the suspect in her back yard. She fired several rounds at him with her handgun. Again, a police report was completed and the local police division continued to expend resources to apprehend the suspect. All these events caused her husband to begin to take his wife to work with him to ensure her safety. Ultimately, the TMU assumed the case and a video camera caught the woman depositing one of the threatening letters on her own doorstep. When confronted, she admitted to fabricating the entire story in order to refocus her husband's attention onto herself.

REVIEW OF THE STALKING RESEARCH

Because the legal definition of stalking did not exist prior to 1990, research on stalking, per se, did not exist. Instead, the stalking research was born from the psychiatric study of erotomania and the psychological study of sexual harassment.

Several early case studies discussed the involvement of erotomanic individuals within the criminal justice system (Goldstein, 1978, 1987; Meloy, 1992; Noone & Cockhill, 1987; Taylor, Mahendra, & Gunn, 1983). Due to the obsessive nature of erotomania, individuals with this disorder frequently displayed "stalking behaviors." Alternately, early psychological research focused on the stalking behaviors themselves and labeled these behaviors "sexual harasssment." In a study of undergraduate university women, Herold, Mantle, and Zemitis (1979) found that obscene phone calls and physical following were common forms of harassment. A more thorough study on female harassment following the termination of a relationship was conducted by Jason, Reichler, Easton, Neal, and Wilson (1984), who found that their community sample experienced a variety of stalking behaviors, including phone calls, home or work visits, verbal or physical threats or physical harm, being followed, and receiving flowers. None of the above studies, however, specifically addressed aggravated stalking. Erotomania research and psychological harassment research were combined in our first study (Zona et al., 1993), within which we detailed the various demographic and clinical characteristics in the three groups noted above.

In a follow-up clincial study to Zona et al. (1993), Meloy and Gothard (1995) analyzed the psychiatric and legal records of 20 obsessional followers and compared them to 30 randomly selected mentally disordered offenders from the San Diego County Superior Court's Forensic Evaluation Unit. Although the authors did not propose a classification system for this study, they did analyze the victim–offender relationship, which consisted of former spouses, former intimates, and strangers.

The third major study on stalking was conducted by Harmon et al. (1995). These authors analyzed the records of 48 individuals charged with harassment, aggravated harassment, and/or menacing who were referred to the Forensic Psychiatric Clinic of the Criminal and Supreme Courts of New York. The cases were classified into a two-dimensional typology based on the offender's motivation for stalking and the victim–offender relationship. There were two offender's motivations for stalking: Affectionate/Amorous, in which the victim is pursued for amorous reasons, or as a result of perceived rejection by the offender; and Persecutory/Angry, in which the offender's pursuit is due to some real or imagined injury, and the victim–offender relationship usually consists of business or professional relations. Victim–offender relationships were separated into the six categories of personal, professional, employment, media, acquaintance, and no relationship.

In a comprehensive review of the literature on stalking and obsessional following, Meloy (1996) compiled the data from 10 case and empirical studies that met subject criteria for obsessional following and resulted in some form of law enforcement or criminal justice intervention. Meloy discussed the various methods these studies used to classify the victim–offender relationship and noted that the current systems lead to confusion in reviewing the literature. Meloy suggested dividing the victims into the categories of prior acquaintances, prior sexual intimates, and complete strangers to solve this problem.

Although we agree with Meloy's proposed classification system, the diction he proposed may lead to still more confusion; the terms prior acquaintance and prior sexual intimate are ambiguous and may exclude victim–offender relationships that would otherwise be included in the proposed categories. For example, the term acquaintance describes both a categorical type of relationship and an actual relationship within that category. Acquaintance does not satisfactorily differentiate among co-workers, professional relations, friends, neighbors, and acquaintances. Similarly, the term prior sexual intimate implies that the victim and offender engaged in sexual intercourse. This implication may not be accurate for some relationships, such as dating relationships where sexual intercourse has not occurred. Additionally, it does not account for the degree of intimacy in that relationship (e.g., casual sexual relationship versus marriage). For these reasons, the most recent Threat Management Unit data collection uses the terms stranger, intimate relationship, nonintimate relationship, self, and unknown relationship to categorize the victim–offender relationship. The use of the terms intimate relationship and nonintimate relationship succinctly clears up any ambiguity in differentiating between subtypes of relationships. Under these category headings are subtypes of relationships that provide a more specific description of the victim–offender relationship. For the stranger category, the subtypes celebrity, political figure, simple stranger (an individual who is not of any particular notoriety), and other stranger are used. The intimate relationship category subtypes include married, engaged, cohabiting, dating, and casual sexual. Due to the wide variety of types of nonintimate relationships, one experiences difficulty in establishing a comprehensive categorical subtype without getting too bogged down in minutiae. For the recent data collection, we used the subtypes of co-workers, professional relations, schoolmates, neighbors, roommates, family members, friends, acquaintances, dated same person, and other nonintimate relationships. Due to the growing number of cases involving individuals who dated the same person (e.g., an ex-girlfriend who stalked her ex-boyfriend's current girlfriend), these cases were isolated from the acquaintance group and given their own category. Table 1 summarizes the Threat Management Unit's classification system and current sample size.

CURRENT FINDINGS

Our data support previous findings that the majority of offenders have personality profiles that fall within the Cluster B group. Although we originally found that 63% of our sample had a major mental illness, we did not differentiate between personality disorders and other mental disorders (Zona et al., 1993). Meloy and Gothard (1995) found that 85% of their sample qualified for a personality

Table 4.1

A summary of the Threat Management Unit's Classification System and Current Sample size (N = 341)

Simple obsessional		Love obsessional (Strangers)	Erotomania	False victimization (Self)	Unknown
Intimate	Nonintimate				
Married (6)	Friends (9)	Celebrity (66)	Intimate (1)		
Engaged (4)	Roommates (2)	Political figure (3)	Nonintimate (5)		
Cohabiting (41)	Neighbors (3)	Simple stranger (12)	Strangers (11)		
Dating (74)	Schoolmates (5)	Other stranger (6)			
Casual sexual (9)	Co-workers (16)				
	Professional relations (39)				
	Dated same person (8)				
	Acquaintances (1)				
$n = 134$	$n = 83$				
$n = 217$		$n = 87$	$n = 17$	$n = 6$	$n = 14$

disorder diagnosis, including antisocial, schizoid, borderline, avoidant, paranoid, and not otherwise specified. However, they noted that in comparison to a random group of mentally disordered offenders, obsessional followers more frequently had a Cluster B diagnosis other than antisocial personality disorder. Harmon et al. (1995) found that 25% of their sample had a primary or secondary Axis II diagnosis that included narcissistic, borderline, schizotypal, and not otherwise specified, but did not include antisocial personality disorder.

It appears that stalking is not a crime typically committed by individuals with antisocial personality disorder or extensive criminal histories. Those stalkers who do have some form of criminal history often have police reports, arrests, and/ or convictions for spousal abuse, assault and battery, assault with a deadly weapon, terrorist threats, or annoying and harassing phone calls. These crimes may be related to the current victim or may be the result of a pursuit of another individual. The majority of diagnosable personality disorders among stalkers include the other Cluster B diagnoses, especially narcissistic and borderline personality disorders. Individuals with these disorders often experience difficulty with both intimate and occupational interpersonal relationships. They do not handle rejection well when these relationships end, and they may react to the termination of these relationships with a vengeance.

As the debate over classifying stalking offenses continues, one variable that has demonstrated significance is the presence of a victim–offender relationship prior to the offense. Our research (Zona et al., 1993) identified 47% of the 74 cases as simple obsessional offenses. We found that the majority of these cases concerned romantic relationships between the victims and offenders. The simple obsessional group has since increased to 65% of 200 cases in our most recent LAPD sample (Zona, Lane, & Moore, 1996). Meloy and Gothard (1995) found that 55% of their sample had prior relationships: 15% of their sample stalked former spouses, while 40% stalked sexual intimates. In the Harmon et al. (1995) study, 71% of the cases consisted of prior relationships: 13% had personal or romantic relationships, 25% had professional relationships, 25% had employment relationships, and 8% were acquaintances. Meloy (1996) noted that as a result of law enforcement's selection bias toward arresting and prosecuting more "high profile" or "stranger" stalkers, there was an underrepresentation of spouse or ex-spouse stalkers in the research. In a presentation to the American Academy of Forensic Sciences, we concluded that the simple obsessional group had the highest rates of substance abuse and personality disorders (Zona et al., 1996). These cases were also found to have the shortest duration of stalking and were the most volatile of the three groups, displaying the highest rates of property damage and physical harm. Because these perpetrators know their victims personally, they directly confront their victims more often, and are more dangerous than the love obsessional and erotomanic groups (Zona et al., 1996).

As we attempt to further enhance our understanding of the significance of specific relationships in stalking, it becomes clear that more refined research must take place. This is critically important for those of us whose challenge it is to interpret risk to the victim, and for the many professionals—mental health and criminal justice alike—who are faced with the crime of stalking as a new century begins.

REFERENCES

American Psychiatric Association. (1994). *Diagnostic and statistical manual of mental disorders* (4th ed.). Washington, DC: Author.

California Penal Code §646.9 (1990).

Goldstein, R. L. (1978). De Clérambault in court: A forensic romance? *Bulletin of the American Academy of Psychiatry and the Law, 6,* 36–40.

Goldstein, R. L. (1987). More forensic romances: De Clérambault's syndrome in men. *Bulletin of the American Academy of Psychiatry and the Law, 15,* 267–274.

Harmon, R. B., Rosner, R., & Owens, H. (1995). Obsessional harassment and erotomania in a criminal court population. *Journal of Forensic Sciences, 40*(2), 188–196.

Herold, E. S., Mantle, D., & Zemitis, O. (1979). A study of sexual offenses against females. *Adolescence, 53,* 65–72.

Jason, L. A., Reichler, A., Easton, J., Neal, A., & Wilson, M. (1984). Female harassment after ending a relationship: A preliminary study. *Alternative Lifestyles, 6*(4), 259–269.

Meloy, J. R. (1990). Nondelusional borderline erotomania [Letter to the editor]. *American Journal of Psychiatry, 147,* 820.

Meloy, J. R. (1992). *Violent attachments.* Northvale, NJ: Jason Aronson.

Meloy, J. R. (1996). Stalking (obsessional following): A review of some preliminary studies. *Aggression and Violent Behavior, 1,* 147–162.

Meloy, J. R., & Gothard, S. (1995). Demographic and clinical comparison of obsessional followers and offenders with mental disorders. *American Journal of Psychiatry, 152,* 258–263.

Noone, J., & Cockhill, L. (1987). Erotomania: The delusion of being loved. *American Journal of Forensic Psychiatry, 8,* 23–31.

Segal, J. (1989). Erotomania revisited: Kraepelin to DSM-IIIR. *American Journal of Psychiatry, 146,* 1261–1266.

Taylor, P., Mahendra, B., & Gunn, J. (1983). Erotomania in males. *Psychological Medicine, 13,* 645–650.

Zona, M., Lane, J., & Moore, M. (1996, February). *The psychology and behavior of stalkers.* Paper presented at the American Academy of Forensic Sciences Annual Meeting, Nashville, TN.

Zona, M., Sharma, K., & Lane, J. (1993). A comparative study of erotomanic and obsessional subjects in a forensic sample. *Journal of Forensic Sciences, 38*(4), 894–903.

CHAPTER 5

The Archetypes and Psychodynamics of Stalking

Glen Skoler, Ph.D.

O, from what pow'r hast thou this pow'rful might
With insufficiency my heart to sway?
To make me give the lie to my true sight
And swear that brightness doth not grace the day?
Whence hast thou this becoming of things ill,
That in the very refuse of thy deeds
There is such strength and warrantise of skill
That in my mind thy worst all best exceeds?
Who taught thee how to make me love thee more,
The more I hear and see just cause of hate?

William Shakespeare
Sonnet 150, Lines 1–10

There must be something about obsessive love triangles, (perhaps old, buried oedipal
residues?) that resonates deeply with our collective unconscious. How else can one explain
the endless fascination with this scenario in every time, place and culture, and among
men and women of all ages and socioeconomic levels? Myth, history, literature, films,
and the current media all abound with examples of the violent processes and sequelae
of unrequited obsessive love.

Helen Singer Kaplan
Erotic Obsession, p. 37

No thoughtful mental health or criminal justice professional can long ponder upon "the violent processes and sequelae of unrequited obsessive love" without reaching the same conclusion as the late human sexuality and paraphilia expert, Helen Singer Kaplan (1996): that the psychodynamics of violent attachments disturbingly resonate in the personal and collective unconscious, and, conversely, that an understanding of the personal and collective unconscious can enlighten the psychodynamics—and even the behaviors—of violent stalkers.

Meloy (1992) first coined the phrase "violent attachments" to underscore that many apparently disparate crimes of violence—murder, rape, malicious wounding, assault and battery, office shootings, even some assassination attempts—are frequently manifestations of violence emanating wholly or partly from unrequited and pathological "love." The psychological concept of violent attachments comprises a larger number of crimes than the legal concept of stalking and serves to psychologically relate the more rare occurrence of violent crime as an end result of stalking to the psychodynamics and processes of stalking itself.

One might ask: Why expend effort understanding the psychodynamic characteristics of stalking offenders? And, even more pointedly, one might ask: What possible relevance could references to modern psychoanalytic theory and to the humanities (history, literature, poetry, and films) have for protecting stalking victims?

First, the relation of stalking, as well as the associated explicit or implicit threat of violence, to the more rare commission of actual violence is empirically unclear—and frequently unpredictable in cases of political, celebrity, and relationship stalking (Dietz et al. 1991a,b; Meloy & Gothard, 1995). The statistical relation between stalking and subsequent violence (or even attempts to approach potential political and celebrity stalking victims) tends to be uncorrelated, negatively correlated, or weakly correlated.

Second, traditional correlates and predictors of dangerousness (such as a history of arrest, prior violence, etc.) also do not hold up well across various studies of various types of stalking—which further complicates the problem of predicting the risk of violence. For example, in a study of criminally charged political threateners and stalkers at St. Elizabeths Hospital in Washington D.C., certain modern psychodynamic constructs, operationalized as constellations of psychological test variables, differentiated, at statistically significant levels, presidential threateners from other similarly diagnosed patients—and even differentiated the more dangerous political threateners and stalkers from the less dangerous (Skoler, 1988). The findings in this sample stood in marked contrast to the lack of statistically significant correlations regarding traditional and supposedly more empirical and scientific predictors of violence, such as a history of arrest, prior violence, and so on.

Third, unless one is aware of the associated psychodynamics and behavioral constellations, the *DSM-IV* (American Psychiatric Association, 1994) Axis I delusional disorders and Axis II personality disorders commonly seen in stalkers are often easy to overlook and difficult to diagnose, particularly during a 1-hour mental health intake or mental status examination. As noted, for example, in the *DSM-*

IV "Criteria C" for delusional, erotomanic obsessions (p. 301): "Apart from the impact of the delusion(s) or its ramifications, functioning is not markedly impaired and behavior is not obviously odd or bizarre."

Fourth, relying on a psychodynamic approach to complement an empirical approach regarding crimes such as serial killings and sexual sadism carries a current criminal justice cachet (Douglas, 1995). However, the semantic efforts law enforcement experts, such as Douglas, purposely make to distinguish their "criminal profiling" from "psychological profiling" reflects an undeniable tension between law enforcement experts and mental health experts.

For years criminal justice experts have understandably been frustrated with outdated Freudian "mother complex" or "father complex" oedipal theories, as well as the less sophisticated but more trendy "inner wounded child" portrayals of criminal offenders. The tension (and sibling rivalry) between clinical psychology and social psychology (social psychologists arguing that their statistical, empirical approach had more validity for law enforcement than clinical descriptions or predictions of dangerousness) exacerbated this alienation between the law enforcement community and the mental health community.

Today, there is a consensus among leading psychoanalytic theorists that the psychodynamics that characterize most mentally disturbed violent offenders generally involve "pre-oedipal"-level character pathology, expressed in personality disorders and delusional disorders. However, modern theories of these disorders were only just being fully developed and accepted in the 1970s and 1980s. And it was not until the late 1980s and early 1990s that the obvious marriage of modern psychoanalytic theory with forensic psychiatry and psychology (Meloy, 1988, 1992; Kernberg, 1992) took place. These modern psychoanalytic theories were also more sympathetic to the law enforcement sentiment that such character pathology or personality disorder does not often reach a level of mental illness to excuse criminal responsibility or to justify criminal insanity.

Yet the very sophistication and complexity of modern psychoanalytic theory, which makes it more relevant to law enforcement concerns and profiling, also poses an obstacle to understanding.

This is the reason why, in training presentations, I began using archetypes in Western culture, as expressed in literature, drama, films, and the media, to render modern psychodynamic constructs of stalkers more convincing and cogent. In fact, this book chapter was developed from just such an approach for an unclassified presentation to psychology staff of the National Security Agency and Central Intelligence Agency.

The following references to psychodynamic theory and literature are not cited to speculate and hypothesize, but rather to explicate and elucidate stalking behavior and psychodynamics, as observed in the evaluation and treatment of actual criminal offenders.

WAS SHAKESPEARE A STALKER?: A MODERN PSYCHODYNAMIC INTERPRETATION OF THE DARK LADY SONNETS

Among the most famous, tortured, and actual love obsessions in Western literature is Shakespeare's sonneteering erotomania for his spurning "dark lady," the "woman colored ill" (*Sonnet 144, Line 4*).

If, as the literary critic Bloom (1994) avers, Shakespeare *is* the center of the Western canon of literature, then a discussion of the archetypes of love obsession might as well start with Shakespeare's own. In fact, archetype is so powerful in illuminating stalking behavior and thinking, that Shakespeare's sonnets shall serve here to introduce a complete outline of the psychodynamics of violent stalkers. ("Though this be madness, yet there is method in 't.")

The educated lay person, from poetry or sonnet anthologies, is probably more familiar with Shakespeare's famous love sonnets whose index of first lines includes, "Shall I compare thee to a summer's day?" (*Sonnet 18*), and "Let me not to the marriage of true minds/Admit impediments. . . ." (*Sonnet 116*). Yet approximately the last 25 or so of the 154 sonnets, and some others, are devoted primarily to Shakespeare's actual love obsession for the "woman colored ill."

At times, Shakespeare's "love sonnets" sound more like "hate sonnets" as his spurned affirmations of love become increasingly vicious, threatening, obscene, paranoid, irrational, desperate, and devaluing both of himself and of her.

Consequently, the dark lady sonnets are not a pretty psychological sight. This discomfort creates a psychic need in some experts and lay readers to argue that the "story" of Shakespeare's love obsession, implied in the sonnet sequence, is more the result of his imaginative genius, rather than the result of an all too human erotomania. Yet even defenders of Shakespeare's psychological objectivity and creativity, particularly those critics and authors with literary acumen (e.g., the poet Wordsworth), concede, in concurrence with most commentators, that Shakespeare's dark lady sonnets are obviously inspired by a personal love obsession.

The curiosity, scholarship, and prodigious speculation devoted to the sonnets, particularly in regard to the identity of the dark lady, is partly fueled by the fact that the sonnets provide one of the few bases for psychoanalysis of Shakespeare. The biographical information on him is sparse, uneventful, and bland (Bloom, 1994). Nor can Shakespeare's personality readily be discerned from his plays, a fact that Bloom relates to the mystery of Shakespeare's genius and creativity. While the characters (e.g., Hamlet, Lady Macbeth, Falstaff, Rosalind, etc.) are subject to psychoanalytic speculation, the playwright is much more psychologically elusive. The humanity in the plays is so vast and so complete that Shakespeare seems almost "too healthy" to psychoanalyze. In the words of Bloom, "Can we locate a blindness in him, a repression, a failing in imagination or in thought?" (1994, p. 50). The relation of this psychological mystery to the creative mystery of Shakespeare's genius renders even more curious and strange his painfully obvious difficulty coping with unrequited, obsessive love.

The "dark lady" sonnets are so called because Shakespeare's betraying beloved is a brunette. Apparently, in Elizabethan England, blondes really did have more fun, being esteemed as beauteous and fair. Shakespeare employs his relentless genius for metaphor and double entendre to play sundry and increasingly embittered variations on the theme of the "black," "dark," "colored ill," "foul," "not fair" character of his spurning, dark-haired obsession.

HISTRIONIC PSYCHODYNAMICS: SEXUAL TRIANGLES, JEALOUSY, COMPETITION, MASOCHISM, INADEQUACY, AND INHIBITION

> So, now I have confessed that he is thine
> And I myself am mortgaged to thy will,
>   *Sonnet 134, Lines 1–2*

This realization (with a sexual pun on his own first name) that Shakespeare's male friend and his adored beloved are having an affair, is a story line implied from the sequence of sonnets. While most of the latter sonnets are addressed to the dark lady, many of the earlier sonnets are addressed to the male friend, a probable patron. (Most critics dismiss the implication of homosexuality, citing conventions of the day, as well as the obvious heterosexual interest in and liaison with the dark lady.) The affair between the friend and the mistress creates an intense love triangle and an unbearable double betrayal for Shakespeare.

Shakespeare ultimately attempts to sublimate this love triangle into a Renaissance metaphor of the struggle in the self between the spirit and the flesh, between good and evil:

> Two loves I have, of comfort and despair,
> Which like two spirits do suggest (tempt) me still:
> The better angel is a man right fair,
> The worser spirit a woman colored ill.
> To win me soon to hell, my female evil
> Tempteth my better angel from my side,
> And would corrupt my saint to be a devil,
> Wooing his purity with her foul pride.
>   *Sonnet 144, Lines 1–8*

Yet despite these efforts at higher level defenses, such as sublimation, Shakespeare also succumbs to inevitable feelings of sexual betrayal, stimulation, jealousy, inadequacy, competition, and inhibition: all suggestive of regression to a constellation of oedipal-level, histrionic psychodynamics.

While the dark lady sonnets push the envelope of sonneteering conventionality, even Shakespeare dare not outright accuse a "Lady" of being a "whore." But he makes the psychological point well enough, quickly generalizing her presumed infidelity with one, to a fantasy of infidelity with many:

> If eyes, corrupt by over-partial looks,
> Be anchored in the bay where all men ride,
> Why of eyes' falsehood has thou forged hooks,
> Whereto the judgment of my heart is tied?
> Why should my heart think that a several (private) plot
> Which my heart knows the wide world's common place?
> Or mine eyes seeing this, say this is not,
> To put fair truth upon so foul a face?
> In things right true my heart and eyes have erred,
> And to this false plague are they now transferred.
>
> *Sonnet 137*, Lines 5–14

In this and the preceding two sonnets (*135* and *136*) Shakespeare alternates between begging to be one of her many presumed lovers and attacking what he imagines to be her promiscuous moral character. The sexual double entendre of being anchored in the bay, or common roadway, where all men "ride" is followed in subsequent lines by references to the dark lady as a "false plague," and to Shakespeare's eyes putting "fair truth upon so foul a face." Both metaphors of a woman's "foulness" and "plague," which Shakespeare will reiterate throughout the dark lady sonnets, are suggestive to the Elizabethan reader of venereal disease.

Shakespeare, punning off his first name ("Will"), actively fantasizes literally about placing his erect penis in the carnal desire ("will") of his mistress, where he imagines so many others to have been:

> Wilt thou, whose will is large and spacious,
> Not once vouchsafe to hide my will in thine?
> Shall will in others seem right gracious,
> And in my will no fair acceptance shine?
>
> *Sonnet 135*, Lines 5–8

This devaluation of the love object appears linked on one psychic level to the fantasized sullied, dirtied character of the beloved, which suggests a kind of mother/whore splitting fantasy first described by Freud (1953) in his *Three Essays on the Theory of Sexuality* as an expression of oedipal-level conflict.

In the penultimate dark lady sonnet Shakespeare combines feelings of sexual betrayal with explicit phallic double meanings of gaining and losing erections, in a manner pathetically suggestive of oedipal stimulation, and frustration:

> For, thou betraying me, I do betray
> My nobler part to my gross body's treason;
> My soul doth tell my body that he may
> Triumph in love; flesh stays no farther reason,
> But, rising at thy name, doth point out thee
> As his triumphant prize. Proud of this pride,

> He is contented thy poor drudge to be,
> To stand in thy affairs, fall by thy side.
>> *Sonnet 151,* Lines 5–12

This "Freudian" mother/whore interpretation may sound theoretical—until Shakespeare suddenly shifts from accusing the beloved of being whore-like, to literally begging her to stop running after his sexual rival and instead turn back to Shakespeare, so as to embrace him, as a mother kisses a child:

> So runn'st thou after that which flies from thee,
> Whilst I, thy babe, chase thee afar behind;
> But if thou catch thy hope, turn back to me
> And play the mother's part, kiss me, be kind.
>> *Sonnet 143,* Lines 9–12

Shakespeare, in the face of obvious sexual rejection and inadequacy, adopts the psychological role not of the "oedipal victor" but of the "oedipal loser," desperately trying to justify his unrequited pursuit based on the purity and primacy of his love, if not on the primacy of his sexuality: a psychosexual elevation of one's inferior sexual position rationalized as an offer of a "pure" (mother) love for an "impure" (whore) lover:

> If thy unworthiness raised love in me,
> More worthy I to be beloved of thee.
>> *Sonnet 150,* Lines 13–14

This deeply repressed theme of sexual inadequacy and frustration is frequently seen in the psychosexual histories of actual stalkers—in unison with the fantasy of "rescuing the whore" from her presumed acts of degrading sexuality into a rationalized more "pure" and "spiritual" union.

BORDERLINE PSYCHODYNAMICS: PSYCHOLOGICAL SPLITTING, PRIMITIVE IDEALIZATION AND DEVALUATION, AND PROJECTIVE IDENTIFICATION

Shakespeare's reliance on mother/whore oedipal-level splitting also appears to mobilize pre-oedipal-, "borderline"-level splitting. Perhaps the most remarkable aspect of the sequence of Shakespeare's dark lady sonnets is his increasing and desperate reliance, in the face of spurned and unrequited love, on the psychological defenses of idealization and devaluation, in concert with splitting. These defenses appear to preserve his idealized object representation from being poisoned into a devalued object representation by his growing frustration, anger, jealousy, and contempt.

Shakespeare at times wonders out loud how he could feel such desperate and disparate extremes for his spurning, unfaithful, obsession:

> Whence hast thou this becoming of things ill,
> That in the very refuse of thy deeds
> There is such strength and warrantise of skill
> That in my mind thy worst all best exceeds?
> Who taught thee how to make me love thee more,
> The more I hear and see just cause of hate?
> *Sonnet 150,* Lines 5–10

Semiconscious of his own psychological splitting, Shakespeare repeatedly utilizes in the sonnet sequence various Renaissance metaphors (eyes versus heart, spirit versus flesh, reason versus body) to express his own split object representations of the beloved—and of himself in relation to her:

> In faith, I do not love thee with mine eyes,
> For they in thee a thousand errors note;
> But 'tis my heart that loves what they despise,
> Who in despite of view is pleased to dote.
> *Sonnet 141,* Lines 1–4

The modern psychoanalytic object relations literature frequently associates the defense of projective identification with the defense of splitting (Kernberg, 1984). And, true to form, Shakespeare, like many love-obsessed men and women, articulates his conviction that he is dominated, controlled, tormented, and even psychologically defined by the object of his own obsession. His confusion in this complex psychological process is reflected by the interrogatory format:

> O, from what pow'r hast thou this pow'rful might
> With insufficiency my heart to sway?
> *Sonnet 150,* Lines 1–2

> Why of eyes' falsehood hast thou forged hooks,
> Whereto the judgment of my heart is tied?
> *Sonnet 137,* Lines 7–8

There are not many instances in the canon of Western literature when one can segue from the writings of William Shakespeare to the writings of O. J. Simpson without missing a psychological beat, but the stalker's conviction of being victimized and controlled by the object of his love obsession is universal. Compare Shakespeare's perceptions of being a victim of his beloved's "pow'rful might" over him and "forged hooks" in him, to O. J. Simpson, in his pre-flight letter arguing, "At times I'v felt like a battered husband or boyfriend but I love her, made that clear to everyone. . . . (Toobin, 1996).

NARCISSISTIC PSYCHODYNAMICS: SELF–OBJECT CONFUSION, DEPENDENCY, AND DISTORTIONS

Despite his devaluation of the love object, at other times Shakespeare tries to devalue himself, so as to preserve both his love for and his idealization of the betraying beloved. Yet Shakespeare turns his own ego upon himself at the price of becoming increasingly narcissistically depressed, depleted, destabilized, and angered, eventually imagining himself to verge on the edge of psychological decompensation and losing almost all sense of psychological "boundary" between himself and his love obsession:

> Prison my heart in thy steel bosom's ward,
> . . . for I, being pent in thee,
> Perforce am thine, and all that is in me.
> *Sonnet 133*, Lines 9, 13–14

> But my five wits nor my five senses can
> Dissuade one foolish heart from serving thee,
> Who leaves unswayed the likeness of a man,
> Thy proud heart's slave and vassal wretch to be.
> *Sonnet 141*, Lines 9–12

Who else but Shakespeare could so consciously articulate the unconscious ambivalence for the narcissistically cathected object by using the oxymoron for being imprisoned in a "steel bosom?"

In the vernacular of popular psychology, one needs only to "dumb down" the language for Shakespeare to sound like the ultimate "co-dependent:"

> Canst thou, O cruel, say I love thee not
> When I against myself with thee partake? . . .
> What merit do I in myself respect
> That is so proud thy service to despise,
> When all my best doth worship thy defect,
> Commanded by the motion of thine eyes?
> *Sonnet 149*, Lines 1–2, 9–12

Shakespeare's conviction in these sonnets that he is "wounded," "imprisoned," and "enslaved" into becoming "the likeness of a man" suggests a regression to levels of narcissistic self–object confusion frequently seen in violent stalkers, who consciously or unconsciously feel the need to destroy their love object in order to regain and stabilize their own fragile sense of self (Meloy, 1992).

ANTISOCIAL AND DELUSIONAL PSYCHODYNAMICS: THREATS AND PREDATION TO CONTROL THE LOVE OBJECT AS A DEFENSE AGAINST PSYCHOLOGICAL DECOMPENSATION

As Shakespeare approaches the role of a threatening stalker in the sonnets, he clearly does so to ward off decompensation fears mobilized by the fragility of his narcissistic defenses and his growing narcissistic anger. One can see in Shakespeare's "love sonnets," of all things, the complex link between the fragility of the self and the mobilization of stalking anger and threats:

> Past cure I am, now reason is past care,
> And frantic-mad with evermore unrest;
> My thoughts and my discourse as madmen's are,
> At randon from the truth vainly expressed:
> For I have sworn thee fair, and thought thee bright,
> Who art as black as hell, as dark as night.
>   *Sonnet 147,* Lines 9–14

Finally, Shakespeare, psychologically trapped by the dilemma of his own obsession, like many an obsessed stalker, tries to control the love object with threats, blackmail, and forebodings of the unpredictable nature of his angry irrationality if he is pressed too far:

> Be wise as thou art cruel: do not press
> My tongue-tied patience with too much disdain,
> Lest sorrow lend me words, and words express
> The manner of my pity-wanting pain.
>
> For if I should despair, I should grow mad,
> And in my madness might speak ill of thee:
> Now this ill-wresting world is grown so bad
> Mad slanderers by mad ears believed be.
>   *Sonnet 140,* Lines 1–4, 9–12

While Shakespeare is not threatening violence here (despite the purposely odd, angry, crazy, and frightening psychological tone), he is threatening something else viciously destructive of the love object. His spurning mistress is presumably of high if not noble class—and, like Shakespeare, is married (*Sonnet 152*). Shakespeare, whose weapon of choice is his words, in *Sonnet 140* chooses slander (presumably accusing an Elizabethan woman of adultery) as his angry threat, to try to pressure and control her. This sense of narcissistic destruction and control of the love object, described by Kernberg (1980), is seen in stalkers who attempt to ruin the reputation (and life) of their victim in the eyes of a spouse or employer.

One also sees in these two "crazy sonnets" the overdetermined nature of stalking anger, which, depending on the case, can coalesce pre-oedipal and oedipal strivings, sexual conflict, and inadequacy; borderline splitting and projective identification; vindictive, malignant antisocial traits of predation; and narcissistic merger, omnipotence/ devaluation, and self-object confusion: as threats and other attempts to psychologically control the love object are utilized to ward off further psychological decompensation, further self-object diffusion, and the further unleashing of primitively condensed aggression and sexuality.

SEPARATION/INDIVIDUATION: LETTING GO

"Was Shakespeare a Stalker?" is not an absurd proposition. Current model stalking statutes do not require an explicit threat to bring a stalking charge, but do require that a "reasonable person" would feel threatened by the unsolicited stalking behavior; this could include chronic, uninvited, bizarre, threatening, and obscene letters. Shakespeare's references to going "mad" and of being "past reason," his threats of slander and angry warnings that he not be "pressed" too far, his venomous and vicious name calling, and his explicitly obscene begging to literally place his erect penis into the vagina he contemptuously portrays as a promiscuous, one-woman venereal plague would certainly appear to meet modern American stalking criteria.

However, the purpose of psychologically illuminating the very darkest side of the "dark lady" sonnets is not to portray Shakespeare as a "stalker," but to make use of his profound artistic ability to consciously articulate the human unconscious (in this case his own). Thus Shakespeare's sonnets provide a means of comprehending the regressive pull in love obsessions toward primitive object relations, distortions of the love object and of the self, and associated psychological defenses—which can break down into violence in cases of actual stalking. It is for this reason that aspects of Shakespeare's sonnets have been organized here according to the personality and delusional disorders that frequently typify stalkers—not to suggest that Shakespeare suffered from a complex of personality disorders.

There is no guarantee that the sonnets are published in the correct order, or that they are even complete. However, the last dark lady sonnet (*152*) suggests that Shakespeare, in fact, did not go the route of a stalker, but instead was able to separate his psyche from the object of his obsession. Backed into his own psychological corner, Shakespeare finally realized that instead of needing to write her, he needed to write her off:

> And all my honest faith in thee is lost;
> For I have sworn deep oaths of thy deep kindness,
> Oaths of thy love, thy truth, thy constancy;
> And, to enlighten thee, gave eyes to blindness,
> Or made them swear against the thing they see;
> For I have sworn thee fair: more perjured eye,
> To swear against the truth so foul a lie.
> *Sonnet 152,* Lines 8–14

PSYCHODIAGNOSES AND PSYCHODYNAMICS OF STALKING

As seen in Shakespeare's dark lady sonnets, stalking fantasies and obsessions frequently coalesce oedipal and pre-oedipal sexuality, as well as several levels of object relations and associated primitive defenses.

To complicate a discussion of stalking psychodynamics further, discrete personality disorder diagnostic categories in the *DSM-IV* (e.g., borderline, narcissistic and antisocial personality disorders) are conceptualized by Kernberg (1984) as being subtypes of one another; borderline personality disorders comprising narcissistic personality disorders, and narcissistic personality disorders comprising some forms of antisocial personality disorders.

Adopting Kernberg's concept of borderline personality organization as comprising a group of *DSM-IV, Axis II,* Cluster B disorders, Meloy's (1989) original distinction between delusional erotomania and borderline erotomania appears to hold up rather well. It is also useful in distinguishing the nature of the stalker's psychological attachment and the nature of the stalker's relationship to the victim.

Meloy and Gothard (1995) noted, for example, that in erotomanic stalking (which usually occurs as a primary diagnosis at a rate of about 10% in studies of criminally charged or investigated stalkers) there has not been an actual relationship between the stalker and victim. Ths victim is usually a celebrity, superior or unattainable, idealized other, often initially "worshipped from afar." In stalking characterized predominantly by borderline personality organization, the severing or spurning of a relationship (or of brief contact the stalker presumed was a relationship) often precipitates the stalking behavior. There are exceptions to these generalizations. Still, this distinction between delusional and borderline erotomania is psychodynamically useful, and has legal ramifications as well, since delusional disorders may, in some instances, qualify for an insanity defense while personality disorders generally do not.

Psychodiagnostically and psychodynamically, this distinction also provides some clarification of the diagnostic confusion in stalking cases, since the rare "delusional erotomania" implies a predominantly Axis I, *DSM-IV* disorder, while "borderline erotomania" implies a predominantly Axis II, *DSM-IV* disorder.

In studies of primarily nondelusional, "borderline erotomania" (as in general studies of borderline personality), the Axis I diagnoses of stalkers can include a misleading mix of mood, anxiety, and substance abuse disorders. However, as Meloy and Gothard (1995) found, there is usually underlying character pathology or personality disorder. Thus while in many studies the focus is often Axis I distinctions, while acknowledging without much interest varying underlying Axis II features, in forensic "borderline erotomanic" stalking cases, the converse may be true; the Axis II features may be of more psychodynamic and psychodiagnostic interest than the Axis I features.

Meloy's "borderline erotomania" concept is also useful for understanding the disturbed psychosexual life of stalkers. Stalking, as does the group of borderline personality organization personality disorders itself, coalesces both oedipal and pre-oedipal sexuality:

Borderline personality organization presents a pathological condensation of genital and pre-genital instinctual strivings, with a predominance of pregenital aggression (Kernberg, 1975). This assumption explains the bizarre or inappropriate condensation of sexual, dependent and aggressive impulses found clinically in borderline (and also psychotic) organization. (Kernberg, 1984, p. 21)

The implication of these theories of borderline sexuality is that the psychosexual life of the average criminally charged stalker is part-object bound, psychologically condensed, complex, largely unconscious—and not easily categorized into any specific level of object relatedness.

If the concept of "borderline erotomania" comprises different *DSM-IV* Axis II personality disorders, so also does the concept of "delusional erotomania" comprise different Axis I psychotic disorders.

The *DSM-IV* is both inadequate and misleading in providing a clear and unified psychodiagnostic picture of delusional stalking. Certainly the *DSM-IV*'s delusional disorder, "erotomanic subtype" does not comprise all forms of delusional stalking. Unfortunately "erotomania" (and its specific *DSM-IV* criteria) is often used synonymously to express generally the concept of delusional stalking.

Part of the confusion is that *DSM-IV*'s erotomanic subtype of delusional disorder describes a very specific disorder historically derived from de Clérambault's syndrome. The *DSM-IV*'s erotomanic subtype requires that the love object usually be of higher status or unattainable, in concurrence with the requirement that the erotomanic patient be convinced that he or she is loved by the love object. (Thus in the case of John Hinckley, Jr., there was debate about whether he really believed actress Jodie Foster loved him, whereas for many stalkers the fantasy is more that they will somehow win over or convince the beloved.)

The *DSM-IV* erotomanic subtype of delusional disorder is also, and paradoxically, both accurate and misleading in suggesting that erotomania usually entails the fantasy of a pure, spiritual, asexual union with the beloved. This is, in fact, a frequent psychodynamic in such cases; however, as described below, it is a psychodynamic fueled by a great deal of psychosexual anxiety, inadequacy, jealousy, preoccupation, and confusion, leaving a highly and often unconscious aggressive and sexualized foundation to diagnostic criteria that describe only the compensatory symptom: the fantasy of a spiritual, pure union—a fantasy that can actually lead to violence.

Another source of diagnostic confusion created by the *DSM-IV* is the distinction between erotomanic and jealous subtypes of delusional disorders, as if they were mutually exclusive diagnostic categories. The jealous components of such love obsessions are sometimes less obvious, and the *DSM-IV* would suggest that delusional jealousy implies a level of preexisting relationship while erotomania does not. Yet in delusional erotomania, because the relationship is more ideational than actual, jealous preoccupations are frequently implied in the love obsession, for example, in the wish that the beloved cease "infidelities" with others.

Based on the foregoing psychodiagnostic considerations, the following discussion of the psychodynamic complexes and archetypes of stalking is organized
primarily by the diagnostic categories of delusional erotomania and "borderline
erotomania," which comprises several *DSM-IV, Axis II, Cluster B* personality disorders.

Archetypes of stalking, like stalking itself, probably are so psychologically
powerful in the personal and collective unconscious precisely because, like Shakespeare's love-obsessed dark lady sonnets, they coalesce different levels of object
relations and associated defenses. A striking example of this psychologically overdetermined and coalescing quality of stalking archetypes is the Madonna/whore
fantasy, which can combine oedipal and pre-oedipal sexual fantasies and which has
a psychological appeal to normal, histrionic, borderline, narcissistic, and delusional
personalities who are love obsessed.

HISTRIONIC PERSONALITY FEATURES

Rescuing the Whore: Male Daydream, Stalking Nightmare

Rescuing the whore with love fantasies from Shakespeare's sonnets and
Freud's turn-of-the-century essays on oedipal sexuality may seem highly theoretical,
and of little relevance to the violent victimization of women in modern society—
until one studies the actual words, behaviors, and fantasies of violent stalkers.

John Hinckley, Jr., became obsessed with actress Jodie Foster when she
played a teenage prostitute who is violently "rescued" from her pimp by a wanna-
be assassin in the film *Taxi Driver.*

Many stalkers and perpetrators of violent attachments obsessively harbor the
fantasy that they will somehow rescue their "beloved" or love obsession from
imagined degradation and defilement with other men—whether they explicitly
or implicitly, consciously or unconsciously, think of her as a "whore" who needs
to be "saved."

Robert Hoskins, convicted of stalking the actress and singer Madonna in
1996, left her a letter titled, "Defiled," claiming he was married to her and that
he wished to save her from a life of imagined "defilement" with other men. One
reason Madonna is a "stalking magnet" is that she, at various times in her career,
has carefully crafted a stage and public persona that deliberately stimulates mother/
whore splitting fantasies and conflict: a crucifix-wearing unattainable "Madonna"
who is nonetheless sexually suggestive and provocative.

When the standard of psychiatric diagnosis, the *Diagnostic and Statistical Manual
of Mental Disorders* (*DSM-IV*), revised criteria for erotomania in 1994, the following
sentence was added to the description of delusional love obsessions: "Some individuals with this subtype [of delusional disorder], particularly males, come into conflict

with the law in their efforts to pursue the object of their delusion or in a misguided effort to 'rescue' him or her from some imagined danger." The fantasy often involves the belief that the beloved will be grateful to be "rescued," cease her "infidelity" with other men, and fall in love with the stalker.

What sounds psychologically theoretical all too often becomes tragically true. The *Tarasoff* case, a civil suit, established a therapist's duty to warn potential stalking victims of dangerous therapy patients. In that California case, Prosenjit Poddar became obsessed with Tatiana Tarasoff after a New Year's kiss followed by her discouragement. He planned to create a disaster from which he would "rescue" her and which, in his deluded mind, would result in her recognition that she loved him. His ill-fated plan turned from love to rage, and he ended up stabbing her to death.

Is this acted-out fantasy in the *Tarasoff* case any more profoundly disturbed and perverted than the following acted-out fantasy?: A teenage boy actually plans and stages an attempted rape of his own mother, perpetrated by himself, harboring the belief that she will finally learn to appreciate his father, whom he hopes will intervene and "rescue" her. In fact, this is not a forensic case study, but the happy ending to the enormously popular family movie, *Back to the Future*. Marty (played by Michael J. Fox) is sent in a time machine to the 1950s, only to have his attractive and precocious teenage mother develop a crush on him. His reverse oedipal task for the rest of the film is to devise some means for his mother to instead fall in love with his pathetically nerdy and passive father-to-be, so that Marty can be born in the future. Marty's plans to stage a rape attempt go awry, and instead his mother is actually threatened with rape by the high school bully. She falls in love with Marty's father, who rescues her—a turn of events that fulfills and affirms the teenage boy's fantasy.

Why is this extremely successful movie script almost identical to the pathological rescuing fantasy described in the *DSM-IV*'s diagnostic criteria for delusional stalkers, and manifested in actual cases of violent stalking such as the *Tarasoff* case? It suggests a psychic symbolism, an archetype of a male rescuing fantasy, which, as soon as one becomes conscious of it, can be readily recognized throughout Western culture, modern American media, and our collective unconscious.

From the days of Mary Magdalene, to the days of the prostitute Sonja in Dostoevsky's *Crime and Punishment,* to the days of *Pretty Woman* and *Leaving Las Vegas,* men, and women, have been intrigued by the fantasy of a man rescuing a prostitute who becomes his nurturing, loving, and faithful companion.

In *Leaving Las Vegas* writer/director Mike Figgis approaches the truth, precisely because he transcends the predictable stereotype and archetype of "rescuing the whore." The prostitute, Sera, played by Elisabeth Shue, is portrayed as having the fantasized loving and nurturing heart of gold for her self-destructive, alcoholic lover, Ben, played by Academy Award winner Nicolas Cage. However, the film becomes poignant and tragic because neither of these flawed but appealing characters is able to rescue the other. He is not capable of rescuing her from the world of prostitution in which she is brutally gang raped, beaten, and sodomized. And she is not capable of rescuing him from his relentless, alcoholic self-destruction. When they move in together, the unconscious audience expectation (or archetypal fantasy) that his love will save her from prostitution, and that her love will save him from himself, is turned on its head, as the new couple commemorates with gifts their mutual understanding that she will keep on whoring and that he will keep on drinking. She gives him a flask. He gives her earrings to feel while she is "fucking" other men. Each gift brings ambivalent tears to the other's eyes.

The Pursuit of Unrequited Love: "Safe Sex" for the "Heterosexually Impaired"

Freud (1953), of course, immediately recognized a repressed oedipal theme in the rescuing the whore fantasy. By this theory the prostitute is a mother figure imagined to be degraded and defiled in acts of sexuality with a powerful, potent father figure, and is perceived (with ambivalent anger and idealization) as a victim who needs to be rescued, in the jealous eyes of the adoring, but sexually immature, male child. Beyond the Freudian interpretation this fantasy is probably so archetypal because it is overdetermined. Themes of rescuing the whore can condense and coalesce several oedipal and pre-oedipal psychodynamics.

The predictable Freudian interpretation, however, helps to explain the counterintuitive paradox: why some erotomanic and obsessional stalkers—who often have rather inadequate heterosexual skills and histories—become obsessed with imagined "whores" and sexual sophisticates such as film stars—women who are perceived as sexually experienced, and threatening, to an obviously fragile and inadequate male ego. However, part of the imagined happy ending of the fantasy is that the union with the "whore" will be a highly idealized pure and spiritual love, devoid of the supposedly degrading and "dirty" sexuality she is expected to cease with other men. Choosing unattainable love objects, such as celebrities, also insulates the stalker from the threat of actual sexual contact.

Stephen Sondheim, in the bizarre musical *Assassins,* dramatizes this heterosexual angst in presidential stalkers by employing the twisted theatrical device of having Squeaky Fromm (Gerald Ford's assailant) seduce John Hinckley. When Fromm senses Hinckley's increasing anxiety, she contemptuously tells him that he wouldn't know what to do with Jodie Foster if he had her. Studies of criminally charged political, celebrity, and relationship stalkers confirm inadequate and anxious heterosexual histories (Skoler, 1988; Meloy, 1996). Thus, in both prostitute films, *Taxi Driver* and *Leaving Las Vegas,* the initial invitation offered the male to do anything he wants to the prostitute results only in his anxious request to talk to her.

Compare this theoretical formulation of pure union with the idealized beloved to actual statements by the paranoid schizophrenic stalker, Arthur Jackson, who stabbed actress Theresa Saldana 10 times during an attack near her apartment: ". . . it was spiritual lovesickness and divine inspiration . . . it's always been aesthetic and Platonic. . . ."[Dietz, 1988].

BORDERLINE PERSONALITY FEATURES

Idealization and Devaluation

As noted in Shakespeare's dark lady sonnets, rescuing the whore with love fantasies also stimulate borderline-level defenses of primitive idealization and devaluation, as well as related narcissistic extremes of omnipotence and devaluation. And, as noted by Kernberg (1984), regarding the psychosexuality of borderline personality organization, idealization of the love object can serve as a defense against primitive rage. These psychodynamic concepts help to explain why in stalking cases the most deep, most ideal, most pure affirmations of love can almost instantly turn to vicious contempt, anger, violence, and sexual degradation.

Hollywood movies rely on a certain kind of psychological "splitting" to make stalking fantasies more palatable and titillating to normal men and women. The woman is usually stalked and/or captured by a bad guy, and, more often than not, eventually rescued by a good guy. In romantic thrillers, such as the films *Witness* and *Speed,* this splitting fantasy is often represented by a bad cop who threatens and captures a woman and a good cop who rescues her. The movie *Klute,* starring Donald Sutherland and Jane Fonda, combines the formula of the stalking thriller with the "good cop" or detective rescuing a "whore" who devotes herself to him.

On a psychodynamic level it is easy to see how facilely the good guy/bad guy or good cop/bad cop splitting fantasy makes more acceptable the otherwise disturbing and repulsive stalking fantasy of the same person imagining himself to be both the good guy and the bad guy, the threatener and the rescuer, in an attempt to control and possess the woman—precisely as the *DSM-IV* describes this fantasy in erotomanic cases such as *Tarasoff.* Yet these films also appear to fuel in disturbed males with borderline personality organization the fantasy that stalking and threatening a woman is a tremendously effective means to both omnipotently control and devalue her into terrified, helpless, and dependent states of vulnerability.

This splitting dynamic in films also allows the audience to become "titillated without guilt" as women are treated very sadistically by men: locked in rooms, tied, bound, gagged, and handcuffed by the "bad guy"—as the audience waits for the "good guy" to rescue a vulnerable, traumatized woman who melts in her rescuer's arms. This is the same kind of treatment that is considered psychotic-inducing torture in actual forensic case studies, or when its horror is more realistically portrayed, as in the chilling true story film *Fargo,* where there is no "romantic rescue" for the housewife who is emotionally, and finally physically, destroyed by being sadistically bound and gagged by a psychopath.

Stephen Spielberg cleverly played off these rescuing and sadistic archetypes in *Raiders of the Lost Ark*. The predictable formula is in place: Indiana Jones' girlfriend is captured by Nazis, threatened with sexual violation and torture, and of course, bound and gagged. Her hero, Indiana Jones, finds her, removes her gag, kisses her—but leaves her tied and puts her gag back in place as she squirms with muffled screams, so that he can do his "guy thing" and pursue the quest for the lost Ark without arousing suspicion. This scene is funny to the audience (and even to the female colleagues who read drafts of this chapter) because it turns on its head the expectable male/female rescuing fantasy and archetype.

Projective Identification in Unrequited Love: Torturing the Torturer

The need to control the stalking victim is a highly overdetermined psychodynamic that coalesces various strains of stalker psychopathology. Certainly projective identification is one of several unconscious dynamics in the stalker's need to control the stalking victim.

As discussed regarding Shakespeare's "dark lady" sonnets, love-obsessed persons as diverse in character, IQ, culture, ethnicity, and sensibility as William Shakespeare and O. J. Simpson perceive themselves as tormented, abused, and literally controlled by the object of their love obsession. Meloy and Gothard (1995) noted the same dynamic in their study of criminally charged stalkers, remarking that one offender felt so psychologically tormented by his love obsession that *he* attempted to obtain a restraining order on *her*.

Kernberg (1977) defined projective identification as:

> 1) the tendency to continue to experience the impulse which at the same time is projected onto the other person; 2) fear of the other person under the influence of that projected impulse; and 3) the need to control the external object (the other person) under the influence of this mechanism. (p. 109)

A striking fictional example of this confusion between aggressor and victim is portrayed in *Taxi Driver,* the film that obsessed John Hinckley, Jr. Even people who have not seen *Taxi Driver* are probably familiar with the scene, repeatedly parodied in pop culture. As the character Travis, played by actor Robert DeNiro, plans to assassinate a presidential candidate, he practices with a gun standing in front of a mirror taunting and threatening himself, with such belligerent posturing as, "Are you talkin' to me?" As he pretends to shoot at the mirror, he is, of course, shooting at an image of himself (Skoler, 1988).

ANTISOCIAL PERSONALITY FEATURES

The typical Hollywood stalking script, while on an unconscious level reinforcing borderline and narcissistic idealization/devaluation fantasies, also reinforces, on a conscious level, several modern myths about stalking: that most stalkers are predatory, psychopathic, and violent; that stalkers will inevitably enjoy threatening their victims; and that otherwise normal people (without an underlying history of criminality, substance abuse, or mental disorder) can suddenly transform into violent and disturbed stalkers at the severing of a relationship. None of these feared stereotypes are supported by the research literature (Meloy, 1996).

Ironically, such movies, by playing off archetypal fears, can actually lull the public into complacency over more common forms of stalking, which can, in certain situations, become violent and lethal.

This is an example of how archetypal fears in the collective unconscious can both elucidate—and obfuscate—an understanding of stalking dynamics. For example, compared to Hollywood movies, actual studies of stalkers show that they do not always make explicit threats during stalking or prior to acts of violence (Meloy, 1996). Such findings led to the revision of model stalking laws, which no longer require an explicit threat to bring a stalking charge.

The power predatory stalking archetypes wield over the human mind may be both a modern and an atavistic preoccupation that evolved to identify and avoid predators. This "primitive brain" fear of and fascination with stalking may sound rather theoretical—until one channel surfs to PBS, the Discovery Channel, or any other family network, which cannot seem to produce enough mesmerizing portrayals of predatory stalkers bringing down panicked and helpless prey. In a study funded by the U.S. Department of Justice, National Institute of Justice, some stalking victims actually report pets being threatened and even killed, as was the pet bunny in the movie *Fatal Attraction*. While this pet killing suggests antisocial personality features, it is nonetheless psychodynamically amazing that such primitive and out of control stalkers can actually incorporate the killing of helpless animals into their disturbed psychosexual world.

Hunting certainly reflects the human fascination with stalking, along with the associated multimillion dollar industry in clothing and gear, including L. L. Bean's latest camouflage "Stalker" pants and pullovers. Some of the most depraved, sadistic, and predatory human killers also purchase this equipment, as did the Virginia man who used a combination of hunting gear (camouflaged clothing and mask, gun, and hunting knife) along with law enforcement gear (handcuffs and a stun gun) to abduct, molest, sodomize, torture, and kill a boy. Men who abduct teenage and adult women to "enslave" them as sexual and sadistic objects (until they are usually killed) often also adopt such hunting/stalking behaviors or fantasies, which may be related to the internal dehumanization and objectification of victims by the "malignant narcissism" (Kernberg, 1984) of sadistic psychopaths. Such case studies emphasize the power of stalking archetypes and fantasies in criminals we usually do not think of as "stalkers" per se, such as predatory psychopaths, serial killers, and sexual sadists.

Narcissistic Personality Features

Stalking as Omnipotent and "Ocular" Control of the Love Object

> Villain, be sure thou prove my love a whore,
> Be sure of it; give me ocular proof.
> > *Othello* III, iii, 359–360
>
> Every breath you take
> Every move you make
> Every bond you break
> Every step you take
> I'll be watching you. . . .
> > Sting
> > "Every Breath You Take"

The hypnotic refrain of this pop/rock classic at first sounds like a love song, yet with the barely conscious but disturbing implication that the absent lover is to know she is psychologically possessed ("Oh can't you see you belong to me?") by being psychologically watched. During the drafting of this chapter, singer Faith Evans released an R & B remake of this song as a tribute to her murdered husband, Biggie Smalls. The refrain is changed from "I'll be watching you" to "I'll be missing you," which alters the implied psychodynamic significantly—from the part-object love of monitoring, controlling, and possessing the absent lover, to the whole-object love implied in mourning the absent lover.

What is most compelling about the archetypes of love obsession is their power, in the words of Kaplan, to fascinate, "in every time, place and culture, and among men and women of all ages and socioeconomic levels" (1996, p. 37). Compare the modern rock refrain of "I'll be watching you" as a means of ensuring the fidelity of an absent lover to the brilliant study by Breitenberg (1996) of "anxious masculinity" in the England of Shakespeare's day, which was manifested by Othello's need for "ocular proof" of Desdemona's infidelity. To use love obsession archetypes to jump back and forth between centuries, like a psychic time machine, compare the Renaissance male preoccupation with "ocular proof" and the "specularization of women" to 1930s, 1940s, and 1950s gumshoe movies about getting the goods on an unfaithful spouse through another form of "ocular proof" in modern times, the camera.

The *Globe* tabloid, in accusing sportscaster Frank Gifford of marital infidelity, played off the all too human need to know and fear to know by assuming that wife Kathie Lee Gifford would act exactly as Othello, and combine with her denial some demand for "proof," which the *Globe* promptly provided in the form of "ocular proof," hidden camera pictures.

Of course, Frank Sinatra would never be caught dead conceding that he also required "ocular proof" of a woman's fidelity, but he sings it better than Shakespeare could ever say it: if you don't want your lady to "blow on some other guy's dice" you tell her, "never get out of my sight" ("Luck Be a Lady," F. Loesser).

The paradoxical obsession in the need to know and the fear to know in obtaining "ocular proof" also involves an unconscious sense of controlling and possessing the sometimes seen and sometimes unseen love object. The murderous stalker Richard Farley took furtive pictures of his love obsession, Laura Black, coming out of an aerobics class to manufacture a fantasy of a joint ski vacation (Meloy, 1992).

Breitenberg (1996), in his study of "anxious masculinity" in an age prior to the "ocular proof" technology of cameras, suggested that the irrationality of male jealousy is partly fueled by the fact that suspicion of infidelity often is beyond proof, creating an "epistemological anxiety," which he relates to what Freud called "epistemophilia" as an aspect of paranoia.

"Till Death Do Us Join": Narcissistic Merger and Rage in Violent Love Obsessions

. . . . I will kill thee,
And love thee after.
Othello, V, ii, 17–18.

"Let's say I committed this crime . . . Even if I did do this, it would have to have been because I loved her very much, right?"

O. J. Simpson
Esquire, Feb., 1998, p. 58

One of the most disturbing archetypes and psychodynamics in love obsession is the fantasy of both union with and possession of the beloved in death. This stalking dynamic is facilitated in narcissistic character pathology by fantasies of merger and union with the love object, as well as omnipotence over, possession of, and devaluation of the love object. Such union in death fantasies are facilitated by both borderline and delusional personality organizations, which can result in regressed confusion and diffusion between self and other, as well as between aggressive and sexual drives.

As described in Shakespeare's "dark lady" sonnets, anger toward and threats to destroy the love object are sometimes mobilized to ward off fears of further psychological decompensation, either from fragile narcissistic or paranoid states. Stalkers and other violent attachment offenders often imagine that, at least in death, the stalker and the "beloved" will finally merge in an exclusive and perfect union—a perverse, forensic version of the Romeo and Juliet fantasy that death is a form of eternal marriage and possession. Such fantasies also mobilize unconscious desires for suicide in some such individuals.

The poet Robert Browning (who, ironically, disdained Shakespeare for the unattractive and personal quality of the "dark lady" sonnets) employs the literary device of the dramatic monologue, first to distance himself as an author, and then to boldly go where Shakespeare had never gone before: using the poem to explore his angry and jealous fantasies of murdering the beloved, so as to narcissistically possess and control her.

In Browning's *Porphyria's Lover* the tormented man, with a "heart fit to break" waits for his lover who arrives with suggestively "soiled gloves" and "damp hair:"

> Too weak, for all her heart's endeavor,
> To set its struggling passion free
>   From pride, and vainer ties dissever,
>   And give herself to me forever. . . .
>
> Be sure I looked up at her eyes
>   Happy and proud; at last I knew
> Porphyria worshiped me; surprise
>   Made my heart swell, and still it grew
>   While I debated what to do.
> That moment she was mine, mine, fair,
>   Perfectly pure and good: I found
> A thing to do, and all her hair
>   In one long yellow string I wound
>   Three times her little throat around,
> And strangled her. No pain felt she;
>   I am quite sure she felt no pain. . . .

The narcissistic character pathology to this point in the poem is bad enough, with the murderer suddenly shifting from questioning the beloved's fidelity, to projecting onto a single look of her eyes that "Porphyria worshiped me," to then deciding at "That moment she was mine, mine, fair/Perfectly pure and good" to strangle her, so as to transfix forever in death the fantasy of her idealization of him and his of her.

But the poem becomes even more bizarre: once she is strangled, he begins to control and manipulate her body, opening her eyelids and imagining them to laugh "without a stain," then kissing her cheek, then literally propping her limp head up on his shoulder:

> The smiling rosy little head,
> So glad it has its utmost will,
>   That all it scorned at once is fled
>   And I, its love, am gained instead! . . .

The observation by a modern female executive that "the guy who wrote that poem must have been a fucking whacko," is actually more of a contribution to the literature than the mental health professional would imagine; for this was the very effect Browning was intending by publishing the poem under the title of *Madhouse Cells* (Browning, 1974).

Browning repeats the narcissistic themes of vengeance, control, and possession by murder of the betraying love object in *My Last Duchess,* as a Duke discusses
"painted on the wall./Looking as if she were alive" the Duchess he presumably
has murdered. The reason becomes obvious:

                                        . . . She had
A heart—how shall I say?—too soon made glad,
Too easily impressed; she liked what'er
She looked on, and her looks went everywhere. . . .
                    . . . She thanked men—good! but thanked
Somehow—I know not how—as if she ranked
My gift of a nine-hundred-years-old name
With anybody's gift. Who'd stoop to blame
This sort of trifling? . . .
                            . . . Oh sir, she smiled, no doubt,
Whene'er I passed her; but who passed without
Much the same smile? This grew; I gave commands;
then all smiles stopped together. There she stands
As if alive. . . .

Do references to Browning's poems and psychoanalytic theories of murdering
the betraying love object to keep her "narcissistically alive" seem arcane, theoretical,
and of no possible relevance to the violent stalking victimization of women in
modern America? Compare Browning's words with both the words of O. J.
Simpson about Nicole Simpson and the words of John Hinckley, Jr., about actress
Jodie Foster.

In the letter he left before fleeing in his Ford Bronco, O. J. Simpson actually
speaks about Nicole Simpson as if she were still alive, "All her friends will confrim
that I'v been tottally loving and understanding of what she's been going through"
(Toobin, 1996, p. 101, spelling uncorrected). That is, he speaks about her, shortly
after attending her funeral, as if she is not quite dead.

Kernberg (1980), in the course of discussing normal and healthy love, emphasized the need in narcissistic personalities to psychologically destroy the love object:

As mentioned before, there has to be an awareness of and a capacity for empathy
with the existence of a psychological field outside of the self, hence . . . the unconscious
destruction of object representations and external objects that are so prominent in
narcissistic personalities destroys their capacity for transcending into intimate union with
another human being. . . . (p. 294)

Compare Kernberg's object relations analysis of the psychic destruction of the
love object in narcissistic character pathology to John Hinckley's simple statement of
what his love for actress Jodie Foster was always really about:

I seem to have a need to hurt those people that I love the most. This is true
in relation to my family and to Jodie Foster. I love them so much but I have this
compulsion to destroy them. . . . My assassination attempt was an act of love. I'm
sorry love has to be so painful. (Caplan, 1987, 129–130)

Perhaps the most recognizable archetype of decompensated jealous rage is Shakespeare's Othello. During the O. J. Simpson criminal and civil trials, comparisons between Simpson and Othello seemed tasteless in our race-conscious and race-conflicted society. However, the parallel is suggested not by race, but by the nature of the crime, which implies narcissistic character pathology, decompensation, and rage. Othello's narcissistic character pathology is suggested by the fragility of his sense of self as he decompensates under jealous fantasies, as well as his self-object confusion and dependency, leaving him no choice but to kill himself after he kills Desdemona.

Again, what is so haunting and disturbing about the archetypes and psychodynamics of stalking are the all too real parallels between cultural archetypes (*Othello*), modern psychoanalytic theory (Kernberg, 1984; Kohut, 1971), and the murder of actual stalking victims. "Narcissistic rage" may sound like a theoretical concept, but when violence does occur in stalking cases, it can be shockingly vicious and uncontrolled. When I worked in a maximum security prison, I was stunned to read police reports detailing the ways in which victims were murdered in some cases of violent attachment. Often it was not psychologically "good enough" for the offender to "merely" kill the victim; rather, there was an attempt to psychologically and physically annihilate the "beloved" by primitive means such as stabbing, strangulation, and burning. In two cases perpetrators sodomized their victims *after* killing them.

Certainly one of the most suspicious pieces of psychological evidence in the O. J. Simpson criminal and civil trials was the way the victims, Nicole Simpson and Ronald Goldman, were murdered with apparent "narcissistic rage." The vicious, annihilating, "overkill" manner in which Nicole Simpson was murdered with multiple stab wounds and subdecapitation certainly suggests a "violent attachment." From a psychodynamic perspective, in the words of former FBI agent and criminal profiling expert, John Douglas, this was a personal killing, which implied a relationship between the murderer and the victim. For people who are capable of whole object love, the loss of love can entail anger and mourning. For people who are only capable of self-object love, the loss of love can entail rage and psychological decompensation.

The narcissistic fragility of the personality organization and defenses in certain cases of violent attachment helps to explain why such criminals often begin their psychological decompensation leading to violence following slights or losses, such as a job firing or a romantic breakup. (The Unabomber suffered both of these stressors about the time of his first alleged bombing.) This is because what is "lost" for these damaged personalities is not the job or the girlfriend, per se, but the psychic cohesion of the fragile self in the face of the loss—with the subsequent harassing and stalking behavior becoming a sick and twisted attempt at psychic self cohesion (or literally "self" defense) in the face of psychological decompensation.

DELUSIONAL PERSONALITY FEATURES

Many of the archetypes, fantasies, and psychodynamics of stalking can be seen in various forms of "borderline erotomania" (Meloy, 1989), as well as "delusional erotomania."

Along with projective identification, political, celebrity, and relationship stalkers can employ primitive defenses of projection as well, which can take several murderous paths. Both unacceptable sexual and aggressive impulses can be projected onto the love object, as well as the suspected "third" party. What makes this psychological process so complex is that the dangerous stalker is not conscious he is often enraged by, threatened by, and defending himself against his own distorted and projected sexual and aggressive impulses. Although projection can occur as a defense along a continuum from normal to psychotic, projection is a primary defensive mechanism in paranoid (delusional) disorders, and it is these disorders that comprise the erotomanic and jealous *DSM-IV* subtypes so common in delusional stalking. Similarly, jealousy, which can occur on a continuum from normal to psychotic, is also a hallmark of paranoid, delusional disorders, generally viewed to be facilitated by the defense of projection.

The current focus on erotomanic delusional disorders diverts attention from the role delusional jealousy plays in erotomanic cases, which is often implied, for example, in the demand that the idealized love object cease his or her sexual contact with others. Thus, in certain cases, there can be a thin and subtle line between jealous and erotomanic preoccupations, which the *DSM-IV* does not at all make clear.

As these psychotic levels are reached, the relationship between the psychodynamics and archetypes of stalking comes full circle. Ironically, the stalking subtypes of delusional disorders in the *DSM-IV* (the jealous and erotomanic subtypes) reflect, in their specific diagnostic criteria, powerful archetypes of love obsession in Western culture and the collective unconscious: the pursuit of unrequited and unattainable love, fantasies of "rescuing" the beloved into a pure, spiritual union; and, of course, paranoid preoccupations with jealousy and fidelity. These archetypal themes are even more dangerous in delusional disorders, as both self-object differentiation and aggressive-sexual drives become more diffused and more condensed. The more delusional stalking fantasies become, the more archetypal they become.

STALKING AS A "MODERN ARCHETYPE" OF "VIOLENT ATTACHMENT"

Heathcliff, in *Wuthering Heights,* would kill everybody on earth to possess Cathy, but it would never occur to him to say that murder is reasonable or theoretically

defensible. He would commit it, and there his convictions end. This implies the power
of love, and also strength of character.

Albert Camus
The Rebel

Camus' (1956) defense of murderous stalking fantasies as implying the "power
of love, and also strength of character" seems incomprehensibly archaic from the
perspective of a modern American culture that, within the past decade, has passed
or revised stalking laws in all 50 states.

Camus' judgment, and the novel it references, symbolize throughout Western
culture the idealization of love obsession, the pursuit of unrequited love, and even
some forms of "violent attachment." Dante's Beatrice, Kierkegaard's Regina,
Shakespeare's dark lady, Heathcliffe's Cathy, as well as modern film (*Il Postino*)
and literature (Marquez's *Love in the Time of the Cholera*) all idealize the pursuit of
unrequited love to the point of obsession. Yet this analysis of stalking archetypes
suggests, beneath the psychic surface of such idealization, a primitive, tormented
and irrational dark side in the collective unconscious.

In studying stalking archetypes and psychodynamics it is difficult not to
speculate whether they suggest a dark side of *our* collective unconscious—or
whether they suggest a dark side of the *male* collective unconscious. Kaplan (1996),
in her study of love obsession, even speculated whether the hormonal basis of
human attachment might in part explain male "mate keeping behavior." It is
thoughtless to ponder upon love obsession without at least lingering a paragraph
or two on the extent to which feminist studies inform an understanding of the
archetypal depth in our collective unconscious of the male pursuit of unrequited
love, of the nature and functions of male jealousy, and of the male perception of
the self as "subject" and the woman as an "object" to be "won" and "possessed."

The feminist perspective, however, does not fully explain why, according to
the *DSM-IV,* women can become just as delusionally and erotomanically obsessed as
men (though at less violent rates). Nor does the feminist perspective of dismissing
these aspects and archetypes of Western society as a reflection of "anxious masculinity" (Breitenberg, 1996) in a male-dominated culture, explain why American men
and women endlessly flock in the millions to movies about the pursuit of unrequited
love, the rescuing of prostitutes, and the stalking of women by men and of men
by women.

Why is a society terrified of stalking also fascinated and titillated by it? This
is a question that can only be answered by an understanding and acceptance of its
archetypal power in the collective unconscious.

Our culture has likewise experienced an archetypal "paradigm shift" in
which male and female pursuit of unrequited love has gone from being grossly
euphemized over the centuries to grossly perjoratized over the past decade in
America. A Western culture that once idealized, romanticized, and even eroticized
the pursuit of unrequited love now outlaws it.

The current emphasis on the paradigm of stalking in American society may reflect our uniquely violent role among industrialized Western nations, our cultural alienation between men and women, our psychological contempt for "codependency," and our unprecedented social and moral acceptance of the initiating—and of the severing—of intimate relationships, by either sex, in or out of marriage.

If "violent attachment" (Meloy, 1992) describes an American culture that knows too much about violence and too little about attachment, then the modern archetype of stalking is truly symptomatic of a psychodynamically and psychosexually troubled collective unconscious.

REFERENCES

American Psychiatric Association. (1994). *Diagnostic and statistical manual of mental disorders* (4th ed.). Washington, DC, Author.

Bloom, H. (1994). *The western canon: The books and school of the ages.* New York: Harcourt, Brace & Co.

Breitenberg, M. (1996). *Anxious masculinity in early modern England.* Cambridge: Cambridge University Press.

Browning, R. (1974). "Porphyria's lover," "My last duchess," In M. H. Abrams et al. (eds.), *The Norton anthology of English literature* (3rd ed. Vol. 2., pp. 1132–1133, 1135–1136). New York: W. W. Norton & Co.

Camus, A. (1956). *The rebel* (A. Bower, Trans.). New York: Alfred A. Knopf. Originally published 1951.

Caplan, L. (1987). *The insanity defense and the trial of John W. Hinckley, Jr.* New York: Dell.

Dietz, P. E. (1988, October). *Interview with Arthur Jackson.* Paper presented at the meeting of the American Academy of Psychiatry and the Law, San Francisco.

Dietz, P. E., Martell, D., Stewart T., Hrouda, D., & Warren J. (1991a). Threatening and otherwise inappropriate letters to members of the United States Congress. *Journal of Forensic Sciences, 36,* 1445–1468.

Deitz, P. E., Matthews, D., Van Duyne, C., Martell, D., Parry, C., Stewart, T., Warren, J., & Crowder, J. (1991b). Threatening and otherwise inappropriate letters to Hollywood celebrities. *Journal of Forensic Sciences, 36,* 185–209.

Douglas, J. (1995). *Mind hunter.* New York: Simon & Shuster.

Freud, S. (1953). Three essays on the theory of sexuality. In *The standard edition of the complete psychological works of Sigmund Freud* (Vol. 7, pp. 125–243). London: Hogarth Press.

Kaplan, H. S. (1996). Erotic obsession: Relationship to hypoactive sexual desire disorder and paraphilia. *American Journal of Psychiatry, 153*(7), 30–41.

Kernberg, O. (1975). *Borderline conditions and pathological narcissism.* New York: Jason Aronson.

Kernberg, O. (1977). The structural diagnosis of borderline personality organization. In P. Hartocollis (ed.), *Borderline personality disorders* (pp. 87–121). New York: International Universities Press.

Kernberg, O. (1980). *Internal world and external reality.* New York: Jason Aronson.

Kernberg, O. (1984). *Severe personality disorders: Psychotherapeutic strategies.* New Haven: Yale University Press.

Kernberg, O. (1992). *Aggression in personality disorders and perversions.* New Haven: Yale University Press.

Kohut, H. (1971). *Analysis of the self.* New York: International Universities Press.

Meloy, J. R. (1988). *The psychopathic mind: Origins, dynamics, and treatment.* Northvale, NJ: Jason Aronson.

Meloy, J. R. (1989). Unrequited love and the wish to kill: The diagnosis and treatment of borderline erotomania. *Bulletin of the Menninger Clinic, 53,* 477–492.

Meloy, J. R. (1992). *Violent attachments.* Northvale, NJ: Jason Aronson.

Meloy, J. R., & Gothard, S. (1995). Demographic and clinical comparison of obsessional followers and offenders with mental disorders. *American Journal of Psychiatry, 152,* 258–263.

Meloy, J. R. (1996). Stalking (obsessional following): A review of some preliminary studies. *Aggression and Violent Behavior, 1,* 147–162.

Shakespeare, W. (1969). *The complete Pelican Shakespeare.* Baltimore: Penguin Books.

Skoler, G. (1988). *Saviors of the nation, assassins of the self: Psychological characteristics of presidential threateners and other Secret Service cases* (Contract No. 87-4076). Study report for the United States Secret Service, Washington, DC.

Tarasoff v. Regents of the University of California, 17 Cal.3d 425 (1976).

Toobin, J. (1996). *The run of his life.* New York: Random House.

CHAPTER 6

The Victims of Stalking

Doris M. Hall, Ph.D

Stalking first received prominent media attention in 1980, with the murder of John Lennon, and again in March 1981, with John Hinckley, Jr.'s assassination attempt on President Ronald Reagan. Hinckley had been obsessed with actress Jodie Foster for many years, and he claimed he shot the President to impress her. But it was not until the 1989 death of Rebecca Schaeffer, a rising young actress, that "stalking" became a household word in America's vocabulary. Since that time, hardly a week goes by without a stalking story in the media. Tales of terror circulate about ordinary people who have been stalked by ex-boyfriends, co-workers, or even a relative stranger such as their postal carrier. Given all the attention stalkers receive in the media it is surprising that only a limited number of studies have been undertaken on the subject. Lack of research, however, has not deterred state legislators from recognizing stalking as a serious crime and passing laws prohibiting the behavior. Unfortunately, these laws do not adequately address important issues when it comes to protecting stalking victims.

Who are the victims of stalking? Who are these so-called stalkers? What kind of relationship, if any, exists between stalker and the victim? In order to understand the larger question of why stalkings happen, one must examine who is being stalked and what type of activities occur. Stalking cases arouse a good deal of interest. Unfortunately the tendency is to look at the more glamorous and sensational aspects of stalking rather than the more common characteristics. Many important aspects that are frequently overlooked are also present in the details of individual cases. While it is enticing to look at the most extreme examples, most stalking cases consist of victims receiving unwanted telephone calls, seeing unfamil-

The Psychology of Stalking: Clinical and Forensic Perspectives

iar cars parked across the street, and feeling watched. The scope of this study examines these and various other aspects of stalking. In addition to demographics, the stalking victims' personality types and the effect the stalking has had on them are considered. All information is examined to determine if any apparent links exist between stalkers and the victims they select.

There is a common misperception regarding the stalking victim. The most popular image is that of a celebrity who is stalked by a crazed fan or a battered woman who has left a physically abusive relationship and is now being stalked by her ex-spouse or ex-lover. While this is the reality for some stalking victims, the majority of cases lie between these two extremes. The public is captivated by the idea of a total stranger becoming obsessed with a victim. Nonetheless, the more common scenario is that of an individual being stalked by someone he or she knows (Meloy, 1996a; Romans, Hays, & White, 1996). In fact, cases involving a stranger fixating on a private citizen are rare and are the least likely type of stalking to end in violence (De Becker, 1997).

To date, the most extensive research in the field focuses on stalkers who have had criminal charges brought against them or who have come to the attention of law enforcement due to their activities. All of the studies on this subject have used nonrandom samples of convenience (Meloy, 1996a). Further, these same studies underrepresent stalkers who have been involved with the victim, such as ex-boyfriends or ex-spouses (also referred to as "post-intimate relationship stalkers"). This is probably due to the early focus on erotomanics and law enforcement's bias toward arresting and prosecuting the higher profile cases, which usually involve strangers, and against prosecuting those cases that have a link to domestic violence (Meloy, 1996a).

Researchers have begun to focus on stalking victims as a source of gathering much needed information on the crime of stalking. Several recent studies have focused on specific populations of stalking victims, such as college students (Fremouw, Westrup, & Pennypacker, 1997) and college counselors and therapists (Romans et al., 1996). Other studies have taken a wider approach and examined stalking victims from all walks of life within large geographical areas (Kong, 1996; Pathé & Mullen, 1997). The study of victims allows researchers the opportunity to examine the crime of stalking from a different vantage point. The emphasis on the victim allows researchers to uncover valuable information that is not available through official records or from interviewing individual offenders.

Victimology has its roots in feminist criminology. Originally the study of victims focused primarily on domestic violence and rape. The field of victimology has been greatly enhanced by the formation of the National Crime Victimization Survey (NCVS) in 1972. According to Zawitz, Klaus, Bachman, Bastian, DeBerry, Rand, and Taylor (1993) the NCVS was a landmark event in building knowledge on crime in America:

> With the advent of the survey, the phenomenon of crime for the first time could be measured directly, from its victims. They are able to tell us about the two

dark figures of crime—crimes that are not reported to law enforcement agencies and crimes which, when reported, go unrecorded.

The extent of the problem of stalking is currently unknown, although it is surmised that stalking behavior is on the rise. According to De Becker (1997) stalking is an epidemic affecting hundreds of thousands of regular citizens per year. During a Senate Hearing in 1993 Senator Dianne Feinstein, a former stalking victim herself, expressed a similar belief:

> I am of the opinion that serious, prolonged, chronic stalking is going to be like serial murder in this country. It is now out there. It has given every kind of mentally aberrant person an idea and it goes on, and I believe it is going to increase and I believe it is extraordinarily serious.

It has been said that 1 out of every 20 women in the United States will be stalked at some time during her life (*Combating Stalking*, 1993). There is much discussion as to whether the crime of stalking is actually increasing or whether this is an artifact of a behavior being labeled as "stalking" due to an increase in legislation. Several studies have explored the prevalence of stalking occurrences within specific populations. In a study conducted on stalking and related behaviors experienced by university counselors and therapists by current or former clients, it was found that 5.6% ($N = 10$) of the respondents reported being stalked on at least one occasion. Contrary to most studies, 60% of the stalking victims were male and 40% were female (Romans et al., 1996). In a study on stalking among college students in West Virginia, 34% of the females and 17% of the males surveyed had been stalked (Fremouw et al., 1997).

Recently researchers have begun to expand their focus and include behaviors that do not necessarily fall within the legal definition of stalking. Viewing these behaviors on a continuum allows researchers to broaden their study to include "relational harassment" to "pathological pursuit" to true criminal "stalking," thus expanding the knowledge on precursors to stalking behaviors. Spitzberg and Cupach's (1996) research on "obsessive relational intrusion" (ORI) examines relatively milder forms of intrusion. ORI is defined by the authors as the "repeated and unwanted pursuit and invasion of one's sense of physical or symbolic privacy by an acquaintance desiring and/or presuming an intimate relationship." Spitzberg and Cupach (1996) contend that at the root of stalking:

> . . . is the idea that someone is attempting to impart, presume, or coerce a type of relationship that is specifically undesired by the target of these affections. As such, stalking is an extreme and obsessive form of relational intrusion. The intrusion is a violation of a person's boundaries of invitation and accessibility; in short, of a person's sense of privacy. (p. 2)

METHODOLOGY

The most reasonable and accessible source of data are the stalking victims themselves. Surveying these people as a group would provide invaluable insight into the characteristics of the crime. Not all victims contact the police, however; nor do police reports cover pertinent information needed to develop patterns of stalking behavior. This study, which is national in scope, used an innovative approach to contact stalking victims within the United States.

The Maverick Group, a national public relations firm based in Santa Monica, California, volunteered to write, with my supervision, a press release to regional and national media outlets to encourage stalking victims to contact the researcher. In this way many people who had defined themselves as stalking victims would be able to take part in the study. Stalking victims were then able to contact the researcher by calling one of the six regional voice mail boxes set up throughout the United States. The target cities consisted of Atlanta, Chicago, Denver, Los Angeles, San Francisco, and Newark, New Jersey. Several months into the study a seventh voice mail box was opened in Columbus, Ohio.

As a result of the press releases the researcher conducted more than 40 radio interviews, numerous interviews for newspaper reporters, and appeared on television in order to promote awareness of the study and the need for stalking victims to participate. Further, articles discussing the study appeared in numerous union newsletters throughout Southern California and in a few magazines. Additionally, in order to include the largest number of stalking victims in the study, flyers were sent to organizations within the target cities that provide assistance to people in need. It was through contact with these organizations that information about the study was placed in numerous newsletters that targeted care providers within domestic violence and sexual abuse clinics.

This approach allowed stalking victims from all walks of life to participate in this study. As a result the participants came from a diverse range of ethnic backgrounds and age groups. Several respondents remarked that this study was the first time they had ever told anyone they had been stalked. In these particular cases the respondents said that the stalking happened prior to it becoming a crime. They did not feel the police would have believed their story and they feared that reporting the experience might further incite their stalker. Therefore, they kept the stalkings a secret.

LIMITATIONS OF THE STUDY

The sample on which these results are based is nonrandom and generalizations to other samples cannot be made. This study focuses only on people who have defined themselves as stalking victims. An unknown portion of the population of stalking victims do not view themselves as being stalked for a variety of reasons: denial, ignorance of the current laws, or an unwillingness to view themselves as victims until the different elements of the crime are described in detail and they begin to recognize the gravity of their own situation.

Potential respondents also had to make the initial contact with the researcher. This included sharing, at the least, a name and a number where they could be reached. Considering the nature of the crime, this took a great leap of faith for the stalking victims since their trusting nature may have long since eroded. Defining oneself as a victim, having to initiate contact with the researcher, and placing trust in an unknown are all steps that each participant had to take. Any of these steps could have resulted in filtering out potential respondents from the study.

This research covers a large geographical area. It is the first study on the subject in which stalking victims throughout the United States were able to participate, and both those who contacted a victim organization or the police and those who did not were targeted in this research. The data collected can be used to build a foundation on which to base future investigations.

RESULTS

Eight-three percent ($N = 120$) of the sample were females, and the remaining 17% ($N = 25$) were males. Early in the data collection process, only 70% of the respondents were women and 30% were men. This proportion of male respondents was astounding. As additional data were collected, the numbers started to more closely reflect the anticipated ratio. After flyers that discussed the project and invited participants were sent to the victim outreach organizations within the target cities, the number of female respondents rose dramatically. The explanation for this increase could be twofold. First, men do not traditionally seek help or support from domestic violence and rape crisis centers. Therefore, men would not necessarily be learning about the study from that particular source. Second, the increase in female respondents might indicate a more accurate proportion of stalking victims.

Throughout this study three categories of stalkers were used: (1) Prior sexual intimates (also referred to in this study as "post-intimate relationship"); (2) prior acquaintances; and (3) strangers who stalk. The first group, post-intimate relationship stalkers, consists of ex-lovers and ex-spouses. Meloy (1996a) referred to this type of stalker as "prior sexual intimates." This term will be used interchangeably with "post-intimate relationship" stalkers, the latter preferred by this researcher because not all relationships that fall under this category are necessarily sexual in nature, as "prior sexual intimates" implies. Individuals can be intimately involved with one another without a sexual component.

Fifty-seven percent of the stalkers in the study were post-intimate relationship stalkers; prior acquaintance stalkers accounted for 35%; and strangers made up 6% of the sample. Two percent ($N = 5$) of the respondents did not know who their stalkers were at the time they completed the questionnaire. A complete summary of these findings is provided in Table 1.

Table 1

Categories of Stalkers

Type	N	%
Post–intimate relationship	82	57
Prior acquaintance	49	34
Stranger	9	6
Unknown	5	3

According to Wright, Burgess, Burgess, Laszlo, McCrary, and Douglas (1996), a stalker may initially communicate with his target through anonymous communications such as calling and hanging-up, obscene or harassing telephone calls, and unsigned letters. "The stalker's identity may remain unknown, or at some point the individual may make his or her identity known through continuous physical appearances at the victim's residence, place of employment, or other location" (p. 496). It is not unusual for a stalking victim to not know her stalker's identity, especially if it is very early in a stalking situation.

Table 2 examines the category of stalker by the stalker's gender in this sample. The vast majority of post–intimate relationship stalkers are male (89% [N = 73] versus 11% [N = 9] female). In this sample male post–intimate relationship stalkers targeted females in 99% (N = 72) of the cases versus 1% (N = 1) male stalkers who targeted males. Sixty-seven percent (N = 6) of the female post–intimate relationship stalkers in this sample targeted males and the remaining 33% (N = 3)

Table 2

Category of Stalkers by Stalker's Gender

Type	N	%
Male		
Post–intimate relationship	73	51
Prior acquaintance	40	28
Stranger	6	4
Unknown	3	2
Female		
Post–intimate relationship	9	6
Prior acquaintance	9	6
Stranger	3	2
Unknown	2	1
Total	145	100

stalked other females. Within this study 5% of the post-intimate relationship stalkers were involved in homosexual relationships. This finding is substantially higher than the estimated occurrence cited in previous studies. According the Meloy (1996a, p. 156), there "are reported cases of homosexual obsessional following, but these appear to be quite infrequent, probably less than 1%."

Female prior acquaintance stalkers are also more likely to target members of the opposite sex in this sample (94% [N = 31]); however, male prior acquaintance stalkers are more likely to target other males (56% [N = 16]). Same sex stalkings by prior acquaintances occurred in 22% (N = 11) of the situations. Whether these same sex stalkings had homosexual overtones is unknown since the data collected did not address this issue.

Strangers who stalk (N = 9) also target members of the same sex. In this sample 38% (N = 3) of the females stalked by strangers were stalked by other females. Additionally, in the only case of a male targeted by a stranger in this sample, the stalker was also a male. Overall, same sex stalkings by a stranger occurred in 44% (N = 4) of the stranger cases. It cannot be determined whether these same sex stalkings by a stranger had homosexual overtones. This is due to the fact that the survey tool did not specifically address this subject matter.

MEN AS VICTIMS

Sixty-four percent (N = 16) of the men were stalked by prior acquaintances, 28% (N = 7) by prior sexual intimates, 4% (N = 1) by strangers, and 4% (N = 1) were unsure who was stalking them. Unlike females who were virtually always stalked by members of the opposite sex, men were almost as likely to be stalked by a male (44%, N = 11) as they were by a female (52% [N = 13]). This finding is similar to that reported in a study conducted by the Canadian Centre for Justice Statistics, wherein 46% of the male stalking victims were stalked by a casual acquaintance, often another male (Kong, 1996).

Male respondents felt that their gender was a handicap in stalking situations, especially if they were being stalked by females. It was the general consensus that law enforcement took their cases less seriously. Indeed, in one tragic case a male stalking victim took his ex-girlfriend to court to obtain a restraining order. The judge in the case told the young man he should be "flattered by all the attention," and issued mutual restraining orders. Several weeks later the female stalker killed the man (interview conducted by author with Susan Fisher, sister of the murdered stalking victim). Another man being stalked by his ex-girlfriend explained, "As a man, my constant calls to detectives for help went unanswered and I felt that if it was a man stalking a woman things would have been different." Another subject reported that male police officers responding to his calls left the impression that,

"A male should never allow himself to become a victim of a female stalker in the first place, but if so, the male victim should take care of it himself."

The focus on victimology, in general, is a fairly new endeavor. Most of the research to date is from a feminist bent investigating the effect of victimization on women. Little is known about the victimization of men despite the fact that most victims of violence are men. Part of the reason is that "we don't envision men's pain as a key issue" (Schwartz, 1996, p. 5). Men themselves are also less likely to view a female stalker as a threat. They see the behavior as an inconvenience or annoyance. This is illustrated by the comment of a male subject in his 30s being stalked by an ex-girlfriend: "This is mainly annoying. It is contributory to my increased vigilance for my personal safety, which is generally advisable anyway." The understanding of a serious situation often leads to men declining to label themselves as stalking victims. It is unknown at this time whether men generally underreport crimes, especially those of a personal nature, such as stalking, rape, or domestic abuse. However, it is not difficult to surmise that if women are not believed or are belittled or blamed for being victims of these types of crimes, men who experience the same type of abuse would be even less likely than women to feel comfortable in discussing these matters or going to the authorities for help.

WOMEN AS VICTIMS

Female respondents were much more likely to be stalked by a post-intimate relationship stalker (63%, $N = 75$) than by a prior acquaintance (28%, $N = 33$). Seven percent ($N = 8$) were stalked by strangers and 3% ($N = 4$) did not know who their stalkers were. Regrouping the Kong (1996) data according to this classification yields the same breakdown for female stalking victims as the percentages reported here. However, in studies from a forensic viewpoint the percentage of stranger stalking was much higher (Meloy, 1996b). This could be due to a historical emphasis on celebrity stalkings and erotomanics in general.

DURATION

Unlike other crimes, stalking can continue for an extended period of time and has been characterized as a "chronic law enforcement problem" (Meloy, 1995). Seventeen percent ($N = 23$) of the respondents said they have been stalked from less than 1 month to 6 months, 23% ($N = 33$) 6 months to 1 year, 29% ($N = 43$) 1 to 3 years, 18% ($N = 27$) 3 to 5 years, and 13% ($N = 19$) more than 5 years. The range of time within this study was from less than 1 month to 31 years. Pathé and Mullen's (1997) findings were similar: their median duration of a stalking lasted 24 months, with a range of 1 month to 20 years.

This study covers cases that span the past 31 years. Several respondents were stalked during the 1960s; one of these involves a stalking that has continued for the past 31 years. This woman described her experience of being stalked by her first husband:

> The police always said that their hands were tied in such cases, because there were no laws to cover such "family" situations (even though the stalking began after we were divorced). So I was thrilled when the Stalking Law and the Three Times and You're Out Law were finally placed on the California books. Yet, I had to fight my local police department to take me seriously. It's a good thing that I dug in my heels, and chose to stand my ground, and demanded to file a report, because if I hadn't, I would have been dead six days before Nicole Simpson. My ex-husband was finally caught, on my block, with a gun and ammo.

PERCEIVED MOTIVATIONS OF STALKERS

Respondents were asked why they thought they were being stalked. Many respondents perceived more than one purpose for the stalking. In this sample 58% ($N = 84$) said that the stalker would not accept the end of the relationship. One respondent reported that after she broke off their dating relationship her ex-boyfriend became obsessed with winning her back. "He started talking about how we were meant to be together and how he wasn't going to give up—even if it took 3 years—like *Shawshank Redemption* he wasn't going to give up. I explained that he needed to move on with his life and let go—my decision was not going to change."

Fifty-six percent ($N = 81$) of this sample felt that the stalker was obsessed with them. One stalker reportedly thought that his target was Jesus Christ. Thirty-two percent ($N = 47$) felt it was in retaliation for a real or imagined slight. Twenty-seven percent ($N = 39$) felt the stalker was jealous. A respondent explained, "He calls it Latino jealousy—I call it psychosis." Twenty-three percent ($N = 33$) said that the stalker wanted to initiate a relationship. A respondent commented, "He wanted more than a friendship and when I ended our friendship it got really bad." Nine percent ($N = 13$) of the respondents did not know why they were the target of the stalker.

A catalyst of stalking behavior occurs when a woman ends an existing relationship or declines to become involved with a man. According to De Becker (1997), "Stalking is how some men raise the stakes when women don't play along. It is a crime of power, control, and intimidation very similar to date rape" (p. 198). Studies on battered women report that the most dangerous time for a woman is when she leaves a relationship (see Walker, Chapter 7). For the past 30 years gender roles and societal expectations of relationships between men and women have been changing. According to McGrath (1994), "Women today are part of a transitional generation, caught in an extraordinary moment in time between a traditional past and a 'liberated' present and future" (p. 10). In the past two decades more women have been initiating divorce proceedings than ever before (Goldberg, 1976). A study on female victims of crime found that separated or divorced women account for 75% of spousal violence even though they account for only 10% of all women surveyed (Harlow, 1991). The old adage, "we only hurt the ones we love," could very well hold true for stalkers.

Some stalking situations begin as an attempt to win someone's love and admiration. An example of this type of persistence and relentless pursuit is illustrated by a Swarthmore College student who was accused of stalking by a fellow freshman. Ewart Yearwood said his behavior, which included lurking outside Alexis Clina-smith's dorm and sending her lewd and threatening messages, was only "aggressive flirting" and that he did nothing wrong. Even after he was found guilty of intimidation, Yearwood claimed that the problem was not with him but with others since "other people don't stand up to his intimidation" (Van Biema, 1994, p. 47). According to De Becker (1997), this would be a perfect example of the need for our culture to teach and then allow women to explicitly reject and to say no. He contends that if more women took that power early on in a relationship, stalking cases would dramatically decline.

It has been suggested that for some individuals stalking is a courtship disorder (Meloy, 1996b). Indeed, the early stages of stalking, "seem to blur the boundaries between 'normal' persistence and obsessive behavior" (Schaum and Parrish, 1995, p. 105). It has also been said that a strong sign of commitment is a man's persistence in courtship (Buss, 1994). De Becker contends that Hollywood films use this message over and over. "Pursuit, even pursuit that ordinarily ought to be considered invasive and abnormal, is glamorized as noble and adventurous" (Schaum & Parrish, 1995, p. 267). Several films seem to support the idea of persistence equaling love. For example, *Indecent Proposal, The Piano,* and *Heaven and Earth* all involve story lines in which the woman was not the least bit interested in a relationship with the male until his insistent pursuit won her over. In the classic movie *The Graduate,* Dustin Hoffman's character uses stalking techniques to get the girl of his dreams. The theme of the movie is, "Persistence will win the war against all odds." De Becker (1997) argued that "Persistence only proves persistence, it does not prove love" (p. 196). In real life, however, this type of behavior does, in fact, sometimes work. As noted by Buss (1994):

> The effectiveness of sheer persistence in courtship is illustrated by a story told by one newlywed: "Initially, I was not interested in John at all. I thought he was kind of nerdy, so I kept turning him down and turning him down. But he kept calling me up, showing up at my work, arranging to run into me. I finally agreed to go out with him just to get him off my back. One thing led to another, and six months later, we got married." (p. 102)

It is stories such as this that makes it hard to discount the theory that persistence pays off—a mating strategy that enhances reproductive success from an evolutionary perspective (Buss, 1994).

Prior acquaintance stalkers consist of individuals, usually men, who hold a grudge that turns obsessive after someone wounds their ego. This grudge can be the result of a date request that is turned down or an imagined slight or insult. The need for revenge or to "teach that person a lesson" becomes a preoccupation. The motivations behind stalkings brought about by rejection usually include a gender issue. Men who target women who do not return their overtures of affection account for 38% ($N = 15$) of prior acquaintance stalkers. Their reasoning that the women "didn't give them a fair chance" is enough justification for the stalker's subsequent behavior. The male ego perceives some obligation from the woman to allow him this "fair chance." One stalker insisted, "She started this when she refused to allow me a valid hearing. She violated the social contract" (Edwards, 1992, p. 37). Further, rejection is a humiliating experience, especially for stalkers. Rejection by the stalking victim can be a direct challenge to the stalker's narcissistic fantasy. According to Meloy (1996a, p. 160), "Disturbance of this narcissistic fantasy, imbued with both a sense of grandiosity and feeling of pride, triggers feelings of shame or humiliation that are defended against with rage." A stalker will often try to assert power and control over someone by frightening or manipulating him or her (Serant, 1993).

Not all cases of acquaintance stalking revolve around the desire for a romantic encounter. In the case of stalkings by neighbors the situation sometimes starts over something as innocuous as a misparked car or stepping on a hose. In addition to typical stalking behaviors such as telephone calls, surveillance of the home and threats, other more personal attacks are common. The following are illustrations supplied from respondents in the current study. One woman reported that a neighbor who was stalking her killed her dog; the neighbor (also a woman) pulled a gun on the victim and threatened her life. Another family reported that their neighbor continually filed false police reports against them, had turned the hose on them numerous times, and had tried to run over their children. One respondent reported that "the neighbor looks into our house from his. The distance is approximately two feet. The police said there was nothing they could do because he was not pressing his face against the windows." A female respondent noted that she spent days trapped in her own home fearing the police would not take the situation seriously because her stalker was a female. Other cases in the current study involving prior acquaintance stalkers included former students, former patients, stepchildren, and former friends.

PAST AND CURRENT STALKING

For the majority of participants in this study the stalking was in the past (55%, $N = 80$). Less than one-fourth (24%, $N = 35$) were currently being stalked and 21% ($N = 30$) were unsure as to whether the stalking was continuing. It often happens that the stalking stops, only to have the stalker turn up months or even years later and for the entire situation to erupt all over again. This was the case with a male respondent who had dated his male stalker several times 8 years before. The relationship was not working out, so the victim ended it. The breakup was followed by a short period of intense stalking that suddenly ended. Three years later the stalker called the victim and said he felt badly about his past behavior and had since gone through counseling. He wanted to make amends and bring closure to the incident and asked if they could meet for coffee. Thinking that this sounded logical and wanting to help with the healing process, the victim agreed. Unfortunately, this meeting resulted in a return to a full-blown stalking that was more violent in nature than the original stalking. This situation has continued for the past 5 years. The stalking victim did not know that meeting with the stalker, even years later, is one of the worst actions a victim can take. According to Meloy (1996a), sporadic contact with a stalker is "intermittent positive reinforcement" and will likely increase the stalking behavior.

DEMOGRAPHICS OF STALKING VICTIMS

Ethnicity and Marital Status

The ethnic background of the respondents in this sample was overwhelmingly White/Caucasian/Anglo at 84%. The next most frequent ethnicity listed was African American (6%), followed by Mixed Ethnicity (3%), Chicano/Latino (2%), Native American (2%), Asian or Pacific Islander (1%), and Other (2%), respectively. When compared to the national average, as reported in the *Statistical Abstract of the United States: 1996* (U.S. Bureau of Census, 1996), this sample of respondents reflects a slight underrepresentation of African Americans. As of 1995 the ethnic background of the United States was 83.0% White, 12.6% Black, and 4.4% "Other." See Table 3 for a comparison of the two populations.

Table 3

Ethnicity of Stalking Victims

Ethnicity	N	This study	U.S. population
White/Caucasian/Anglo	123	84	83
African American	8	6	13
Other	14	10	4
Total	145	100	100

At the time they were stalked, the majority of respondents in this sample had either never been married (34%) or were divorced (28%). In descending order, the remaining respondents were: married first time (15%), separated (12%), remarried (6%), living with significant other (3%) or widowed (3%). A complete summary of these findings is in Table 4.

Age Range and Education

The range of ages of stalking victims in this sample is widespread: from 16 years old to several respondents who were in their mid-70s (see Table 5). The mean age of respondents was 35 years. Fifty-seven percent of the respondents were between the ages of 26 and 46 when they were stalking victims. it is interesting to note that 11% ($N = 17$) were 51 years or older at the time of the stalking. In a study by Pathé and Mullen (1997) the reported age range was from 14 years old to over 50 years old. According to Meloy (1996a), "Victims do appear, on the average, to be older than one would expect in a general crime victim population" (p. 157).

Elderly stalking victims can be in as much danger from their stalkers as their younger counterparts. Recently a 70-year-old man, William Smillie, pleaded no contest to a misdemeanor stalking charge after he was jilted by his 71-year-old ex-girlfriend. Smillie's behavior was similar to that of stalkers half his age. He harassed his ex-girlfriend, called her constantly, and even crept into her backyard in the middle of the night to rearrange her patio furniture. It was Smillie's threat, however, to buy a cheap gun and kill his ex-girlfriend and then himself that got the court's attention ("Jilted, jealous," 1996). Senior citizens can also be the targets

Table 4

Stalking Victim's Marital Status at the Time of Stalking

Martial status	N	%
Never married	49	34
Divorced	41	28
Married, first time	21	15
Separated	18	12
Remarried	8	5
Living with significant other	4	3
Widowed	4	3
Total	145	100

Table 5

Age Range of Stalking Victims When Stalked

Age range (years)	N	%
Under 18	5	3
18–25	35	24
26–30	21	15
31–35	18	13
36–40	21	15
41–50	28	20
51–60	11	8
61–70	2	1
Over 70	2	1
Total	143[a]	100

[a] Two cases did not respond to this item.

of prior acquaintance stalkers. A retired couple from this study reported being stalked by a business acquaintance following a minor disagreement. Another respondent in her 70s reported that the police refused to take her case seriously because her stalker was both a female and a senior citizen.

Most respondents reported having completed a relatively high level of education at the time of their stalking. In this sample 45% ($N = 65$) had completed some college, 20% ($N = 29$) had college degrees (which included both associate and bachelor), 9% ($N = 13$) had received some graduate training, and 16% ($N = 23$) possessed graduate degrees. The remaining 10% ($N = 15$) had either completed some high school or were high school graduates. These numbers are much higher than the national average reported in the *Statistical Abstract of the United States: 1996* (U.S. Bureau of Census, 1996), which lists the average percentage of the population with some college at 17.6%, an associate degree at 7.1%, a bachelor degree at approximately 15.2%, and those with graduate degrees at 7.8%.

The education level of the sample of stalking victims could be skewed by the fact that the type of person who would willingly volunteer to participate in a research project on a socially sensitive subject may tend to have a more extensive educational background than those in the general population. The use of mailed-out questionnaires can also account for the discrepancy. According to Labovitz and Hagedom (1981) there is a high degree of self-selection in using questionnaires as survey tools. "Those most interested (in the topic) or highly educated are most likely to respond" (p. 69). The target audience of radio and newspapers also may have a different educational level than the average citizen. These are all variables to be considered when interpreting these data.

Most of the stalking victims in this study have made career choices that reflect their high level of education. A breakdown of the respondent's occupations when stalked is provided in Table 6. A recent study of stalking victims conducted in Australia reports similar findings; 36% of the respondents were employed as professionals at the onset of the stalking (Pathé & Mullen, 1997).

STALKER DEMOGRAPHICS

Gender, Ethnicity, and Age Range

In this sample 84% ($N = 122$) of the stalkers are male and 15% ($N = 21$) are female; 1% ($N = 2$) of the stalkers are of unknown gender. These findings differ slightly from those reported by Meloy and Gothard (1995), wherein 90% of the obsessional followers were male and only 10% were female, and to a much greater degree from those reported by Harmon, Rosner, and Owens (1995), wherein 66% of the stalkers were male and 33% were female.

The ethnic background of the stalkers is more diverse than that of their stalking victims. In this sample, 67% ($N = 97$) of the stalkers were White/Caucasian/Anglo; 10% ($N = 15$) were African Americans; 6% ($n = 9$) were Chicano/Latino; 4% ($N = 6$) Asian or Pacific Islander; 3% ($N = 5$) mixed ethnicity; 6%

Table 6

Stalking Victim's Occupation at the Time of Stalking

Occupation	N	%
Professional	46	31
Executive/managerial	29	20
Clerical/sales	23	16
Student	17	12
Technical	17	7
Musician/actor/artist	6	4
Retired	5	3
Homemaker	4	3
Disabled/handicapped	1	1
Other	4	3
Total	145	100

($N = 8$) were identified as "Other"; and 3% ($N = 5$) of the ethnic backgrounds were unknown to the stalking victim (see Table 7). As compared to the national average in 1995, 83.0% of the population is White, followed by 12.6% Black, and 4.4% listed as "Other" (U.S. Bureau of Census, 1996). Previous studies on stalkers have reported a wide range of ethnicities in the sample population. Harmon et al. (1995) reported that 67% of their sample was White, 13% Black, 10% Hispanic, 3% Asian, and 4% Unknown. Meloy and Gothard (1995) reported a more diverse population—35% White, 25% Black, 15% Hispanic, and 25% Unknown—perhaps reflecting the Southern California location of their study's sample.

Like the stalking victims, the stalkers' age range is quite large, varying from 18 years into their 70s. Like the stalking victims, the majority of stalkers (63%, $N = 92$) are from 26 to 50 years old. In this sample stalkers appear to be slightly older than their victims; and 15% ($N = 22$) of the stalkers are 51 years or older, compared to only 11% of the stalking victims (see Table 8 for further details). This finding is consistent with previous research on stalkers. In Harmon et al. (1995) the average age of stalkers was 40 years, with a range of 22 to 66; while Zona, Sharma, and Lane (1992) had an average age of 34.6 to 35.3 years; Meloy and Gothard (1995) reported a very similar average age of 35 years, with a range from 20 to 50 years. Stalkers are generally older than the usual criminal offender.

Occupation

Since the stalker's demographic background is only provided by the stalking victim in this study, there is a portion of this population for which not much background information is known. This missing information becomes even more

Table 7

Ethnicity of Stalkers

Ethnicity	N	%
White/Caucasian/Anglo	97	67
African American	15	10
Chicano/Latino	9	6
Other (foreign born)	8	5
Asian or Pacific Islander	6	4
Mixed ethnicity	5	3
Unknown	5	3
Total	145	100

Table 8

Stalker's Age Range

Age range (years)	N	%
18–25	25	18
26–30	20	14
31–35	17	12
36–40	21	15
41–50	34	24
51 or older	22	15
Unknown	3	2
Total	142[a]	100

[a] Three cases did not respond to this item.

apparent as the questions become more personal in nature. In this sample the stalkers' occupations cover a wide range, and suggest more of a working class background than that of the stalking victims. A frequency distribution is used in Table 9 to summarize these data.

In this sample only 3% of the stalkers were described as unemployed at the time of stalking. Meloy and Gothard (1995) found, "The majority of the subjects were unemployed or underemployed or had very unstable work histories at the time of their offenses (p. 259)." Similarly, Pathé and Mullen (1997) found that 43% of their sample was unemployed. The discrepancy between these findings could be influenced by the fact that the sample of obsessional followers were in custody versus the current study, in which it would appear that a very small number of the stalkers were currently incarcerated. Further, the current study took a superficial look at the stalker's occupation and did not address issues such as underemployment or the individual's work history.

Although findings from other studies suggest that the majority of stalkers had erratic employment histories, it is important to remember this is not always the case. Powerful and influential persons with stellar employment histories have been known on occasion to stalk. One example is Sol Wachtler, the former New York State Chief Judge, who was "poised to run for governor against Mario Cuomo" (Duggan, 1995, p. A17). Wachtler was arrested by the FBI after stalking Joy Silverman, who had ended their affair (Somerson, 1995). Silverman has since become one of several official spokespersons for the National Victim Center (Duggan, 1995) and Wachtler is now out of prison and has become a vocal advocate for prison reform.

Table 9

Stalker's Occupation

Occupation	N	%
Professional	25	17
Executive/managerial	14	10
Clerical/sales	14	10
Precision/crafts/repair	14	10
Student	13	9
Technical	10	7
Retired	9	6
Unemployed	5	3
Military	4	3
Disabled/handicapped	4	3
Musician/actor/artist	3	2
Homemaker	1	1
Other	9	6
Unknown	19	13
Total	144[a]	100

[a] One case did not respond to this item.

The current study did not address the issue of formal education of the stalkers. With 27% of the sample's occupation listed as either professional or executive/managerial, however, it would suggest that this population has at least a high school education, and validates previous studies by Harmon et al. (1995) and Meloy and Gothard (1995). Harmon's study found that all of the stalkers had some high school education and 40% were college graduates. Meloy reported that most of the obsessional followers in his sample had a high school education. All these findings would suggest that stalkers tend to be better educated than the average criminal offender.

Stalker's Personal Background

It has been suggested that certain personality traits, behaviors, and backgrounds may predispose rejected lovers to become obsessive. Respondents to this study were asked about the stalker's background regarding a number of issues that may provide insight into a propensity to stalk. Naturally, a large portion of the stalking victims were not privy to such sensitive issues in their stalker's history.

Table 10

Stalker's Prior History

Does stalker have a history of:	Yes (%)	No (%)	Unknown (%)
Drug/alcohol abuse	52	19	29
Mental illness	30	16	54
Violence or physical abuse	49	10	41
Criminal record	34	24	42
Violent family background	31	13	56
Stalked another person(s)	30	8	62

The results, shown in Table 10, are nonetheless noteworthy. Regardless of the large number of "unknowns," the percentage of stalkers who scored positive on mentioned indicators is high. Not all previous studies on stalkers addressed the issue of the stalkers' prior history, and those that did had only limited statistics available. Nonetheless, these findings do coincide with the current study's findings. Harmon et al. (1995) reported that 46% of their sample had a history of prior offenses for stalking. Meloy and Gothard (1995) reported that 60% had a history of either inpatient or outpatient psychiatric treatment and 70% had a history of substance abuse or dependence.

STALKING BEHAVIORS

Stalker's behaviors run the gamut from anonymous telephone calls in the middle of the night to sexual assault and kidnapping. It has been said that, "the alleged stalker's behavior, not motives, should be the most significant factor in determining whether to file charges" (Bureau of Justice Assistance, 1996, p. 4). Respondents were asked about the various types of contact that the stalker made. The questionnaire limited the choices to those in Table 11, although space was provided to add other types of contact. Studies conducted by Meloy and Gothard (1995); Hammell, Hoyt, and Lipson (1995); and Pathé and Mullen (1997) had similar findings (Table 12).

Since the development of the survey instrument many additional typical contacts made by stalkers have come to light. These were not listed individually in this project but could be included in future research on stalking victims. These include, but are not limited to, the following: going through mail or stealing it, entering the home to move around objects without taking anything, using other persons to help in the stalking, stealing underwear, going through the victim's garbage, threatening suicide, wiretapping the victim's telephone, telephoning the

Table 11

Contact Made by Stalker

Type of contact indicated	N	%
Telephone calls	126	87
Surveillance of home	122	84
Followed	116	80
Drive by home	112	77
Appearing at workplace	78	54
Sent letters	73	50
Made other types of contact	71	49
Spread gossip	69	48
Property damage	63	43
Left things on property	62	43
Threatened to harm others	60	41
Broke into home	57	39
Sent unwanted gifts	56	39
Hit or beat victim	55	38
Sexual assault	32	22
Injured or killed pets	19	13
Kidnapping	11	8
Sent packages containing[a]	5	3
Arson	2	1
Other[b]	71	49

[a] Urine, semen, dead animals, blood, or locks of hair.
[b] All other behaviors not listed specifically in questionnaire.

victim at work, going through the victim's handbag/briefcase, verbal abuse, filing false police reports or law suits against the victim, ordering items in the victim's name, canceling things in the victim's name (such as utilities, leases, and subscriptions), and harassing the victim's neighbors, friends, family, or children. Several of these types of contact were mentioned by respondents in this study. However, many were suggested by Joan Zorza, a board member of both the New York State Coalition against Domestic Violence and the National Coalition against Domestic Violence, to be included in future research on stalking victims. Zorza has done extensive work with stalking victims and is familiar with the idiosyncrasies of stalking behavior.

Stalking victims also reported a variety of unusual incidents. These included finding their clothes cut into pieces, finding a dildo wrapped in the female victim's

Table 12

Contact Made by Stalker—A Comparison of Several Studies

Type of contact made	Hall (current study) (%)	Meloy & Gothard (1995) (%)	Hammell, Hoyt, & Lipson (1995) (%)	Pathé & Mullen (1997) (%)
Telephone calls	87	40	n/a	78
Went to victim's home	77	60	n/a	n/a
Followed	80	n/a	n/a	71
Sent letters	50	25	n/a	62
Property damage	43	n/a	35	36
Threatened to harm others	41	45	71	58
Sent gifts or unsolicited materials	39	10	n/a	50
Physically assaulted	38	25	28	31

underwear, being stalked at church, finding semen on the car steering wheel, and being held hostage by the stalker and forced to play "Russian Roulette" with a loaded gun. One stalker mailed several teeth and locks of his hair, along with a pair of his underwear, to his stalking victim. One female respondent told of how she woke up in the middle of the night to find her ex-boyfriend sleeping beside her after having broken into her home, a real-life *Sleeping with the Enemy*.

Stalking victims report experiences that are almost too strange to believe. In fact, the more bizarre the stalking incident, the more difficult it is to convince others it is truly happening. Several respondents reported that the stalker broke into their home with the sole purpose of moving things around so that it would be obvious they had been there. One can imagine the victim's frustration in trying to convince a police officer that someone broke into her home and moved the candlesticks to the bathroom, without taking or doing anything else.

A stalker's behavior can be frustrating as well as frightening. This is illustrated by an excerpt provided by a respondent in this study:

> One Sunday morning, he pulled his car into my driveway so that I couldn't open my garage door to leave. He rang the doorbell continuously. I called the police to have him removed from my property. They arrived within 10–15 minutes and forcefully told him to leave and to cease all contact with me. Within a half hour he phoned me, and with great vivacity, told me how exciting I'd made his life.

EFFECTS ON THE VICTIM

Respondents concur that the experience of being stalked for months and even years at a time is akin to psychological terrorism. Their entire lives change.

Many move or quit jobs, some change their names, others have gone underground, leaving friends and family behind in order to escape the terror. Several stalking victims changed their appearance by dyeing their hair, gaining weight, and even getting a breast reduction in the hopes that their stalker might not recognize them. In a separate study, stalking victims reported that they were at a loss as to the right thing to do and everything they tried turned out wrong (Roberts and Dziegielewski, 1996). The profound effect of stalking takes a toll on all aspects of the victim's life. Not surprisingly, 83% ($N = 121$) of the respondents reported that their personalities changed as a result of being stalked: 86% ($N = 103$) of all the female respondents and 68% ($N = 18$) of all the male respondents. Stalking victims in this study reported new behaviors following the stalking: 88% ($N = 127$) now were cautious, 41% ($N = 59$) often felt paranoid, 52% ($N = 75$) were now easily frightened, and 27% ($N = 39$) were much more aggressive. These findings are even more interesting when compared with the personality traits and behaviors reported prior to being stalked. See Table 13 for a summary of findings.

Many female respondents in this study added that they now were less trusting, especially of men. Some mentioned being very suspicious of other's motives and now were leading more lonely and isolated lives. One stalking victim noted, "I cannot stress how my life has changed since this happened. I do not trust men any longer. My stalker took away my loving trusting nature." Another wrote, "I would say that this whole episode [stalking and assault] was one of the most significant events of my life." One woman who had been stalked by a rapist said that she "dropped out of school and went through at least five years of grief and

Table 13

Personality Traits and Behavior Reported prior to and after Stalking

Personality traits and behaviors	Percentage reported prior to stalking	Percentage reported after stalking
Friendly	89	53
Outgoing	78	41
Cautious	15	88
Easily frightened or startled	4	52
Paranoid	2	41
Aggressive	17	27
Introverted	9	20
Shy	10	11
Quiet	15	19
Passive	18	9

condemnation from my family." Another tried to see some positive gain from the experience:

> I wanted to say also that even though this situation drastically changed and reshaped my life, I feel I am a better person now for what I learned. Please don't get me wrong, I realize I did not deserve to be treated this way. Particularly as I now live with a disability as a result of this situation.

Although many of the respondents in this study felt that their stalkings had ended, they still live in fear that the stalker will find them, and the entire experience will start all over again. This is expressed by one stalking victim who wrote, "His last contact was 2 years ago, but part of me is still afraid of him and when he'll pop up again. Logically I know he won't, but sometimes it still scares me." Even the fact that their stalker is in jail is of little comfort to some stalking victims. "I continue to live in fear that on release my stalker will return to finish the job he started. Although I have changed jobs and am moving, my finances are seriously disrupted, I feel it will never be enough." Another victim concluded, "The only reason I am not currently being stalked is because he is in jail. . . . I believe that stalking will resume as soon as he is released."

CONCLUSIONS

The results of this study shed more light on a subject about which so little is actually known. While this area of research is growing, certain critical aspects remain elusive at this time. The information offered by the stalking victims provides a profile that may be expanded upon in future research. Since this information was gathered from the victims of stalkings who were survivors and not from the stalkers, however, certain data are missing with regard to stalkers' demographics and prior history. When the data from this study are compared to the data available from studies on stalkers from a forensic population, there are many similarities. The average age of stalkers is similar throughout several studies, as is the gender of the victims, and the types of contact made by the stalkers.

The data suggest that the majority of stalking victims are women who are being stalked by men who wish to either reestablish or initiate a relationship with them. In this sample the women, in general, are outgoing and friendly (or at least perceived themselves to be prior to being stalked), are between the ages of 26 and 46 and have a higher educational background than the general public. The results illustrate that men are also stalking victims and deserve the same respect and help as female stalking victims. Further, not all stalkers seek a relationship; some are bent on revenge.

Stalking behaviors experienced by the respondents ranged from anonymous telephone calls to sexual assault and kidnapping. The vast majority of respondents reported that they had received unwanted telephone calls and letters and that their stalker regularly followed them and often drove by their homes. The ominous threats, constant surveillance, and intrusion into the victims' lives have long-term, damaging psychological effects. Living in fear takes a toll on the quality of human life. It is through understanding this unique crime and the various aspects of it that the criminal justice system and other agencies may become better prepared to help stalking victims. The need for more research to fully understand this crime, its victims, and its perpetrators is paramount.

REFERENCES

Bureau of Justice Assistance. (1996, June). *Regional seminar series on developing and implementing antistalking codes.* (NCJ-156836). Washington, DC: U.S. Department of Justice.

Buss, D. (1994). *The evolution of desire: Strategies of human mating.* New York: Basic Books.

Combating stalking and family violence: Hearing before the Committee on the Judiciary, Senate, 103d Cong., 1st Sess. (1993).

De Becker, G. (1997). *The gift of fear: Survival signals that protect us from violence.* Boston: Little, Brown.

Duggan, D. (1995, February 16). Joy ends unhappy silence. *New York Newsday.*

Edwards, L. (1992, December). Trespassers of the heart. *Details.*

Fremouw, W. J., Westrup, D., & Pennypacker, J. (1997). Stalking on campus: The prevalence and strategies for coping with stalking. *Journal of Forensic Sciences, 42,* 664–667.

Goldberg, H. (1976). *The hazards of being male: Surviving the myth of masculine privilege.* New York: New American Library.

Hammell, B. F., Hoyt, D., & Lipson, G. (1995, March). *San Diego County stalking survey.* Paper presented at the Stalking the Stalker Conference, San Diego, CA.

Harlow, C. Wolf. (1991). *Female victims of violent crime.* Washington, DC: U.S. Department of Justice.

Harmon, R. B., Rosner, R., & Owens, H. (1995). Obsessional harassment and erotomania in a criminal court population. *Journal of Forensic Sciences, 40,* 188–196.

Jilted, jealous 70-year old told to steer clear of his ex. (1996, November 14). *Pleasanton (California) Valley Times.*

Kong, R. (1996). Criminal harassment. *Statistics Canada. Juristat Publication, Canadian Centre for Justice Statistics, 16,* 1–13.

Labovitz, S., & Hagedom, R. (1981). *Introduction to social research* (3rd ed.). New York: McGraw-Hill.

McGrath, E. (1994). *When feeling bad is good.* New York: Henry Holt.

Meloy, J. R. (1995, August). *The psychodynamics of stalking.* Paper presented at the fifth annual meeting of the threat management conference. Anaheim, CA.

Meloy, J. R. (1996a). Stalking (obsessional following): A review of some preliminary studies. *Aggression and Violent Behavior, 1,* 147–162.

Meloy, J. R. (1996b). A clinical investigation of the obsessional follower: "She loves me, she loves me not . . ." In L. Schlesinger (Ed.), *Explorations in criminal psychopathology* (pp. 9–32). Springfield, IL: Charles C. Thomas.

Meloy, J. R. & Gothard, S. (1995). Demographic and clinical comparison of obsessional followers and offenders with mental disorders. *American Journal of Psychiatry, 152,* 258–263.

Pathé, M., & Mullen, P. E. (1997). The impact of stalkers on their victims. *British Journal of Psychiatry, 170,* 12–17.

Roberts, A. R., & Dziegielewski, S. F. (1996). Assessment, typology, and intervention with the survivors of stalking. *Aggression and Violent Behavior, 1,* 359–368.

Romans, J. S. C., Hays, J. R., & White, T. K. (1996). Stalking and related behaviors experienced by counseling center staff members from current or former clients. *Professional Psychology: Research and Practice, 27,* 595–599.

Schaum, M., & Parrish, K. (1995). *Stalked: Breaking the silence on the crime of stalking in America.* New York: Pocket Books.

Schwartz, M. (1996, January/February). The study of masculinities and crime. *The Criminologist.*

Serant, C. (1993, October). Stalked: Any woman can become a victim of this heinous crime. *Essence.*

Somerson, M. D. (1995, April 23). Shy woman speaks up for victims of stalkers. *The Columbus (Ohio) Dispatch.*

Spitzberg, B. H., & Cupach, W. R. (1996, August). *Obsessive relational intrusions: Victimization and coping.* Paper presented at the International Society for the Study of Personal Relationships, Banff, Canada.

Taylor, P., Mahendra, B., & Gunn, J. (1983). Erotomania in males. *Psychological Medicine, 14,* 645–650.

U.S. Bureau of Census (1996). *Statistical Abstract of the United States: 1996* (116th ed.). Washington, DC: Author.

Van Biema, D. (1994, January 24). Semester break. *Time.*

Wright, J. A., Burgess, A. G., Burgess, A. W., Laszlo, A. T., McCrary, G. O., & Douglas, J. E. (1996). A typology of interpersonal stalking. *Journal of Interpersonal Violence, 11,* 487–502.

Zawitz, M. W., Klaus, P. A., Bachman, R., Bastian, L. D., DeBerry, M. M., Jr., Rand, M., & Taylor, B. (1993, October). *Highlights from 20 years of surveying crime victims: The national crime victimization survey, 1973-92.* (NCJ-144525). Washington, DC: U.S. Department of Justice.

Zona, M., Sharma, K., & Lane, J. (1994). A comparative study of erotomania and obsessional subjects in a forensic sample. *Journal of Forensic Sciences, 38,* 894–903.

CHAPTER 7

Stalking and Domestic Violence

Lenore E. Walker, Ed.D. and J. Reid Meloy, Ph.D.

The identification of domestic violence as a major social, legal, and health problem with the potential to destroy millions of families—in an age in which family values appear to be a widely desired goal—has captured the attention of scholars and practitioners across the world during the past two decades (Walker, in press). New laws have been passed to better protect battered women and their children (cf. Hart, 1988; Schechter, 1982; Schneider, 1986). Psychologists have developed clinical treatments for battered women (Dutton, 1992; Walker, 1994), batterers (Dutton, 1995; Gottman et al., 1996; Sonkin & Durphy, 1982; Sonkin & Walker, 1994), children who are exposed to violence (Goodman & Rosenberg, 1987), and families (Geffner, 1997; Geffner, Barrett, & Rossman, 1995; Hansen & Harway, 1993; O'Leary, 1993). Researchers have studied the various aspects of the problem from different points of view, such as epidemiological and sociological perspectives (Gelles & Straus, 1988; Straus, 1993; Straus & Gelles, 1988; Straus, Gelles, & Steinmetz, 1980), dangerousness (Dunford, Huizinga, & Elliot, 1990; Dutton, 1995; Edwards, 1989; Harrell, 1991; Jones, 1981, 1994; Sherman & Berk, 1984; Sonkin, 1997), feminist perspectives (Rosewater & Walker, 1985; Yllo, 1993; Walker, 1994), and reviews of the psychological research (APA, 1996; Barnett & LaViolette, 1993; Geffner, 1997; Koss, Goodman, Browne, Fitzgerald, Keita, & Russo, 1994; O'Leary, 1993). Legal arguments protecting battered women who may harm or kill the batterer in self-defense have been put forward (Browne, 1987; Ewing, 1987; Schneider, 1986; Walker, 1989). From 1985 to 1995, the United Nations assigned high priority to getting member countries to better protect women and children from gender-based violence by holding conferences, collect-

The Psychology of Stalking: Clinical and Forensic Perspectives

ing statistical data, and declaring the abuse of women a violation of their human rights. In the United States as well as in many other countries (Heise, 1994; Walker, in press), systems of shelters and protection for battered women and their children were established and funded by the federal government during the 1980s. By 1995 the U.S. Congress passed the Violence Against Women Act, which defined any physical or sexual abuse against a woman as a gender-based crime designed to take away a woman's civil rights.

Domestic violence has been conceptualized as an abuser's attempt to use physical, sexual, or psychological force to take away a woman's power and control over her life. Perhaps the most successful method used by batterers to accomplish their goal to control the woman is the systematic isolation of the woman from family, friends, and other community support systems. Although difficult to measure because the behavior used is often only the extreme form of typical behavior between a couple—such as questions about one's activities, telephone calls to find out how one's day is going, or offering opinions about one's friends or family whose flaws irritate the batterer in some way—when it reaches the point of monitoring, surveillance, and overpossessiveness, and induces fear, it approaches *stalking*. Like many other patterns of psychological manipulation, the beginning of this behavior goes unnoticed because of its close approximation to normal interaction between couples (Walker, 1996). Not until the power balance becomes lopsided, with the man using his knowledge of the woman's thoughts and feelings to control her behavior and isolate her from others, while still holding the right to do as he pleases without the same level of input from her, does the intended outcome of these attempts at control become clear. It is not unusual to hear a battered woman comment in retrospect about how she liked the man's attention focused on her until it became too stifling. For example, occasional telephone calls during the day to say hello are nice; but, when they increase to several per hour, they take on a monitoring function. Studies of the more extreme forms of isolation and stalking behavior have helped us to learn how it begins, which can help women gain better control prior to more serious abuse.

HOMICIDE STUDIES

Studies of battering relationships have elucidated the dynamics that propel their development until the woman feels like she has become captive. By the time professionals see the domestic violence relationship, being battered has often put a woman in a no-win situation. If she tries to terminate the battering relationship, which is the commonsense solution to the problem, the battered woman often finds herself in more danger than if she stays in the relationship and accepts whatever controls and violence the batterer chooses to deliver. Statistics of the number of women murdered in the United States indicate that women are most likely to be killed either during their preparation to leave or soon after they successfully separate from the batterer (APA, 1996; Browne, 1987; Ewing, 1987; Walker, 1989). In fact, the American Psychological Association's Presidential Task Force on Violence and the Family found that the highest risk factor for being harmed in the family is to be female (APA, 1996). Even so, the number of women who are actually killed by their batterers is quite small, especially when compared to the number of women who are battered each year. Estimates of the numbers of battered women in the United States range between $2\frac{1}{2}$ and 4 million women, and estimates of the number of women killed by their abusers range from 1200 to 4000 women per year (less than 10% of homicides; most victims of homicide are men). We have no good estimates of the number of additional women who somehow escape from murderous threats. Among stalkers in general, homicide rates appear to be less than 2% (Meloy, 1996), while at least half of stalkers threaten their victims or property.

Most battering relationships do end in divorce, often putting the woman at the highest risk for further harm or actual death from the point of separation to about 2 years post-divorce. In relation to the number of women who are battered by their partners, few batterers kill their partners. Even fewer battered women kill their abusers, although some believe that more women are now defending themselves against unwanted assaults. Some behaviors, such as murder, occur so infrequently that their prediction is expected to be inaccurate. Campbell (1995) reminded us that when homicide occurs at a base rate of 9 in 100,000 and domestic violence occurs at a base rate of 16,000 in 100,000 [which is an underestimate according to other researchers; see Browne (1993)], any predictions of homicide based solely on a history of domestic violence would be no better than chance. It is equally accurate, however, to tell battered women that as a group they are at higher risk of being killed than are non-battered women, although recent statistics indicate that half of all women who are murdered by their partners were never physically abused prior to the homicide (NCVS, 1995). The two best sources of such data in the United States are the National Institute of Justice's National Crime Victim Survey (NCVS) and the FBI's Uniform Crime Reporting System (UCRS), but even these reports underestimate both domestic violence and spousal homicides.

One way to escape the threat of being murdered is to kill the abuser in self-defense. Approximately 1000 to 2000 battered women per year kill their batterers, although numbers vary depending on how believable their claims of self-defense are to the prosecutors and their defense attorneys. Browne (1993) and Browne and Williams (1989) suggested that the number of women killing batterers is decreasing, particularly if there are other services and resources available to the woman. In those same communities, however, it appears that more women are being killed by batterers. Perhaps they are not encouraged to take the threat of being murdered by the batterer seriously when they access services that they believe will protect them. The sad truth learned when working in this field is simple: *there is nothing we can do to stop a batterer who is determined to kill a woman.* We can help her learn to better protect herself and her children, we can protect her by keeping her in a shelter for a while, and we can incarcerate the batterer for a short period of time, but we cannot stop him from using surveillance and eventually finding her. As Meloy (1989, 1992, 1996) has shown, a man who is obsessed with a woman and stalks may kill her to possess her.

STALKING IN BATTERING RELATIONSHIPS

Stalking is the name given to a combination of activities that batterers do to keep the connection between themselves and their partners from being severed. This can include following the woman, hiring others to do surveillance, and harassing the woman by unwanted telephone calls, monitoring, letters, gifts, and other ways of keeping in contact and in control. There are many more battered women being stalked by their batterers than are actually killed (Browne & Williams, 1989; Dunford et al., 1990; Dutton, 1995; Geffner, in press; Meloy, 1992; Pence & Paymar, 1993; Sonkin, 1997; Walker, 1989). However, predicting who will be the stalker and what relationship stalking behavior has to injury or death of the victim is not clearly known in the field of *domestic violence* per se.

Advocates believe that the most dangerous batterers can be identified by their stalking behavior that helps keep a woman more isolated even while they are living together (Hart, 1988), and psychologists believe that stalking behavior and obsessive thinking are highly related behaviors (Meloy, 1996). In fact, advocates for battered women helped persuade legislators in many states to pass the anti-stalking legislation that swept the United States in the early 1990s, and current research indicates that most stalking victims were prior sexual intimates of the perpetrator (see Meloy, Chapter 1). However, most of the data used to persuade us of the relationship between stalking and dangerousness are based on retrospective rather than prospective information. Thus, if it is known that a batterer threatened to kill a woman whom he later kills, it cannot be considered predictive that this batterer was at higher risk to kill than a batterer who has never threatened to kill. The same is true for a batterer who engages in stalking behavior. One reason is the high frequency—and poor discriminative or predictive power—of stalking and threats in all domestic violence cases. Earlier research suggested that 86% of the battered woman sample believed that the batterer could kill them (Walker, 1984). But stalking is a risk factor for further physical abuse or a lethal incident just by virtue of the tenacious proximity seeking toward the victim, and especially if it occurs in combination with several other high risk behaviors. It needs to be identified at its earliest stages even before the behavior becomes serious enough to bring in law enforcement.

IDENTIFYING WOMEN AT HIGH RISK

Most advocates for battered women understand that a battered woman is at higher risk than a non-battered woman to be seriously harmed or killed. Statistics from the U.S. Department of Justice NCVS telephone surveys of victims of crimes, and statistics from the FBI's UCRS, which tabulates information from law enforcement agencies, both suggest that experiencing previous violence, stalking, threats to kill, and actual attempts to kill are related to a higher risk for women to be seriously harmed or killed than not experiencing these behaviors. On the other hand, the statistics indicate that only 40–60% of all murdered women were previously battered. The lower percentage was Caucasian women who lived in nonviolent neighborhoods; the higher percentage was African-American women living in poor urban areas who were in danger of violence from many different sources, including their partners. If we reverse these figures, 40 to 60% of women murdered by their partners were not known to have been previously battered. The odds are about 50/50 that if a woman is killed, it will be by her prior batterer.

Anecdotal review of local news in most locales demonstrates that murder/suicides often occur in domestic violence families when the woman has attempted to leave the relationship, consistent with research (Cooper & Eaves, 1996; Feltous & Hempel, 1995; Marzuk, Tardiff, & Hirsch, 1992). Prior to the new focus on violence and the family, these reports typically stated that the family was having domestic problems, but none of the family or friends who knew the couple suspected anything like this might happen. In many cases they were described as "keeping to themselves" or "new to the area," which could actually be the typical social isolation seen in domestic violence families. In more recent publicized cases those who knew the victim(s) are more likely to state that the woman had told someone that she was terrified she would be killed by the man who had made such direct threats. Following the Nicole Brown Simpson and Ron Goldman murders, reported batterers have used a new verb to threaten to kill the woman: "I'm going to OJ you!" Sometimes neighbors report that the man was seen "hanging around the house" even though he was no longer living there. Others report that he made numerous telephone calls to them to try to find his family to persuade them to come home; and in some cases, he might try to enlist the help and support of the person to whom the call was made. Rarely was there information in the news stories about prior violence. Sometimes, if the case stayed in the news more than that 1 day, reports of previous arrests for domestic violence were revealed—but that is not the norm (Meloy, 1997a).

Although there are high risk factors that may help identify women who are in serious danger, it is important to remember that one-half of women who are killed by partners did not let it be known that there was any identifiable risk.

Psychologists know that past violent behavior is the best predictor of future violence; but Campbell (1995) found that mental health clinicians have a prediction accuracy rate of around 40% at best. This corresponds to Hansen and Harway's (1993) findings that most marriage and family therapists ignored (40%) or minimized (91%) the danger cues presented by their abused clients. Figley (1997) suggested that one reason professionals do not take violence threats seriously is their attempt not to develop a secondary victimization syndrome, which comes from listening to too much trauma. Professionals may guard against feeling traumatized by victims' stories by finding ways not to believe the offender could really be so dangerous. Societal norms that set expectations for women to be more emotional than men in describing their situation, some women's styles of telling their stories by adding many extraneous details and going off on tangents that often serve the purpose of blocking the reexperiencing of emotional pain and fear when retelling what happened to them, and men's often more rational ways of describing their experiences all contribute to the difficulty in believing women's reports of domestic violence and stalking [cf. Walker (1994) for further description].

Given these rather inconclusive data, advocates for battered women still tell all battered women that they are at a higher risk than non-battered women for being stalked and killed, and they preach the message that although battered women need to leave the relationship, they must take precautions to do so safely. Battered women and their families have been encouraged to report abuse to the authorities, and it has become easier for most women to apply for and receive civil restraining and protective orders from courts. Meloy and his colleagues (Meloy, Cowett, Parker, Hofland, & Friedland, in press) found that in the majority of studies, obtaining a domestic protection order was followed by a reduction in criminality and violent criminality toward the protectee, but these studies did not focus specifically on stalking as a component of domestic violence.

Law enforcement officers seem to take calls from women who have obtained such protection orders more seriously, and the women themselves appear to be empowered by them, often perceiving themselves as better able to take other protective steps (APA, 1996; Walker, 1979, 1989). Criminal and civil prosecutions of batterers increased dramatically in the 1980s once barriers to reporting criminal assaults were removed. One of the main changes was allowing law enforcement officers to sign the complaint when they believed there was probable cause to make an arrest, rather than insisting the victim "press charges" against her abusive partner. Training law enforcement officers in making arrests upon probable cause has been another important change (Edwards, 1989). Having victim's advocates help battered women learn what resources are available and treatment programs as an alternative to jail sentences for the batterers have also helped victims cooperate with the system. In Denver, Colorado, for example, which instituted a special domestic violence court around 1985, the number of complaints filed went from 3000 per year to over 10,000 in the first year. In Miami, Florida, a similar phenomenon occurred. Cases increased from approximately 3000 to over 12,000 the first year, with steady increments over the past five years, especially when the domestic violence and drug treatment courts were combined. Specially trained judges and prosecutors help keep cases from getting lost in the system. The new stalking laws passed during the 1990s also permitted prosecution of the often nonviolent crimes involving surveillance and following of the victim that could escalate into serious levels of violence.

REDUCING RISK FOR BATTERED WOMEN

At the Domestic Violence Institute's affiliate offices we have been collecting information about ways to identify women at high risk for being seriously injured or killed. We first developed a list of behaviors that we found to be associated with domestic violence relationships. This list often helps a battered woman or her family and friends to assess whether there actually is abuse in the relationship (see Table 1).

Table 1

Battered Woman's Checklist

Does the person you love . . .

1. Have to know where you are all the time?
2. Constantly accuse you of being unfaithful?
3. Discourage your relationships with family and friends?
4. Want you to stop working or attending school?
5. Criticize you for little things?
6. Anger easily especially when drinking or using drugs?
7. Control all the finances and make you account for every penny you spend?
8. Refuse to keep a job and force you to pay all the bills?
9. Humiliate you or insult you in front of others?
10. Destroy your personal property or sentimental things?
11. Demand sex even when you do not want it?
12. Hit, punch, slap, push, pull your hair, shake, kick, twist your arms or legs, bite you or your children?
13. Threaten to hurt you or your children?
14. Threaten to or actually use a weapon against you or your children?
15. Coerce or force you to perform sexual acts you don't want to engage in?

If you check off more than 5 of these items or items 12, 13, 14, or 15, then there is too much violence in your home and you need to do something to help your family survive right now!

We have also developed a list of high risk factors that we distribute in our training programs and other materials. This list of what we call *lethality factors* can be found in Table 2. Many of the items have been taken from various research studies, particularly those in which women attempted to kill or killed their spouses because they believed their lives were in danger.

Others have looked at risk factors in lethal outcomes of violence as a discriminating factor. For example, from her research with battered women who killed in self-defense, Browne (1987) suggested several high risk factors for escalation of domestic violence to lethal levels. The six factors from her analysis are the first six items in this current lethality list, and include an increase in frequency and severity of physical violence, threats to kill, abuse of children, alcohol and/or drug abuse, and sexual abuse. Campbell (1995) added more formalized dangerousness assessments after analyzing mortality data, while Hotaling and Sugarman (1986) reviewed the literature and found no risk markers for batterers who kill other than witnessing or experiencing violence in their childhood home. It is common knowledge among advocates, however, that combinations of these lethality or high risk factors do place women at higher risk for danger and harm (Browne & Williams, 1989).

Table 2

Lethality Guide[a]

1. Frequency of man's use of violence is escalating.
2. Severity of man's violence is escalating.
3. Man threatens to kill woman or others.
4. Frequency of intoxication from alcohol and other drug use.
5. Man threatens to harm children.
6. Man forced or threatened sex acts.
7. Man's or woman's suicide threats or attempts.
8. Weapons kept at home or easily accessible.
9. Psychiatric impairment of man or woman.
10. Proximity of man and woman—how close to where they both work and live.
11. Man's need for control of contact around the children.
12. Current life stresses in man's or woman's lives.
13. Man's previous criminal history.
14. Man's attitudes toward violence.
15. Presence of a new relationship for either man or woman.

[a] These factors have been found to be important in taking precautions against further escalation of domestic violence, although the best predictor of future violence is past violence.

BATTERER TYPOLOGIES

The mandatory reporting laws for domestic violence and subsequent court-ordered treatment programs in the United States have recently provided better access to and understanding of abusive men. This expanded knowledge both calls into question and enhances much of what was known about the dynamics of domestic violence during the past 20 years, most of which came from victims' self-reports. While the details that these new studies (cf. Holtzworth-Munroe & Stuart [1994] for a review) present are very exciting in guiding the development of new approaches to both understanding and stopping violence in the family, it is critical to integrate this new information into the context of an already established database to protect the victims.

Batterers, like battered women, come from all different demographic groups (Sonkin, Martin, & Walker, 1985). In fact, the label, *batterer* and its subsequent description of the behavioral acts of violence until now have sufficed as descriptors. Studies measuring mental and personality disorders (Dutton & Starzomsky, 1993; Hamberger & Hastings, 1986; Saunders, 1992), dangerousness (Campbell, 1995), deterrence (Dunford et al., 1990; Sherman & Berk, 1984), recidivism (Harrell, 1991), and physiological differences (cf. Gottman et al., 1996), however, challenge the domestic violence community's notion that batterers can all benefit from the same type of psychoeducational treatment. They provide strong evidence that may help explain why some of the current intervention and treatment approaches do not work with a large number of batterers, and why others are more effective with some batterers in stopping domestic violence.

The various perpetrator typologies have been based on clinical and anecdotal, as well as empirical, research data, an absolute necessity since so many more batterers have been observed by clinicians than by researchers. Some classifications are based on levels of severity of the actual violent acts. This is only a partial discriminator since some cases have a continued escalation of abuse, while others do not (Campbell, 1995; Dunford et al., 1990; Geffner, in press; Harrell, 1991; Gelles & Straus, 1988; O'Leary, 1993). Others look more at the target of the abusive behavior. Initially, batterers were thought to fall into two major groups: those who were violent only within their families and those who also were violent outside the home. The more recent understanding of typologies includes three major groups (Walker, 1996).

1. *Power and control batterers* use violence mostly in their homes and are primarily motivated by abnormal power and control needs. This group often can choose to stop their abuse with some psychoeducation about anger management and sex-role attitude readjustment, although in some cases the psychological manipulation and maltreatment becomes greater when the physical abuse ceases (Geffner, in press; Harrell, 1991; Lindsay, McBride, & Platt, 1992; Pence & Paymar, 1993; Sonkin, 1997; Sonkin & Durphy, 1982).

2. *Mentally ill batterers,* in addition to their abnormal power and control needs, also have serious psychological problems, including depression, disordered thinking and obsessive–compulsive behavior, paranoid disorders, borderline traits, and other serious mental disorders. They often need individual and group psychotherapy as well as a trial on medication (Dutton & Starzomski, 1993; Geffner, in press; Hamberger & Hastings, 1986; Lindsay et al., 1992; O'Leary, 1993; Saunders, 1992; Sonkin, 1997).

3. *Criminal–psychopathic batterers* commit other violent and nonviolent crimes as well as assaults within the home. They are often diagnosed with antisocial personality disorder (*DSM-IV*) for which there is little known treatment at this time (Meloy, 1995). Depending on their degree of *psychopathy* (Hare, 1991), incarceration may be the only method known to protect battered women and their families (Dutton & Starzomski, 1993; Lindsay et al., 1992; Sonkin, 1997; Walker & Sonkin, 1995).

The first two groups may benefit from psychoeducational and offender-specific treatment groups that are popular in North and South America as court-ordered interventions for the batterer. The second group, however, may also need long-term individual psychotherapy and perhaps medication to manage psychological and emotional problems, some of which are chronic. The latter group is the least likely to stop their violence without external controls such as confinement in jail or prison, and the identification of batterers in this group by psychologists and psychiatrists provides important information for battered women in deciding what to do about their relationship. Although psychology has much to offer in deciding to which group an individual offender belongs, it is not yet known which group might be more likely to stalk women, even though the last two groups are considered the most dangerous. All of these types of batterers fall within the "simple obsessional" group of stalkers identified by Zona, Sharma, and Lane (1993), the most violent group among their three-group typology of stalkers.[1]

IDENTIFYING DANGEROUS DOMESTIC VIOLENCE STALKERS

Gottman et al. (1996) suggested that the most dangerous batterer may not be the one whose rage is out of control, but rather the one whose rage is quiet, "cold," and totally under his control: what Meloy (1988) referred to as "predatory" rather than "affective" violence. This batterer has a mean streak that metes out

[1]In a recent presentation they reported a rate of 18.4% physical harm and 33.6% destruction of property, with an overall "damage done" figure of 42.9% in a large sample (>200) of "simple obsessionals" followed by the LAPD Threat Management Unit (M. Zona and R. Palarea, Seventh Annual Threat Management Conference, Los Angeles, August, 1997).

cruel and vicious acts against his partner. If stalking behavior includes the calculated and continuous harassment, surveillance, and monitoring of the woman, then it is necessary for the batterer who stalks to be purposeful in his behavior. Lindsay et al. (1992), Sonkin (1997), and Walker and Sonkin (1995), however, suggested that batterers who stalk are more likely to have cognitions that are based on faulty reasoning. Lindsay said that the need for revenge, as well as a need for vindication, motivate many batterers who stalk; while Sonkin suggested that dysfunctional cognitive thinking propels stalking behavior. Using a model similar to Beck's (1976) cognitive model of depression, Sonkin (1997) devised a treatment approach for domestic violence stalkers that can be added to many mandatory domestic violence treatment programs. It is based on the original program developed for the JurisMonitor Project described below.

In any case, it is as difficult to predict the *domestic violence* stalker as it is to predict who will stalk in general. One of the most confounding tasks is to differentiate between the lover who cannot relinquish the relationship and the dangerous domestic violence stalker. Following are several cases that illustrate this point.

James is a 66-year-old man who lived for the past 20 years with Helen, a 62-year-old woman, in her home. They were both known to drink alcohol, and in fact were considered alcoholics by their physicians. Helen developed serious health problems that prevented her from drinking any more alcohol. Soon after becoming sober, she no longer wanted to put up with James' abusive behavior when he was drunk. Claiming to more clearly see the abusive behavior for what it was, Helen tried to get James to go into treatment. When he refused, she told him to leave her home. He protested leaving the only home he knew but she successfully had the locks changed. Having nowhere to go and no resources, James hung out on the street outside Helen's house and slept at night in his car parked across the street. Helen became scared of James' behavior and called the police who arrested James, citing him with the stalking statute. But was he really stalking Helen or was he simply hanging out there because he couldn't shift and find another home?

Take this same case a few months later: James was released from jail and went back to hanging out in the front of Helen's house until the police asked him to move. He refused and kept returning to the house. He began calling Helen on the telephone, begging her to let him return, and promising not to drink alcohol anymore. Although Helen was tempted to let him back home, her children intervened and would not permit it. James became angry and started vandalizing the house, but then hiding in the bushes around the neighborhood so it was difficult to locate him. During one telephone call, Helen told James she was leaving all his clothes outside the house for him to pick up. James scattered the clothes around the front of the house, destroying them by ripping and slashing them with a knife. Helen called the police who arrested him again, believing that he was becoming more dangerous. Although he still had not physically harmed Helen, was his increased abusive behavior toward inanimate objects and his telephone calls an indication that he was becoming more dangerous?

James was incarcerated for another few months while the lawyers sorted out the charges and tried to find another home for him. There was no facility, however, that he was willing to consider that could provide him with companionship and activities. He kept obsessing about going back to live with Helen and called her from jail whenever he could get to the telephone. Although she refused his collect calls, his harassing behavior and threats left on her answering machine terrified her. She believed he was definitely going to harm her when he got out of jail. How much was Helen's reaction due to a realistic fear of James' dangerousness, and how much was it a result of hypervigilance that came from the earlier abuse, which was no longer occurring? And was the risk of violence from James greater with the escalation of his observable dependency on Helen?

In this particular case, James was incarcerated for more than 6 months because he would not promise not to stalk and harass Helen. Finally, the court could no longer exercise control over him and he was released; he went right back to Helen's house to begin his vigil all over again. Helen's children helped her to sell her house and move away, which finally stopped him from stalking her once he knew that she was no longer there. He moved into a trailer nearby and continued to live a marginal life.

Or take the case of stalking that was reported by the media during O.J. Simpson's trial for the murder of his former wife, Nicole Brown, and her friend Ron Goldman: According to investigation, O.J. did hang around outside Nicole's new home after they separated in January 1992. For several months, he called her trying to persuade her that they needed to work things out, brought her flowers and left them on her doorstep, and showed up at neighborhood restaurants they used to go to in hopes of seeing her there. He says he just couldn't believe that their marriage really was over until the March night that he looked in the front window and saw her having oral sex with Keith Zomlovitch, her then current boyfriend. O.J. said that he was shocked out of his denial and realized then that their marriage really was irretrievably broken. Although much was made out of the confrontation with Zomlovitch and Nicole the next morning, unlike most batterers, O.J. did not lose his temper either the night before, when he left without telling them he was there, or that morning when he says he told Nicole that she should think about the children when she has sex with a man and they are home. He claims never to have followed her again. Shortly afterward, O.J. met his new girlfriend, Paula Barbieri, and they began their relationship. Was this the action of a lovesick man who did not want to face the end of his relationship just yet, or is it domestic violence stalking? Obviously, time can help tell the difference because in non-obsessed persons lovesickness does eventually pass.

In this case, there was also evidence that after O.J. and Nicole were divorced, later that year in October 1992, their relationship around the children seemed to deteriorate and for several months they had minimal contact. Visitation with the children was arranged by his secretary and they were dropped off and picked up with the assistance of O.J.'s housekeeper and office staff. By March 1993, Nicole was seen following O.J. around on the golf course several times, pleading with him to try a reconciliation. She also hung out around his house and used her key to enter the house at night and get into his bed to sleep with him. At her persuasion, O.J. stopped dating Paula and agreed to try a reconciliation with Nicole, which lasted through the following spring, 1994. Was Nicole stalking O.J. when she followed him on the golf course or at his home? Or was she simply someone who felt she made a mistake in breaking up their marriage and was trying to get his attention to see if he was willing to reconcile?

These are difficult questions to answer in trying to determine what is domestic violence stalking and what is a nondangerous attempt to keep a relationship together. Following is another case in which the woman stalked the man to better protect herself from his violent behavior: Jan was married for 16 years to Dan, who had never sold his apartment when they were married. At first he had it rented and then he let his daughter from a prior marriage live there for a short period of time. Jan, however, was very jealous of Dan's ability to easily come and go. She couldn't understand why Dan wouldn't get rid of the apartment. He would often provoke a fight, batter her, and then leave their home, sometimes not coming home for several days. Jan believed he went to the apartment during these battering incidents. In her panic at being left alone and frightened at the possible continuation of the abuse when Dan returned, Jan would go out to try to find him. She frequently ended up at the apartment, sneaking around outside, and throwing stones at the bedroom windows to see if he would appear so she would know for sure that he was there. She also called him on the telephone every 15 minutes or so, at the apartment and at his office during the day, again trying to see where he was and monitor his mood, which she believed was helping her to stay safe.

In yet another case, Chris followed Nancy around no matter where she went: Chris and Nancy were married for 10 years when she finally filed for divorce, stating that she no longer could trust him to be around her or their three small children. She knew that he seemed to be obsessed with her, following her around the house like a lost puppy dog, always wanting to know what he could do to help, but then never actually doing any tasks. Money was not an object because of Nancy's wealth, but she had hoped he would find some work that interested him instead of staying home all day with her, the nanny, and the children. Nancy says he gave her the "creeps": every time she would look up there was Chris staring at her, putting his face in hers, or trying to engage in whatever she was doing. Chris also wandered the neighborhood talking to others, usually with a friendly demeanor that hid his vicious temper. Sometimes the questions he asked them bordered on insensitivity and a need for power and control over Nancy.

Despite their discomfort, reports indicate that Chris managed to get people to divulge secrets and other information designed to make things easier for him to stalk and control Nancy, who rarely left the house. At one point, Nancy felt so uncomfortable with her own fears about leaving the home that she had bars installed on the windows to keep burglars from getting inside the home. Chris had them immediately removed. This caused her to believe that Chris wanted something bad to happen to her and increased her level of fear of him. By this time it was difficult to separate out which of Nancy's fears were reasonable and which were a product of her own internal experiences. Nancy fought for sole custody of the children in a state where shared legal custody was presumed by law to be best for children, except in cases of physical domestic violence. Within 1 day of being told that by the assigned custody evaluator, Nancy and Chris got into an altercation in which as he was leaving the home and she tried to stop him he attempted to throw obstacles at her to cause her to trip and fall downstairs. Nancy immediately reported the incident to the police, went to the hospital emergency room for treatment, and took pictures of her injuries. The custody evaluator had difficulty deciding if this incident occurred because she was manipulating the situation to gain sole custody of the children, or because she stopped placating Chris and made a demand that he was not going to meet so he became violent. Although the custody evaluator said that everyone involved with this family described Chris as "slimy," no one thought he was capable of physically harming either Nancy or the children. Even the incident when he caused her to fall downstairs and got away by harming Nancy did not fully convince them that Nancy was telling the truth. Perhaps the only way to keep Nancy and the children safe over the long term is to design a parenting plan that makes it more in Chris's self-interest to keep a good relationship with them than not to do so. But how to encourage that behavior is a question that will take creativity and new ways of looking at parenting children who have been exposed to domestic violence.

These cases are not the typical domestic violence incidents that we think about when discussing stalking. Such cases are more closely patterned after ones described in the following section on the JurisMonitor project. These cases are important for a full understanding of the complexity of the issue and the potential for not adequately exploring the facts when analyzing the interpersonal dynamics of various domestic violence relationships. It is also important to accept that many battered women do recognize the dangers from their husband's stalking behavior even if it cannot be legally proven, or has not reached the threshold that will permit the justice system's involvement. Health and mental health professionals need to keep a close watch on these cases and help women to feel that they can do some things to keep themselves and their children as safe as possible. Other community members' help needs to be elicited, sometimes to build a circle of protection around the victim until she feels more comfortable (Meloy, 1997b). Some would argue that protecting the victim often steps on the abuser's rights;

this may sometimes happen, particularly when young children are present. But the research data on impact of divorce on children indicate that it is the quality of the relationship between the parents, not the frequency or infrequency of time with one parent, that makes the difference in their adjustment (Liss & Stahly, 1993). Calming down the situation and protecting the mother may need to be the first step in a long-term parenting plan.

THE JURISMONITOR PROJECT

In the early 1990s the number of domestic violence offenders who were arrested and charged with assaultive behavior significantly increased, putting a strain on the criminal justice system to detain and keep them incarcerated. A corporation that had alliances with those who were pioneering monitoring technology for early release of nondangerous criminals developed an ankle bracelet that could be worn by a domestic violence offender whose partner agreed to have a monitoring system placed in her home. The couple could not be living together if they participated in this program. The system was designed with the typical domestic violence stalker in mind: Ronald had been arrested more than one time for physical and sexual assault on his partner, Lisa. He refused to obey the restraining order issued to protect her from his harassment and stalking. He called and harassed her, alternating between charming and threatening behaviors. He put flowers one time and dead rats another time on her doorstep. He wrote her letters, chased after her while both were driving cars, and hid in the bushes watching her house while he waited for her to get home. He held himself out to be above the law, and told the children to tell their mother that he would "get her" if she didn't meet him to talk. She agreed to meet at a public place, a nearby busy restaurant, when they exchanged the children after visitation. The meeting soon deteriorated into his calling her names and threatening to kill her when she refused to consider reconciliation. He kept repeating the same things over and over, so Lisa decided to end the meeting and started to leave. Ron quickly got into his car and followed her. He kept ruminating about Lisa's refusal to be intimidated or persuaded to do what he demanded, and in his anger banged his car into hers, causing her to panic and drive to the closest police station. When Ron drove up, he was arrested for violation of the domestic violence restraining order, but not stalking. Ron was offered a chance to be released from jail if he was willing to wear the ankle bracelet and not go near Lisa's house, where she agreed to have a monitor placed. The alarm went off at the monitoring center twice during the 12 weeks he wore it, indicating that either Ron was within the 500 feet radius or the alarm itself was faulty. He also entered the JurisMonitor Stabilization Program, which helped him learn new ways to get his needs met. Lisa had filed for divorce by then, and was not interested in keeping the marriage together. She stated that she was able to relax and really enjoy herself for the first time in many years once she knew that Ron was wearing the electronic device that would set off signals at the monitoring center if he came close enough to follow, surveil, or harass her. By the end of the program, which included cognitive behavioral conditioning to help stop the domestic violence and stalking, Ron had begun to get his own life together and was able to leave Lisa alone.

The ankle bracelet was successful in about two-thirds of the first 10 cases we saw. One man left the state but was thoughtful enough to remove the bracelet and return it before he absconded. Most of the women involved chose not to return to the batterer after the 12-week period of forced separation. When women were interviewed after the program was completed, they were uniform in their agreement that knowing where their abusive partner was most of the time was helpful and relieving. Although some advocate organizations were concerned that battered women might be lulled into failure to take responsibility to protect themselves, we found that most women knew the limitations of the electronic monitoring systems. Knowing that their homes were safe zones permitted them to lower their vigilance, often accompanied by the sense of "walking on eggshells" all the time, so they could make better decisions based on good judgment rather than abject fear. Cindy was one of the more vocal battered women whose husband, Tony, was released from jail wearing the JurisMonitor ankle bracelet that served both as a domestic violence and a home arrest monitoring system. He was unable to leave his residence (which could not be with Cindy because of the domestic violence charge) because of another criminal charge pending and had to be there when random calls were made to him by the monitoring system. Cindy said that she felt safe for the first time in many years. She was even able to engage in simple pleasures, like planting a garden close enough to the house so that if Tony came by the alarm would go off in the monitoring station. She said she had not been able to just sit in the sunshine without fear for so long that she cried the first day she felt she could do it.

PSYCHOLOGICAL TECHNIQUES OF BATTERING

It is important for professionals to understand the psychological techniques of batterers so that when women report these lower levels of abuse they are quickly recognized and not ignored. Sonkin (1997) has developed a comprehensive list of psychological techniques that are typically used for coercion. These are listed in the latter portion of his *Spouse Abuse History Form* (see Tables 3 and 4). Many of these techniques are routinely seen in nonviolent as well as violent couples. It is the frequency, severity, and pattern with which they are used that seem to be important in differentiating the two groups. Sonkin has developed a card sort that can be used on a Macintosh computer so that professionals can rate their clients

Table 3
Psychological Torture[a]

Isolation

_____ Locked in a house, room, or closet

_____ Tied up with rope, chains, handcuffs, etc.

_____ Forced to live in isolated settings

_____ Frequent moves

_____ Controlled socialization with family or friends

_____ Monitored use of telephone/mail

Degradation

_____ To curse, name-call, such as stupid, worthless, etc.

_____ To depreciate or devalue

_____ Public humiliation

_____ Private humiliation

_____ Denial of power or competency

_____ Forced prostitution or sex acts with others

_____ Forced pornography

_____ Rejection (emotional, intellectual, social, sexual, affectional)

Denial of reality

_____ Denial of power or competency

_____ Told or convinced person is mentally ill

_____ Lying and manipulating partner

_____ "Gaslighting" techniques

Induced debility producing physical distress or exhaustion

_____ Forced to take on role of servant

_____ Forced to clean house or work excessively long hours

_____ Obsessive needs for cleanliness, such as towels placed just right

_____ Interference with sleep patterns

_____ Interference with eating and nutrition

_____ Not allowed personal or rest time

Alcohol or drug administration

_____ Forced to use alcohol or other drugs

_____ Forced to participate in sale/distribution of drugs

_____ Induced dependence on drugs

Monopolizing of perceptions

_____ Pathological jealousy

_____ Controlled activities

_____ Economic control

_____ Checking on where partner is (surveillance)

(*continues*)

Table 3 (*continued*)

———— Forced partner to live up to abuser's expectations

———— Refuses discussions or negotiations

Threats

———— Threats to kill partner or children

———— Threats to kill others

———— Threats to commit suicide

———— Threats using weapons

———— Sham executions

———— Threats to kidnap or keep children

[a] This chart has been adapted from Sonkin (1997).

Table 4

Common Domestic Violence Stalking Acts[a]

———— Mailing cards or other cryptic messages

———— Breaking windows, breaking into or vandalizing partner's home

———— Taking partner's mail

———— Leaving things such as flowers on doorstep or at work

———— Watching partner from a distance

———— Hang up calls on the telephone

———— Following partner with a car

———— Following partner on foot

———— Hiding in bushes or other surveillance of partner's home

———— Surveillance of partner at work

———— Other trespassing

———— Vandalizing partner's property

———— Destroying property to scare or intimidate partner

———— Stealing things from partner

———— Breaking into partner's house or car

———— Filing numerous pleadings in court cases

———— Filing for custody of children regardless of their needs

———— Not respecting visitation limitations

———— Harassing telephone calls or notes

———— Violation of restraining orders

[a] This checklist has been adapted from Sonkin (1997).

Table 5

Clinical Assessment for Survivor Therapy

- Obtain informed consent
- Mental status examination
- Clinical interview
  Obtain victim's own story with open-ended Q & A
    Leave adequate time
    Nonjudgmental attitude
    No interpretation
    No victim-blaming remarks
    No suggestions
- Relevant histories
  Childhood history
  Relationship history (friends and family)
  Abuse history
- Psychological test data
  MMPI-2, MCMI-III
  Projective tests (Rorschach)
  Cognitive tests (WAIS-III)
- Neuropsychological test data
- Physical injury history
- Physical illness history
- Lethality assessment
- Alcohol and drug assessment
- BWS & PTSD diagnosis?
- Other clinical diagnosis?

using this method. It can be found on his home page on the Web.[2] Men appear to be better at reporting their own use of these techniques in a group of other admitted batterers, while women are better at reporting when they are less frightened of further abuse or retaliation. Using standard psychological methods for making assessments along with specialized domestic violence assessment techniques (Walker, 1994) provides assurance that the interviewer is getting the best information possible. See Table 5 for some of the more common assessment techniques.

It is crucial to clarify whether the assessment is being used for treatment planning or forensic evaluations. There is much more latitude in the former—the client's credibility can be assessed over a period of time—than in the latter, where the courts need a reasonable degree of psychological certainty that evidence presented is based on sound clinical inference and admissible facts. For example, it is

[2]Daniel Sonkin can be found at: http://www.member.dsonkin@aol.com.

important to know how well the client observes emotionally laden as well as everyday events and can report them. If her perceptual and cognitive skills are less accurate when emotional stimuli are present, then some of her reporting may be compromised. On the other hand, battered women often do report details of incidents, some of which may not be important to those who are not familiar with the interpersonal dynamics of a battering relationship. Battered women often talk about details peripheral to the recalled assault as a way to dampen their rising emotional responses. Knowing the psychodynamics of battering victims can help determine credibility, a most important element in forensic cases. Walker's descriptions of battered women (1979, 1984, 1989) and Meloy's (1992) descriptions of stalkers' borderline reality testing and abnormal attachments also help clarify credibility of reports that usually do not have witnesses. Melton, Petrila, Poythress, and Slobogin (1997) provide an excellent resource for forensic examinations.

CONCLUSIONS

It is clear from the anecdotal and clinical reports of battered women that far more batterers than are known to the justice system follow, harass, surveil, and frighten their partners or ex-partners, engaging in what functionally can be called stalking. While some of these stalking behaviors will meet threshold criteria (provable elements, see Saunders, Chapter 2) for criminal stalking, others are more likely designed to psychologically control the victim and may not be prosecutable. It is important for us to look more closely at the relationships between all forms of domestic violence, stalking, and batterers' typologies, so that we can better understand how to predict which women are more likely to be seriously assaulted or killed by batterers who will not leave them alone. Such research has yet to be done (Kurt, 1995).

The *obsessional* aspect of batterers who begin their stalking during the relationship and continue it even after the women make it clear that they want the relationship to end may be a key to prediction and risk management. Battered women must also be helped to respect their own sensitivity to cues of danger, especially when dealing with a batterer who does stalk them. Consistent responses on the part of the woman toward the man may help break some of the obsessional ties to her, although the research on stalking behaviors in nondomestic situations suggests that the internal psychological dynamics for the man are far more important than the external reward system (Meloy, 1996). Domestic violence is not one act of violence, but a pattern of physical, sexual, and psychological abuse that causes fear in its victims so that they give up their power to the abuser (APA, 1996). Stalking behaviors are an important prelude and means to such control. Battered women and their families need to be reempowered to become survivors, and that often means cutting off all contact so they are protected from further abuse.

Stopping domestic violence stalking will take creative community solutions that help batterers to understand the consequences of their acts.

ACKNOWLEDGMENTS

Dr. Walker acknowledges appreciation to Daniel Sonkin and Michael Lindsay for their work together on the JurisMonitor project.

REFERENCES

American Psychological Association (1996). *APA presidential task force on violence and the family report*. Washington, DC: Author.

Barnett, O. W., & LaViolette, A. D. (1993). *It could happen to anyone: Why battered women stay*. Newbury Park, CA: Sage.

Beck, A. T. (1976). *Cognitive therapy and emotional disorders*. New York: Basic Books.

Browne, A. (1987). *When battered women kill*. New York: McMillan Free Press.

Browne, A. (1993). Violence against women by male partners. *Am Psychologist, 48*, 1077–1087.

Browne, A., & Williams, K. (1989). Resource availability for women at risk and partner homicide. *Law and Society Review, 23*, 75–94.

Campbell, J. C. (Ed.) (1995). *Assessing dangerousness: Violence by sexual offenders, batterers, and child abusers*. Newbury Park, CA: Sage.

Cooper, M., & Eaves, D. (1996). Suicide following homicide in the family. *Violence and Victims, 11*, 99–112.

Dunford, F., Huizinga, D., & Elliot, D. (1990). The role of arrest in domestic assault: The Omaha Police experiment. *Criminology, 28*, 183–206.

Dutton, D. (with Golant, S. K.) (1995). *The batterer: A psychological profile*. New York: Basic Books.

Dutton, D. G., & Starzomski, A. J. (1993). Borderline personality in perpetrators of psychological and physical abuse. *Violence and Victims, 8*, 327–337.

Dutton, M. A. (1992). *Healing the trauma of woman battering: Assessment and intervention*. New York: Springer.

Dutton (Douglas), M. A., & Walker, L. E. A. (Eds.) (1988). *Feminist psychotherapies: An integration of psychological and feminist systems*. Norwood, NJ: Ablex.

Edwards, S. M. (1989). *Policing domestic violence: Women, the law and the state*. England: Sage.

Ewing, C. (1987). *Battered women who kill*. New York: Lexington.

Fagan, J., Stewart, D., & Hansen, K. (1983). Violent men or violent husbands? Background factors and situational correlates. In D. Finkelhor, R. Gelles, G. Hotaling, & M. Straus (Eds.), *The dark side of families: Current family violence research*. Beverly Hills, CA: Sage.

Feltous, A., & Hempel, T. (1995). Combined homicides–suicides: A review. *Journal of Forensic Sciences, 40*, 846–857.

Figley, C. R. (Ed.). (1997). *Compassion fatigue: Coping with secondary traumatic stress disorder in those who treat the traumatized*. New York: Brunner/Mazel.

Geffner, R. (1997). Family violence: Current issues, interventions, and research. *Journal of Aggression, Maltreatment, & Trauma, 1*, 1–25.

Geffner, R. (with Mantooth, C.). (in press). *Ending spouse/partner abuse: A psychoeducational approach for individuals and couples*. New York: Springer.

Geffner, R., Barrett, M. J., & Rossman, B. B. (1995). Domestic violence and sexual abuse: Multiple systems perspectives. In R. H. Mikesell, D. D. Lusterman, & S. H. McDaniel (Eds.), *Integrating family therapy: Handbook of family psychology and systems theory* (pp. 501–517). Washington, DC: American Psychological Association.

Gelles, R. J., & Straus, M. (1988). *Intimate violence: The causes and consequences of violence in the American family.* New York: Simon & Schuster.

Goodman, G. S., & Rosenberg, M. S. (1987). The child witness to family violence: Clinical and legal considerations. In D. J. Sonkin (Ed.), *Domestic violence on trial: Psychological and legal dimensions of family violence* (pp. 97–126). New York: Springer.

Gottman, J. M., Jacobson, N. S., Rushe, R. H., Wu Short, J., Babcock, J., La Taillade, J. J., & Waltz, J. (1996). *Journal of Family Psychology, 9.*

Hamberger, L. K., & Hastings, J. E. (1986). Personality correlates of men who abuse their partners: A cross-validation study. *Journal of Family Violence, 1,* 323–341.

Hansen, M., & Harway, M. (Eds.). (1993). *Battering and family therapy: A feminist perspective.* Newbury Park: Sage.

Hare, R. D. (1991). *Manual for the psychopathy checklist (revised).* Toronto: Multihealth Systems.

Harrell, A. (1991). *Evaluation of court-ordered treatment for domestic violence offenders.* Washington, DC: The Urban Institute.

Hart, B. (1988). Beyond the "duty to warn": A therapists' "duty to protect" battered women and children. In K. A. Yllo & M. Bograd (Eds.), *Feminist perspectives on wife abuse* (pp. 234–248). Newbury Park, CA: Sage.

Heise, L. (with Pitanguy, J., & Germain, A.). (1994). *Violence against women: The hidden health burden* (World Bank Discussion Paper 255). Washington DC: The World Bank.

Holtzworth-Monroe, A., & Stuart, G. L. (1994). Typologies of male batterers: Three subtypes and the differences among them. *Psychological Bulletin, 116,* 476–497.

Hotaling, G. T., & Sugarman, D. B. (1986). An analysis of risk markers in husband to wife violence: The current state of knowledge. *Violence and Victims, 1,* 101–124.

Jones, A. (1981). *Women who kill.* New York: Fawcett.

Jones, A. (1994). *Next time, she'll be dead: Battering and how to stop it.* Boston: Beacon Press.

Koss, M. P., Goodman, L. A., Browne, A., Fitzgerald, L. F., Keita, G. P., & Russo, N. (1994). *No safe haven: Male violence against women at home, at work, and in the community.* Washington, DC: American Psychological Association.

Kurt, J. L. (1995). Stalking as a variant of domestic violence. *Bulletin of the American Academy of Psychiatry and the Law, 23,* 219–230.

Lindsay, M., McBride, R., Platt, C. (1992). *AMEND: Philosophy and curriculum for treating batterers.* Denver, CO: McBride.

Liss, M., & Stahly, G. (1993). Domestic violence and child custody. In M. Hansen & M. Harway (Eds.), *Recovering from battering: Family therapy and feminism* (pp. 175–187). Newbury Park, CA: Sage.

Marzuk, P., Tardiff, K., & Hirsch, C. (1992). The epidemiology of murder–suicide. *Journal of the American Medical Association, 267,* 3179–3183.

Meloy, J. R. (1988). *The psychopathic mind.* Northvale, NJ: Aronson.

Meloy, J. R. (1989). Unrequited love and the wish to kill: Diagnosis and treatment of borderline erotomania. *Bulletin of the Menninger Clinic, 53,* 477–492.

Meloy, J. R. (1992). *Violent attachments,* Northvale, NJ: Jason Aronson.

Meloy, J. R. (1995). Antisocial personality disorder. In G. Gabbard (Ed.), *Treatments of psychiatric disorders* (2nd ed., Vol. 2, pp. 2273–2290). Washington, DC: American Psychiatric Press.

Meloy, J. R. (1996). Stalking (obsessional following): A review of some preliminary studies. *Aggression and Violent Behavior, 1,* 147–162.

Meloy, J. R. (1997a). Predatory violence during mass murder. *Journal of Forensic Sciences, 42,* 326–329.

Meloy, J. R. (1997b). The clinical risk management of stalking: "Someone is watching over me . . ." *American Journal of Psychotherapy, 51,* 174–184.

Meloy, J. R., Cowett, P. Y., Parker, S., Hofland, B., & Friedland, A. (in press). Domestic protection orders and the prediction of criminality and violence toward protectees. *Psychotherapy.*

Melton, G., Petrila, J., Poythress, N., & Slobogin, C. (1997). *Psychological evaluations for the courts* (2nd ed.). New York: Guilford Press.

National Crime Victim Survey (1995). Washington, DC: National Institute of Justice.

O'Leary, K. D. (1993). Through a psychological lens: Personality traits, personality disorders, and levels of violence. In R. J. Gelles & D. R. Loeske (Eds.), *Current controversies on family violence* (pp. 7–30), Newbury Park, CA: Sage.

Pence, E., & Paymar, M. (1993). *Working with men who batter: The Duluth model.* New York: Springer.

Rosewater, L. B., & Walker, L. E. (Eds.) (1985). *Handbook on feminist therapy: Psychotherapy for women.* New York: Springer.

Saunders, D. G. (1992). A typology of men who batter women: Three types derived from cluster analysis. *American Orthopsychiatry, 62,* 264–275.

Schechter, S. (1982). *Women and marital violence: The visions and struggles of the battered women's movement.* Boston: South End.

Schneider, E. M. (1986). Describing and changing: Women's self-defense work and the problem of expert testimony on battering. *Women's Rights Law Reporter, 9*(3–4), 195–222.

Sherman, L. W., & Berk, R. A. (1984). The specific deterrent effects of arrest for domestic assault. *American Sociological Review, 49,* 261–271.

Sonkin, D. J. (1997). *Domestic violence: The perpetrator assessment handbook.* (Available from Daniel J. Sonkin, Ph.D., 1505 Bridgeway, Suite 105, Sausalito, CA 94965; E-mail: dsonkin@aol.com.)

Sonkin, D., & Durphy, M. (1982). *Learning to live without violence: A book for men.* San Francisco: Volcano Press.

Sonkin, D., Martin, D., & Walker, L. E. (1994). *The male batterer.* New York: Springer.

Straus, M. A. (1993). Physical assaults by wives: A major social problem. In R. J. Gelles & D. R. Loeske (Eds.), *Current controversies on family violence* (pp. 67–87). Newbury Park, CA: Sage.

Straus, M. A., & Gelles, R. J. (1988). How violent are American families? Estimates from the National Family Violence Resurvey and other studies. In G. T. Hotaling, D. Finkelhor, J. T. Kirkpatrick, & M. A. Straus (Eds.), *Family abuse and its consequences* (pp. 14–36). Newbury Park, CA: Sage.

Straus, M., Gelles, R., & Steinmetz, S. (1980). *Behind closed doors: Violence in America.* New York: Doubleday.

Walker, L. E. (1979). *The battered woman.* New York: Harper & Row.

Walker, L. E. A. (1984). *Battered woman syndrome.* New York: Springer.

Walker, L. E. A. (1989). *Terrifying love: Why battered women kill and how society responds.* New York: Harper & Row.

Walker, L. E. A. (1994). *Abused women and survivor therapy: A practical guide for the psychotherapist.* Washington, DC: American Psychological Association.

Walker, L. E. A. (1996). Assessment of abusive spousal relationships. In F. Kaslow (Ed.). *Handbook of relational diagnosis* (pp. 338–356). New York: Wiley.

Walker, L.E.A. (in press). Domestic violence around the world: Introduction to the international psychology section on domestic violence. *American Psychologist.*

Walker, L. E. A., & Sonkin, D. J. (1995). *JurisMonitior stabilization and empowerment programs.* Denver, CO: Endolor Communications.

Yllo, K. A. (1993). Through a feminist lens: Gender, power, and violence. In R. J. Gelles & D. R. Loeske (Eds.), *Current controversies on family violence* (pp. 47–62). Newbury Park, CA: Sage.

Zona, M., Sharma, K., & Lane, J. (1993). A comparative study of erotomanic and obsessional subjects in a forensic sample. *Journal of Forensic Sciences, 38,* 894–903.

CHAPTER 8

The Stalking of Clinicians by Their Patients

John R. Lion, M.D. and Jeremy A. Herschler, M.D.

This chapter reflects our knowledge of and involvement with several dozen cases in which patients (or their relatives) have formed pathologic attachments to clinicians. By pathologic attachment, we mean conduct that transcends the usual terms of treatment wherein the patient tacitly understands the limitations of a professional relationship: that is, the office visit is limited to the scheduled hour, phone calls are for emergencies, and there is no outside contact. When such boundaries are not adhered to, the patient begins to excessively phone the therapist at work and at home, converses with other family members, sends inappropriate letters or other articles, makes unscheduled visits to the office, and eventually follows the therapist to his home or maintains a presence in his neighborhood. These behaviors culminate in written or verbal threats made by mail, hand–delivered notes, or messages left on telephone answering machines. Unlike erotomanic stalking, which is characterized by a delusional belief that the perpetrator is loved by his or her victim, patients who stalk clinicians typically do so because they feel misunderstood, wronged, or mistreated. In the case of mental health providers, stalking may reflect one facet of an intolerable love/hate ambivalence with which the patient struggles. For other clinicians, such as those in the medical specialties of surgery or obstetrics, stalking may be the direct result of an undesired or dissatisfying outcome such as a bad cosmetic repair or a failure on the doctor's part to heal a spouse or child. Plastic surgeons have long known that patients with unreasonable expectations might react to any operative outcome with extreme anger.

The Psychology of Stalking: Clinical and Forensic Perspectives

Those clinicians who contacted us were either actively treating the stalking patient or had in the past treated the stalker. Years, even decades, might have passed since patient and clinician had contact with one another. In these cases, it became apparent that the patient was still somehow bound to his caretaker in memory or fantasy. This conscious or unconscious bond was a surprising aspect of the stalking, for the clinician was usually quite unaware of it. But we encountered other instances in which the clinician underestimated the severity of an ongoing therapeutic enmeshment. For example, some clinicians who treated patients with borderline illness found themselves the focus of an idealization that was stronger and more brittle than they initially thought. This idealization was somehow not sufficiently explored and when it ultimately became shattered, the patient manifested the rage of disappointment. Other therapists who overlooked the powerful intimacy evoked by therapy found themselves in the role of someone who once abused or abandoned the patient. In the intensive psychotherapeutic treatment of patients with dissociative identity disorder or multiple personality disorder, certain clinicians discovered themselves the object of violence by a specific alter. We have referred to the pathologic emotions evoked by treatment as a *deranged transference* and comment further on this phenomenon below.

Although a variety of workers have studied stalking behavior (Dietz et al., 1991; Harmon et al., 1995; Kurt, 1995; Meloy, 1989; Miller, 1985), the incidence of stalking against the medical profession is largely unknown. Two studies shed some light on the subject. Miller (1985), surveying harassment of forensic psychiatrists, found that 55% of 480 clinicians reported having been physically threatened, 14% actually attacked. More recently, Buckley and Resnick (1994) surveyed clinicians attending a March 1994 annual meeting of the Oregon Psychiatric Society. In their study, stalking was defined as "intentionally, knowingly, or recklessly alarming or coercing another person by engaging in repeated and unwanted contact with the other person." Of 90 questionnaires returned by members, 26 indicated that they had experienced persons stalking them by coming into visual or physical contact with them. Another 24 indicated that they had experienced persons waiting outside their place of business or their home, and 13 related incidents wherein they had incurred damage to their home, property, or workplace. More noteworthy, however, were some data showing several clinicians to have been stalked multiple times. This raises the question of whether there exist certain clinicians who may be more prone to incur threats and stalking, either by virtue of the patients they chose to treat or their own personalities and behavior. Brown and co-workers (1996) are attempting to look at repeated threats and assaults on clinicians in order to understand this phenomenon.

Both Miller's study and that of the Oregon group suggest a high level of stalking in clinical practice. It is our general impression that dangerous stalking behavior is rare, though many clinicians have encountered inappropriate curiosities on the part of disturbed patients they have treated; for instance, a patient drives by their home or waits outside their office. But these behaviors do not typically escalate into something of a threatening nature. We divide stalking behavior into short term—weeks or months—and that which is more chronic and years in duration. Some stalking involves physical danger to the clinician/victim, while other forms of stalking appear to be more benign and involve peripheral and intermittent contact on the part of the patient/perpetrator; that is, the stalker is seen once every few months, or disappears for years, or shows himself on the anniversary of, say, termination from therapy. The following case examples depict different forms of stalking. Certain features of the cases are altered for purposes of confidentiality.

CASE EXAMPLE 1

A hospital-based psychologist called to discuss an outpatient who had left inappropriate remarks on her answering machine. The patient was a young man with temper proneness whom she had been seeing for 6 months. He had antisocial and paranoid personality traits and a substance abuse problem as well; during the phone calls, he sounded intoxicated. He spoke of "coming after her" and warned her to "be careful." Next, he came to the ward unannounced and demanded to see her. It was at this point that the therapist phoned for assistance.

In previous writings, Lion (1995) has discussed the problem of denial in dealing with dangerousness, and this example illustrates the process. By the time the psychologist asked for consultation, months had elapsed. Yet even when advised to terminate with the patient, she was reluctant to do so. Denial plays a pivotal role in rationalizing threatening behavior as the therapist thinks that "this will stop by itself" or "the patient is sick" or "you have to expect this sort of thing with these kinds of patients." Obvious questions are raised about the psychodynamics of the therapist's continued engagement with this disturbed man. Often, therapeutic zeal—in the face of danger—is difficult to address without an exploration tantamount to psychotherapy, but such inquiry may be needed to break the cycle. For example, an underlying dynamic may relate to the therapist's need to rescue the patient, much as he or she did as a child in dealing with an alcoholic father.

Fear of confronting the threatener and stalker is very common. Clinicians often declare that they are frightened of exacerbating threats by reporting them to the police. This phenomenon is seen in domestic abuse as well. In our experience, confrontation—and even counter threats—are important responses to what otherwise is an uncontrolled situation in which the patient has the upper hand. For example, the clinician who receives a threat or has a former patient stalk him or her should warn the patient to cease and desist and consider formally notifying the patient (via an attorney) in writing that legal action will be taken if stalking continues. There should be no illusions, however, that this is a simple matter. A formal warning is but the first step in a process that requires legal assistance and the cooperation of law enforcement officials. Patients who stalk have transcended a large psychological barrier, and simple exhortations to stop will not be easily heeded. In some situations, the patient may incorporate the injunction into his existing perception of the clinician as "mean" or "uncaring." Even family members may be brought into the picture and join the patient in seeing the clinician as harassing; thus one of us (J.R.L.) is aware of a case in which a patient's parents, when confronted with their son's stalking behavior, accused the therapist of homosexually molesting their son. Nevertheless, the clinician must be diligent and forceful. Limit-setting is the key to deterrence and resolution. Threats escalate in the absence of confrontation; after all, a threat begs attention. If the clinician ignores the threat, the patient will cry louder to be heard (Lion, 1995).

CASE EXAMPLE 2

A male psychiatry resident-in-training agreed to take on in treatment a 39-year-old borderline woman prone to alcohol abuse and self-mutilation. Within the hospital, she had engaged in much splitting, pitting staff against the resident whom she idealized. Once an outpatient, she began calling the resident at home in an intoxicated state and also reached his fiancee who became most alarmed by the calls. Long messages were left on the resident's answering machine during which she continued to idealize the therapist. Next, a note of "thanks" was left at the front door of the resident's home, and the patient left house plants at a neighbor's house. Next, she began sending letters and photographs of herself. The resident maintained a stance of acceptance of these behaviors until such time as his patience gave way to anger. Expressing this anger to his supervisor, he was encouraged to tell the patient that he would notify the police if she continued to harass him. She ultimately required hospitalization at which point treatment with the resident was terminated and the behavior ceased.

This case illustrates the dangers of idealization in characterologically primitive patients. Of interest is the extension of the patient's attachment from the clinician to his fiancee, and to at least one neighbor. The fiancee began listening to the tapes of the patient, reading the mail she sent, and studying the photographs. Patients who stalk therapists do not set about to create this complexity, but the effects of stalking clearly extend far beyond the therapist alone. Jealousy may be evoked in spouses or intimate partners, and alarm might spread to the entire family as concerns for safety amount. The above case also illustrates the problem of excessive tolerance for disturbed behavior. Residents are not the only clinicians who can erroneously condone behavior that should be challenged. Indeed, we have seen seasoned clinicians endure harassing behaviors that should otherwise be grounds for termination of therapy.

CASE EXAMPLE 3

This case highlights the complexities of confrontation and prosecution: A psychiatrist took on in treatment a borderline patient with a history of sexual abuse and intermittent suicidal ideation. Because of uncontrolled drinking and other noncompliant behavior, the psychiatrist terminated treatment. Subsequently, he received a package without any return address. It contained a blurred Polaroid photograph of his house. Another envelope contained a montage of pictures that must have been taken from the backyard of a nearby house. Other articles arrived in the mail, including candles. Next, some lighter fluid was poured on the carpet in the hallway outside the therapist's office. A month later, a dead bird was placed outside the office. The psychiatrist was sure that all these acts were carried out by his ex-patient, but proof was lacking and legal action could not easily be taken.

In this case, photographs blatantly proved that the stalker had access to the clinician's house, while candles, lighter fluid, and a dead bird were obvious symbols of rage. The themes of intimacy and fury were thus intertwined. But this case also highlights the complications of prosecution. In the absence of definitive evidence, confrontations may be limited to acting on a "hunch." The psychiatrist in this case was virtually certain that his former patient was responsible for the threats, but his attorney also viewed formal action as unwise in the absence of proof. One possible course of action in such cases is to speak with the patient and present to him or her one's suspicions, indicating that police will be informed about any further act of stalking. Such a confrontation must be skillfully done, for there are obvious hazards. Contact with a former patient may again activate the relationship, and the stalker may react to perceived harassment with intensified behavior. Still, to do nothing at all in the face of ongoing threats can be a license for more threats; a "counter threat" signals to the stalker that the behavior has at least been noticed and is viewed as unacceptable. As each case of stalking behavior is unique, the best a clinician/victim can do is to assemble as much forensic consultation as possible. It has been our experience in this regard that traditional psychotherapists may not have the requisite experience to serve as advisors. What is more needed are experts in the forensic and law enforcement arena who know the judicial system and can help the therapist/victim deal with those clinical and administrative strategies applicable to criminal populations. In short, it requires a different mind set to deal with stalking.

Prosecution of stalkers remains problematic (Dietz, 1984; Kurt, 1995). In most states, violation of anti-stalking laws is only a misdemeanor. As of this writing, federal statutes making such behavior a felony have just been passed. Clinicians may chose to bring charges of stalking, harassment, or assault, depending on the evidence they have at hand (a good reason to keep answering machine tapes as documentation). A restraining order may be another option. Good legal consultation is crucial. The following case illustrates this further.

CASE EXAMPLE 4

A 40-year-old female psychiatrist and single parent practicing in a large, academic teaching hospital agreed to treat a 20-year-old who had a borderline personality disorder. As treatment progressed, the patient decompensated and became more paranoid. He called colleagues of the therapist and accused her of having sex with him. Then, he began leaving threatening messages on the therapist's answering machine. These threats escalated to the point that he stated he would kill her and firebomb her 3-year-old son. He began to follow her car as she drove home from the hospital. The therapist considered commitment, but realized that this would be limited in duration; under state statute, a longer commitment of 6 months was possible if initiated by the hospital, but the hospital attorney was very bureaucratic and was not helpful. The therapist moved her office, installed panic alarms, changed automobiles, and ultimately moved her residence as well.

In this distressing case, the primary advice given the clinician/victim was to hire her own attorney to force the hospital to intervene. A private attorney can be of great assistance in the advocacy of the situation, such as dealing with the police, and assist in resolution of the tremendous helplessness that inevitably accompanies the drama. But the choice of attorney is important. Civil-rights-minded lawyers may equivocate in vigorously pursuing a restraining order or making demands on the police or institution for adequate investigation and protection. A criminal lawyer or labor attorney is often more suited for the task. In this case, the victim secured her own lawyer who pressed the hospital into taking out a petition for commitment of the patient. Subsequently, the threats ceased entirely.

CASE EXAMPLE 5

This case illustrates the problem of telephone harassment. It is our impression that patients who physically stalk their clinicians do not use the phone, and vice versa.

A 50-year-old psychiatrist began receiving numerous harassing telephone calls during which a male voice shrieked and repeatedly called him a "son of a bitch." The voice then said "I'm gonna kill you." The clinician was completely mystified by the identity of this voice and eventually had the telephone company track the call to a distant trailer park in which resided a schizophrenic man who, 20 years earlier, had been the psychiatrist's patient. When examined, the patient stated that he had stopped his antipsychotic medications and was smoking marijuana. He also indicated that he had been embarrassed by the clinician's exploration of his sexuality those many years ago, and harbored the anger over this lengthy period. Now, psychotic and delusional, the rage surfaced. Charges of telephone abuse were pressed by the clinician. The patient went to trial, was placed on probation, and was ordered by the court to seek treatment. No further threats ensued.

When we initially began to review threats on the lives of clinicians, we believed that such threats occurred only within the context of ongoing therapy. Clearly, this case shows that old encounters may still resonate in the minds of certain patients. How long a pathological attachment typically lasts is not known. In some cases we have seen, the attachment continues as long as the patient and therapist have a relationship and stops when therapy is halted; indeed, there is reason to halt treatment with a patient who transgresses the boundaries of therapy. When and how the clinician interprets behavior as a transgression warranting termination is a subjective matter, and collegial consultation might be useful, for the decision has medicolegal abandonment implications. Transferring such cases may be difficult, as any prospective clinician may well be leery of accepting a patient who has already stalked the previous clinician. Hospitalization may be required to defuse matters. Assignment of the patient to a hospital-based clinician or group of clinicians (to dilute the transference) may be an alternative.

CASE EXAMPLE 6

This case reveals the scope of stalking behavior and the impact it can have on a clinician's professional life: A child psychiatrist treated a patient with dissociative identity disorder who had been physically and sexually abused. The therapy was characterized by initial idealization of the therapist on the part of the patient, but anger erupted when the therapist refused to complete a disability form. Subsequently, the therapist noted mail missing and found her office broken into. Next, dead squirrels with hearts excised were left at the office. Her house was then broken into and several neighbors' cars had their tires slashed. Additionally, a fire was set in the basement of her office. The patient was ultimately arrested but immediately released. Detectives were hired and cameras installed, but the patient— now out of treatment—was never visualized. Some 7 years later, the stalking continued on a sporadic basis.

There is an enormous burden in dealing with stalking, in terms of both emotions and finance. For most clinicians, the sudden awareness of danger is quite overwhelming and leads to panic and despair; after all, they have chosen a highly cognitive profession and one that would appear to be far removed from concerns about safety issues. The doctor in this case had great difficulty seeing the other patients in her practice, and eventually took some time off to deal with the logistics of protection and her own anxiety. While private security is routinely hired by movie stars and other public figures who are the targets of stalkers, the fees quickly become prohibitive for the average clinician in practice. We have seen several clinicians install security devices in their homes and offices. At a minimum, this would include a panic alarm wired to a security firm or the police. In one case, the acquisition of a gun, coupled with practice sessions at a local pistol range, was sufficient to mobilize the therapist's anger to the point that he took decisive action in successfully prosecuting the stalking patient. Previously, he had used much denial and reacted to danger by assuming a passive, helpless role.

CASE EXAMPLE 7

This case is an extreme example of stalking: A young psychiatrist treated the wife of a gambler with suspected underworld connections. The woman was diagnosed with a borderline personality disorder. Therapy proceeded uneventfully until such time as the psychiatrist went on summer holiday with his wife and noted the patient at the same beach resort. In treatment, the patient stated that she loved the therapist, and no one else should. The therapist perceived this as a manifestation of the transference, and increased the frequency of therapy in an attempt to resolve matters. But the patient eschewed any interpretations, insisting that the clinician should love her. As he refused, the patient became angry and threatened violence. Leaving the parking lot one night, the therapist was assaulted by an unknown youth who beat him; he sustained a rib fracture. Next an explosive device was found in the therapist's garage. Police suspected the patient, but the absence of any evidence made an arrest impossible. The therapist, deeply fearful for his life, moved his entire family to another city.

This case raises many concerns. Stalking evolves out of the panoply of thoughts and fantasies that reflect a deranged transference. In many instances, the development of this derangement is heralded by dreams or conscious thoughts about therapy and about the therapist. Some of these feelings and thoughts are accessible to the clinician. It was unclear in the above case whether the therapist monitored the transference as it emerged, or possibly dismissed early warning signs. Therapists must keep a finely tuned ear to seemingly innocuous remarks, jokes, playful acts, or any other products of imagination, desire, anger, or even hatred. It was also unclear to the consultant (J.R.L.) whether the clinician in this case erred by intensifying his contact with the patient, thus possibly worsening the disturbed relationship.

CASE EXAMPLE 8

The susceptibility of surgical specialists to stalking has already been mentioned. Plastic surgeons bear a special risk by virtue of the intense expectations fueled by the procedures they undertake to correct: beauty, desirability, social acceptance, even love. These wishes can easily be crushed, as illustrated by this case.

A 40-year-old plastic surgeon operated on a 60-year-old woman who wanted a face lift. The patient was an unhappy person who had saved money for this operation, and she underwent a blepharoplasty and chin repair without incident. Some months after surgery, she began to experience pain and hair loss. She made unscheduled visits to the surgeon's private clinic and spent hours in the waiting room. The surgeon became dismayed by the patient and contacted his malpractice carrier, sensing that her unhappiness might translate into a lawsuit. He also urged psychiatric treatment for the patient, but was not successful. The patient demanded the repair of her surgery, and the doctor was ambivalent. The patient secretly purchased a handgun. A month later, she hid in the surgeon's office at the end of the day, killed him, and then went home and killed herself with the same weapon. She left a note which blamed him for the pain she had endured ("Patient blamed," 1991).

This frightening example illustrates the complexity of choosing which patient to operate on, and how to select those who have deviant expectations of surgery (Goin & Goin, 1981). Some plastic surgeons will not perform an elective rhinoplasty on any male over 40, sensing that such a patient will most likely be critical of any outcome. Plastic surgeons will sometimes psychologically screen patients by referring them for evaluation. The point, however, is to anticipate who might become problematic. Psychiatrists and mental health workers need to adopt the same posture of caution in, say, working with deprived and abused populations who are at risk for developing a pathologic attachment based on deep-seated neediness and loneliness. Some patients ought to be seen in public places, not in private offices during evenings and weekends. And certain patients may need to be discharged as the clinician senses events swirling out of control. The following case is relevant to this point.

CASE EXAMPLE 9

A psychiatrist who treated a schizophrenic woman was subject to criticism by the patient's husband. The patient eventually developed dyskinesia, and the husband sued the doctor. The case was settled out of court. But the husband continued to have sporadic contact with the clinician. He wrote to the director of the hospital in which the psychiatrist practiced and asked for a joint meeting to protest the doctor's malpractice. He also asked to meet alone with the psychiatrist. In each case, the latter refused. Ultimately, the husband came to the office to talk with the doctor. The doctor still insisted that he had nothing to say to the man, whereupon the latter produced a revolver. The psychiatrist physically subdued the husband, and during the violent struggle that followed, strangled his assailant. No criminal charges were filed (Seeds, 1991).

This case raises obvious questions about the strategy of ignoring a potential stalker's repeated request for contact. Perhaps a refereed meeting might have spared the resulting deadly encounter, though once stalking escalates and becomes an obsessive preoccupation, discussion is most likely to be counterproductive. As repeatedly mentioned above, the clinician must intervene early and as soon as he senses any inappropriate attachment occurring. This case also draws attention to the rarer behavior of administrative harassment, whereby the patient serves to punish the clinician by making complaints to the state medical board or to the head of the hospital or medical school. The translation of anger into legal action might seem safer for the clinician, but it encumbers him with the need to defend himself and document his propriety with licensing agencies and malpractice carriers. The burdens here may be quite onerous.

SUMMARY

The following points are important for the recognition and management of stalking. First, the clinician should be attuned to early inappropriate behaviors that reflect a deranged transference. These inappropriate behaviors develop gradually over time, thus giving the clinician opportunity to intervene. Second, the clinician who encounters boundary violations should at least ponder the possibility of such violations escalating to the point of physical danger. And third, legal and forensic consultation should be sought early, preferably prior to an intervention, which should include a clear confrontation and statement of consequences.

REFERENCES

Brown, G. P., Dubin, W. R., Lion, J. R., Garry, L. J. (1996). Threats against clinicians: A preliminary descriptive classification. *Bulletin of the American Academy of Psychiatry and the Law, 24*(3), 367–376.

Buckley, R., & Resnick, M. (1994). *Stalking survey: Oregon Psychiatric Society, Portland, OR, March 4–5, 1994.* Unpublished manuscript.

Dietz, P. E. (1984). A remedial approach to harassment. *Virginia Low Review, 70,* 507.

Dietz, P. E., Matthews, D. B., Martell, D. A., Stewart, T., Hrouda, D. A., & Warren, J. (1991). Threatening and otherwise inappropriate letters to members of the United States Congress. *Journal of Forensic Sciences, 36,* 1445–1468.

Goin, J. M., & Goin, M. K. (1981). Psychological screening of the rhinoplasty patient. In *Changing the body: Psychological effects of plastic surgery* (pp. 137–144). Baltimore, MD: Williams & Wilkins.

Harmon, R. B., Rosner, R., & Owens, H. (1995). Obsessional harassment and erotomania in a criminal court population. *Journal of Forensic Sciences, 40*(2), 188–96.

Kurt, J. L. (1995). Stalking as a variant of domestic violence. *Bulletin of the American Academy of Psychiatry and the Law, 23*(2), 219–230.

Lion, J. R. (1995). Verbal threats against clinicians. In B. S. Eichelman and A. C. Hartwig (Eds.), *Patient violence and the clinician* (pp. 43–52). Washington, DC: American Psychiatric Press.

Meloy, J. R. (1989). Unrequited love and the wish to kill: Diagnosis and treatment of borderline erotomania. *Bulletin of the Menninger Clinic, 53,* 477–492.

Miller, R. (1985). The harassment of forensic psychiatrists outside of court. *Bulletin of the American Academy of Psychiatry and the Law, 13*(4), 337–343.

Patient blamed in plastic surgeon's death. (1991, April 17). *Seattle Post-Intelligence.*

Seeds, G. M. (1991, June). When a psychiatrist is assaulted in the line of work [Perspective and commentary]. *Clinical Psychiatry News.*

CHAPTER 9

Preventing Attacks on Public Officials and Public Figures:
A Secret Service Perspective

Robert A. Fein, Ph.D. and ASAIC Bryan Vossekuil

Assassination of political leaders and other public figures is a rare, but significant, problem in the United States. Since 1835, there have been 11 attacks on
U.S. presidents (four of them resulting in the death of the president). Since 1949,
there have been two attacks on presidential candidates, two attacks on members
of Congress, several assassinations of national political leaders, a number of attacks
on state and local elected officials, and more than two dozen instances in which
planned attacks on political leaders were intercepted before the attacker came
within lethal range of his or her target. In addition, there have been a number of
murders of federal and state judges and several well-publicized attacks on celebrities
and business leaders.

Acts of violence directed against public officials and public figures have
caused immeasurable harm to the political and social fabric of the nation and to
the basic ideal of a free and open society. Mention of the political murders of
President John F. Kennedy, the Reverend Martin Luther King, Jr., and Senator
(and presidential candidate) Robert Kennedy causes deep pain for most citizens.
More recent attacks on Governor (and presidential candidate) George Wallace,
President Gerald Ford, and President Ronald Reagan have heightened the public's
awareness of and concern about the potential for violent attacks on its political
leaders. The assassination of former Beatle John Lennon, the attack on actress
Theresa Saldana, and the murder of actress Rebecca Schaeffer, likewise, underscore
the vulnerability of public figures in society.

The United States Secret Service is the federal law enforcement agency
mandated to protect the president, the president's family, the vice president and

The Psychology of Stalking: Clinical and Forensic Perspectives

family, former presidents, visiting heads of states, candidates for president during a campaign year, nominees for president and vice president and their spouses, and certain other national leaders.

To aid in fulfillment of its protective responsibilities, the Secret Service has sponsored conferences of experts to investigate the phenomenon of assassination (Takeuchi, Solomon, & Menninger, 1981). The Secret Service has also conducted research related to assassination.

The Secret Service Exceptional Case Study Project (ECSP) is the latest such effort. The ECSP is a study of all persons in the United States known to have attacked, or approached to attack, a prominent public official or figure since 1949. The study has focused on the thinking and behavior of attackers and near-attackers in the days, weeks, and months before their assaults or near-lethal approaches. The ECSP is the first study of the known universe of recent American assassins and near-assassins.

This chapter reports on the Secret Service Exceptional Case Study Project. We describe three myths about American assassins and present data about assassins and near-assassins. We then offer some observations about assassination in America and present two case studies, one of a near-lethal approacher, the other of an attacker.

THE SECRET SERVICE EXCEPTIONAL CASE STUDY PROJECT

PURPOSES

The primary goal of the Exceptional Case Study Project is to gather information and develop knowledge that might aid law enforcement organizations to fulfill protective responsibilities for public officials and public figures.

There are two related components to protection. Protection encompasses a range of functions and services aimed at deterring or stopping an assault on a protected person. For example, uniformed and plainclothes security officers may maintain positions around a protected person. These protectors are prepared to stop an assailant and to shield the protectee from harm. This protection is obvious and observable.

The other aspect of protection is discreet and less visible. "Protective intelligence" seeks to prevent lethal access to a protectee. Protection is most effective if persons and groups with the intention and capacity to mount an attack on a protected person are identified and stopped before they come near a protectee.

Protective intelligence programs and systems, therefore, are designed to:

- solicit and gather information about persons who appear to have unusual or inappropriate interest in a protectee;

- investigate any such persons who have come to attention;
- evaluate the information gathered;
- assess whether a person or group poses a risk of violence to a protectee;
- manage the risk and thereby prevent an attack.

The Secret Service Exceptional Case Study Project was developed to generate knowledge useful to both physical protection and protective intelligence functions. The study was designed to be operational. The ECSP has focused on gathering and analyzing information that law enforcement officials can or could gather during the course of investigations.

Previous assassination studies either examined the demographic and psychological characteristics of a relatively few assassins or studied persons who made threats but never came close to mounting an attack. The Secret Service Exceptional Case Study Project has been a departure from this mode. Unlike studies about threateners, the subject group of the ECSP is *persons who have acted in lethal or near-lethal ways*. Unlike most studies of assassins, the ECSP focuses on the *thoughts and behaviors* of study subjects before their attacks and near-attacks, not on demographic characteristics or clinical status.

POPULATION

Assassination of a prominent person of public status is a discrete form of targeted violence, in which a potential assailant identifies, then attempts to harm a particular target (or targets) (Fein, Vossekuil, & Holden, 1995). Experience and information suggest that many public official assailants and threateners focus their interests on the *office* and its prominence (and its current holder), rather than on a particular individual as a target. In addition, many of the persons who are evaluated as presenting the greatest risk of directing violence toward a public official or figure have had interests in *more than one* public official or public figure.

It was decided to study persons who had selected public officials *or* public figures as targets. Selection of this subject population would permit analysis of whether subjects who selected public officials as targets also considered public figures (and vice versa) and would increase the number of persons in the study.

The population to be studied in the ECSP was defined as all people known to have attacked, or approached to attack, a prominent person of public status in the United States since 1949. This definition was chosen for these reasons:

- The study was designed to provide useful information for law enforcement organizations with responsibilities for protection of public officials and public figures.
- Cases were known in which subjects had been apprehended near or approaching public officials and public figures, with weapons, with the apparent intention of attacking.

- Attacks and assassinations of prominent persons of public status are rare.[1] It was decided to include people who had *approached* prominent persons of public status *with lethal means* (weapons) with the apparent intent to attack. Including people who approached with weapons increased the total number of subjects while maintaining the study's focus on behavior that could result in lethal attack.

While subjects who made an approach with weapons and also made threats were included in the study, people who made threats *without* making approaches with weapons did not qualify for inclusion. Similarly, people who traveled to visit or who approached prominent persons of public status, and who did not have weapons with them, were not included.

"Prominent persons of public status" were defined as:

- persons protected by the Secret Service (the president, the vice president, their families, former presidents, candidates for president, visiting heads of states);
- other major federal officials and office holders (cabinet secretaries, members of Congress, federal judges);
- important state and local public officials (governors, mayors of large cities);
- celebrities, such as sports figures, and movie, television, radio, and entertainment notables;
- presidents and chief executives of major corporations.

The "principal incident" was defined as the most violent of the following types of acts:

- assassination of a prominent person of public status;
- attack on a prominent person of public status;
- approach to a prominent person of public status with a lethal weapon.

The time frame, 1949 to the present, was chosen because the first major public figure and public official attacks after World War II occurred in 1949 and 1950. In 1949 Ruth Ann Steinhagen stalked and shot Philadelphia Phillies first baseman Eddie Waitkus. In 1950 Oscar Collazo and Griselio Torresola attempted to assassinate President Truman at Blair House, across the street from the White House.

Once the population of the study was defined, efforts were made to search for cases that met study inclusion criteria. These efforts included:

- review of books, articles, studies, and media accounts about assassinations, attacks, and near-lethal approaches;
- review of Secret Service files;

---

[1] Since 1949 there have been 34 known assassinations or attacks in the United States in which the target was a prominent person of public status.

- consultation with experts knowledgeable about public official and public figure protection;
- requests to selected federal and state law enforcement agencies for cases that might meet study inclusion criteria.

Eighty-three subjects were identified. These subjects comprise the universe of persons known to have attacked, or to have come close to attacking, a prominent public official or figure in the United States from 1949 to 1996.

DATA COLLECTION

The study plan involved two kinds of data collection and review. First, all available archival information about each subject was gathered and coded. This record review enabled aggregate analysis of information about all subjects in the study. Second, interviews were conducted with living subjects. Interviews permitted in-depth exploration of the subject's ideas, motives, behaviors, and activities in the days and weeks before the attack or near-lethal approach.

Archival Information

Three categories of information were determined to be of primary importance:

- *Information about the principal incident* (PI) that brought the subject into the study. Information about the PI included a description of the event, the subject's apparent motives, the subject's behaviors immediately before the event, injuries or deaths caused by the PI, legal consequences to the subject, and results of mental health evaluations or contact precipitated by the event.
- *Demographic and descriptive data about the subject* at the time of the principal incident. In addition to variables like age, gender, level of education, and employment status, information was gathered and coded about each subject's criminal history, history of contact with mental health professionals and institutions, history of involvement with fraternal, religious, political, professional, and other organizations, history of weapons use, travel history, interest in assassination, violence history, and history of harassment of others.
- *Information about "attack-related" behaviors* other than those exhibited in the principal incident. These behaviors included:
  - sustained interest and consideration of harm of any public official or figure (including the target of the PI);
  - communications to or about any public official or public figure (including direct or indirect threats);

- visits to homes, offices, or temporary sites visited by public officials or figures;
- approaches to contact public officials or public figures;
- following/stalking behaviors directed toward public officials or figures;
- previous attacks on public officials or public figures.

Once key study variables were identified and defined, a codebook that permitted orderly capture of archival information about each subject was written. The codebook contained more than 700 variables. It was piloted, tested, and revised until deemed acceptable for use.

Multiple efforts were made to gather information. For each subject, a Nexis search was conducted to gather newspaper and other media information. For subjects who had been investigated by the Secret Service, considerable information was available. For other subjects, information was obtained from law enforcement, private security, prosecutors, courts, probation, correctional institutions, and public records. For example, one-fourth of the subjects had been in the custody of the Federal Bureau of Prisons. The correctional files were reviewed for each of these subjects. In addition, one investigator studied all available books and scholarly articles written about ECSP subjects. In a number of cases, trial transcripts were obtained.

Each case was coded separately. After a case was coded by two coders, it was reconciled. The coders met to discuss each question. For variables that had been coded differently, the coders discussed the question until they agreed on a response. In the rare circumstances in which the coders could not agree, a third coder was asked to resolve the difference.

All codebooks for the 83 subjects were keypunched and entered into a Statistical Package for the Social Sciences database.

Interviews

The research design of the study involved two principal components: archival reviews, as detailed above, and interviews. The interview was seen as the primary vehicle to get detailed information about the subject's motives, target selection, movement from idea to action, expectations, planning process, previous interest in, and activity concerning assassination.

A subject interview protocol was developed to guide questioning. Sections in the protocol covered topics such as:

- idea to action;
- target selection;
- communications;
- preincident behaviors;

- planning;
- symptoms of mental illness and violence;
- key developmental experiences.

The interview explored the subject's thinking and behavior regarding the target of the principal incident. Questioning then moved to other public official and public figure targets that the subject had been interested in or had considered attacking.

Interview teams were composed of one Secret Service agent and one mental health professional. Agents brought the skills and skepticism of criminal and protective intelligence investigators. Mental health professionals brought expertise interviewing persons with serious emotional and mental health problems who had acted violently.

An informed consent form was developed for study interviews.

Ultimately, interviews were completed with more than 20 subjects. Some subjects were interviewed several times.

ECSP FINDINGS

MYTHS ABOUT ASSASSINS

There are three prevalent beliefs about assassination. These beliefs are widespread in the popular culture. They are largely unsupported by data that have been gathered and analyzed about persons who have carried out attacks on public officials and figures in the United States. They do not withstand critical thinking about assassination behaviors. These beliefs are myths because they are untrue.

The Profile

Myth 1: There is a "profile" of "the assassin."

Fact: Attackers and near-lethal approachers do not fit any one descriptive or demographic "profile" (or even *several* descriptive or demographic profiles).

Much has been written about "profiles" of assassins. But, in reality, there are no accurate descriptive or demographic "profiles" of American assassins, attackers, and near-lethal approachers. American assassins and attackers have been both men and women. They range across ages, educational backgrounds, employment histories, marital status, and other demographic and background characteristics.

Findings about the histories and personal characteristics of attackers and near-lethal approachers of ECSP targets include:

- The age range was from 16 to 73.
- Almost half had attended some college or graduate school.
- Attackers and near-attackers often had histories of mobility and transience.
- About two-thirds of all attackers and near-lethal approachers were described as social isolates.
- Few had histories of arrests for violent crimes or for crimes that involved weapons.
- Few had ever been incarcerated in state or federal prisons before their public figure-directed attack or near-lethal approach.
- Most attackers and would-be attackers had histories of weapons use, but few had formal weapons training.
- Many had histories of harassing other persons.
- Most are known to have had histories of explosive, angry behavior, but only half of the subjects are known to have had histories of violent behavior.
- Many had indicated to someone their interest in being violent toward a public figure.
- Attackers and near-attackers often had interests in militant/radical ideas and groups, though few had been members of such groups.
- Many had histories of serious depression or despair.
- Many are known to have attempted to kill themselves, or are known to have considered killing themselves at some point before their attack or near-lethal approach.
- Almost all had histories of grievances and resentments. Many had histories of grievances or resentments against a public official or public figure.

While there is no assassin profile, there are "common denominator" behaviors and activities that potential attackers engage in before their attacks. Mounting an attack on a prominent person is a type of violence that requires a number of preincident decisions, behaviors, and activities. A potential assassin must choose a target, figure out where the target is going to be, decide on and secure a weapon, survey security, develop a plan for attack, and consider whether to escape (and if so, how). While not every public figure attacker and near-attacker engaged in all of these activities and behaviors, most engaged in several of them.

Mental Illness

Myth 2: Assassination is a product of mental illness or derangement.

Fact: Mental illness only rarely plays a role in assassination behaviors.

Many believe that attacks on public figures are deranged behaviors, without rational or understandable motives, and, therefore, that perpetrators of these crimes must be mentally ill. In most cases, however, mental illness does not appear to be a primary cause of assassination behavior. Attacks on persons of prominent public status are actions chosen by persons who see assassination as a way to achieve their goals or solve problems.

Many persons who demonstrate unusual or inappropriate interests in, or make threats against, public officials and figures are mentally ill. But most near-lethal approachers, and the great majority of attackers and assassins, are *not* mentally ill.

No attacker or near-lethal approacher has been a model of emotional well-being. Almost all had psychological problems. However, relatively few suffered from serious mental illnesses that caused their attack behaviors.

Even for those attackers who were mentally ill, in almost every case an attack was a means to achieve some ends, such as calling attention to a perceived problem. Moreover, in cases where mental illness clearly did play a role in assassination attempts, symptoms of mental illness generally did not prevent the subject from engaging in attack-related activities such as rationally planning an attack. In most situations involving persons with severe and untreated mental illness, the symptoms disable the person's usual problem-solving abilities. However, most mentally ill attackers and near-lethal approachers remained organized and capable of planning and mounting an attack.

Labeling an attacker or near-lethal approacher as mentally ill, whether accurate or not, does not explain or help predict assassination behavior. It also contributes little to enhancing our ability to investigate potential attackers.

Mental health histories of attackers and near-lethal approachers indicate:

• Many had contact with mental health professionals or care systems at some point in their lives before their attack or near-lethal approach. But few indicated to mental health staff that they were considering attacking a public official or public figure.

• Almost half had histories of delusional ideas. But only in a few cases did delusional ideas lead directly to a near-lethal approach or an attack.

• Few had histories of command hallucinations.

• Relatively few had histories of substance abuse, including alcohol abuse.

Threats and Communications

Myth 3:   Explicit threateners are the persons most likely to carry
          out attacks.

Fact: Persons who *pose* threats most often do not *make*
          threats, especially explicit threats.

Much thinking about assassination links threateners and attackers, as if the two categories are one. The assumption of many is that those who *make* threats *pose* threats. While some threateners may pose threats, most often those who make threats do not pose threats. Frequently, those who pose threats do not make threats. For example:

• None of the 43 assassins or attackers communicated a direct threat about their target to the target before their attack.

• Fewer than a tenth of all 83 attackers and near-attackers communicated a direct threat about their target to the target or to a law enforcement agency.

These data do not suggest that investigators should ignore threats that are sent or spoken to or about public officials or public figures. Many persons may have been prevented, or deterred, from taking action because of a prompt response to their threatening communications. These data do suggest, however, that attention should be paid to identifying, investigating, and assessing persons whose behaviors suggest that they might pose threats of violence, but who do not communicate direct threats to their targets or to the authorities.

• While few assassins and would-be assassins communicated a direct threat to their target(s) or to law enforcement, two-thirds are known to have spoken or written in a manner that suggested that they were considering mounting an attack against a target. Would-be assassins told family members, friends, work colleagues, and associates about their thoughts and plans, or wrote down their ideas in journals or diaries.

KEY OBSERVATIONS ON ASSASSINS

A number of key observations about assassins and their behaviors have emerged from the ECSP. These observations are as follows:

• Assassination is the end result of a discernible and understandable process of thinking and behavior.
• For most persons who attack others, the violence is perceived as a means to a goal, or a way to solve a problem.
• There is a direct connection between a subject's motives and selection of target(s) for attack.

These observations are discussed below.

The Product of Organized Thinking and Behavior

Assassinations and attacks on public officials and public figures are the end results of understandable, and often discernible, processes of thinking and behavior.

Assassinations, attacks, and near-attacks, almost without exception, are neither impulsive nor spontaneous acts. The notion of attacking the president does not leap into the mind of a person standing at a political rally attended by the president. Assassins are not impelled into immediate violent action by sudden new thoughts that pop into their heads.

Ideas of assassination develop over weeks and months, even years. They are stimulated by television and newspaper images, movies, and books. Potential assassins seek out information about assassination, the lives of previous attackers, and the protectors of their targets. They may deliberate about which target or targets to choose. And they may transfer their interest from target to target.

Thoughts about assassination percolate in an attacker's mind. Attackers and near-lethal approachers ruminate about assassination, decide on targets, develop plans, and sometimes rehearse, before mounting an attack. Some attackers and potential assailants are preoccupied by thoughts of assassination. Their days are shaped by their planning activities: Which kind of weapon shall I use? Where will the target be? How will I get close? What should I wear? What should I carry with me? Should I leave a letter in case I am killed?

For some would-be attackers, such thinking organizes their life, providing a sense of meaning and purpose, or an ending point when they believe their emotional pain will cease.

Often thinking about assassination is compartmentalized. Some potential assassins engage in private, ongoing internal discussions about their attacks, while maintaining outward appearances of normality and regularity. In every case, assassination was the end result of an understandable process, involving the attacker's pattern of thoughts, decisions, behaviors, and actions that preceded the attack.

Motives: Assassination as a Means toward a Goal

Few assassins in the United States, even those whose targets were major political leaders, have had purely "political" motives.

Other than the Puerto Rican nationalists who attacked President Truman in 1950 and members of Congress in 1954, most recent assassins, attackers, and near-lethal approachers held motives that had nothing to do with politics or political causes.

Examination of the thinking and behaviors of the 83 American attackers and near-lethal approachers suggests that they held combinations of eight major motives, most of which were personal:

- to achieve notoriety or fame;
- to bring attention to a personal or public problem;
- to avenge a perceived wrong; to retaliate for a perceived injury;
- to end personal pain; to be removed from society; to be killed;

- to save the country or the world; to fix world problems;
- to develop a special relationship with the target;
- to make money;
- to bring about political change.

Many attackers and near-lethal approachers craved attention and notoriety. Others acted to bring attention to a problem. A number of assailants of public officials or figures were consumed with wishes to avenge a perceived injury or harm. A few attacked public officials or figures, or came close to attacking, in the hope of being killed, being removed from society, or ending their mental pain. Several believed that assassination of their target was a way to save the world or responded to voices or beliefs that they felt ordered them to attack a national leader. A number of subjects approached a celebrity with a weapon in order to force the target into a special relationship. And a few persons attacked a public official or public figure for money, either because they were paid to kill the target, or as part of an attempt to secure a ransom.

Motive and Target Selection

Targets are selected on the basis of a subject's motives, not primarily because of a subject's feelings about, or hostility toward, a particular target or office. Whether a subject likes or hates a particular office holder may be irrelevant if the subject's motive is to achieve notoriety. The policies or politics of a given official may not matter to a subject whose motive is to be removed from society. An attack on the target will achieve the goal. "I would have voted for him," said one would-be attacker, "if I hadn't been in jail charged with trying to kill him." Thus targets are instrumental; they are a means to an end.

Consistent with their motives, many attackers and would-be attackers considered more than one target before moving to attack. For example, several subjects whose primary motive was notoriety considered attacking public officials like governors and members of Congress before ultimately deciding to attack a president or vice president. These subjects calculated that an attack on the president or vice president would receive more attention than one on another elected official. Assailants often made final decisions about which target to attack because an opportunity for attack presented itself, or because they perceived a target as unapproachable, not because of personal animosity toward a target.

Two Case Studies

JD

JD, age 45, was working in a West Coast city as a delivery man. He was married, but a self-described "loner." JD was interested in guns and rifles and shot regularly at a range with a number of other gun aficionados. A fan of action movies, JD had seen *Day of the Jackal*, a movie about assassination, six times (more than he had seen other films). JD had been deeply distressed in 1963 by the assassination of President John F. Kennedy, whom he thought was leading the country in the right direction. But he had little respect for the current president, whom he believed was taking the country in the wrong direction.

Within a period of several months, JD's wife left him and he was fired from his job. Taking his cash savings of about $18,000, JD packed his belongings in his car and started driving. He also took a sniper rifle, which he had modified, and a number of bullets he had filled with mercury, to make them devastate a target on impact. JD was feeling deeply depressed about his life. He was filled with anger, seeing his life moving in a downward spiral.

JD first went to visit his elderly mother, with whom he had had a strained relationship. The visit did not go well. He next drove to see his sister. From there, he drove across the country, then visited Canada.

Back in the United States, driving in the Southwest, JD began to think of assassinating the president. He reasoned that if he killed the president, the country would no longer be led in the wrong direction. He figured that he would be killed in the attempt, which would resolve another problem: he wanted to die, but feared he didn't have the guts to kill himself. Also, assassinating the president would bring him notoriety: he would no longer be a nonentity.

JD traveled toward Washington, D.C. On his way, he bought a tape recorder and recorded a number of statements about his intention to kill the president. He did not identify himself on the tapes. Wearing gloves (to avoid fingerprints), JD put the tapes in envelopes, addressed the envelopes "To the FBI," and dropped them in mailboxes.

When he arrived in Washington, D.C., JD looked for sites where he might be able to shoot the president. JD then drove to visit several cities in the Northeast that he thought the president was likely to visit. He then returned to Washington, D.C., where he got a hotel room and spent several days thinking about how to shoot the president. Frustrated by the difficulty of attempting an assassination, he left Washington.

Several weeks later, JD was feeling desperate. He sold his car and traveled by bus to Washington. He spent several days walking around the White House and sitting in Lafayette Park, across from the White House. Increasingly troubled, he spent hours sitting in a church debating within himself whether it was right to assassinate the president. He wrote several letters that he did not send. In one he said:

> Every time I awake in the morning, I am in mortal fear for my life. I do not know if I can go through with this plan to kill the president. I have even contemplated suicide, but I do not know if I can do it. I have never killed anything in my life and I don't want to start now. You may think that I am crazy, maybe I am and maybe I'm not. I do not know. All I do know is that I am scared of what I may do if I am not

stopped soon. I know that I need help but I am afraid to ask for it. Will someone help me or am I asking too much?

Shortly thereafter, the Secret Service received a call from a man who identified himself as "Smith." The caller said that he had observed a man hanging around Lafayette Park who was there to kill the president. Smith called to report the same information the next day. A day later, he called again and told an agent that *he* was planning to kill the president and would turn himself in if the agent would agree to aid him to get help and if he could keep his Bible. Shortly thereafter JD was arrested across the street from the White House.

JD was sent by the court to a psychiatric hospital. Ultimately he pled guilty to threatening the president. He remained hospitalized for several years.

For JD, the "process" of assassination took place over a 6-month period. Consideration of assassination appeared to be precipitated by major changes in JD's life (loss of marriage and job) and feelings of hopelessness, desperation, and rage.

Although the first thought about assassinating the president occurred to him while he was driving across the country, JD had prior interest in assassination. JD saw assassination as a solution to his problems: he would stop the president from (in his view) taking the country in the wrong direction, get himself killed, and achieve a degree of notoriety. His feelings about the wrongfulness of killing ultimately led him to turn himself in before he attempted harm.

Arthur Jackson

Born and raised in Scotland, Arthur Jackson traveled to the United States in 1955 and enlisted in the Army. While serving in Germany, Jackson gradually became convinced that there was an Army–CIA mind control plot afoot that was pressuring him to become homosexual. Hospitalized for psychiatric reasons, Jackson was discharged from the military. He traveled around the United States until he was deported in 1961 after he had written a letter to President Kennedy that was perceived as threatening.

Jackson lived in Scotland and England for the next 20 years, while occasionally taking trips to other countries. In early 1981, Jackson, a movie buff, saw *Raging Bull*, a movie in which the actress, Theresa Saldana, played a minor role. Jackson became convinced that Saldana was connected to the Army–CIA mind control conspiracy he had experienced in 1955. He decided that he must embark on a mission to kill Theresa Saldana and thereby force the U.S. government to execute him.

In December 1981, Jackson departed Scotland to begin his "mission." Believing that he would die as a result of his actions, he visited Europe to see the sights before traveling to the United States. Jackson arrived in New York in January 1982. He attempted to determine Saldana's whereabouts by pretending to be a journalist. He learned that she was living in Los Angeles.

Traveling by bus, sleeping in bus stations, keeping careful track of his money, and writing a detailed journal, Jackson visited cities in the East, South, and West before arriving in Los Angeles in March. He wanted to get a handgun, because he believed that it would be more "merciful" to kill Saldana by shooting her, but he was not able to procure one. He could not buy one because he did not have proper identification. He considered attacking a police officer in the dark, knocking him out, and stealing his service revolver, but did not find the opportunity to attempt such an attack.

After being unable on his own to discover Saldana's address in Los Angeles, with his money supply dwindling, Jackson spent $100 to pay a private investigator to find Saldana's address. Two days later, he walked in front of the apartment building in which she lived. He carried a knife and a hammer with him. In his knapsack was a "manifesto" in which he explained that he was on a mission to kill Saldana and requested to be executed by the federal government at Alcatraz Prison.

On March 15, 1982, Jackson went to Saldana's home early in the morning. He had never laid eyes on Theresa Saldana, other than in the movies. He saw a woman leaving the building whom he identified as Saldana. Walking quickly, he grabbed her from behind and stabbed her repeatedly in the chest. A bystander came to Saldana's rescue and pulled Jackson off Saldana while Jackson screamed at her.

Saldana staggered back to her home and collapsed. She had suffered multiple injuries. An ambulance rushed her to a hospital that fortunately was only several minutes away. Despite being gravely wounded, Saldana survived her attack. She was hospitalized for $3\frac{1}{2}$ months and then again on subsequent occasions for follow-up surgery and care.

Jackson was arrested and tried and convicted of attempted murder. In 1996, after completing his original sentence, and a second sentence he was given for threatening Saldana in the late 1980s, Jackson was extradited to England to be tried for a murder he was alleged to have committed in 1976.

Arthur Jackson's journey toward assassination was thoughtful and deliberate. Once he had selected his target, he made determined efforts to locate her address, to acquire a weapon, and to secure her and his fates. Although clearly mentally ill, Jackson remained focused and organized. He kept a detailed journal of his travels and his stalking of Ms. Saldana, though he never communicated directly with his target. He did not communicate threats of harming Ms. Saldana to others.

SUMMARY AND CONCLUSIONS

An assassination attempt is the *end result of a process* of thinking and behavior. Many attackers and near-lethal approachers move through life on a path that leads them to consider assassination of one or another prominent person of public status as an acceptable way to improve their situations or resolve their problems. These persons are often relatively bright and/or well educated. They may appear to be socially isolated, but they often look, dress, and act in ways that do not readily distinguish them from others.

Assassins, attackers and near-lethal approachers may have histories of harassing others. Some feel threatened by close contact with other people. Many hold on to grievances and resentments, especially toward public officials and leaders. Often they have histories of acting impulsively, angrily, or explosively. Significantly, while more than half have a history of a juvenile or adult arrest, only one-fourth have a history of an arrest for a crime involving a weapon and only one-sixth have a history of an arrest for a violent crime. Three-fourths of attackers and near-lethal approachers have no history of incarceration. Those who have been in jail have usually been there for pretrial detention, not while serving a sentence.

Many attackers and near-lethal approachers are evaluated by mental health professionals at some point before they step out on the path toward assassination. Some have histories of inpatient psychiatric hospitalization. Few, however, remain in mental health treatment for an extended time. And, significantly, unlike most persons with mental illness, attackers and near-lethal approachers who are seriously mentally ill maintain the capacity to plan and carry out organized activities.

Many assailants and near-assailants of public officials and public figures have considered killing themselves. They may have talked of suicide, threatened to kill themselves, or made a suicide gesture or attempt.

At some point—often after a life crisis—attackers and near-lethal approachers begin to see the idea of assassination as acceptable and desirable. They may gather information about previous assassins, take special interest in one or more potential public official targets, and/or begin to view assassination as a way to achieve their objectives, such as becoming famous or notorious, being removed from society, or getting killed. Some write about their ideas and activities in a journal or diary. Others tell friends, family, or colleagues—but usually not the target—about their thoughts and intentions.

The fact that few attackers and near-attackers communicated explicit threats to their targets or to law enforcement authorities underscores the importance of careful attention to attack-related behaviors as indicators of potential attacks.

Persons who continue along the path to attack often carefully consider how to carry out an attack. They may travel to visit an office, home, or temporary visiting place of a target. Their travels may take them far from home. Many with an interest in the president visit the White House on their journey toward attack. Attackers and near-lethal approachers may practice with a weapon they have chosen for assassination. They may try to learn about security arrangements, and see the presence (or absence) of security as a deterrent (or as an opportunity).

Attackers and near-lethal approachers often consider more than one target, ultimately choosing a target for attack after concluding that an opportunity for attack exists and that an attack on the chosen target is likely to fulfill their goals. But many of these persons have mixed feelings about actually attacking. Some who feel propelled to move along the path to assassination search for reasons why they should not attack and are stopped from mounting attacks by the belief that they will not be successful.

Some prospective assassins think about—and plan for—escaping after their attack. Others approach their assassination attempts with the expectation they will be killed, or, for the *purpose* of being killed.

Few attackers or near-lethal approachers possessed the cunning or the bravado of assassins in popular movies or novels. The reality of American assassination is much more mundane, more banal, than assassinations depicted on the screen. Neither monsters nor martyrs, recent American assassins, attackers, and near-lethal approachers engaged in preincident patterns of thinking and behavior. Understanding these patterns of ideation and action may permit those with protective responsibilities to prevent future attacks.

ACKNOWLEDGMENTS

This project was supported under Award Number 92-IJ-CX-0013 by the National Institute of Justice, Office of Justice Programs, U.S. Department of Justice, and by the U.S. Secret Service, Department of Treasury.

REFERENCES

Fein, R.A., & Vossekuil, B. (1997a, May). *Preventing assassination: A literature review* (A report from the Secret Service Exceptional Case Study Project, prepared under NIJ Grant 92-IJ-CX-0013). Washington, DC: U.S. Department of Justice, National Institute of Justice.

Fein, R.A., & Vossekuil, B. (1997a, May). *Preventing assassination: A monograph* (A report from the Secret Service Exceptional Case Study Project, prepared under NIJ Grant 92-IJ-CX-0013). Washington, DC: U.S. Department of Justice, National Institute of Justice.

Fein, R.A., & Vossekuil, B. (1997c, May). *Preventing assassination: A selected bibliography* (A report from the Secret Service Exceptional Case Study Project, prepared under NIJ Grant 92-IJ-CX-0013). Washington, DC: U.S. Department of Justice, National Institute of Justice.

Fein, R.A., Vossekuil, B., & Holden, G. (1995). *Threat assessment: An approach to prevent targeted violence* (NCJ 155000). Washington, DC: U.S. Department of Justice, Office of Justice Programs, National Institute of Justice.

Takeuchi, J., Solomon, F., & Menninger, W.W. (1981). Behavioral science and the Secret Service: Toward the prevention of assassination. In J. Takeuchi, F. Solomon, & W.W. Menninger (Eds.), *Behavioral science and the Secret Service: Toward the prevention of assassination.* Washington, DC: National Academy Press.

CHAPTER 10

De Clérambault On-Line: A Survey of Erotomania and Stalking from the Old World to the World Wide Web

Robert Lloyd-Goldstein, M.D., J.D.

In recent years, there has been a burgeoning of interest in erotomania and its clinical variants, which had hitherto been relegated to the dubious status of "rare, unclassifiable, collective and exotic psychotic syndromes" (Arieti & Meth, 1959). Likewise, there has been a spectacular outpouring of media glare and attention from the law enforcement community and legislators over the phenomenon of stalking. Sensational headlines are an almost everyday occurrence, trumpeting the stalking of celebrities, as well as otherwise anonymous individuals. The relentless torments visited upon the victims, the psychological profiles of the stalkers, the grotesque dramas (including maimings and murders) that may ensue have become the subject of serious scholarly study (Meloy, 1996; Segal, 1989), as well as fodder for the popular culture (e.g., tabloids, television talk shows, and movies such as *Play Misty For Me, The Story of Adele H.,* and the genre's magnum opus, *Fatal Attraction*). Unsurprisingly, the growth of new technologies, such as the proliferation of computers and the ubiquity of the World Wide Web, has been accompanied by the emergence of electronic surveillance, e-mail stalking, and Internet harassment, among other forms of on-line crime.

Quaint Old World clinical curiosities, where monarchs and members of the nobility were amorously pursued (usually from afar) by lovesick individuals (invariably women "of a certain age"), were described in the early literature by Kraepelin (1921), De Clérambault (1921/1942), Hart (1921), and others (Krafft-Ebing, 1879). It appeared to some to be so quintessentially a phenomenon of the Ancien Régime, deeply rooted in continental culture, that one early psychiatrist described erotomania as a "syndrome essentiellement Française," (Reik, 1963).

The Psychology of Stalking: Clinical and Forensic Perspectives

One of the original cases described by De Clérambault in his classic work *Les Psychoses Passionelles* (1921/1942) was representative of this clinical entity:

> A 53-year-old Frenchwoman became absolutely convinced that King George V of England was in love with her. She was certain that English sailors and tourists in France were messengers sent by the King to proclaim his love for her. . . . During several trips to England, starting in 1918, she waited patiently outside the gates of Buckingham Palace; once when she saw a curtain moving in a window, she interpreted this as a signal from the King. She claimed that news of their love was known throughout London, but she also insisted that the King was disrupting her travel plans and that he had arranged for the loss of her luggage, which contained money and portraits of him. Despite these difficulties, which might have been interpreted as attempts to discourage her affections, she persisted in her belief that there was a special relationship between the King and herself, saying, "The King might hate me, but he can never forget. I could never be indifferent to him, nor he to me." (p. 343)

Similar cases were reported by Kraepelin (1921), Hart (1921), and Spitzka (1889), utilizing the nosology, phenomenology, and scientific methodology of their time. Prior to the advent of psychiatry as we know it, this syndrome in one form or another was known to the ancients; described by Hippocrates, Galen, and Plutarch; reported by various physicians of the Middle Ages; and portrayed in classic works of literature, such as the *Decameron* of Boccaccio (Enoch, Tretho-wan, & Barker, 1967).

In more recent years, we have witnessed the transplanting of this Old World syndrome to the soil of the New World, where it has taken root and flourished in ways that could not have been foreseen. Feder (1973) was one of the first to remark on this phenomenon:

> It is every clinician's experience to come across a case from time to time which hews closely to some classic description of disease. This is no less true in psychiatry, and it is all the more striking when one observes a clinical picture originally described in one cultural context making its appearance in another. Such a case tends to reaffirm that psychopathology—in fact, mental functioning in general—transcends its individual appearances in time and place and, indeed its very content. (p. 240)

This transmogrification of erotomania has kept pace with many other trendy sociological vogues of our time, evoking the peculiarly American overtones of glitzy sensationalism, lurid "made for Hollywood" melodrama, overt violence and sadism, and pop commercialization (as a mega-cottage industry has sprung up, of concerned politicians, law enforcement entrepreneurs, and celebrity forensic psychiatrists, striving mightily to cash in on the bonanza). This Americanization of erotomania and stalking has taken us full cycle, from the clinical esoterica of a bygone era (with vignettes of genteel modistes and old maids, enmeshed in their romantic fantasies with Kings and clergymen), to the thoroughly hip modern celebrity stalkers of Madonna and David Letterman, to the startling instances of violence that have prompted anti-stalking legislation in all American jurisdictions, and most recently of all, to the vast new frontier of *cyberstalking*. The rekindling of an interest in the forensic aspects of erotomania, with its potential for stalking and serious violence (particularly in men, who often predominate in these forensic populations), was initiated by Goldstein (1978, 1986, 1987) and by Taylor, Mahendra, and Gunn, (1983) barely 20 years ago. During this brief span, erotomania and stalking have come of age, prompting a plethora of serious scientific inquiries that have added to our knowledge of the nosology, demographics, and clinical and forensic dimensions of this important entity.

NOMENCLATURE AND DIAGNOSIS

The nosological and diagnostic controversies over erotomania have apparently been resolved for the time being by *DSM-IV* (APA, 1994), which lists it as the erotomanic subtype of the diagnostic category delusional disorder (which represents a new diagnostic designation, first introduced by *DSM-III-R* [APA, 1987]). Prior to that, the appropriate *DSM-III* (APA, 1980) diagnosis for the condition was the nonspecific atypical psychosis. Before *DSM* conferred its authoritative imprimatur, erotomania had languished for many years in "a kind of diagnostic limbo" (Segal, 1989), truly "a symptom in search of adequate conceptualization. . . [having] been incorporated into diagnostic systems in many different ways" (Rudden, Sweeney, & Frances, 1990, p. 625). Despite *DSM*'s official fiat, individual cases may pose lingering questions that defy easy categorization. Mullen and Pathé (1994a) point out that *DSM* credits erotomania with being an occasional symptom of 22 categories of disorder, ranging from schizophrenia to multi-infarct dementia. These cases of "secondary" erotomania would necessarily exclude an Axis I diagnosis of delusional disorder. Thus, erotomanic symptoms in themselves do not dictate diagnosis. Patients with erotomania are a heterogeneous group, with diagnoses that may fall into two main categories—*primary* erotomania (i.e., delusional disorder, erotomanic subtype) or *secondary* erotomania (i.e., the delusion is superimposed on another psychotic condition, e.g., schizophrenia, schizoaffective disorder, bipolar disorder) (Rudden et al., 1990). With an increased interest in erotomania and stalking, more cases are identified and reported in the literature than ever before. More precise diagnostic determinations will assist researchers to refine our ability to better predict clinical course, response to treatment, future dangerousness, and other variables (often in a forensic context).

PRIMARY EROTOMANIA

De Clérambault diagnosed primary (or "pure") erotomania as a monodelusional disorder, in which there is a precise and explosive onset, with no significant psychiatric symptoms apart from the elaborate erotomanic features. The patient (invariably a woman, according to De Clérambault) holds the delusional belief that a man, usually older and of elevated social status, sometimes a public figure, is passionately in love with her, despite paradoxical conduct by him, during which he may appear to deny his love for her vigorously, even to hate or harm her, when in fact he really does love her and is merely testing her love (or trying to throw others off the track) (De Clérambault, 1921/1942).

As Segal (1989) emphasized, it was not De Clérambault, but Kraepelin who originally described erotomania in modern terms, as a subcategory in his schema of paranoia (Kraepelin, 1921). Kraepelin noted that erotomanic patients are usually mature women with persistent delusions of being loved, which serve as "a kind of psychological compensation for the disappointments of life" (Kraepelin, 1921, p. 259). He described a prototypical case as follows:

> A female patient noticed that the reigning sovereign bowed with special respect to her in the theatre and made his children greet her. . . . Very soon the signs of the secret misunderstanding increased in number. Every chance occurrence, clothing, meetings, reading, conversations, acquired for the patient a relation to his imagined adventure. His love was an open secret and an object of universal interest; it was talked about everywhere, certainly never outspokenly, but always in slight indications, the proposed meaning of which he understood very well. . . . (p. 259)

This discrete monodelusional entity, unaccompanied by a generalized psychotic process, has been given official recognition and enshrined in our diagnostic lexicon (*DSM-III-R* and *DSM-IV*) as the erotomanic subtype of delusional disorder, "in a return to the original Kraepelinian formulation" (Segal, 1989, p. 1261).

While the primary syndrome is recognized by most authorities, there is a difference of opinion regarding its true incidence. Samples of erotomanic patients reported in the world literature are a heterogeneous group with respect to diagnosis. In a nonforensic sample of erotomanic patients, Rudden et al. (1990) reported that 7 of 28 subjects (25%) warranted a diagnosis of delusional disorder, erotomanic subtype. (Three of these were given an additional Axis I diagnosis of mood disorder.) In another nonforensic sample of erotomanic psychiatric inpatients, Menzies, Fedoroff, Green, and Isaacson (1995) diagnosed primary erotomania in 2 of 13 patients (15.4%). A predominantly forensic cohort of erotomanic patients was described by Mullen and Pathé (1994a), in which 5 of 16 subjects (31.3%) received a diagnosis of delusional disorder, erotomanic subtype. Harmon, Rosner, and Owens (1995) reported cases from a court clinic in New York City, where 48 stalkers were evaluated. Six of 48 cases (12.5%) were confirmed as suffering from primary erotomania. (There were 8 other cases of delusional disorder: 3 of the persecutory subtype and 5 of the unspecified subtype.) Zona, Sharma, and Lane (1993) investigated a forensic cohort of stalkers and, in the absence of systematized clinical data, suggested that 10% could be classified as primary erotomania. Meloy and Gothard (1995), in the first reported comparative clinical study of stalkers, found that 2 of 20 subjects (10%) warranted a single Axis I diagnosis of delusional disorder, erotomanic subtype.

SECONDARY EROTOMANIA

De Clérambault distinguished his *pure* cases of erotomania from *secondary* cases, in which the distinctive delusion was but one manifestation of a more generalized psychotic illness, usually with a disorganized and deteriorating clinical course. The sudden onset and paradoxical features were typical of the former (*pure* or *primary* type). Although some investigators maintain that erotomania is *always* symptomatic of schizophrenia (i.e., that it never exists as a separate entity) (Ellis & Mellsop, 1985; Hayes & O'Shea, 1985), the evidence does appear to be rather conclusive that a primary form does indeed exist and is best conceptualized and classified as a subtype of delusional disorder (Segal, 1989). The sudden explosive onset, described by De Clérambault as a sine qua non of pure erotomania, has not been observed by most investigators.

Traditionally, the secondary cases were almost always diagnosed as paranoid schizophrenia (Rudden et al., 1990). Rudden's group (1990) identified a larger number of accompanying affective symptoms and a greater number of cases of mood disorder than have traditionally been described for erotomanic patients in the world literature. Manic symptoms were especially prominent in their sample. Twenty-five percent of their erotomanic patients were diagnosed as schizoaffective disorder, manic type, and 7% had bipolar disorder. As noted above, erotomanic symptoms may occur in 22 different diagnostic categories in *DSM* (Mullen & Pathé, 1994a). At least two-thirds of these secondary cases are best diagnosed as schizophrenia. The second most common diagnosis appears to be mood disorder.

OTHER VARIANTS OF EROTOMANIA

Meloy (1989) has identified a form of nondelusional erotomania, which he terms "borderline erotomania." It is characterized by an intense and tumultuous attachment to an unrequited love, in the absence of an erotomanic delusion of being loved in return. These patients are usually organized at a borderline personality level, with an obsessional attachment to an unattained (or former) love object. Segal (1990a) regarded this syndrome of obsession without erotomanic delusion as a pathologically exaggerated reaction to an actual rejection by the love object, more common than erotomania per se, more frequent in males, and more likely to erupt into violence. Mullen and Pathé (1994a) have described a similar clinical entity, terming it "morbid infatuation." The morbid infatuation preoccupies patients to the exclusion of other interests, results in serious disruption of their lives, and leads to a relentless pursuit of the love object, often with escalating intrusiveness:

> The patient doggedly pursued his "God chosen bride" over several years. His life became dominated by the quest, and all his other interests were subordinated. He created chaos for the object of his affections, put the lives of others into danger, and totally destroyed the fabric of his own life, culminating in long-term incarceration. Throughout this time he never claimed that the object of his affection returned his love, stating only that if others stopped poisoning her mind against him she might come to return his affection. (Mullen & Pathé, 1994a, p. 617)

Two cases of historic significance that were characterized by an individual's intense and obsessive attachment to an unrequited love object (in the absence of erotomanic delusions) were John Hinckley, Jr. (who attempted to assassinate President Reagan in response to his all-consuming infatuation with the actress Jodie Foster) and Prosenjiit Poddar, who stalked and killed Tatiana Tarasoff (which became arguably the most famous case in the annals of modern forensic psychiatry) (Goldstein, 1995).

A number of cases of erotomania associated with other uncommon delusional conditions have been reported: Sims and White (1973) reported a case of De Clérambault's syndrome and Capgras syndrome in combination. Pearce (1972) reported a case of erotomania associated with shared paranoid disorder (folie à deux). Menzies et al. (1995) reported three cases of erotomania secondary to schizophrenia associated with delusional misidentification syndromes. Mullen and Pathé (1994a) conceptualized a spectrum of *pathologies of love,*

> which at one end [of a continuum] overlaps with extreme examples of such reactions in normal people, and at the other with bizarre variants which are to be found embedded in a schizophrenic psychosis. [These pathological extensions of love usually involve a mixture of morbid infatuation and a morbid conviction of being loved, although the former may occur by itself. They occur in both a primary form and a symptomatic form, as part of an underlying psychosis.] Extracting a clear description of these disorders from the chaotic richness of clinical realities may present formidable difficulties. (pp. 618–619).

In these erotomanic spectrum disorders, the boundary issues are especially acute in cases in which there has been some form of real relationship, albeit a fleeting one, between the patient and the love object. Zona and his colleagues (1993) suggested a classification into three distinct groups:

1. An erotomanic group (diagnosed as delusional disorder, erotomanic subtype),

2. A love obsessional group, with a primary psychiatric diagnosis (in addition to erotomania, if present), and

3. A simple obsessional group, wherein an actual prior relationship with the love object had soured or led to lingering grievances about mistreatment. [In the

first two categories, there was never any prior relationship between the stalker and victim.]

McAnaney, Curliss, and Abeyta-Price (1993) proposed a theoretical typology of stalkers that includes primary erotomania, borderline erotomania, "former intimate" relationship, and sociopathy (e.g., serial killers and rapists).

DEMOGRAPHICS, DANGEROUSNESS, AND DYNAMICS

In a series of papers and books, Meloy has played a leading role in augmenting our scientific knowledge about the complexities of erotomania and stalking behavior (Meloy, 1988, 1989, 1992, 1996; Meloy & Gothard, 1995). Research in this intriguing area is still in its early stages and many questions remain unresolved, awaiting further empirical investigation by studying larger patient samples in various clinical and forensic settings. This section succinctly reviews these issues, relying on the innovative work of Meloy (1988, 1989, 1992, 1996; Meloy & Gothard, 1995), Mullen & Pathé (1994a,b), Zona and his colleagues (1993), and others, who have contributed to our body of knowledge about these pathological extensions of love, by using increasingly sophisticated research methodology.

DEMOGRAPHICS

Gender Prevalence

Erotomania, stalking, "violent attachments" (Meloy, 1992), and other pathologies of love occur in men and women, in Western and non-Western cultures, and have been written about for thousands of years. Although there has been a dramatic increase in media fascination with stalking that would suggest that its base rate is escalating in the population, there is no hard empirical data to warrant such a conclusion to a reasonable degree of scientific certainty. Only one study reports any data on this issue: Harmon et al. (1995) found that the percentage of referrals to a court clinic in New York City for stalking types of behavior showed a relative increase of 0.6% to 1.7% (a nearly threefold rise), between 1987 and 1993.

Traditionally, erotomania was considered to occur almost exclusively among women. Hart (1921) pointedly referred to the disorder as "Old Maid's Insanity." However, even the original cases reported by De Clérambault (1921/1942) included one male patient (20% of his original five cases):

> Aged 34 years, he had a morbid passion towards his ex-wife. Although she maintained she did not love him, he claimed her attitude always belied her words. After

her re-marriage, he said she would once again become his mistress and that when he had satisfied his pride he would again reject her. He was constantly writing, ambushing her, and striking her in public. He carried a razor, threatening "if you remarry, I'll get you both." He alleged that her divorce from him was null and void. (p. 364)

It is noteworthy that the very first case of De Clérambault's syndrome reported in a male patient exhibited violent behavior toward the love object, triggered by the core symptomatology (Goldstein, 1987).

Segal (1989; 1990b) estimated that erotomania occurs in men in 20–30% of cases. Mullen and Pathé (1994a) reported findings on a forensic cohort of 16 erotomanic patients. Five subjects were diagnosed as primary erotomania (i.e., delusional disorder, erotomanic subtype). Three of these were men (60% of the primary erotomanics). Eleven subjects suffered from secondary erotomania, of which 8 were men (72.7% of the secondary erotomanic cases). These findings were consistent with reports by Goldstein (1986, 1987) and Taylor et al. (1983) that erotomanic patients in a forensic setting were more likely to be men. Meloy and Gothard (1995) evaluated a group of 20 stalkers, two of whom suffered from primary erotomania. Both were men. In the largest study to date of a forensic cohort, Zona et al. (1993) found that 6 of 7 erotomanics were women (85.7%). Harmon et al. (1995) found that 100% of their 6 erotomanic patients referred for stalking behavior were women. In an analysis of preliminary research on stalking between 1978 and 1995 (gleaned from clinical reports on 186 subjects published in the world literature), Meloy (1996) found that the aggregate data suggested (but did not conclusively establish) that (1) erotomanic stalkers are more likely to be women than are stalkers with different diagnoses or motivations, and (2) the relative proportion of erotomanics who are women is likely to be greater in samples derived from nonforensic populations. Stalking cases in which the perpetrator and victim are of the same sex (homosexual stalking) are quite infrequent (less than 1%) (Meloy, 1996). Meloy emphasized that there is still an insufficient scientific basis for definitive conclusions to be drawn regarding gender prevalence in erotomania (Meloy, 1990). Preliminary data suggest that 75% of stalkers (of which 10% are erotomanics) are men (Meloy, 1996).

Other Demographic Variables

The early case reports of erotomania noted that the patients were usually *mature* women. Kraepelin (1921) reported that the patients were generally over 30 years of age. De Clérambault's original cases were four women and one man (respectively aged 55, 53, 50, 33, and 34) (De Clérambault, 1921/1942). Contemporary cases are in line with these findings in regard to age. It has been suggested that chronic failures in social and sexual relationships during young adulthood may be a necessary precursor to the development of erotomanic symptomatology (Meloy, 1996). Mullen and Pathé (1994b) found that the average age of their group of primary erotomanics was 43.6 years (with the average age of their total group of combined primary and secondary cases being 39 years). Harmon et al. (1995) reported an average age of 40 years. Meloy and Gothard (1995) found an average age of 35 years in their study of stalkers, exactly replicating the findings of Zona et al. (1993). Stalkers are generally significantly older than comparison groups of criminal offenders (Meloy and Gothard, 1995).

The literature suggests that most stalkers are more intelligent and better educated than other types of offenders. Most had a high school education and one study found a high percentage of college graduates; however, they usually demonstrated unstable work histories with elevated rates of unemployment or underemployment (Meloy, 1996). Most were unmarried, isolated, and had a clear-cut history of failed social and sexual relationships over many years (Segal, 1989). Some erotomanic patients have been described as notably unattractive physically (Hollender & Callahan, 1975). In some cases, the disturbance seemed to arise after marital separation, divorce, loss of a loved one, job failure, or termination of psychotherapy (Raskin & Sullivan, 1974).

There appears to be overwhelming evidence that stalkers are likely to have a history of prior psychiatric difficulties,[1] as well as a history of prior criminality (related or unrelated offences).[2] Meloy and Gothard (1995, p. 260) were emphatic on this point: "Our findings do *not* support the notion that stalking . . . is an aberrant behavior committed by an otherwise law-abiding and mentally healthy individual."

Another interesting finding is that a significant percentage of stalkers (possibly as high as 10%) are foreign-born immigrants. This is especially the case in diagnosed erotomanics (Meloy, 1996). The psychosocial stress associated with immigration and its inevitable extreme social dislocation and potential for maladaptation and alienation have been recognized as contributing factors to the genesis of delusional disorder in general (Pederson, 1949).

DANGEROUSNESS

Psychiatrists today are decidedly more circumspect and unassuming regarding their expertise in predicting future dangerousness than they were even a few years ago. The paucity of empirical scientific support for their supposed predictive gifts in this area has had its sobering effect (Monahan & Steadman, 1994). (Witness the spectacle of the American Psychiatric Association, in its amicus brief, protesting

---

[1]Eighty-five percent of stalkers had both Axis I and Axis II diagnoses: mostly substance abuse and dependence (35%) and mood disorders (25%) on Axis I and a Cluster B personality disorder other than antisocial personality disorder on Axis II (Meloy, 1996).

[2]Only the simple obsessional subgroup described by Zona et al. (1993) had a majority of first-time offenders.

to the Supreme Court that psychiatric testimony on the issue of predicting future dangerousness is almost entirely unreliable [*Barefoot v. Estelle,* 1983].) Nevertheless, given a social phenomenon of the magnitude of stalking which has aroused such an extraordinary amount of attention from the media, the criminal justice system, and the political establishment, it is inevitable that there will be an emphasis on developing a better clinical understanding of the potential for violence in these individuals and, if possible, how to identify and quantify the parameters that may assist law enforcement agencies and the courts to take appropriate measures to contain the risk.

The potential for violent behavior and stalking was clearly identified in erotomanic patients 150 years ago by Morrison: "Erotomania sometimes prompts those laboring under it to destroy themselves or others, for although in general tranquil and respectful, the patient sometimes becomes irritable, passionate and jealous" (Mullen & Pathé, 1994b, p. 470).

Esquirol reported the case of a man suffering from erotomania who lifted up the skirt of an actress he was stalking and later attacked her husband, who was impeding his access to his beloved (Esquirol, 1845/1965). The question is whether or not erotomanic fixations inevitably progress from fantasy to escalating intrusiveness (telephoning, letter writing and gift giving, without respite), to ever more ominous stalking approaches (following, face-to-face confrontations, staking out the victim's workplace or residence, threats, breaking into the victim's home, physical and sexual assaults, and single or multiple homicides). Which subgroups are most likely under certain circumstances to become dangerous and eventually to make an attempt on the life of their victim or others who are perceived as standing in the way? What are the triggering circumstances likely to be? Have the empirical studies provided any guidelines that are helpful in attempting to predict dangerous behavior in erotomanics and other stalkers with varying diagnoses and motivations? Which patients are likely to resort to violence, when pathological loving gives way to hatred and resentment, after prolonged pursuit and repeated advances remain unrequited by the object of affection?

Dietz (1988) opined that erotomania was not so rare as previously believed, that it was not necessarily predominantly a female condition, that fewer than 5% of patients become violent, and that the most likely target of any violence was a third party seen as impeding access to the beloved object. Zona et al. (1993) reported that none of their erotomanic or love obsessional subgroups engaged in physical violence and only two subjects in their simple obsessional category inflicted bodily harm (an overall incidence of violence of only 2.7%). Mullen & Pathé (1994b) reported a much greater incidence of intrusiveness and overt violence in a forensic context, with predominantly male subjects. Thirty-six percent assaulted their victims; another 43% sexually attacked them; and 36% destroyed their property. There is some controversy about sexual aims in erotomania. Thirty years ago, Enoch et al. (1967) noted:

> Erotomania is certainly not founded upon platonic love. On the contrary, De Clérambault showed that most patients craved for a sexual relationship. The writings of some patients surpass the imagination in sexual crudity. Some have even been arrested following attempted or actual assaults upon the objects of their affections. (p. 21)

It is noteworthy that in the report by Mullen & Pathé (1994b), sexual attacks were perpetrated only by subjects diagnosed with secondary erotomania. Only one of their five primary erotomanics would admit to even entertaining any overt sexual fantasies about the love object. One of the latter group, when queried as to whether he had any sexual fantasies about his beloved, became agitated, "claiming the very question demeaned and soiled the purity of his love" (Mullen & Pathé, 1994b, p. 473). It may be that primary or *pure* erotomania, as some earlier psychiatrists believed, is more likely to be characterized by the idealized and spiritual, rather than the carnal aspects of love. As Spitzka (1889) observed:

> As a rule the affection for the adored object remains as chaste and pure as it begins; a sort of distant romantic worship . . . which consequently assumes such a predominating position in the patient's mental horizon as to entirely overshadow it. (p. 348)

Meloy and Gothard (1995) reported a 25% incidence of physical assault in their forensic cohort of stalkers. Harmon et al. (1995) reported a 21% incidence of assault in their court-referred sample of stalkers. Meloy (1996) found four cases of homicide altogether in his review of the world literature on stalking, for an incidence of 2%. Menzies et al. (1995) reported a 23% incidence of assaultive behavior in a nonforensic sample of 13 men with erotomania (including two physical assaults and one sexual attack). The authors go on to conclude that the presence of multiple love objects and a history of prior serious antisocial behavior (unrelated to the erotomanic delusions) are useful predictors of dangerous behavior in men with erotomania. Utilizing a combination of these two variables, it was possible to predict dangerousness with an accuracy of 88.9%.

Overall, assaults by stalkers reported in the world literature varied in frequency between 3% and 36%, mostly committed without a weapon. The most likely target of violence is the love object herself or himself (80%). Third parties seen as standing in the way were the second most common victims of violence (Meloy, 1996). Mullen & Pathé (1994b) identified two other subgroups of targets of violence, innocent bystanders and the stalkers themselves (by suicide or attacks by others). It hardly needs to be pointed out that despite the statistical fact that most stalkers are not violent[3] (and that the risk and extent of actual physical harm posed by the erotomanic subgroup may be less than for other categories of stalkers), nonetheless, the subjects invariably bring chaos to the lives of their victims. The merciless harassment and pursuit inflict enormous psychological and social disruption and

---

[3]Most stalkers even after a year or more of pursuit will not physically attack their victim (Zona et al., 1993).

damage, often escalating over a period of many years. Victims may be reduced to living in an unrelieved state of siege:

> It is the constant presence of the stalker which unnerves them, particularly when [a] sudden appearance reveals a knowledge of the victim's plans and movements which they had believed confidential. . . . It is difficult to overstate the fear produced in most victims of stalkers simply by the repeated and intrusive contacts. . . . It is often the perceived threat in the constant and escalating attentions which discomforts the victims. (Mullen & Pathé, 1994b, p. 475)

DYNAMICS

No broad consensus exists on a single psychodynamic explanation for erotomania, which is hardly surprising, given the relative paucity of published cases, the absence of in-depth psychoanalytically oriented case studies (in patients who are notoriously resistant to recognizing a need for treatment in the first place), and the multiplicity of psychodynamic schools of thought. Notwithstanding the absence of clinically detailed knowledge of the inner lives of these individuals, "leaving any causal theory more speculative than substantiated" (Segal, 1989, p. 1264), psychoanalytically oriented psychiatrists and psychologists have not hesitated to pursue their predilections to search for theoretical insights in the form of various dynamic formulations. This review of the main psychodynamic hypotheses is limited, given the constraints of space, to a brief overview.

Many of these subjects are described as shy, awkward, lacking in confidence, isolated from others, feeling (or actually) physically unattractive, and "facing a life which appeared to them bleak, unrewarding and bereft of intimacy" (Mullen & Pathé, 1994a, p. 620). Kraepelin (1921, p. 25) suggested that erotomanic delusions served to provide "a kind of psychological compensation for the disappointments of life." An ego defect has been postulated, resulting in part from deep feelings of being unloved or unlovable. The specific erotomanic delusion is understood as an attempt to overcome narcissistic blows by transmuting them into grandiose fantasies. The symptom serves the purpose of warding off intolerable depression and loneliness, while providing an outside source of nurturance and love from an exalted personage (Raskin & Sullivan, 1974). The fact that in many cases the love object has a distinctive cachet, being a public figure, a politician, entertainer, or even a member of a royal family, serves the patient's narcissistic needs: "The patient feels herself [or himself] to have been plucked from . . . obscurity and singled out for the object's love . . . [which bestows] the ultimate form of approval" (Segal, 1989, p. 1264)

Feder (1973, p. 246) contended that the syndrome is a "defensive facade of a delusional, histrionic, romantic love, behind which lies the drama of an ontogenetically earlier phase of life elaborated in psychosis." Under conditions of regression, there is an attempt at restoration of the earlier blissful union with the mother figure (Feder, 1973). The search for a safe and erotized father figure and the need to ward off homosexual impulses are alternative dynamics discussed in the literature (Enoch et al., 1967).

In a number of papers, Meloy has given an elegant description of the borderline-level defenses and operations of these subjects and their narcissistic character pathology (Meloy 1989, 1990, 1992, 1996; Meloy & Gothard, 1995). He discusses the character traits that help to determine the overt behavior of stalkers, including narcissism, hysteria, paranoia, and psychopathy. Stalkers tend to use projection, projective identification, and other primitive defenses (they often report feeling harassed by the love object and, in one case, the stalker tried to obtain a restraining order against the victim!) (Meloy & Gothard, 1995). Meloy (1996) pointed out that his observations about the psychodynamics of stalkers should be treated as "testable hypotheses," to be investigated in individual cases through comprehensive clinical interviews, psychological testing, and objective measures of behavior independent of self-reports by the subjects. The pathologies of attachment in these individuals suggest early developmental disturbances during the differentiation and practicing subphases of separation–individuation (Mahler, Pine & Bergman, 1975).

In concluding that an explosion of violence in these individuals is usually "affective," driven by narcissistic rage at acutely or chronically perceived rejection by the love object, Meloy and Gothard (1995) noted:

> For those obsessional followers who have had a prior relationship with the victim, abandonment rage arising out of a narcissistic sensitivity appears to defend against the grief of object loss, which then drives the obsessional pursuit. For those subjects without a prior relationship with the victim, fantasy or delusion defends against feelings of loneliness and isolation. When the subject seeks actual contact with the stranger victim, a rebuff then stimulates abandonment rage. (p. 262)

The emphasis on psychogenic explanations for erotomania does not mean that subtle biological factors play no role in the etiology of this group of disorders. Even De Clérambault himself believed that the primary cause of erotomania "was an ill-defined organic brain lesion that he called *automatisme mental*" (Segal, 1990a).

STALKING

The dictionary defines *stalking* as "moving threateningly or menacingly; tracking prey or quarry; or pursuing by tracking stealthily" (American Heritage Dictionary, 1992, p. 1751). In a legal context, stalking has been defined as "willful, malicious, and repeated following and harassing of another person that threatens his or her safety" (Perez, 1993, p. 264). Following the murder of actress Rebecca Schaeffer in 1990 by a fan who had stalked her, California became the first state to enact an anti-stalking law. In response to other high-profile cases (involving celebrities and ordinary citizens) and the recognition that Orders of Protection and other existing measures provided inadequate protection,[4] all states (and the District of Columbia) followed suit by passing similar legislation. Although celebrity stalking and stranger stalking have received the greatest attention, it appears that a majority of stalkers pursue prior sexual intimates and the rest are divided in some unpredictable ratio between prior acquaintances and strangers. Stalking as a variant of domestic violence is a serious public health problem that has only recently begun to receive scientific scrutiny (Kurt, 1995). Many victims are also seemingly chosen in passing, at work, in the course of receiving medical or legal services, or after chance encounters, for example, seeing someone on the street. "We are all potential objects for the disordered attentions of the erotomanic" (Mullen & Pathé, 1994b, p. 477).

Most studies report that the stalker has one victim, although multiple victims are found in 33% and 22%, respectively, in two studies of forensic cohorts (Mullen & Pathé, 1994b; Harmon et al., 1995). Sequential victims have also been reported (Taylor et al., 1983). About one-half of all stalkers eventually threaten their victims, with increased likelihood if there was a prior intimate relationship (Zona et al., 1993) or an injury (real or imagined) experienced in a business or professional context (Harmon et al., 1995). Seventy-five percent of threats were *not* followed up with actual physical violence (Meloy, 1996). Paradoxically, a few studies report that some stalkers who never threatened the victim can suddenly and unexpectedly become assaultive (Meloy & Gothard, 1995; Mullen & Pathé, 1994b).

As noted above, most stalkers are found to be older, smarter, and better educated than a comparison group of offenders with mental disorders (Meloy & Gothard, 1995). This may account for the finding that they are particularly resourceful and manipulative in tracking down and pursuing their victims, despite attempts to elude them by moving, changing telephone numbers, and other evasive tactics (Meloy & Gothard, 1995).

The Los Angeles Police Department established a national model to combat the problem of stalking by setting up a unit exclusively devoted to that mission, the Threat Management Unit (TMU). This elite unit pursues stalkers aggressively, emphasizing victims' rights and a policy of proactive policing. Stalkers are confronted and restraining orders directing the stalker to cease approaching the victim are routinely obtained. In addition to aggressive police intervention, victims are instructed to cut off *all* contact with the stalker. (Only about 10% of the TMU's caseload involves celebrity stalking, even though they are located in the heart of the entertainment industry.)

---

[4]Dietz believes that restraining orders often do more harm than good and may often serve to inflame the subject, who in turn may increase the harassment of the victim (especially if the stalker is mentally ill) (Toobin, 1997). A study of restraining orders against stalkers found that more than half resumed unwanted contacts within 3 months of the first order (Toobin, 1997). Other studies contradict these assertions (see Meloy, Chapter 1).

A number of private security consulting firms have sprung up to advise corporate clients and others on dealing effectively with stalkers and violence prevention. They generally favor a policy that emphasizes safety as a paramount value over police intervention. This usually involves advising victims to move, change telephone numbers to unlisted ones, and even to change their jobs. Such strategic retreats for victims are commonplace in the corporate sector: the victim is counseled to leave his or her job and in return the company provides a fair financial settlement and outplacement. Confrontations with the stalker are almost always avoided, except in the unusual case where a felony arrest or long-term hospitalization appears to be a highly probable option (Toobin, 1997).

A number of vignettes culled from newspapers across the country are illustrative of the phenomenon of stalking:

CASE 1

Mr. C., 31, met a well-known lawyer over a business matter. Although his meeting with the woman was casual, Mr. C. "knew" she was in love with him and, to declare his love, began besieging her with calls, letters and flowers. Although she denied any interest in him and finally filed charges of harassment, he saw her reactions as a "test of love." He left his wife and abandoned his business to pursue the lawyer. When she continued to rebuff his advances, he sent threatening letters and was finally committed to a psychiatric hospital. (*New York Times,* Tuesday, October 31, 1989, p. C-1)

CASE 2

[A fan had been stalking a prominent teenage tennis player for one year, alarming the girl's mother.] His shadowy presence at her daughter's junior tournaments over the last year, his phone calls to her coaches, had been emotional terrorism. Since the 1993 stabbing of Monica Seles on a court in Germany, the fear of an obsessive fan becoming violent had haunted sports. It is no empty fear, according to the head of the Los Angeles Police Department's Threat Management Unit, the country's first anti-stalking squad; as sports stars become as glamorous as music and movie stars, they become as appealing a target for stalkers. . . . [When the girl's mother confronted the subject] he merely sat there. In what she described as a polite, educated voice, he told her that he was on his way to the house of a famous basketball player to reveal himself as the superstar's father . . . [He] then confided that he had sired many pro basketball stars as well as many world-class tennis players. The Central Intelligence Agency had used his sperm in an experiment. Her daughter was his child too. (*New York Times,* Sunday, June 29, 1997, Sect. 8, p. 1)

CASE 3

The man who shot and killed seven people Tuesday in Sunnyvale inhabited a fantasy world in which the woman who rejected him in real life was his constant loving companion, according to letters obtained yesterday. Richard Farley, a burly 39-year-old ex-Navy seaman expected to be charged with those murders, believed that he and Laura Black had taken vacations together and even tried to pass faked photographs as proof that the dates happened. When his dream lover refused to acknowledge his fantasy, he issued dark warnings that "something bad" might happen. "This is going to escalate and soon. Oh, God the s--- is going to hit the fan. All because you think I'm a joke and refuse to listen or to understand that I'm gravely serious," he wrote on November 13. When Black continued to spurn his advances, he went gunning for her. . . . [She] had recently won a temporary restraining order to keep him away. . . . As it turned out, the court order apparently enraged Farley, who took out his frustration by bursting into ESL on Tuesday and [killing seven people]. (*San Francisco Chronicle,* Thursday, February 18, 1988, p. 1)

MANAGEMENT

Although some clinicians are more sanguine about the management of erotomania per se and feel there is a misplaced pessimism about the therapeutic outcome (Mullen & Pathé, 1994a), most reports indicate that the overall prognosis for these subjects is rather gloomy (and that the lives of their victims as a consequence may be in disarray for many years, plagued by merciless pursuit and, in extreme cases, sudden violence) (Segal, 1989). Careful differential diagnosis of both Axis I and Axis II disorders is critical for appropriate therapeutic intervention and effective risk management (Meloy, 1996). Cases of secondary erotomania, most commonly due to schizophrenia or a mood disorder, should be treated accordingly (the response to treatment reflecting the nature and severity of the underlying condition) (Mullen & Pathé, 1994a). Treatment of primary erotomania with psychotropic medication is likely to produce a modest improvement at best, reducing the intensity of the delusion and associated ideas of reference, but leaving the core delusion intact (Segal, 1989). Other modalities, such as psychotherapy and ECT, have provided no convincing evidence of clinical efficacy (Segal, 1989). Containment of the patient, in order to prevent the infliction of distress and potential violence on the victim, is the keynote of successful risk management. Enforced separation from the victim, by involuntary hospitalization or incarceration, is necessary in the most refractory cases (Mullen & Pathé, 1994a). The typical course is a chronic one, although waxing and waning and even periods of full remission may occur (one of De Clérambault's cases persisted for 37 years) (Enoch et al., 1967). Although most stalkers will not become violent, Meloy (1996) emphasized that the incidence of violence is sufficiently high to warrant ongoing concern. Periodic violence risk assessment of the stalker is indicated (Meloy, 1996). Ninety percent of stalkers do not suffer from erotomania. Whether successful treatment of the Axis I and Axis II disorders in these nonerotomanic stalkers will have a significant impact on future stalking and violence is a question of great import that deserves, and will no doubt receive, further study.

EROTOMANIA IN CYBERSPACE

When criminals turn to computers, is anything safe? (Kolata, 1992)

In cyberspace, no one can hear you scream. (text taken from a lithograph by Portal Publications Ltd, 1995)

The computer revolution has transformed the communications culture[5] for better or for worse. Infinitely powerful computers and vast computer networks have built the "information superhighway" and generated global interlocking databanks, brimming with invaluable personal information on almost everyone (e.g., names, addresses, telephone and fax numbers, photographs, fingerprints, medical histories, work resumés, credit data, and much more). As with all revolutionary advances in technology, the overwhelming benefits for society are to a greater or lesser extent offset by the potential for misuse and criminal exploitation. It was predictable that interlopers would begin to roam the darkest alleys of cyberspace for their own sinister purposes, trespassing and penetrating the soft underbelly of computer databanks containing a vulnerable goldmine of online personal information. The advertising slogan "we're all connected" takes on a new darker meaning when we consider the many ways that stalkers, erotomanics, and other malicious intruders[6] can wreak havoc on their victims by perversely wielding these new high-tech tools.

Cyberstalking confirms our deepest concerns that whether on-line or in the outside world, people have the same desires and emotions, as well as the same capacities for deranged behavior. It may be that the computer underworld, with its alternative universes, virtual realities, and cyberpunk counterculture, with the blurring of lines between fantasy and fact that it nourishes, will serve to quicken and potentiate the twisted fixations of the stalker, thereby creating a new and more challenging set of problems in the years to come.

There have been many examples of cyberstalking crossing over to the real world. The following cases have recently sparked a great deal of attention from the media and the law enforcement community.

CASE 1

Andrew Archambeau and a female schoolteacher communicated via *America Online* and then arranged to meet. The woman quickly became uneasy and frightened as he immediately began to talk about marriage and having children together. After she

[5]Most people do not realize that the World Wide Web is more than a system of communication, but is in fact a virtual highway, stretching the entire earth, with exits into millions of homes and offices.

[6]On-line crime by a variety of perpetrators has involved pedophiles, pornographers, credit card fraud artists, rip-off traders, and other dark-side hackers.

made it clear that she had no romantic interest in him, he persisted with e-mail, telephone messages and letters. Within a two month period, he sent her 20 e-mail messages and 10 postal letters and packages. His electronic communiqués acquired an ominous tone when she continued to rebuff him, at one point threatening to share the details of their "relationship" with other *AOL* subscribers, her family and friends. He informed her that he sometimes watched her through the window of an ice cream shop near the school where she taught. "I've been trying to court you, not stalk you. If you let me, I would be the best man, friend, lover you ever could have. You've turned my innocent and somewhat foolish love for you into something bad in your own mind," he wrote to her via e-mail. Despite her warnings that she would contact the police, he persisted, parking near her school and waving to her. Then he called her answering machine and left the chilling message "I stalked you for the first time today." He was prosecuted under the toughest antistalking law in the country: Michigan is the only state that has expanded such legislation into the electronic realm, specifically banning electronic stalking. (*New York Times*, Friday, September 16, 1994, p. 45)

CASE 2

[Headlines recently blared] Student held on cybersex 'rape.' Jake Baker, a University of Michigan student, was arrested by the FBI for publishing a lurid fantasy of rape, torture and murder that was posted in a Usenet newsgroup and read around the world. He used the name of a woman student in his class and corresponded with another man on where and how to carry out the attack. He wrote via e-mail "Just thinking about it any more doesn't do the trick. I need to do it." Another transmission read "Torture is foreplay, rape is romance, snuff [killing] is climax." One of his transmissions described how he would kidnap the classmate at gunpoint, rape her, force her to strip, and torture her with a clamp and spreader bar before killing her. He was charged with interstate transmission of a threat to injure, a felony offense under federal law. (*New York Post*, Saturday, February 11, 1995, p. 15)

CONCLUSIONS AND SUMMARY

A survey of erotomania and stalking, from the earliest cases and classic phenomenological descriptions of De Clérambault (1921/1942) and Kraepelin (1921), evoking a romantic aura of Old World culture, to more modern manifestations of celebrity stalking and e-mail stalking, provides a historical context for an overview of the clinical scientific investigation of these entities. Once regarded as rare and exotic psychiatric curiosities, erotomania and stalking have emerged as weighty public issues of the first magnitude, exciting unprecedented media attention, legislative and law enforcement activity, and ever more rigorous scientific research efforts. A state-of-the-art review of the nosological and diagnostic status, demographic characteristics, psychodynamics, and potential for violence of erotomania and its variants has been presented. Stalking, as a legal, sociological, and public health phenomenon in its own right has been described, its relationship to erotomania outlined, and strategies for effective therapeutic and risk management set forth. As our scientific mastery of these issues continues to advance, more focused and methodologically sophisticated research studies promise to enhance our in-depth understanding of both stalkers and their victims, as well as to provide more effective means of psychiatric intervention and social control.

REFERENCES

American heritage dictionary of the English language (3rd ed.). (1992). Boston: Houghton Mifflin.

American Psychiatric Association. (1980). *Diagnostic and statistical manual of mental disorders* (3rd ed.). Washington, DC: Author.

American Psychiatric Association. (1987). *Diagnostic and statistical manual of mental disorders* (3rd ed., revised). Washington, DC: Author.

American Psychiatric Association. (1994). *Diagnostic and statistical manual of mental disorders* (4th ed.). Washington, DC: Author.

Arieti, S., & Meth, J. M. (1959). Rare, unclassifiable, collective and exotic psychotic syndromes. In S. Arieti (Ed.), *American handbook of psychiatry* (Vol. I, pp. 548–563). New York: Basic Books.

Barefoot v. Estelle, 463 U.S. 880 (1983).

De Clérambault, G. (1942). Les psychoses passionelles. In *Oeuvres Psychiatriques* (pp. 323–443). Paris: Presses Universitaires de France. (Original work published 1921).

Dietz, P. (1988, October). Presentation of research data concerning threats against celebrities, American Academy of Psychiatry and the Law, San Francisco, CA.

Ellis, P., & Mellsop, G. (1985). De Clérambault's syndrome—A nosological entity? *British Journal of Psychiatry, 146,* 90–93.

Enoch, M. D., Trethowan, W. H., & Barker, J. C. (1967). *Some uncommon psychiatric syndromes.* Bristol: John Wright & Sons.

Esquirol, J. E. D. (1965). *Mental maladies: A treatise on insanity* (R. De Saussure, Trans.). New York: Hafner. (Original work published 1845).

Feder, S. (1973). Clérambault in the ghetto: Pure erotomania reconsidered. *International Journal of Psychoanalytic Psychotherapy, 2,* 240–247.

Goldstein, R. L. (1978). De Clérambault in court: A forensic romance. *Bulletin of the American Academy of Psychiatry and the Law, 6,* 36–40.

Goldstein, R. L. (1986). Erotomania in men [Letter to the editor]. *American Journal of Psychiatry, 143,* 6.

Goldstein, R. L. (1987). More forensic romances: De Clérambault's syndrome in men. *Bulletin of the American Academy of psychiatry and the law, 15,* 267–274.

Goldstein, R. L. (1995). Paranoids in the legal system: The litigious paranoid and the paranoid criminal. In *The Psychiatric Clinics of North America, 18*(2) (*Delusional Disorders*), 303–315.

Harmon, R., Rosner, R., & Owens, H. (1995). Obsessional harassment and erotomania in a criminal court population. *Journal of Forensic Sciences, 40,* 188–196.

Hart, B. (1921). *The psychology of insanity.* Cambridge: Cambridge University Press.

Hayes, M., & O'Shea, B. (1985). Erotomania in Schneider-positive schizophrenia. *British Journal of Psychiatry, 146,* 661–663.

Hollender, M. H., & Callahan, A. S. (1975). Erotomania or De Clérambault syndrome. *Archives of General Psychiatry, 32,* 1574–1576.

Kolata, G. (1992). When criminals turn to computers, is anything safe? *Smithsonian, 23*(8), 116–124.

Kraepelin, E. (1921). *Manic-depressive insanity and paranoia* (G.M. Robertson, Trans). Edinburgh: E. & S. Livingstone.

Krafft-Ebing, R. (1879). *Text book of insanity.* (C. Chaddock, Trans.) Philadelphia: F.A. Davies.

Kurt, J. L. (1995). Stalking as a variant of domestic violence. *Bulletin of the American Academy of Psychiatry and the Law, 23,* 219–231.

Mahler, M., Pine, F., & Bergman, A. (1975). *The psychological birth of the human infant.* New York: Basic Books.

McAnaney, K., Curliss, L., & Abeyta-Price, C. (1993). From imprudence to crime; anti-stalking laws. *Notre Dame Law Review, 68,* 819–909.

Meloy, J. R. (1988). *The psychopathic mind: Origins, dynamics and treatment.* Northvale, NJ: Jason Aronson.

Meloy, J. R. (1989). Unrequited love and the wish to kill: The diagnosis and treatment of borderline erotomania. *Bulletin of the Menninger Clinic, 53,* 477–492.

Meloy, J. R. (1990). Nondelusional or borderline erotomania [Letter to the editor]. *American Journal of Psychiatry, 147,* 820–821.

Meloy, J. R. (1992). *Violent attachments.* Northvale, NJ: Jason Aronson.

Meloy, J. R. (1996), Stalking (obsessional following): A review of some preliminary studies. *Aggression and Violent Behavior, 1*(2), 147–162.

Meloy, J. R., & Gothard, S. (1995). Demographic and clinical comparison of obsessional followers and offenders with mental disorders. *American Journal of Psychiatry, 152,* 258–263.

Menzies, R. P. D., Fedoroff, J. P., Green, C. M., & Isaacson, K. (1995). Prediction of dangerous behavior in male erotomania. *British Journal of Psychiatry, 166,* 529–536.

Monahan, J., & Steadman, H. (1994). *Violence and mental disorder: Developments in risk assessment.* Chicago: University of Chicago Press.

Mullen, P. E., & Pathé, M. (1994a). The pathological extensions of love. *British Journal of Psychiatry, 165,* 614–623.

Mullen, P. E., & Pathé, M. (1994b). Stalking and the pathologies of love. *Australian and New Zealand Journal of Psychiatry, 28,* 469–477.

Pearce, A. (1972). De Clérambault syndrome associated with *folie à deux. British Journal of Psychiatry, 121,* 116–118.

Pederson, S. (1949). Psychological reactions to extreme social displacement. *Psychoanalytic Review, 36,* 344–356.

Perez, C. (1993). Stalking: When does obsession become a crime? *American Journal of Criminal Law, 20,* 264–280.

Raskin, D. E., & Sullivan, K. E. (1974). Erotomania. *American Journal of Psychiatry, 131,* 1033–1035.

Reik, T. (1963). *The need to love.* New York: Farrar, Strauss.

Rudden, M., Sweeney, J., & Frances, A. (1990). Diagnosis and clinical course of erotomanic and other delusional patients. *American Journal of Psychiatry, 147,* 625–628.

Segal, J. H. (1989). Erotomania revisited: From Kraepelin to DSM-III-R. *American Journal of Psychiatry, 146,* 1261–1266.

Segal, J. H. (1990a). Erotomania, obsessive love not uncommon but difficult to treat. *The Psychiatric Times: Medicine & Behavior, VII*(7), 22–24.

Segal, J. H. (1990b). Reply to J. R. Meloy: Nondelusional or borderline erotomania [Letter to the editor]. *American Journal of Psychiatry, 147,* 820–821.

Sims, A., & White, A. (1973). Coexistence of the Capgras and De Clérambault syndromes: A case history. *British Journal of Psychiatry, 123,* 635–637.

Spitzka, E. C. (1889). *Insanity, its classification, diagnosis and treatment.* New York: E.B. Treat.

Taylor, P., Mahendra, B., & Gunn, J. (1983). Erotomania in males. *Psychological Medicine, 13,* 645–650.

Toobin, J. (1997). Stalking in L.A. *The New Yorker, LXXIII*(2), 72–83.

Zona, M., Sharma, L., & Lane, J. (1993). A comparative study of erotomanic and obsessional subjects in a forensic sample. *Journal of Forensic Sciences, 38,* 894–903.

CHAPTER 11

Cultural Factors in Erotomania and Obsessional Following

Judith Meyers, Psy.D.

As obsessional followers have gained increasing attention in the media and forensic literature, researchers have removed the concept of erotomania from the arcane annals of psychiatric and psychological literature and made it more clinically relevant to the understanding of obsessional following, stalking, and domestic violence (Meloy, 1996). Erotomania is no longer regarded as merely a variant of psychosis that affects only women (De Clérambault, 1921/1942), but rather a subgroup of delusional disorder that affects a larger percentage of men and is a precipitating factor in some forensic cases (Dietz et al., 1991; Goldstein, 1987; Meloy, 1989).

Erotomania, as a delusional disorder (*DSM-IV*, APA, 1994), is also understood as a variant of pathological mourning (Evans, Jeckel, & Slott, 1982), a disorder of attachment, identity disturbance, and a reflection of poor reality testing (Meloy, 1989, 1997). Other authors cite erotomania as a reaction to loss (Fenichel, 1945), or as part of a paranoid disorder (Feder, 1973; Goldstein, 1987). Meloy's psychodynamic formulation of obsessional followers makes similar comparisons (1996).

In their extensive group study of erotomanic and obsessional forensic subjects, Zona, Sharma, and Lane (1993) noted a strikingly high number of foreign-born subjects in their erotomanic group; 43% were from other cultures with nonexistent or limited family support, compared to 3% in the love obsessional subgroup, and 5% in the simple obsessional subgroup. The *DSM-IV* also cites immigration as a possible stressor in this disorder. Despite this empirical evidence, no one has researched the role of culture in the formation of these delusional disorders of attachment. Theoretical evidence suggests the link is clinically sensible, but the

The Psychology of Stalking: Clinical and Forensic Perspectives

relationship between erotomania, obsessional following, and acculturation problems remains unexplored.

THEORETICAL FRAMEWORK

A theoretical link exists between the concepts of erotomania and culture shock in the psychoanalytic literature. Both have been described as variants of pathological mourning (Evans et al., 1982; Garza-Guerrero, 1974), suggesting similar dynamics in the role of object loss in the shaping of symptoms. Fenichel (1945) noted in his discussion of erotomanic symptoms that males at the psychotic end of the continuum frantically search for an object in the face of imminent object loss. Culture shock has also been described as a painful longing, an admixture of anxiety, desperation, and sadness in the face of the loss of culture (Garza-Guerrero, 1974).

Identity problems have also been discussed in the dynamic formulation of both culture shock and erotomania. Culture shock has been described as a precipitant in identity problems, since an individual may temporarily experience a break in the continuity of the self as it interacts with an unfamiliar environment (Garza-Guerrero, 1974; Zaharna, 1989). Meloy stated that the identity disturbance seen in the borderline erotomanic is evidenced by their intense yet tumultuous attachment to their love object (Meloy, 1989).

SOCIAL ISOLATION

The link between social isolation and obsessional followers, whether erotomanic or not, is quite strong. Meloy (1996) described obsessional following, in part, as a "maladaptive response to social incompetence" (p. 159). Meloy and Gothard (1995) reported a history of impaired social relationships and failed courtship attempts in their subjects. Many men never had a significant long-term relationship. Zona et al. (1993) found that 72% of their erotomanic subgroup had never married. Segal stated that erotomanics lead lonely, socially vacuous lives, and the delusions "may provide solace for a few lonely souls, who might otherwise spend their lives in unrelieved isolation and solitude" (Segal, 1989, p. 1265).

Failures in acculturation may relate to an individual's interpersonal difficulty in engaging people who are different from himself, a lack of flexibility or ethnocentrism, or an inability to establish a support group within the host culture. Social isolation may result from intrapsychic problems such as schizoid tendencies that would manifest in any culture, or feelings of mistrust toward the dominant host culture. Conversely, marginalization is frequently rooted in the culture's response to the individual, based on race, ethnicity, or social/political status. Due to stereotypes, prejudices, and institutionalized restrictions, the individual perceives that he or she will never be integrated into the mainstream of the new culture (Berry, 1997; Berry, Kim, Minde, & Mok, 1987).

REALITY TESTING

Impaired reality testing is a cardinal feature of erotomanics and obsessional followers, since the distortion in their perception of the relationship is the basis for the unwelcome pursuit. If psychotic, the individual is characterized by delusional and persecutory ideation. If nonpsychotic, there is an impairment in self–other differentiation, wherein the individual has difficulty understanding the origin of his feelings and thoughts (Meloy, 1996).

The accuracy of one's reality testing also affects the acculturation process. Perceptual acuity (Meyers, 1990; Kelley & Meyers, 1992; Meyers & Meloy, 1994) has been cited as a critical skill for adapting to the new cultural environment. It is a trial and error process in which one learns to make accurate assumptions about the norms of the new culture and avoids negative attributions based solely on one's internal needs. It is the ability to process information within the context of the new culture and deal effectively with ambiguity. It involves both empathy and perceptual accuracy.

One factor that contributes to poor perceptual acuity is the inability to comprehend nonverbal cues. For example, an individual from another culture may completely misconstrue the behavior of the love object, simulating the delusional quality of erotomania. A male from a heterosexually repressed culture who immigrates to a more sexually open, westernized culture, could attach romantic meaning where there is none, or misinterpret social friendliness. This is particularly likely in an individual with borderline or psychotic functioning where the reality testing is already compromised, or the individual may fail to modify his discrepant beliefs, social customs, and mores to better align with those of the host culture. This is due to an impairment in the feedback loop in which he is unable to recognize or comprehend negative social reinforcement, or alter his behavior in response to it.

LOSS, MOURNING, AND IDENTITY

Since severe culture shock and erotomania are both considered variants of pathological mourning, the issue of loss has been cited as an important psychodynamic in both (Garza-Guerrero, 1974; Levy-Warren, 1987). A successful transition to another culture involves the same psychological mechanisms as in the mastery of any separation or loss—a stable internal image of the need-satisfying object (in this case, the culture of origin), libidinal object constancy, and the ability to mourn. Garza-Guerrero (1974) stated:

> Culture shock is a reactive process stemming from the impact of a new culture upon those who attempt to merge with it as a newcomer. Culture shock profoundly tests the overall adequacy of personality functioning, is accompanied by mourning for the abandoned culture, and severely threatens the newcomer's identity. (p. 410)

Levy-Warren (1987) discussed normal culture shock as a loss experienced in the environment, whereas severe culture shock is experienced as a profound loss of self, similar to pathological mourning.

If one is unable to adapt to the new culture, one is vulnerable to psychological distress (Berry, 1997) and even pathological regression (Garza-Guerrero, 1974). This failure to acculturate can also be understood as a disorder of attachment, because the individual suffers through a period of distress and isolation and an inability to attach to the new environment. Similar to pathological mourning, the individual may hunger for lost objects with which to bond and identify.

When erotomanic behavior or obsessional pursuit is seen in foreign-born individuals, its relationship to acculturation stress should be explored. Individuals usually will have a history of early loss or deprivation (see Kienlen, Chapter 3) and an acculturation process marred by trauma, loss of status, and difficulty assuming meaningful new roles in this culture. The individual vacillates between a yearning for the lost culture and a tumultuous encounter with the new (Garza-Guerrero, 1974). While there are many variants of culture shock, pursuit behavior within the context of immigration suggests an inability to deal with multiple losses inherent in a cross-cultural move. The frantic pursuit of the love object emerges as a mechanism to ward off depression, a defense against mourning, and a substitute for identity loss. Paranoid reactions to the new culture, often a feature of the disorganization phase of culture shock (Newhill, 1990), take on delusional proportions. The more disparate the customs and social cues between the two cultures, the more vulnerable the individual (David, 1971; Meyers & Meloy, 1994). The following case illustrates these salient points.

CASE 1

Tarasoff v. Regents of the University of California (1976) is a well-known forensic case that redefined the concept of confidentiality in the psychotherapy relationship. What is less known is that the case involved an erotomanic attachment that resulted in the death of the love object. Prosenjit Poddar was a foreign student from Bengal, India, who was born into the untouchable caste. He entered U.C. Berkeley as a graduate student in September 1967, residing at the International House. One year later, while attending folk dancing classes, he met Tatiana (Tanya) Tarasoff. They dated during the fall of 1968. On New Year's Eve, they kissed, an act which he believed signified a serious relationship. When she learned of his feelings, she actively discouraged him and indicated that she did not wish to enter into an intimate relationship. Despite this, he developed a delusional fixation on her as a love object.

As a result of the rebuff, Poddar seriously regressed. He became depressed, withdrew socially, and neglected his studies and his appearance. He continued to deteriorate into the summer of 1969. He would meet occasionally with Tanya during this period and tape record their conversations to ascertain why she did not love him.

Tanya left that summer for several months, and Poddar improved and consulted a therapist. However, when Tanya returned in October, he stopped seeing his psychologist. On October 26, 1969, he went to her house to talk to her and Tanya was not home. Her mother told him to leave. He returned later, armed with a pellet gun and a kitchen knife. This time Tanya was alone. He planned to create a disaster from which he would rescue her and cause her to recognize her love for him. However, his plans went awry. When she refused to talk to him, he would not leave. She screamed. At this point, he shot her with the pellet gun. She ran from the house, but she was caught and fatally stabbed.

At the sanity phase of his criminal trial, three psychiatrists and one psychologist testified that his mental capacity was diminished by paranoid schizophrenia. His former treating psychologist opined that his psychotic delusions about the deceased rendered him incapable of comprehending what he was doing. The testimony of an anthropologist shed light on the cross-cultural determinants in this case. He testified that Poddar had been having a difficult time adjusting to American college life. He stated that the precipitant for his illness was a failed cross-cultural adaptation and discussed his illness in terms of culture shock. He testified to the fact that Tanya had provided the only meaningful social contact that he had, and when he was rebuffed, he became delusional (*People v. Poddar,* 1974).

EVALUATING CULTURE SHOCK AND ACCULTURATION STRESS

The process known as culture shock (Oberg, 1960) is actually the anxiety that results from the confrontation with the new culture, the mourning that takes place in relation to the lost culture, and the threat to identity that results from the loss of the known, familiar, and expectable. It is my contention that severe culture shock can precipitate erotomanic reactions in borderline or psychotic males, particularly when they are from heterosexually repressive cultures. This may be particularly true for men from traditional Islamic cultures, or Middle Eastern and Arab men who have been marginalized in Western culture.[1] These groups have learned very different social mores and sociosexual cues regarding heterosexual relationships and behavior. They are likely to have a devalued position in this culture and feel estranged from the cultural norms of Western society, which values individualism rather than collectivism (Hofstede, 1980; Feghali, 1997) and sexual equality over male dominance. This discrepancy is known as cultural distance, which is the degree of psychological difference between one's native culture and the host culture. It includes differences in values, language, and religion. The greater the cultural differences, the less positive is the adaption (Newhill, 1990; Ward & Searle, 1991; Berry, 1997). Cultural distance also results in the negative expectation that one will not be integrated into the larger society, resulting in feelings of isolation. These factors are quite strong for Middle Eastern and Arab men in our culture, unless they have found a supportive subculture (Hoffman, 1991).

CASE 2

Patient A was a 37-year-old Libyan male evaluated to determine his violence risk toward a young American woman. He had never personally known her, but she had sat in front of him during a college course. He had subsequently pursued her for 5 years, sending her gifts and flowers, several letters, and, on one occasion, a blood-soaked feather. He had telephoned her, her mother, and her employer, and he intermittently approached her in public places. She became anxious and fearful and entered psychotherapy. Prior to his evaluation, Patient A violated five temporary restraining orders issued by the Superior Court.

The patient was born in Libya to an intact family with two older brothers and eight younger sisters. He finished high school and then began working in the family business. His life was very constricted by Western standards, and he was quite bound to his family. It was difficult to assess, from his self-report, whether this level of enmeshment was consistent with his cultural norm or an early indicator of social problems. He dated very little and, when he did, he was chaperoned by family members, which he reported as customary. He eventually became engaged to his cousin, but she terminated the relationship after 2 years. In response to his rejection, he immigrated to the United States at age 27. He lived alone in a large American city, worked at menial jobs, and took some college courses. While at college, he first saw the victim.

During the clinical evaluation, he denied that he was in pursuit of the victim or intended to harm her, but rather was responding to "the way she looked at

---

[1] The reader is referred to Feghali's (1997) framework for an understanding of the cultural/ political background of these groups and the boundaries attached to these terms. Her exhaustive bibliography is compiled from a multidisciplinary perspective and covers Arab history, religion, and cultural communication patterns.

me, the way she did her hair, she gave a smile from a distance like she wanted to engage in a puzzle . . . the challenge is what keeps me going" (Meyers & Meloy, 1994, p. 906). Psychological testing confirmed an individual organized at a psychotic level of personality who had difficulties with reality testing, identity diffusion, and modulation of affect. While his self-esteem was low, he had an idealized grandiose self, which meant that aspirations far outstripped his abilities.

> Formal thought disorder was apparent, and content analysis of his Rorschach indicated a plethora of symbiotic merging responses. His IQ was in the bright normal range (110–119). His diagnosis was delusional disorder, erotomanic subtype (DSM IV). Further, the patient's misperception of social friendliness as serious romantic intent was a partial product of his attempt to integrate two widely divergent interpersonal cultures. But it was exacerbated by a psychotic personality organization which seriously impaired his reality testing. The motivational dynamics involved a pathological mourning for the lost culture, as well as the losses sustained in that culture, threats of loss of identity due to a marginalized position in the new culture, an inability to process the complexities of the new culture, and an affectional hunger for the new object, that would defend against his losses. (Meyers & Meloy, 1994, pp. 906–907)

In order to better analyze the degree that cultural factors could be contributing to the expression of symptoms in foreign-born obsessional followers, it is important to understand the concepts of acculturation, acculturation stress, and cultural identity.

Acculturation is a continuous process of unfolding when an individual comes into constant contact with a new cultural environment. It involves psychological, cultural, behavioral, and social changes. While culture shock is an expected reaction to the initial phases of acculturation, the degree of culture shock can vary, depending on factors such as prior cross-cultural experience, the degree of volition involved in the move, and current social supports. Factors such as age, education, and predeparture status are also influences (Baron & Heras, 1991).

Acculturation stress, as it states, is the specific type of stress that results from the process of acculturation. It is the symptom of culture shock that results in lowered health status and, typically, confusion, anxiety, depression, feelings of marginality and alienation, heightened psychosomatic symptoms, and identity confusion (Berry et al., 1987).

> Acculturation stress is thus a reduction in the health status of individuals, and may include physical, psychological and social aspects. To qualify as acculturation stress, these changes should be related in a systematic way to known features of the acculturation process as experienced by the individual. (Berry et al., 1987, p. 493)

There are several moderating factors that affect the degree of acculturation stress. The first has to do with the degree of volition and sense of permanence attached to the move. The less choice involved in the move, the more difficult the acculturation process. For example, political refugees who were forced to relocate would experience more stress than immigrants who made a voluntary choice to relocate. Those who plan to permanently settle in a location and who establish a social network do better than sojourners without permanent social systems (Berry et al., 1987).

The mode of acculturation also contributes to the degree of acculturation stress. This also gives important information as to how the individuals resolved their conflict regarding *cultural identity* (Berry et al., 1987; Berry, 1997; Dana, 1993). When an individual does not wish to maintain his native culture and identity, sheds this culture, and seeks daily interaction with the dominant host culture, the mode is assimilation. This is associated with an "approach" style of social interaction. In contrast, when value is placed on holding on to one's original culture and avoidance of interaction with the host culture, then separation is the mode. This is also termed "traditional" because the individual holds on to his original value system, often to the exclusion of the host culture's norms. An "avoidance" style of social interaction is associated with this approach. When there is interest in maintaining one's culture, as well as daily interaction with the other, integration is the mode. It is also termed "bicultural" because the individual maintains ties and practices rituals within the context of two cultures. This is associated with a "flexible" style. Finally, an enforced cultural loss, such as with refugees, coupled with little interest in the host culture, is associated with marginalization. This social style is associated with psychopathology (Berry, 1997).

It should be noted that marginalization can be a result of an individual's desire to withdraw, or discrimination on the part of the host culture. In either case, there is enforced cultural loss. This means the presence of hostility, much reduced social support, and alienation. Acculturation strategies have been shown to have a substantial relationship to the levels of positive adaption. Integration is usually the most successful; marginalization the least; and assimilation and separation strategies moderately successful (Berry, 1997).

The coping mechanisms used in the process of acculturation are important predictors of the degree of acculturation stress that will be experienced. Kelley and Meyers (1992) developed a self-assessment measure, *The Cross-Cultural Adaptability Inventory,* which describes four dimensions essential to cross-cultural effectiveness: emotional resilience, flexibility/openness, perceptual acuity, and personal autonomy. Emotional resilience is correlated with the ability to bounce back from setbacks and maintain a positive attitude. It is associated with a sense of adventure and emotional equilibrium. Flexibility and openness is associated with the ability to deal with ambiguity, openness to novelty, and a nonjudgmental approach to new people and experiences. Perceptual acuity is the ability to pay attention to verbal/nonverbal cues and to interpret communication in terms of the context as well as the content. Personal autonomy is a strong internal locus of control and a clear personal value system that allows one to maintain his or her identity within the new culture. These coping mechanisms help the individual adapt effectively and lower the effects of acculturation stress. Other moderating factors such as education, preacculturation status, motivation, and positive expectations also help in the adaption process.

In order to best assess these acculturation factors, a careful clinical interview should be the cornerstone of the diagnostic formulation. *DSM-IV* gives recommendations for the information to be included in the clinical interview of culturally diverse people (pp. 843–844). The goal is to augment the standard diagnostic interview with information regarding the individual's culture of origin, cultural identity, and the perceived relationship to the host culture. This would include the mode of acculturation as well as current support systems (Lu, Lim, & Mezzich, 1995).

If the individual is a recent immigrant, a migration history should include the predeparture status, degree of volition in the move, and any displacements, internments, or refugee camps. Given the centrality of loss and mourning in the dynamics of these individuals, clinicians need to explore the extent of the losses, traumas, separations, and disappointments experienced (Jacobsen, 1988; Lu et al., 1995).

It is also important to understand the cultural idioms for mental illness, how feelings of distress are expressed, and how illness is explained by the cultural reference group (Hughes, 1993). Finally, clinicians must assess the differences in culture and social status between patients and themselves, and determine whether difficulties in communication or transference/countertransference issues may impede the diagnostic interview. If such is the case, the use of an interpreter to facilitate communication and/or a cultural consultant to function as a cultural liaison is recommended. Ideally, the latter should be a mental health professional familiar with the individual's culture of origin in order to explain the norms and values of the culture, assist in identifying culture-bound symptoms, and help avoid biases and misdiagnoses (Lu et al., 1995).

TREATMENT CONSIDERATIONS

Clinical risk management for stalking is complicated, and a multidisciplinary team approach is usually necessary before the behavior will cease. Clinical management involves strategic planning that factors in the potential of the perpetrator to respond to treatment, the role of the criminal justice system, and the response of the victim. Each case must be handled on an individual basis, based on the dynamics of the individual and the effectiveness of outside sanctions. As Meloy (1997) succinctly stated: "In most cases, mental health and criminal justice responses are both necessary, but each insufficient" (p. 181).

Factoring in cultural issues may appear to add yet another level of complexity to an already complicated clinical issue. However, focusing on a cultural formulation enhances the usefulness of the biopsychosocial model, as it highlights the effect of culture on the expression of symptoms, definition of illness, and treatment (Lu et al., 1995; Hughes & Wintrob, 1995). For example, one would want to evaluate whether stressors related to immigration and acculturation were the primary precipitants in the pursuit behavior. If the symptoms were a reaction to feeling marginalized and alienated in this culture, then the intervention would primarily target Axis IV psychosocial stressors. In this case, the team approach would emphasize a case management model, with attention to providing social supports to the individual. The unwelcome behavior may be related to cross-cultural differences in courtship patterns, misinterpretation of social cues, or other failures in perceptual acuity. Such behaviors, while tenacious, annoying, and intrusive, might not be dangerous. "The clinician should view these 'obsessional relational intrusions' along a continuum, and recognize that most of these behaviors will not rise to the threshold of criminal behavior" (Meloy, 1997, p. 174). In this type of case, the team approach should involve an external sanction that will give a clear message that the behavior is unacceptable, coaching of the victim to ensure that the behavior is not reinforced, and cognitive–behavior therapy for the perpetrator that emphasizes social skill-building, preferably in a group setting.

In most cases of stalking, however, prior criminal, psychiatric and substance abuse histories exist (Meloy, 1996). Axis I and Axis II must be assessed, and the presence of an affective disorder, psychosis, delusional disorder, or character pathology would be seen as the primary consideration in treatment planning. Acculturation stress may be the precipitating factor in these diagnoses, or the preexisting conditions may have contributed to the acculturation problems. This is one of the challenges in the diagnostic formulation of these patients. While certain schizophrenic and manic-depressive disorders, substance abuse disorders, and organic conditions show less variability across cultures (Johnson, 1988), conduct, adjustment, anxiety, somatoform, dissociative, personality, and dysthymic disorders show greater variation across cultures (Kleinman, 1988).

It is important that clinicians judge possible symptoms of psychopathology against a knowledge of the cultural norms of the patient's cultural identity (Hughes & Wintrob, 1995). This is essential in the treatment of erotomania and obsessional following, for the determination of the primary diagnosis predicts response to treatment and future dangerousness.

SUMMARY

I have shown the relationship among erotomania, culture shock, and pathological mourning in forensic cases of foreign-born individuals. The unifying theme is loss related to the immigration experience, which results in a yearning and searching for a new object. In erotomania, the pursuit takes on delusional proportions. In obsessional following, abandonment rage may be a displacement from the original loss. Other factors include their premorbid personalities, early history of trauma, the disequilibrium fostered by the cultural transition, and the suspicion and mistrust engendered by the new culture.

I have outlined how the clinician can gain more relevant diagnostic information from the patient by investigating his culture of origin, cultural identity, current environmental stressors, support system, and relationship to the host culture. By combining the data regarding his ego organization, affective stability, and character structure with sociocultural factors, the clinician should be able to make a sensitive diagnostic formulation, while meeting the treatment needs of the individual and the safety needs of his potential victim.

REFERENCES

American Psychiatric Association. (1994). *Diagnostic and statistical manual of mental disorders* (4th ed.). Washington, DC: Author.

American Psychological Association. (1993). Guidelines for providers of psychological service to ethnic, linguistic, and culturally diverse populations. *American Psychologist, 48*, 45–48.

Baron, M. S., & Heras, P. (1991, November). Acculturation. *Academy of San Diego Psychologists Newsletter.*

Berry, J. W. (1997). Immigration, acculturation and adaption. *Applied Psychology, 46*(1), 5–68.

Berry, J. W., Kim, U., Minde, T., & Mok, D. (1987). Comparative studies of acculturative stress. *International Migration Review, XXI*(3), 491–511.

Bowlby, J. (1961). Processes of mourning. *International Journal of Psychoanalysis, 42*, 317–340.

Dana, R. H. (1993). *Multi-cultural assessment perspectives for professional psychology.* Massachusetts: Allyn and Bacon.

David, K. H. (1971). Culture shock and the development of self-awareness. *Journal of Contemporary Psychotherapy, 4*, 44–48.

De Clérambault, C. (1942). Les psychoses passionelles. In *Oeuvre Psychiatrique* (pp. 323–443). Paris: Presses Universitaires de France. (Original work published 1921)

Deitz, P. E., Matthews, D., Martell, D. A., Stewart, T., Hrouda, D., & Warren, J. (1991). Threatening and otherwise inappropriate letters to members of the United States Congress. *Journal of Forensic Sciences, 36*, 1445–1468.

Evans, D. L., Jeckel, L. L., & Slott, N. E. (1982). Erotomania: A variant of psychological mourning. *Bulletin of the Menninger Clinic, 46*, 507–520.

Feder, S. (1973). Clérambault in the ghetto: Pure erotomania reconsidered. *International Journal of Psychoanalytic Psychotherapy, 2*, 240–247.

Feghali, E. (1997). Arab culture communication patterns. *International Journal of Intercultural Relations, 21* (3), 345–378.

Fenichel, O. (1945). *The psychoanalytic theory of neurosis.* New York: Norton.

Furnham, A., & Bochner, S. (1982). Social difficulty in a foreign culture: An empirical analysis of culture shock. In S. Bochner (Ed.), *Cultures in contact* (pp. 161–198). Oxford: Pergamon Press.

Garza-Guerrero, A. C. (1974). Culture shock: Its mourning and the vicissitudes of identity. *Journal of the American Psychoanalytic Association, 22*, 408–429.

Goldstein, R. L. (1987). More forensic romances: De Clérambault's syndrome in men. *Bulletin of the American Academy of Psychiatry and the Law, 15*, 267–274.

Hoffman, D. M. (1991). Beyond conflict: Culture, self, and intercultural learning among Iranians in the U.S. *International Journal of Intercultural Relations, 15*, 63–182.

Hofstede, G. (1980). *Culture's consequence: International differences in work-related values*. London: Sage.

Hughes, C. C. (1993). Culture in clinical psychiatry. In A. C. Gaw (Ed.), *Culture, ethnicity, and mental illness* (pp. 3–41). Washington, DC: American Psychiatric Press.

Hughes, C. C., & Wintrob, R. M. (1995). Culture-bound syndromes and the cultural context of clinical psychiatry. In J. M. Oldham & M. B. Riba (Eds.), *American Psychiatric Press review of psychiatry* (Vol. 14, pp. 565–597). Washington DC: American Psychiatric Press.

Jacobsen, F. M. (1988). Ethnocultural assessment. In L. Comas-Diaz & E. H. Griffith (Eds.), *Clinical guidelines in cross-cultural mental health* (pp. 135–147). New York: Wiley & Sons.

Johnson, F. A. (1988). Contributions of anthropology to psychiatry. In H. Goldman (Ed.), *Review of psychiatry* (2nd ed., pp. 167–181). Norwalk, CT: Appleton and Lange.

Kelley, C., & Meyers, J. (1992). *The cross-cultural adaptability inventory*, Minneapolis, MN: NCS Assessments.

Kleinman, A. (1988). *Rethinking psychiatry*. New York: Free Press.

Levy-Warren, M. H. (1987). Moving to a new culture: Cultural identity, loss, and mourning. In J. Bloom-Feshback & S. Bloom-Feshback (Eds.), *The psychology of separation and loss* (pp. 300–315). San Francisco: Jossey-Bass.

Lu, F. G., Lim, R., & Mezzich, J. E. (1995). Issues in the assessment and diagnosis of culturally diverse individuals. In J. M. Oldham & M. B. Riba (Eds.), *American Psychiatric Press review of psychiatry* (Vol. 14, pp. 477–507). Washington DC: American Psychiatric Press.

Meloy, J. R. (1989). Unrequited love and the wish to kill: Diagnosis and treatment of borderline erotomania. *Bulletin of the Menninger Clinic, 53,* 477–492.

Meloy, J. R. (1996). Stalking (obsessional following): A review of some preliminary studies. *Aggression and Violent Behavior, 1,* 147–162.

Meloy, J. R. (1997). The clinical risk management of stalking: "Someone is watching over me . . ." *American Journal of Psychotherapy, 51,* 174–184.

Meloy, J. R., & Gothard, S. (1995). Demographic and clinical comparison of obsessional followers and offenders with mental disorders. *American Journal of Psychiatry, 152,* 258–263.

Meyers, J. (1990). *Assessing cross-cultural adaptability*. Paper presented at the Society for Personality Assessment, San Diego, CA.

Meyers, J., & Meloy, J. R. (1994). Discussion of "A comparative study of erotomanic and obsessional subjects in a forensic sample" [Letter to the editor]. *Journal of Forensic Sciences, 39,* 906–907.

Newhill, C. E. (1990). The role of culture in the development of paranoid symptomatology. *American Journal of Orthopsychiatry, 60*(2), 176–185.

Oberg, K. (1960). Culture shock: Adjustment to new cultural environments. *Practical Anthropology, 7,* 177–182.

People v. Poddar (1974). 10 C.3d 750; 111 Cal. Rptr. 910, 518 P.2d 342.

Rohrlich, B. F., & Martin, J. N. (1991). Host country and reentry adjustment of student sojourners. *International Journal of Intercultural Relations, 15,* 163–182.

Segal, J. H. (1989). Erotomania revisited: From Kraepelin to DSM-III-R. *American Journal of Psychiatry, 146,* 1261–1266.

Searle, W., & Ward, C. (1990). The prediction of psychological and sociocultural adjustment during cross-cultural transitions. *International Journal of Intercultural Relations, 14,* 449–464.

Tarasoff v. Regents of the University of California, 17 Cal.3d 425 (1976).

Ward, C., & Searle, W. (1991). The impact of value discrepancies and cultural identity on psychological and sociocultural adjustment of sojourners. *International Journal of Intercultural Relations, 15,* 209–225.

Zaharna, R. S. (1989). Self-shock: The double-binding challenge of identity. *International Journal of Intercultural Relations, 13,* 501–525.

Zona, M., Sharma, K., and Lane, J. (1993). A comparative study of erotomanic and obsessional subjects in a forensic sample. *Journal of Forensic Sciences, 38,* 894–903.

CHAPTER 12

False Victimization Syndromes in Stalking

**Kris Mohandie, Ph.D., Chris Hatcher, Ph.D.,
and Det. Douglas Raymond**

The phenomenon of false victimization has been noted since biblical times. The case of Potiphar is described in the Book of Genesis, Chapter 39. Potiphar, a captain of the Pharaoh's guard, had employed Joseph to take care of his household. Joseph was an attractive man, and Potiphar's wife tried to seduce him day after day, to no avail. Upset over his refusal to have sex with her, she cried rape. She told her husband that when she screamed for help, Joseph ran off leaving his cloak behind. Her husband was furious and placed Joseph in the King's prison where he spent 2 years before the Pharaoh eventually released him, based on Joseph's ability to interpret dreams (Macdonald, 1995). Such allegations of the false single crime have been noted throughout the centuries in a variety of cultures. More recently, false allegations in the crime of stalking have been recorded (Zona, Lane, & Moore, 1996; Zona & Palarea, 1997; Truscott & Evans, 1997).

There are currently no professional references or publications dedicated to the issue of false allegations of stalking, referred to by some stalking researchers as false victimization syndrome (Zona et al., 1996). Two references where the phenomenon is identified mention it in passing, while addressing the typology of stalkers encountered in a municipal law enforcement population (Zona et al., 1996; Zona & Palarea, 1997). These references do not offer any description, explanation, or interventions for these types of cases, which occur at an estimated 2% of all reported stalking cases. Studies from this Los Angeles Police Department database show that false cases occur at a base rate of 1 in 50 cases: In the 1993 study this amounted to 2 false cases out of a total of 102 cases, while in the 1997 report this amounted to 6 false cases out of a total of 341 cases (R. Palarea, personal

The Psychology of Stalking: Clinical and Forensic Perspectives

communication, November 1997). In these studies, cases were categorized as false cases if the "victim" confessed or the investigators determined that the case was not credible (M. Zona, personal communication, November 1997). Even the term *syndrome* might be considered misleading, since it implies a single homogeneous and distinct presentation. In this chapter, we offer a typology of related "false victimization syndromes" that vary according to the victim's account of the source of the victimization and whether a perpetrator is identified.

Our professional career history has involved assisting victims of violent crime and assisting in the development of intervention strategies to prevent perpetrators of violent crime from acquiring additional victims. Our collective experience base involving literally hundreds of cases has produced a very significant empathy for those individuals who, through no fault of their own, become the object of terror and violence by another.

Over this experience base, on rare occasions, a case would emerge in which the initial self-identified victim subsequently acknowledged that the crime had never occurred or was convicted in a court of law of making a false allegation. As the "false" victims discussed the reasons for having presented themselves to law enforcement as actual victims, themes of need for attention and/or need for a meaningful identity in life emerged, among others. At first, we found this phenomenon to be both puzzling and thought provoking, but the observations were always overshadowed by the need to return to the service of the large number of actual crime victims. However, over time, we have determined that this phenomenon, however limited, does exist and warrants thoughtful attention.

Although relatively rare, these false cases do impact the criminal justice system in five ways: First, the time and energy devoted to investigating false claims takes away valuable, and increasingly scarce, resources from genuine crimes and victims. Second, unsolved and frequently high-profile cases involving these kinds of serious allegations can result in negative publicity and political problems for the investigating agencies, as well as any other organizations involved in the false claim. Third, innocent people can be wrongly accused, and in extreme situations this can result in wrongful imprisonment. For example, Gary Dotson received a 25- to 50-year sentence for a rape he did not commit and served 6 years in an Illinois prison, before having his sentence commuted in 1985. The alleged victim, Kathleen Webb, stated that the suspect had torn her clothing and scratched her with broken glass, including a scratch in her vaginal area. Based on her description of the assailant, an artist created a sketch that led to Gary Dotson's arrest. Based on Ms. Webb's testimony he was subsequently convicted. Later, Ms. Webb became a Christian and confessed to making the whole thing up because she believed she was pregnant by her boyfriend. She further stated that she had scratched herself with broken glass. DNA testing showed that the semen in her underwear matched her boyfriend's. The case judge did not respond to her retraction, but the Illinois governor commuted the sentence to 6 years already served (J. Macdonald, personal communication, October 1997).

Another case involved consequences for the wrongful accuser. A Nebraska woman, Elizabeth Richardson, was sentenced to a 6-month jail sentence for lying under oath that a man had raped her. The alleged perpetrator, who was married, was arrested, jailed, and lost his job, and his children were taunted in school. She later admitted to making the story up to get her husband's attention (J. Macdonald, personal communication, October 1997).

Fourth, civil litigation at the initiation of the victim and/or the wrongfully accused can be costly. And fifth, desperate and troubled individuals who may benefit from mental health assistance go untreated or enter the health care system and are treated as "legitimate" victims. These kinds of cases have serious and important consequences.

The purposes of this chapter are to: (1) overview the available references to false victims in the scholarly literature; (2) offer a model with three hypothesized false victim types; (3) present three illustrative case examples of stalking-related false victimization syndrome (with appropriate protection of the identities of the individuals involved); (4) analyze the case examples by the authors' model; and (5) promote discussion and further study of the false victim phenomenon.

REVIEW OF THE LITERATURE

We offer a cautionary note in regard to any discussion of false allegations. The exploration of this issue should not in any way undermine the important advances made by modern law enforcement in responding to crime victims. Specifically, in the investigation of certain types of crime where women are the primary victims and men the primary offenders, such as rape, there have been problems overcoming a bias that such a crime may have, in some way, been victim precipitated. All victim reports warrant careful, complete, and timely investigation characterized by professionalism and respect that will prevent any secondary victimization by the investigating process. The ensuing review is designed to open a dialogue about these exceptional cases. It would be a misuse to employ this review to question the legitimacy of the overwhelming majority of stalking reports.

In this review, we offer a conceptual model for categorizing false allegations (see Table 1). The model suggests that there is not one false victimization syndrome (FVS), but rather several syndromes that vary by characteristics, secondary gains, and interventions. Further, as one moves from Type 1 through Type 3, the model indicates a progression in complexity of motives and sophistication of methods on the part of the false victim. There are three types of false victimization syndrome. Type 1, in which the victim reports physical symptoms without a known physical cause, includes three subtypes: Type 1a, hysterical paralysis; Type 1b, Munchausen

Table 1

False Victimization Syndrome Typology

FVS type	Characteristics	Secondary gains	Interventions
1. a. Hysterical paralysis	1. Paralysis of limbs. 2. Inconsistent with known physical cause. 3. Victim of some internal phenomena. 4. Incidence declines as society becomes technologically more advanced. 5. Less sophisticated.	1. Relatively quick relief from emotional stress or successful restriction from having to participate in a future event. 2. Anxiety about past or future event is "bound up" in the paralyzed limb. 3. Very limited medical resources devoted to diagnoses and treatment. 4. Very limited personal and family resources devoted to care and rehabilitation.	1. If hysterically paralyzed limb, then paralyze some other extremity through the use of hypnosis.
b. Munchausen c. Munchausen by proxy	1. Various medical complaints. 2. Various medical complaints for a dependent. 3. Complaints consistent with known physical cause. 4. Victim of some internal phenomena. 5. Prevalence may coincide with increase in medical sophistication of society.	1. Successful at attention from health care providers and from family members. 2. Attention over time begins to wane forcing individual to present over time as a "true medical mystery," and placing an even higher requirement on continued symptom credibility. 3. Demands an increasingly higher knowledge of medical conditions by the individual. 4. Extensive personal and family resources devoted to daily care.	1. Requires substantial medical resources devoted to diagnoses and treatment. 2. Eventual frustration by treating physicians leads to suspicion, which is characteristically confirmed when true extent of prior treatment and surgical procedures becomes known.
2. Known perpetrator a. Single event b. Multiple event (stalking)	1. Almost always some prior relationship. 2. Victim of an identifiable other. 3. Series of incidents over time in which victim has been alone and accessible to a perpetrator without a third party to witness.	1. Limited medical attention, diagnoses, and treatment. 2. Limited family and personal resources devoted to physical care and rehabilitation. 3. Substantial use of law enforcement resources for investigation.	1. Extensive allocation of law enforcement investigative resources does not lead to case resolution. 2. Consideration of potential false reports results in highly emotional response from reporting victim and family.

4. Critical event(s) is/are characterized by initial noncriminal contact that progresses rapidly to contact of a criminal nature.
5. Victim acquires ideas for reported criminal events from popular culture or from someone known to the individual who has reported these types of events.
6. Rape kits, injuries, letters/cards, threatening/harassing telephone calls, being followed or chased.

3. Unknown perpetrator
   a. Single event
   b. Multiple event (stalking)

1. Victim of an unknown suspect.
2. Suspect almost always indeterminable.
3. Series of incidents over time in which victim has been alone and accessible to a perpetrator without a third party to witness.
4. Critical event(s) is/are characterized by initial noncriminal contact that progresses rapidly to contact of a criminal nature.
5. Victim acquires ideas for reported criminal events from popular culture or from someone known to the individual who has reported these types of events.
6. Rape kits, injuries, letters/cards, threatening/harassing telephone calls, being followed or chased.

4. Substantial use of victim witness program and psychological services for emotional distress and victim-focused psychological treatment.
5. Need by law enforcement, family, therapist, and others for crime incident and post-crime incident details.
6. Enhanced media coverage if victim is openly distressed and articulate.

1. Limited medical attention, diagnoses, and treatment.
2. Limited family and personal resources devoted to physical care and rehabilitation.
3. Substantial use of law enforcement resources for investigation.
4. Substantial use of victim witness program and psychological services for emotional distress and victim-focused psychological treatment.
5. Need by law enforcement, family, therapist, and others for crime incident and post-crime incident details.
6. Enhanced media coverage if victim is openly distressed and articulate.

3. Preponderance of evidence leads to confrontational law enforcement interview resulting in confession and recanting prior reports.

1. Extensive allocation of law enforcement investigative resources does not lead to case resolution.
2. Consideration of potential false report results in highly emotional response from reporting victim and family.
3. Preponderance of evidence leads to confrontational law enforcement interview resulting in confession and recanting prior reports.

syndrome; and Type 1c, Munchausen syndrome by proxy. Type 2, in which the victim reports a crime or a series of crimes for which there is a known perpetrator, includes two subtypes: Type 2a, when there is a single crime event such as a rape or assault; and Type 2b, when there are multiple crime events over time, such as stalking. Type 3, in which the victim reports a crime or series of crimes for which the perpetrator is unknown, includes two subtypes: Type 3a when there is a single crime event such as rape or assault; and Type 3b, when there are multiple crime events over time, such as stalking.

FVS Physical Symptoms Without a Known Physical Cause

Type 1a: Hysterical Paralysis

Early historical references to false victim cases involved physicians such as the French neurologist Jean-Martin Charcot whose patients reported symptoms such as limb paralysis that had no known cause (Ellenberger, 1970). Charcot became suspicious as the nature of the paralysis did not correspond with 19th century knowledge of anatomy. Charcot experimented with the use of hypnosis with these patients and was able to dramatically eliminate the symptoms. The theory was that the patient wished relief from emotional stress or release from having to participate in a future event. With the focus of all attention being on the paralyzed limb, the patient had achieved a socially acceptable exclusion from having to meet certain expectations of himself and others. While there was a cost to this adaptation (loss of limb use), the net gain was acceptable to the patient. Freud was sufficiently impressed with the work of Charcot that it had a substantial impact on the development of psychoanalytic theory; for example, unexpressed emotional conflicts could emerge as physical symptoms. Other physicians in a variety of cultures around the world have also seen this phenomenon of hysterical paralysis. Although still not completely understood, it has been noted that the incidence of hysterical paralysis declines as a culture or society becomes more technologically advanced, leading to a rapid diagnosis, a high success rate of symptom removal by hypnosis, and a concurrent loss of effective victim status.

Type 1b: Munchausen Syndrome

As early as 1863, reports began to appear in the medical literature concerning patients who traveled from one physician to another and from one hospital to another reporting various illness symptoms (Gavin, 1863; Jones, 1995). Richard Asher coined the term Munchausen syndrome to describe these patients, after the famous Baron von Munchausen, a traveler of the world who told many dramatic and untruthful stories (Asher, 1951; Raspe, 1944; Jones, 1995). In contrast to hysterical paralysis symptoms, these patients reported symptom patterns that were initially quite credible and consistent with known physical causes (Goodman, 1994; Levin & Sheridan, 1995). However, the symptoms would be unresponsive to conservative treatment, resulting in complex and invasive diagnostic procedures and treatment courses. Early cases were brought to light only after the patients had successfully convinced a series of surgeons to operate on them. Over the years, investigators have noted that Munchausen syndrome is more often seen in women than men, requires a certain level of medical knowledge, is often accompanied by having previously observed genuine illnesses in a family member or close friend, and represents a socially acceptable adoption of the "sick" role as a means of avoiding conflict and/or responsibility (Levin & Sheridan, 1995; Goodman, 1994).

Levin and Sheridan (1995) reported that individuals suffering from this disorder may function relatively normally until confronted by particular triggers that are threatening to their unique psychological niche. Goodman (1994) saw it as a patient's attempt to overcome the stresses of life and an attempt to master a profound sense of powerlessness and lack of control. Loss, in particular, is hypothesized to be the most powerful trigger. Levin and Sheridan (1995) specified that the feigning of illness as a way of coping is a result of a mental disorder or personality style that interacts with the individual's experiences during her formative years, including cultural, societal, and family influences as they affect the perception of physicians and medical services.

In 1997 some individuals are even getting paid to report false symptoms to medical professionals in a variant of the "mystery shopper" technique used by retail stores (Benac, 1997). A series of hospitals have employed patients who get themselves admitted to the hospital via a report of false symptoms in order to assess the appropriateness of medical referral and service delivery. Devon-Hill Associates in La Jolla, California, charges $12,000 to $15,000 for what is usually a 3-day hospital stay that can carry a mystery patient to the brink of surgery.

Type 1c: Munchausen Syndrome by Proxy

Recognition of false victimization in which another family member (frequently a primary caretaker such as mother or childcare worker) stimulates or fabricates an illness pattern is relatively new (Meadow, 1977; Schreier, 1996). As with Munchausen syndrome, this new set of false victims came to public attention after extensive medical procedures were applied, often to very young children. These children were later shown to have had their symptom patterns stimulated or fabricated by a primary caregiver, and some actually died as a result of the actions of their adult caregiver. Schreier (1996) reviewed a series of cases in which the mother's desire appeared to be to maintain a relationship with individuals in positions of authority: physicians in cases of child physical illness and law enforcement officers/child protection workers in cases of child sexual abuse allegations. As with Munchausen syndrome itself, the involved primary caregiver needs to have a reasonable degree of medical sophistication in order to make the "medical mystery ailments" of the child plausible. Extensive personal and family resources can become vital to the daily care and ongoing search for proper diagnosis. The fabricating primary caretaker's behavior is often the initial clue to the real explanation, marked by repeated child symptom reports without the expected physical or laboratory findings, immediately changing portions of the account when questioned about the veracity of prior statements, or actually performing acts in the child's hospital room to further the child's illness. Anecdotally, it has been noted that fabricator behavior includes a pattern of exaggeration about prior events in their lives, past abnormal illness symptoms for the fabricator, suicide attempts, or other episodes of tragic loss apparently designed to elicit sympathy and extra attention from the listener (Schreier, 1996; Levin & Sheridan, 1995).

FALSE CRIME REPORTS—GENERAL DISCUSSION

False victim reports of a crime might be related to early prior studies of pathological lying. As early as 1921, Deutsch attempted to understand the phenomenon of pathological lying in her exploration of "pseudologia phantastica," the active creation or elaborate fabrication of an untruth that is grounded in contact with reality (as reported by Deutsch and Roazen [1982]). She astutely observed that patients who exhibit this behavior do so in order to control their anxiety, avoid past unresolved conflicts, attain revenge for imagined or real deceits or conflicts from childhood, create enjoyment over deceiving others, or create an imaginary world that is more exciting than their mundane experience. She described one particular case where the patient reported that she was being aggressively pursued by an interested suitor, who brought her flowers, sent romantic letters, and arranged amazing rendezvous in forbidden places, all of which were memorialized by this patient in a detailed diary over 3 years. The falsehoods were later revealed through the course of her analytically based psychotherapy (Deutsch & Roazen, 1982). According to Snyder (1986), characteristics of *pseudologia phantastica* are seen most frequently in subjects who suffer from borderline personality disorder and include lying in order to enhance their self-esteem, a strong fantasy life that quickly dissipates in the face of contradictory evidence, and a compulsion to project blame and their own deficits and misdeeds onto others.

Those who suffer from borderline personality disorder diagnoses may also engage in self-mutilative behavior as defined by Walsh and Rosen (1988). They define Category III self-mutilative behavior when the individual's injuries are mild to moderate, such as wrist or body cutting, and indicate that the individual's psychological state prior to the episode is one of psychic crisis. While dramatic in appearance, these mutilative behaviors often require an explanation to significant others, and fabrication of stories to cover up this type of behavior is common.

While there is little scholarly research on the subject of false rape allegations, as representative of a single or multiple reported event with or without a known perpetrator, the literature that does exist offers some interesting observations. It appears that there are three primary reasons or motives why complainants, usually women, make false rape allegations. One reason is to provide an alibi for regretted sexual activity or unplanned pregnancy; another is to inflict revenge against an uninterested suitor or a man who unilaterally terminates what the woman believes was a desirable relationship, in other words to punish the rejecter; and, another is for attention seeking or to obtain sympathy (Kanin, 1994). In Kanin's study (1994), 56% of the cases are of the alibi type, 27% of the revenge type, and 18% of the attention-seeking type.

According to Macdonald (1995), the existence of a double standard within society—female virginity is lauded, while adolescent male virginity is denigrated— may contribute to behaviors designed to protect one's own sense of morality or culpability by projecting blame onto others. These often occur to cover up regretted sexual activity or an unplanned pregnancy. Consequences of the alibi and revenge types of false rape allegations are usually more serious since there is a named perpetrator, while the attention-seeking type may be least detrimental since there is rarely an alleged perpetrator named (Kanin, 1994). The attention-seeking type of false allegation is said to be motivated by the enormous efforts our society has made to protect women who are raped by providing shelter, medical, and psychological assistance, and to portray some of those who openly acclaim their traumatizing experience, often on talk show venues, as modern day martyrs (Kanin, 1994). Some women may also feel comfortable making a false claim without fear of being detected, considering televised reports of low crime clearance rates (Schrink & LeBeau, 1984).

From the law enforcement perspective, retired Special Agent Roy Hazelwood (Hazelwood & Burgess, 1987; Hazelwood, 1983) of the Behavioral Science Unit of the FBI is a nationally recognized investigator of sex crimes and of false allegations of sex crimes. Hazelwood's long criminal case experience base suggests that there are different motives for cases when there is an identified or known perpetrator (Type 2) then when there is an unidentified or unknown perpetrator (Type 3). The former are motivated by revenge, excuses, and alibi while the latter involve more self-induced violence and varying motives (R. Hazelwood, personal communication, October 1997).

We note that stalking-related false victimization syndromes may represent less of a threat to the esteem of the victim when reported, and thus represent a more attractive option to the individual who is motivated to make a false report than an allegation of a sex crime. McDowell and Hibler (1987) noted that the kinds of sex acts described by false rape complainants tend to be fairly restricted to more conventional forms of sexual behavior (for example, allegations of penile penetration and fondling), which is in contrast to many actual rape cases that often include oral and anal sex, acts that the false claimant may find personally humiliating and unnecessarily demeaning to accomplish whatever the various goals of the false report; therefore, these types of events are not likely to be included in descriptions of the crime. Stalking as a behavior, then, is even less threatening to the esteem of the claimant and thus represents an attractive option. Invasive and intrusive forensic procedures, such as rape kits, are also avoided.

The motives in Types 2 and 3 are instrumental. The individuals are seeking secondary gains such as attention and sympathy, particularly with someone in a position of power; attempting revenge and retaliation, particularly in response to perceived rejection; trying to prevent abandonment and initiate reconciliation with a withdrawing or unavailable intimate; avoiding responsibility, covering up or providing an alibi or smokescreen for some other behavior such as self-mutilation; or seeking to maintain a dependent relationship with someone in a position of power. We believe that this particular differentiation is useful in stalking in that there are different descriptors, degrees of sophistication, case dynamics, and interventions among the broad categories. We believe that these designations account for those false victimization syndromes most frequently encountered in a criminal justice population.

Type 3 cases are similar in characteristics to Type 2 cases. Among experienced investigators and police psychologists, it has been hypothesized that false victims reporting a Type 3 case are more sophisticated in that unnamed, undescribed perpetrators are inherently more difficult to find. This increases the potential for the accuser to maintain an enduring status as a victim of unknown terror, and continued attention from law enforcement. A disadvantage of Type 3 reports is that the accuser must continue to either provide new information about a Type 3a single crime event, or must report a new crime to add to the list of events that already compose a Type 3b multiple crime event. Such elaboration about a single crime, or reports of new crimes, become increasingly difficult for the false victim to prepare and execute without being discovered.

Type 2a: FVS Single Crime Event with Known Perpetrator

As previously referenced, false victimization extends back to biblical times. Through history, such cases have most frequently involved a prior relationship between the accuser and the accused in which the two have or could have been alone without a third-party witness. Initially the contact between the accuser and the accused is noncriminal in nature, but progresses rapidly into contact of a criminal nature. Accusers appear to acquire the ideas for these reported criminal events from movies or books and/or someone known to the accuser who has reported being a crime victim recently. Attention is provided by boyfriends, girl-friends, and law enforcement.

However, the actual amount of money or time in help from others that is extended to the accuser is far less than the support system resources in Type 1 cases. The accuser may also display high usage rates of victim/witness programs and psychological counseling, with low usage rates of women's shelter or crime victims' group counseling. This may be due to the relatively unconditional accep-tance of the accuser's account of events in her life to a victim/witness and/or psychotherapist, as contrasted to the characteristically more confrontational style of peer groups. In such cases, law enforcement may devote extensive resources to the investigation without any progress whatsoever. Eventually, this leads to a law enforcement consideration of the possibility of a false report. Subsequent interviews focused on the inconsistencies in the accuser's story result in recantation accompa-nied by an offered explanation that is often attention-seeking based.

The earliest documented contemporary case of this nature was a false allega-tion of rape in Scottsboro, Alabama, in 1931. Eight young black men in their midteens to early twenties were accused of raping two white women, Victoria Price and Ruby Bates, on a freight train. All of the individuals involved were hobos, and there were three criminal trials. Upon arrest, these young men were nearly lynched. In the original trial the young men were sentenced to death, and it would be 19 years before the last man was freed. Finally, it was determined that neither woman had been raped, and Ruby Bates eventually repudiated the entire story. What had happened, in fact, was that these young black males had thrown some white males off the train. When these white males, and young women accompanying them who were dressed as boys, were picked up by the police for riding the train illicitly, they attempted to deflect the attention off of themselves; and these young women had had sex and did not want anybody to know it. Defense attorney Samuel Liebowitz defended the accused in the midst of major racial tensions within the community, including conflicts between the Communist Party on one side and the NAACP on the other (M. Olshaker, personal communi-cation, October, 1997).

A more recent famous false allegation case occurred in 1989 in Dutchess County, New York, and involved Tawana Brawley, a 15-year-old black female. She alleged that six Caucasian males, including a man with a badge, had abducted her for 4 days, did not feed her or allow her to drink liquids, raped her vaginally, anally, and orally, defecated and urinated upon her, and then scrawled racial epithets on her body with a soot-like substance. A neighbor found her hopping around a townhouse her family used to own with a green garbage bag over her head. This neighbor called for assistance and the supposedly comatose victim was rushed to the hospital. When interviewed afterward about what had happened, Brawley wrote the words "White cop" on a sheet of paper.

Public reaction to the case was extensive. New York Governor Mario Cuomo named a special investigator to the case and a task force was established by the Attorney General of New York, composed of experts from the New York Bureau of Criminal Investigation, the Federal Bureau of Investigation, attorneys from the Attorney General's office, and other experts. Bill Cosby and the publisher of *Essence* magazine offered a $25,000 reward. Mike Tyson told Brawley he would provide her with a $50,000 scholarship, and then took the Rolex watch from his wrist and gave it to her. After a seven month investigation, a grand jury determined that Brawley had faked her story, possibly to avoid punishment for staying out late. The grand jury cited that Brawley was not malnourished, not suffering from exposure, hospital tests for rape were negative, and she was seen stepping into the plastic bag in which she was found. She chose to name police officers as her perpetrators because of her family's expressed dislike of law enforcement. (R. Hazelwood, personal communication, October, 1997). Brawley, who attended Howard University, has reportedly changed her name and is now living in the Washington, D.C. area.

During the aftermath of the case, Brawley's advisors, Reverend Al Sharpton and lawyers Vernon Mason and Alton Maddox, Jr., stated in press conferences and on television that one of her assailants was Steven Pagones, a young Caucasian Dutchess County assistant district attorney. Sharpton stated: ". . . Steven Pagones, the assistant district attorney, did it. If we're lying, sue us . . . dare them to sue us."

Now a decade after 15-year-old former high school cheerleader Tawana Brawley was found in a garbage bag in Dutchess County, New York, Pagones did just that with the filing of a $170 million defamation suit (Goldman, 1997). Sharpton, a defendant, has become involved in politics, placing third in the Democratic U.S. Senate primary and second in the recent New York Democratic mayoral primary. Maddox was suspended in 1990 from practicing law after he was charged with not cooperating with a bar association ethics committee investigating charges that he impeded justice in the Brawley matter. Mason was disbarred in 1995 from practicing law for professional misconduct, and is now a seminary student. Pagones, 36, has gone on to become an assistant New York State attorney general. Since he was a local prosecutor at the time of the allegations, he must prove in his civil case that the statements by Sharpton, Maddox, and Mason were malicious and had reckless disregard for the truth.

While such cases typically present through a law enforcement agency, they can appear in civil or government agency contexts as well. Truscott and Evans (1997) presented three case studies of false claims for workers' compensation benefits (WCB) whereby the victim alleged that a sexual assault took place at work. One of these cases involved a Type 2a event where there was a named perpetrator. In this case the victim later confessed that it was not a sexual assault but a consensual sex act. Surveillance cameras in the first case disconfirmed the victim's account of the sexual assault. The victim's arms and face were cut up with a knife and she alleged that she was trying to defend herself from a customer who had assaulted her. In the surveillance video it is revealed that the encounter was consensual. The knife cuts were also inconsistent with the kind of attack she described. Further investigation revealed a history of childhood sexual abuse, and the victim admitted later that the act was consensual. She felt enormously guilty and did indeed self-mutilate out of guilt and self-disgust. She had called her supervisor who had made a lot of assumptions about the victim's call and presentation. This supervisor then called the police and initiated the claim to WCB. Fraud charges were not pursued as the police were convinced that she never intended to perpetrate a fraud.

Type 2b: FVS Multiple Events Over Time with a Known Perpetrator

While the majority of the Type 2 cases noted in modern times have involved a single crime event, the second half of the 20th century has produced more false victim reports involving multiple crime events over time. However, in our review of the literature, we were unable to discover any accounts of multiple events over time with a known perpetrator. In these cases, following, harassing, stalking, assault, or rape form a pattern of behavior blamed on the accused, who is identified and known by the accuser. In our case history section, we present a Type 2b case example.

Type 3a: FVS Single Event with an Unknown Perpetrator

In the Type 3a event, the victim reports a single event, often an assault or a rape, but does not report an identifiable assailant. Often the victim's descriptions are sufficiently vague to prevent the apprehension of an innocent person as well as discovery of the falsehood by forcing a confrontation over the veracity of the allegation with any named perpetrator.

A recent case of this type occurred in 1996 at the Galleria at Tysons II, an upscale shopping center in Virginia. A young woman in her early twenties claimed she was walking back through the parking lot in the afternoon when she was abducted at gunpoint, driven around suburban areas for several hours, sexually assaulted, taken back to the mall, and thrown out of the car. She called the police, filed a report, and gave a description. The victim witness coordinator did not feel the facts of the case and the victim's behavior added up. The victim was a woman who had recently moved to Virginia from Pakistan, was educated, and was living with two cousins. When the victim witness coordinator went to the house, the woman seemed upset, but not overly so, and the roommates did not seem upset. While she was willing to look at lineups, ID books, or anything else, her affect was subdued. She was in the same clothes and had not showered, even though she had already had the rape examination by the medical staff. There was some evidence of sexual activity including minor genital abrasions. This event was widely reported in the media. Her mother traveled from Pakistan to be with her. The motive for this event was not money. Rather, subsequent investigation showed that she was lonely in this new country and wanted attention. She confessed to making the false allegations, which her roommates had suspected, and was charged with filing a false report but did not serve jail time (Douglas & Olshaker, 1998).

Truscott and Evans (1997) presented two case studies of false claims for WCB whereby the victim alleged that a sexual assault took place at work with an unidentifiable perpetrator. In these two cases the individuals withdrew their claims after they were confronted about inaccuracies. The first case involved a female security guard at an industrial site who claimed that an individual approached from behind, bound and gagged her, and then sexually assaulted her. Police found no physical evidence of any kind. She was unable to explain any of the details of this alleged assault. Further investigation revealed an extensive psychiatric history, primarily Borderline Personality Disorder (*DSM-IV*), with previous claims of sexual assault and numerous suicide attempts. Information revealed in counseling indicated that her brother came upon her at home, saw she was upset and crying, and she relayed the story of this alleged sexual assault at work. He initiated the complaint to the police and a claim to WCB. Later it was revealed that she had met someone on a sadomasochistic Internet chat line and had made arrangements to meet him. It was the belief of the investigators that she met the man, engaged in the sadomasochistic sexual behavior, regretted it and was distraught, but could not tell her brother what really happened. Again, fraud charges were not pursued. The second case involved a woman working as an apartment caretaker who claimed that two masked men accosted her at a new apartment building. She reported buzzing them in and they entered her apartment with masks on. One took her jewelry and the other allegedly squeezed her breasts enough to leave bruising. She went to the emergency room and there was bruising. The investigators became suspicious of her account of events and asked her to take a polygraph. She refused the polygraph and complained that she was being harassed by the police. She was later sent to counseling and refused to talk about the incident. However, this 43-year-old woman said she was afraid of her father and that he was going to kill her. The claim was denied and she did not contest it. She later filed another claim that she injured herself falling down the stairs. It was the belief of the investigators that she was being abused by a significant male in her life and was using these reports to cover up the abuse. In both of these cases the victims were psychologically very upset; thus, fraud would not necessarily be suspected. Truscott and Evans (1997) indicated that these cases suggest the importance of scrutiny of the stories, reviewing collateral data, and viewing the false victim as a distressed person rather than as a fraud.

False allegations may also occur in the context of hate crimes. Since 1990, almost 100 faked hate crimes have been noted (Levine, 1997). As faked hate crimes often involve property damage to the reporting person, some insurance industry observers view the rise in substantiated hate crimes as responsible for the apparent increase in false reports. Dennis Jay, executive director of the Coalition Against Insurance Fraud, contends that many perpetrators are provided with the idea of filing a false hate crime report by two factors: The sympathetic media attention given to hate crimes in general and the sense of being an oppressed minority taken advantage of by the insurance system. The false report enables them to get back at the system in a more morally defensible way. As illustrated in the following examples, false allegations of hate crimes can occur in a variety of circumstances.

In August 1997, Sandra Benson and Freeman Berry, an interracial couple, were charged with 23 counts of fraud in a series of incidents eventually leading to the arson of their Jonesboro, Georgia home. The arson destroyed their home and a reported $200,000 in computer equipment. The home and the fence around their property had been spray painted with swastikas and misspelled racial slogans. The case will be tried in 1998 (Levine, 1997).

In 1995, Pastor DeWayne Byrdsong, an African–American minister from Coralville, Iowa, filed a report that his Mercedes Benz automobile had been spray painted with racial epithets. When Mr. Byrdsong's insurance company was reluctant to pay for the damage, he took his case to the media including contacting the *Oprah Winfrey Show*, indicating the insurance company's lack of responsiveness was based in racism. However, the resulting publicity to his case produced calls from local auto body repair shops indicating that Byrdsong had obtained estimates about repainting his car before the spray painting incident occurred. Byrdsong was found guilty of making false crime reports. When asked about Mr. Byrdsong's motivation for the crime, Coralville chief of police Barry Bedford stated "My best guess is that he wanted this car repainted very badly." While Chief Bedford's analysis may be somewhat tongue-in-cheek, it is notable that many false allegations involve a high degree of risk of public exposure and disgrace for an often limited financial reward (Levine, 1997).

In September 1997, Angela Jackson, a law student and Chicago based seller of African–American art, was charged with attempting to defraud the United Parcel Service. Ms. Jackson alleged that UPS employees apparently opened four of her packages in transit and defaced the art works with racial slurs. Prosecutors have stated that she also shipped 27 other packages with racial slurs on UPS letterhead to civil rights leaders, in order to lend credence to her own claim. The case will be tried in 1998 (Levine, 1997).

In 1997, Al Rubin, a Miami mechanic, and his son Steven arranged to have the Hillel Community Day School (where Steven was employed) vandalized with anti-Semitic statements. Both individuals, who were subsequently convicted, hoped to get the repair contract to fix the damaged school (Levine, 1997).

Type 3b: Multiple Events over Time with an Unknown Perpetrator

In the Type 3b event, the victim reports multiple crime events over time (such as stalking), but does not report knowing the identity of the alleged perpetrator.

In what may be the first documented stalking-related false victimization syndrome, Swanson, Chamelin, and Territo (1984) described a 47-year-old woman who reportedly was terrorized for a period of 4 years beginning in the late 1970s, in a series of incidents by a mysterious individual identified as "the Poet" due to the versed form of the threatening letters sent to her. Other tormenting acts she experienced were receiving a butcher knife at Christmas, having her telephone line cut, having chunks of concrete thrown at her home, and being kidnapped and stabbed in her lower back. When the woman was discovered mailing letters from "the Poet" along with her bills and normal correspondence, she admitted there was no "Poet" and that she had even stabbed herself to lend credence to her story. A psychologist working on the case speculated that an assault on the woman when she was 16 years old was the motivating force for her false reports. She had allegedly been the victim of a sexual assault at the age of 16 during which she was drugged and branded; this report may also have been false (Swanson et al., 1984; "Mystery poet," 1981).

A more recent case took place in the Pacific Northwest during the late 1980s. A college girl reportedly received telephonic death threats and would look out the window and see someone watching her from the woods. When a third party with her in the house would look outside, he or she would not see anybody. When wiretaps were put on the phone, there were no phone calls; and when the wiretaps were removed, the phone calls would begin again. While in a restaurant with her boyfriend she went to the restroom; she claimed that on her way back, she was confronted by a man who threatened to kill her and stuck a gun in her vagina. A medical exam determined that there were, in fact, tears in her vagina. The last major event involved her being abducted while on her way to the library. Consultation with profiling experts at the Behavioral Science Unit of the FBI in Quantico, Virginia, was sought. Based on their experience with victim and perpetrator behavior in sexual assault cases, it was their analysis that the allegations and events were likely to be false. However, they did encourage the next steps taken by the victim's family in order to draw the victim out. Her father went on television professing his love and begging for the release of his daughter. The victim later showed up staggering back to campus, claiming to have escaped, an event that had been predicted by the profilers. It was determined that her grades had taken a recent turn for the worse, she had become pregnant and had an abortion, and had been begging her teachers for some relief. In a sense, stable points in her life had been collapsing around her. After the investigative interview, she confessed to making the whole thing up, saying she was seeking attention and that her life and support systems were dissolving (J. Douglas, personal communication, October 1997).

Another false stalking case occurred in St. Louis in the 1980s and was known as the Red Heart case; 60 complaints were filed by a woman over a 6-month time period. She made a variety of allegations, including discovering her panties with red hearts drawn on them in lipstick from her house, that her house had been broken into on multiple occasions, and that several blood-soaked teddy bears were left on the garage door so that they would fall on people when the door closed. She also alleged that someone moved her car from the driveway to the center of her street. These events culminated with a blood-soaked teddy bear being left in her infant's crib. The victim went to the media, holding news conferences complaining about the lack of interest by the police. During the course of the investigation, she was caught on videotape placing another teddy bear on the garage door. The motivation was originally believed to be to force her husband to change his working hours, but later it was determined that she wanted to move to a new house. By causing this constant disruption, she had hoped to make it so uncomfortable for her husband that they would move. The investigators felt that she was a risk of danger to her child, due to her apparent progression to events involving her child. The woman was sent for psychiatric care and her child was removed from her custody (R. Hazelwood, personal communication, October 1997).

A celebrity false stalking case of this sort occurred in Los Angeles in 1995 involving Cyndy Garvey, the ex-wife of professional baseball player Steve Garvey. In the aftermath of a relationship breakup with a Los Angeles area restauranteur, she reported a number of stalking incidents to the police, including that she was receiving notes and flowers and that someone had scribbled an "X" on her front door. She made desperate phone calls to the police pleading for protection and ended up at the police station with a black eye and an injured nose. Upon investigation it was determined that she had been harassing her estranged boyfriend and that a similar pattern of harassment had taken place when she separated from Steve Garvey. She eventually confessed to the police that she had made up the story that an unknown person was stalking her as a way of getting revenge on her ex-boyfriend (Siegel, 1995; B. Melekian, personal communication, November 1997; J. Butts, personal communication, November 1997). She was charged with filing false police reports.

FALSE VICTIMIZATION TYPES MOST LIKELY ENCOUNTERED BY LAW ENFORCEMENT

Law enforcement agencies are most likely to encounter false victims who report a crime or series of crimes. Accordingly, three detailed case histories of Type 2b and Type 3b cases involving false allegations of stalking are presented.

CASE 1: FVS TYPE 2b, KNOWN PERPETRATOR

The victim in this case was 45-year-old Caucasian female married to a financial company executive. The husband's responsibilities involved a significant amount of time away from home due to business-related travel. Several years prior to the current series of complaints, she had an appointment with her dentist, where she was receiving regular care for an ongoing condition, when she reported that she had met a man in the elevator who made her feel uncomfortable. In the weeks that ensued, she reported being followed and receiving threatening calls and several letters from this unknown person. She reported these incidents to her husband and her dentist, and filed one police report before the events suddenly stopped.

At the time of these initial reports, the victim scheduled her ongoing appointments with this dentist so that she could be the last patient at the end of the day, and when she traveled she often sent cards to him signed, "with love." She wrote letters to him about how grateful she was for his special attention and caring and about what a special person he was. Office personnel commented that it seemed like she "had a crush on him." The dentist and others interpreted her behavior as somewhat overly friendly, but thought little else about it.

Some time later, when her husband was diagnosed with a complicated medical condition that required ongoing significant care, the victim reported that she had begun to receive strange letters that would sometimes be threatening and other times offer a warning about impending danger to her. She did not report these incidents to her husband until much later on, citing concern about his medical condition. When his condition improved, she notified him about the occurrences, and some time later a police report was filed and an investigation initiated. She began to implicate her dentist as the source of these letters, occasional gifts, and obscene phone calls. The dentist vehemently denied making these contacts and there was no evidence to support his involvement. The victim had her husband write to the dentist several times, asking him to cease the contacts and inquiring about billing issues. In these various letters they threatened several times to complain to the dentist's regulatory board, but never followed through.

The victim began to get more animated and demanding with the investigators, insisting that they interrogate the dentist and/or arrange a meeting between her and her alleged perpetrator. She enlisted her husband to increase the pressure on the investigators to handle her case. Her focus of concern was primarily on the progress of the investigation and when the investigators were "going to haul him into the station for questioning." Due to numerous concerns about the veracity of her complaints, a surveillance was set up, during which the victim was found mailing letters and packages to herself. She confessed to making the whole thing up out of her anger and hurt over the dentist's refusal of her advances and her attempt to gain her neglectful husband's attention. Charges were not filed, but the victim's social worker, who had been treating her for trauma and borderline personality disorder, was informed about the false nature of the complaints so that he could modify his treatment. Conversations with the husband and the treating social worker revealed a history of major childhood abandonments and a description of the victim as an insecure person who was repeatedly hospitalized for nervous breakdowns, which would occur when significant others in her life went away.

CASE 2: FVS TYPE 3b, UNKNOWN PERPETRATOR

The victim, a single hispanic female in her early twenties, attending an East Coast university, reported an attempted sexual assault incident to the university's department of public safety. The incident was memorialized in an internal document, but the alleged crime was not reported to the police until 2 weeks later. In her statement to the university, and later to local police, the subject stated that the suspect grabbed her from the rear, pushed her head into a door, then pulled her backward into another dormitory room across the hall. The subject then described in great detail how during the attack the suspect pawed at her clothing and body. As a reported result, she sustained scratches on her body as well as tears to both outer- and undergarments. During the investigative interview with local law enforcement, the subject described certain things in great detail, for example, "he looked at me in the eyes and smiled," but she was unable to describe the suspect's general facial features.

The subject then told police that the suspect left an envelope containing a poem, and half of her bra that was torn during the attack, underneath the door mat at her dormitory apartment. She reported that she was visiting with her boyfriend nearby, when she "got a bad feeling" and returned to her dormitory room to find the articles. The subject brought the articles with her to the police station and they were booked into evidence when she finally reported the assault that day.

The subject claimed that she recognized the voice of her assailant while walking on campus, and an initial suspect, another student, was identified. The subject could not make an eyewitness confirmation and the suspect and these incidents were investigated by sexual assault detectives, but their efforts failed to develop any further investigative leads; therefore, the case was placed in inactive status. The initial suspect was expelled from the university.

Meanwhile, the victim began reporting to family members and others in her life that she was receiving hang up phone calls, threatening calls, cards, and followings for 6 months after the initial incident. The subject was given special security considerations on campus, including a reserved parking space. These events culminated in the subject reporting to the police 6 months later that she had received a mutilated and dismembered Barbie doll, which was covered with a red substance. The doll was inside a cardboard box, which also contained a threatening letter. All of the reported behaviors, and the receipt of the Barbie doll, took place with no witnesses, other than someone hearing the phone ring and seeing the subject answer it.

Because the pattern of conduct was long term and contained elements of stalking behavior, a specialized group of detectives with expertise in threat and stalking cases assumed investigative responsibility. These detectives contacted the subject and were scheduled to meet with her to discuss the prior criminal incidents. The day before this meeting was to occur, the victim was attending a two hour evening class at the university. Because of the prior reported incidents, the university had assigned campus security officers to escort her to and from classes. Approximately 60 minutes into the lecture, the instructor decided to cancel the class and dismissed the students early. The subject then decided to go to the student lounge and listen to some music without a security escort; she alleged that upon entering she was attacked from behind and forcefully pushed into the room, which rendered her unconscious. When she awoke, she found herself lying face down tied to a desk in the room, on her stomach, with her hands bound at the wrist. Her jeans were pulled down around her ankles and her body was covered with long scratches and superficial lacerations. She was discovered by a classmate who called security. The victim was transported to a rape crisis center by a rescue ambulance and examined by a physician specializing in rape trauma. Photographs of the victim in the hospital room revealed almost a smile or smirk on her face, consistent with her seeming enjoyment of all the attention she was getting. The crime scene was secured and investigators responded to gather evidence. The incident became a local media event, and near hysteria erupted among students on campus when warning flyers were distributed.

The detectives were notified of the incident that evening and the following day they interviewed the subject at her family home. The interview was very comprehensive and chronicled the events from the first incident through the alleged rape from the night before. As the victim spoke, subtle inconsistencies began to emerge. It was evident that the stalking scenarios being offered were not consistent with known stalking behavior patterns, and clearly two different types of rapists were being portrayed. The subject's mother was a champion of rape victim's rights and reported that she had been raped many years prior. The subject's brother suffered from depression and an eating disorder.

Detectives conducted dozens of interviews with incidental witnesses, analyzed critical evidence, and consulted with other experts over the next several months. Other relevant material came forward, including allegations of physical abuse by the subject's boyfriend. The subject had begun dating another student around the time that the mysterious phone calls began, and the abuse by her boyfriend stopped while he was protecting her from the alleged stalker. In addition, the boyfriend with whom she later reconciled reported an instance of what he believed was a feigned pregnancy by the subject and that she had told him that her pierced navel was to commemorate a gang rape that she had survived in high school. It also became apparent that the subject was having a difficult time with her upcoming graduation and the social pressure to "grow up."

This information, coupled with critical forensic evidence indicating that she might have falsified the allegations of stalking and rape, resulted in several attempts to interview the subject to reconcile the inconsistencies. She canceled several times with vague reasons. Finally an interview was scheduled and attended. Detectives confronted her with the inconsistencies in her stories. After approximately 90 minutes she admitted that she had made up the allegations of attempted rape, stalking, and rape. Tearfully, she talked about hating herself, the suicide attempt that she was trying to cover up during the first incident, and her confusion over her lack of direction in life and the pressure to achieve. The subject was granted immunity on the condition that she be truthful with her family and pursue appropriate treatment. Her treating therapist, who had been treating her for several months for post-traumatic stress disorder from the rapes, was informed and there have been no further complaints. The litigation that the family had against the university was dropped.

CASE 3: FVS TYPE 3b, UNKNOWN PERPETRATOR

The victim, a married Caucasian female in her late twenties, was employed as an administrative assistant in a large corporation. She reported to her supervisor that at approximately 10:20 a.m. she had entered the women's restroom and found "Mary will die" written in lipstick on the mirror. Her supervisor notified both the company's human resources and corporate security. Corporate security appropriately filed a timely police report.

Subsequent investigation revealed that the company had a large number of male and female employees on three floors of a high-rise building at this particular work site. There was one men's and one women's restroom on each floor. The entrance to the women's restroom was not observable from any of the desks or workstations in the company. Consequently, no other employees were observed who had been in the restroom immediately prior to Mary. Interviews of other female employees who had used that restroom on that morning revealed that only two known female employees had been in the restroom, and they had entered and left at the same time. These two female employees were assigned to a different work unit than Mary and stated that they did not even know who Mary was.

An interview with Mary determined that she was a 2-year employee of the company with average to below average performance ratings. Mary had been married for 3 years and did not have any children. She stated that she did not know who could have done this; she did not believe that she had any enemies. Mary stated that she had informed her husband of the incident, he was most concerned, and she requested several days' absence, which were granted. Corporate security advised Mary of the need to notify the company and law enforcement of any further suspicious events and to take reasonable personal safety precautions.

Interviews of Mary's supervisors and co-workers did not produce evidence of any disagreements or relationship problems that might be related to this incident. A review of corporate security and law enforcement records did not reveal any similar incidents within the past 2 years.

After 4 days off of work, Mary returned to her job. The investigation continued, but there were no further leads. Mary sought and obtained a referral to the company's employee assistance program and began seeing a counselor. Mary was provided with a parking space close to the building and a security officer escort to her car if she left work after dark. Mary remained distressed about the incident, visiting human resources and security representatives several times over the next week. She was assured that the company and law enforcement had done all that could be done at the present time, pending any further developments.

Three weeks after the women's restroom incident, Mary again contacted her supervisor. She was in considerable distress, and produced a single sheet of white paper with the computer-printed sentence, "I will get you." The note had been received in an intraoffice mail envelope that was unsealed. Mary's name had been printed on a computer label and affixed to the envelope. The paper was a common variety used throughout the company. The three floors of the company had numerous drop-off bins for intraoffice mail, making identification of the drop-off point impossible. Mary left work that afternoon for an emergency visit with her employee assistance counselor. Her husband left his job early and returned home to be with her after the conclusion of her counseling visit. Corporate security, law enforcement, and human resources continued the investigation, which was limited due to the lack of leads.

After another week of absence, Mary again returned to her job. Two weeks passed, and then another note appeared in the intraoffice mail. This time, all intraoffice mail addressed to Mary was being diverted by corporate security at the request of law enforcement, and the second note was discovered through this diversion process. The note said "I will come and find you" and was addressed in a manner identical to the first note. Mary once again left work. A follow-up interview with Mary's husband found him to be upset, but not able to offer any suggestions as to the origins of these communications. He did report that he was now devoting all of his free time to be with his wife. He further indicated that his wife's interests had become focused on security measures and repetitive speculation concerning who might be responsible for the communications.

Two weeks later, Mary indicated that she would not be returning to work and did not wish to have any further investigation of the incidents. In an additional follow-up interview with Mary's husband, he stated that he now realized that his wife had been under stress and had not been receiving as much attention as she needed and that he did not believe that the communications came from somebody else. The two of them had started to go to counseling together to discuss how this had all started and gotten out of hand. Accordingly, the investigations were closed. No further communications of any kind toward Mary or any other employee were ever received.

FVS Known and Unknown Perpetrator Types—Case Discussion

These cases exemplify several points about Type 2b and Type 3b false victimization syndromes, as summarized in Table 2. First, in all of these cases the victims presented themselves as victims and attributed the experience to some sort of criminal activity without going through the initial denial commonly encountered. Second, these individuals presented themselves in a manner inconsistent with usual victim behavior: in Case 1 the victim requested a meeting with her supposed stalker and did not seem to be concerned about her vulnerability; in Case 2 the victim did not appear particularly traumatized; and in Case 3 the victim appeared to be having reactions beyond the realm of reactions ordinarily encountered in true victims. Third, all of these victims enlisted the support of others in a way that suggested they were deriving a significant amount of new attention and sympathy. Fourth, each of these individuals presented with significant psychological data: all three clearly evidenced a personality disorder from Cluster B of the *DSM-IV* (APA, 1994), most notably Borderline Personality Disorder, and the victim in Case 2 also self-mutilated. Fifth, all three presented historical clues, such as past lying or some victim role familiarity, having been or known a prior victim. Sixth, all of these cases show problems with the suspect's described behavior; the suspect either had a good alibi or the profile was consistent with popular culture, but not real case dynamics. In fact, these victims presented sensational and dramatic events that are nearly absent in true stalking cases. Seventh, all of the victims had motives for their false allegations including attention, sympathy, and reconciliation, and in one case revenge over rejected advances. Eighth, these cases demonstrated a reporting rhythm in which the incidents coincided with life stressors and a decline in significant other interest or involvement in their lives. Ninth, these cases lacked any forensic or medical evidence to support the allegations. Further, details in Cases 2 and 3 were notably inconsistent, the victim able to recall certain important details and not others. Tenth, each of these victims had a significant issue around abandonment, loss, and rejection, and had been behaviorally reinforced for being in the victim role. Eleventh, all of these victims likewise had a dysfunctional relationship with their significant other that appeared to be related to the ongoing events. And finally, in each of these cases, investigators intuitively sensed that something was awry prior to being able to articulate it.

These cases also support that a primary difference between the named and unnamed perpetrators is the motive and previous relationship with the identified "perpetrator"; the revenge motive is usually absent in the unnamed perpetrator

Table 2

False Victimization Syndrome Descriptors

Descriptors	Case 1: Known perpetrator	Case 2: Unknown perpetrator	Case 3: Unknown perpetrator
1. Initial attributions	Present	Present	Present
Denial absent	√	√	√
2. Victim presentation	Present	Present	Present
Trauma-free or overeract	√	√	√
Vulnerability absent	√	√	
3. Enlistment of others	Present	Present	Present
Obvious secondary gains	√	√	√
Jumping through hoops	√	√	√
4. Psychological data	Present	Present	Present
Personality disorder "B"	√	√	√
Personal/life crises	√	√	√
Self-mutilation		√	
5. Historical clues	Present	Present	Present
Lying	√	√	√
Victim role familiarity	√	√	√
6. Suspect problems	Present	Present	Present
Popular culture profile	√	√	√
Mixes profiles	√	√	√
7. Motives	Present	Present	Present
Alibi/excuse		√	
Reconciliation	√	√	√
Revenge	√		
Attention/sympathy	√	√	√
8. Reporting rhythm	Present	Present	Present
Waning interest reports	√	√	√
Phantom suspect reports	√	√	√
Coincide with stressors	√	√	√
9. Forensic–medical	Present	Present	Present
Evidence inconclusive	√	√	√
Pseudocorroboration	√	√	√
Detail problems	√	√	√
Unbelievably lucky		√	
10. Situational stressors	Present	Present	Present
Abandonment/loss/reject	√	√	√
Developmental stress	√	√	√
11. Family dynamics	Present	Present	Present
Dysfunction with significant other	√	√	√
Victim reinforcement	√	√	√
12. Intuition	Present	Present	Present
Gut reactions	√	√	√

category. As McDowell and Hibler (1987) noted in false rape cases, a false allegation of stalking with an unidentified perpetrator enables the victim to elude detection more effectively, and may be a more useful ploy in the service of attention seeking and sympathy. A named perpetrator, on the other hand, is more of a high-risk option, since it forces a confrontation around the veracity of the allegations. While it may appear that there was an identified perpetrator in Case 2, we note that the identification of the suspect in this case was more happenstance. Such a vague description was given in this case that there should have been a failure to identify the suspect. However, as unfortunate as it may be, the victim got "carried away" trying to justify herself and an innocent person was identified.

These cases also exemplify the tremendous consequences involved. In all of these cases law enforcement, private security, or mental health resources were deployed. Negative publicity for the university and the dentist resulted from allegations, and in the case of Mary, there was much anxiety for co-workers in the corporate setting. A student's career was adversely affected, and the dentist nearly lost his license. Once again, the importance of the impact of false allegations should not be minimized.

FALSE VICTIMIZATION SYNDROME DESCRIPTORS

When suspicions arise that a stalking complaint might not be legitimate, there are at least 12 categories of descriptors that should be assessed to determine the presence of a potential false victimization syndrome. Each of these factors is discussed individually and they are presented in summary form in Table 2. This list is not exhaustive nor additive, and the complex relationship of these factors in each case may lend one factor to be more or less relevant than another.

INITIAL ATTRIBUTIONS

Initial attributions pertain to the victim's first interpretation of what is happening to her when confronted with a problematic criminal behavior. Generally most true victims, when initially confronted by stalking behavior, do not immediately conclude, "I am a victim." More commonly there is denial and disbelief, with victims often feeling that they have somehow been responsible for the deviant behavior and making statements to themselves and others such as "this can't be happening." In false cases, on inquiry the victim does not go through this initial disbelief or denial and goes straight to the conclusion, "I am being stalked."

VICTIM PRESENTATION

Victim presentation refers to the kinds of behavior engaged in by the victim, and whether this behavior is consistent with typical victim behavior. With the initial decision to come forward, it is common for true victims to receive significant prodding from supportive others to "do something about it"; while in false cases, the victim often comes forward confidently and gleefully. When coming forward and participating in law enforcement recommended intervention, the true victim is often very reluctant and ambivalent, fearing that she will exacerbate the situation or precipitate retaliation. In contrast, the false accuser expresses little ambivalence or fright, knowing that there is no one to fear. Fear and feelings of vulnerability in general are also absent, often replaced by a seeming indifference to relay concerns about the events, a matter of fact presentation of events, and engaging in behaviors without regard to security precautions. Occasionally, however, it may be just the opposite, with gross overreaction to a fairly minor report. In dramatic cases, the victim might seem to be enjoying the attention, or even engage or seek contact with the supposed stalker when there is an identified suspect. The false accuser is a lot more pushy and demanding about what she wants during the investigation and may try to control how it is done, while the true victim is much more ambivalent and unsure.

ENLISTMENT OF OTHERS

Enlistment of others refers to the manner in which the complainant interfaces with her support system around the incident. In some cases of false victimization it is not at all uncommon to clearly see the obvious secondary gains that the victim is getting out of the allegations. Significant others are rallying all around them, doing things for them, and jumping through all kinds of hoops. If the context of the event is the work or school environment, there may be special parking places, new working hours, and other special accommodations. True victims are often embarrassed and would rather not draw too much attention to themselves.

PSYCHOLOGICAL DATA

Psychological data refer to whether there are any mental health problems in the victim's background. We have anecdotally noted many false victims who have been diagnosed or would qualify for *DSM-IV* Cluster B personality disorders, most notably borderline and histrionic personality disorders. This makes sense since criteria for these types of disorders include manipulativeness, dramatic attempts to avoid perceived or real abandonment, intense inadequacy, and acting out. Our observations are consistent with McDowell and Hibler's (1987) observations of hysterical and borderline features in those who falsely accuse others of rape. In addition, many of our observed cases have involved individuals who present as highly insecure about family or work, have a tendency to exaggerate or draw attention to themselves, have a history of past self-mutilation or suicide attempts and previous hospitalizations, and have had a recent significant personal or life crisis.

HISTORICAL CLUES

Historical clues include information gleaned from the history of the complainant and other collateral sources that may point in the direction of a false allegation. Historical clues that may suggest a false claim of stalking include lying and manipulativeness, attention-seeking behavior, telling "tall tales," having observed others known to them go through the "real thing," having been a victim before under similar mysterious circumstances, having a history of feigning illness or excessive medical care for dramatic illnesses, sexuality problems, or a previous attraction to and rejection by the supposed perpetrator in named perpetrator scenarios.

SUSPECT PROBLEMS

Suspect problems refer to problems with the victim's description of the suspect, often centering around the notion that the victim's characterization of the suspect conflicts with known suspect behavior. Often false victims derive their ideas about how suspects act from the popular culture's movies, sensational news reports, and the print media. As a consequence, there may be sharp discrepancies between how the suspect is portrayed and how real suspects actually behave. For example, it is extremely rare for there to be a mysterious unidentified stranger as portrayed in Hollywood movies; more often than not, the suspect will become known fairly quickly in an actual case. Another obvious suggestion of a false report with a named or identified suspect is when the suspect has a good alibi and there does not appear to be evidence of someone knowingly or unknowingly conspiring to help the suspect carry it off undetected. The false complainant may also mix two mutually exclusive profiles of stalkers, such as the erotomanic and the simple obsessional, in their reporting of behavior and incidents.

MOTIVES

The motives descriptor simply means that there is an obvious discernible motive for the complainant to falsify an allegation of stalking: the need for an alibi or excuse for personal behavior, such as carrying on an illicit affair and needing a story to cover up phone calls and "mysterious" and unexplainable events; the desire for reconciliation or a closer attachment to someone who has been perceived as withdrawing or abandoning by putting them in the role of rescuer; the need for revenge against someone who has rejected them or threatens their security, such as the manufacturing of a stalking complaint at work when performance has been down; and, nearly always present, the desire for attention and sympathy.

REPORTING RHYTHM

Reporting rhythm refers to the manner in which the victim makes the crime complaints. Suspicions of a false allegation may be supported if the reports come on the heels of a significant life or developmental stressor, or after a similar crime received major publicity. We also see a tendency for reports to be generated when it appears that law enforcement and other interest in the form of follow-up phone calls and concern might be waning. In these circumstances, the victim may in fact increase the intensity of the reported behaviors, particularly if she feels that her credibility is beginning to be questioned. It is interesting to note the "phantom suspect" reporting behavior where the victim claims that "it just happened, you just missed him," and the events always seem to occur in that brief window of opportunity when no independent third parties are present to corroborate them.

FORENSIC–MEDICAL

The forensic–medical descriptor refers to the fact that in most true stalking cases, there is either a clearly identified and known suspect or forensic evidence available in the form of fingerprints and handwriting to confirm the existence and identity of the suspect. In false cases this is often notably absent, and when there are injuries to the victim they are often consistent with self-mutilation. Supposed corroboration in the suspected false case needs to be closely scrutinized since such corroboration often fails to truly corroborate the event. We call this "pseudocorroboration." For example, the victim who receives telephone calls while her boyfriend is present and says, "he heard the phone ring"; however, at no point did he actually listen in on the call. Further, some of the behaviors that false victims engage in to corroborate their claims can be quite creative, including asking a stranger at an airport to mail a letter from his destination so that it will have an out-of-state postmark, or asking a fellow shopper at the supermarket to take a picture of the victim in the supermarket to create supposed surveillance photos.

In addition, details of the event may be remarkably inconsistent and ambiguous. For example, the victim reports that she is being followed and states, "it was a blue Dodge Intrepid, with a dent in the front bumper, but I can't recall any of the license" or "he smiled at me and had Nike Air Jordans but I can't recall his face." If the victim is attacked, often times she seems "amazingly lucky" and the physical injuries look worse than they actually are. If investigators are saying its amazing and unbelievable, perhaps it is.

SITUATIONAL STRESSORS

Stressors associated with the creation of false stalking claims include those that center around abandonment, loss, or rejection; developmental stress around the individual moving from one life stage to the next and unconsciously wanting to maintain a more dependent life stage; and relationship problems, especially having an affair or recently being sent to the family "doghouse." These types of stressors may serve as triggers for the false accuser who uses the events as a way of coping with these various life dilemmas and avoiding or resolving conflicts.

FAMILY DYNAMICS

Current family dynamics may likewise indicate a context that precipitates the victim to file a false report or series of reports. The dynamics we have observed in a number of cases include relationship problems with the victim's significant other, abuse and/or pressure within the family constellation that is lessened or mitigated by the events, and strong reinforcement within the family for being in the victim role.

INTUITION

Tenured investigators with extensive experience in victim and suspect interviews develop over time an ability to sense when things just do not seem right. These kinds of "hunches or gut instincts" can compel an investigator to look more closely at cases in a linear, systematic fashion, and should not be discounted.

INTERVENTION SUGGESTIONS

The first step is to thoroughly and exhaustively gather data to rule out the possibility that the case is, in fact, a legitimate stalking case. This data gathering frequently includes forensic and medical tests, handwriting analysis, surveillance, and comprehensive interviews with the complainant, as well as any other potential data sources. Consultation with stalking case experts, including mental health consultants, can also be helpful.

Proactive techniques might also draw the person out. For example, investigators have told suspected false claimants what their expectations are about the next perpetrator behaviors, such as "right about now, I would expect that he'll start to involve himself by calling us"; in one case this was followed by a series of hang up calls to the investigator (J. Dunn, personal communication, October 1997). Other implausible suggestions may be offered as "real" behaviors to expect. Amazingly, as with Charcot's induction of paralysis in hysterics, the false claimants will then engineer the behavior to support their claim. Each of these demonstrated suggestions become data points to refute the veracity of the claims during the confrontation.

Once the investigators are strongly convinced that the allegations are false, an interview should be arranged with the victim to gently confront and hopefully gain a confession regarding the false claims. It is our experience that a beneficial approach is to clearly state that the "events did not occur as you told us" and then allow a face saving exit for the victim by portraying the falsehood sympathetically as a "cry for help." We have found the most effective interrogation and interviewing techniques utilize this firm but sympathetic, nonjudgmental, and supportive approach. McDowell and Hibler (1987), in their discussion of interview approaches with rape false accusation cases, advocated using someone other than the primary investigator for the confrontation, in order to act as a buffer and preserve the ability of the primary investigator to maintain rapport.

It should be determined beforehand whether charges of perjury or filing a false police report are going to be pursued. It is rare for most of these cases to be charged criminally, and if this decision is known prior to the confrontational interview, this becomes a potential bargaining chip with the victim.

Mental health intervention is a more common outcome. The investigator who gets a confession from the victim may be well served by following up to ensure or even strongly insist that the victim pursue mental health assistance as an alternative to prosecution. The investigator may also gain permission from the victim to contact any current or future treating therapist to relay accurate information, thus ensuring appropriate follow-up and treatment. Similar communications may be facilitated with significant others. This may also remove some of the stigma and pressure on the person from having to face others lied to, thereby facilitating some modification in dysfunctional relationship patterns.

SUGGESTIONS FOR FURTHER RESEARCH AND INVESTIGATION

We believe that further research and statistical tracking of the prevalence of these syndromes is indicated. We recommend that the descriptors that we have hypothesized be further examined to determine their usefulness in discriminating between real cases and false cases. In-depth psychological assessments of those who make these kinds of false allegations would also be useful to shed some additional light on the dynamics of these individuals.

We have attempted to provide a thorough review of the unique and interesting topic of false victimization syndromes. We have organized these phenomena into a useful typology, and have shared information regarding case dynamics and descriptors for stalking-related false victimization syndromes. We hope that our contribution will stimulate interest, further exploration, and continued discussion. While occasionally a person does cry wolf, we still must initially treat every situation as if there really is a wolf.

REFERENCES

American Psychiatric Association. (1994). *Diagnostic and statistical manual of mental disorders* (4th ed.). Washington DC: Author.

Asher, R. (1951). Munchausen's syndrome. *Lancet, 1,* 339–342.

Benac, N. (1997, October 27). Medical spies check in to check out care. *Associated Press.*

Deutsch, H., & Roazen, P. (1982). On the pathological lie (pseudologia phantastica). *Journal of the American Academy of Psychoanalysis, 10*(3), 369–386.

Dohn, H. H. (1986). Factitious rape: A case report. *Hillside Journal of Clinical Psychiatry, 8*(2), 224–231.

Douglas, J., & Olshaker, M. (1998). *Obsession.* New York: Scrivner.

Dulit, R. A., Fyer, M. R., Leon, A. C., Brodsky, B. S., & Frances, A. J. (1994). Clinical correlates of self-mutilation in borderline personality disorder. *American Journal of Psychiatry, 151*(9), 1305–1311.

Ellenberger, H. F. (1970). *The discovery of the unconscious: The history and evolution of dynamic psychiatry.* New York: Basic Books.

Gavin, H. (1863). *Feigned and factitious diseases, chiefly of soldiers and seamen.* London: J & A Churchill.

Goldman, J. (1997, November 18). Rape defamation case rubs new salt in old wounds. *Los Angeles Times,* p. A15.

Goodman, B. (1994). *When the body speaks its mind: A psychiatrist probes the mysteries of hypochondria and Munchausen's syndrome.* New York: Putnam.

Hazelwood, R. R. (1983). Behavior-oriented interview of rape victims: The key to profiling. *FBI Law Enforcement Bulletin, 52*(9), 8–15.

Hazelwood, R. R., & Burgess, A. W. (1987). *Practical aspects of rape investigation: A multidisciplinary approach.* New York: Elsevier.

Hazelwood, R. R., & Harpold, J. (1986). Rape: The dangers of providing confrontational advice. *FBI Law Enforcement Bulletin, 55*(6), 1–5.

Jones, R. M. (1995). Factitious disorders. In H. I. Kaplan & B. J. Sadock (Eds.), *Comprehensive textbook of psychiatry* (6th ed., pp. 1271–1279). Baltimore, MD: Williams & Wilkins.

Kanin, E. J. (1984). Date rape: Unofficial criminals and victims. *Victimology: An International Journal, 9*(1), 95–108.

Kanin, E. J. (1994). False rape allegations. *Archives of Sexual Behavior, 23*(1), 81–92.

Levin, A. V., & Sheridan, M. S. (Eds.). (1995). *Munchausen syndrome by proxy: Issues in diagnosis and treatment.* New York: Lexington Books.

Levine, A. (1997, November 3). The strange case of faked hate crimes. *U.S. News and World Report,* p. 30.

Macdonald, J. M. (1995). *Rape: Controversial issues, criminal profiles, date rape, false reports, and false memories*. Springfield, IL: Charles C. Thomas.

McDowell, C. P., & Hibler, N. (1987). False allegations. In R. R. Hazelwood & A. W. Burgess (Eds.), *Practical aspects of rape investigation* (pp. 275–299). New York: Elsevier.

Meadow, R. (1977). Munchausen syndrome by proxy—The hinterland of child abuse. *Lancet, 2*, 343–345.

Melges, F. T., & Swartz, M. S. (1989). Oscillations of attachment in borderline personality disorder. *American Journal of Psychiatry, 146*(9), 1115–1120.

"Mysterious poet" assailant proves to be victim herself. (1981, October 3). *Atlanta Journal Weekend, Atlanta Constitution*, p. 3–A.

Raspe, R. E. (1944). *The surprising adventures of Baron Munchausen*. New York: Peter Pauper.

Schreier, H. (1996). Repeated false allegations of sexual abuse presenting to sheriffs: When is it Munchausen by proxy? *Child Abuse and Neglect, 20*(10), 985–991.

Schreier, H., & Libow, J. (1993). *Hurting for love: Munchausen by proxy syndrome*. New York: Guilford Press.

Schrink, J., & LeBeau, J. (1984). *Forcible rape: Myths and myth making*. Paper presented at the Academy of Criminal Justice Sciences Annual Meeting.

Siegel, J. (1995). Look who's stalking. *Los Angeles, 41*(5), 70–73.

Snyder, S. (1986). Pseudologia fantastica in the borderline patient. *American Journal of Psychiatry, 143*(10), 1287–1289.

Swanson, C. R., Chamelin, N. C., & Territo, L. (1984). *Criminal investigation* (3rd ed.). New York: Random House.

Truscott, D., & Evans, J. (1997, November). *Fraud or false attribution? Three case studies of WCB claims involving sexual assault*. Paper presented at the thirteenth annual meeting of the international society for traumatic stress studies, Montreal, Canada.

Walsh, B., & Rosen, P. (1988). *Self-mutilation: Theory, research, and treatment*. New York: Guilford.

Zona, M. A., Lane, J. C., & Moore, N. (1996, February). *The psychology and behavior of stalkers*. Paper presented at the 45th annual meeting of American Academy of Forensic Sciences, Nashville, TN.

Zona, M. A., & Palarea, R. (1997, August). *The psychology and behavior of stalkers*. Paper presented at the Association of Threat Assessment Professionals, annual conference, Anaheim, CA.

CHAPTER 13

Stalking, Erotomania, and the Tarasoff Cases

Glenn S. Lipson, Ph.D. and Mark J. Mills, J.D., M.D.

The Tarasoff record is one that is rich in judicial review and subsequent professional commentary. In addition to the civil suit brought by the Tarasoff family against the Regents of the University of California, professionals, and the campus police, there is the criminal case that involved the trial of Prosenjit Poddar. That criminal case underwent the scrutiny of both California Appellate and Supreme Court review (*People v. Poddar*, 1972; *People v. Podder*, 1974). As a result of the civil negligence trial brought by the Tarasoffs, two rulings were published by the California Supreme Court in 1974 and in 1976 (*Tarasoff v. Regents of the University of California*, 1974; *Tarasoff v. Regents of the University of California*, 1976), establishing the unprecedented duty of a therapist to protect others from the harm a patient intimates he or she may cause.

Discussions of the Tarasoff case focus on legal obligations that may be imposed on a therapist if a client threatened to seriously harm others. This duty has evolved in scope and definition through the evolution of case law. Questions, however, still remain. Does the Tarasoff duty apply only to identifiable victims (*Schuster v. Altenberg*, 1988)? Does it also apply to property or those in the so-called "zone of danger" (*Leonard v. Iowa*, 1992)? How specific does the threat have to be (*Peck v. Counseling Services of Addison County*, 1985; *Leonard v. Latrobe Area Hospital*, 1993)? How does the "duty to protect" impact inpatient treatment plans, including discharge decisions (*Jablonski v. United States*, 1983; *Lipari v. Sears Roebuck*, 1980)? How does the patient's status as an inpatient or outpatient affect this duty, and what steps are needed to fulfill the particular state's statutory requirements?

The Psychology of Stalking: Clinical and Forensic Perspectives

In the wake of the Tarasoff rulings, it is easy to miss that the issues involved in this case not only address the duty owed by therapists to clients and foreseeable third parties at risk, but also provide a well-documented case of stalking. Stone (1984) was one of the first individuals to recognize that the Tarasoff case involved De Clérambault's syndrome, or erotomania. Retrospectively, the reported historical details can provide a starting point for the thoughtful analysis of erotomanic individuals who stalk.

CASE HISTORY

Prosenjit Poddar was a native of a village in India where he belonged to the lowest caste (the untouchables). During his early years, he had minimal contact with people from Europe or America. He was considered academically gifted, however, and was able to advance to the top of the Indian University System; beginning in 1967, he pursued graduate studies in electronics and naval architecture at the University of California, Berkeley (Winslade, 1981).

Poddar's academic success suggests that he was able to function well in school. Thus, with structure and clear expectations, he was able to succeed intellectually. The areas in which individuals function well speak to their strengths, and the meaning of success or failure needs to be explored individually. For example, does being successful match individuals' sense of their abilities? Are individuals' achievements motivated by a compensatory desire to convince themselves and others that they are worthwhile? Finally, do their accomplishments seem well suited to their abilities, or do they feel like an impostor, unable to acknowledge the genuineness of their accomplishments?

Poddar had been able to move into a new cultural context and initially met the demands of a graduate program in another country. This suggests that his weaknesses were at that time held in check. Emotional and interpersonal problems can impact memory, concentration, and the efficiency of thought processes in general. Someone's habitual style of dealing with affects, relationships, and conflicts is the province of personality. Poddar's apparent academic success masked areas of functional weaknesses. Psychotherapists can miss the extent of a person's difficulties when their client's accomplishments, in and of themselves, suggest that he or she is resourceful and effective. This success may be attained at a high cost, obfuscating emotional and interpersonal weakness. Problems related to personality defects come to the fore contextually, brought on by success or failure, and often in the course of relationships with others.

When evaluating a stalker, cultural issues need to be explored. One's identity via others and one's world view are uniquely individual derivatives of experience. Poddar had historically and contemporaneously belonged to the Harijan or untouchable caste in India, which would have some impact on his identity (Vande

Creek & Knapp, 1993). A sensitive cultural assessment involves familiarity with the culture and its practices regarding intimacy, role expectations, and the meanings assigned to actions. This evaluation needs to be tailored to the individual. If culture represents the fabric, the individual fit is influenced by moderator variables, including socioeconomic status, education, travel, extended family, and level of tradition. Personality remains an important variable since not all members of a caste or group respond in the same way to discrimination and other life events.

Prosenjit Poddar met Tatiana Tarasoff through a folk dance group while at the University of California. Tatiana had herself come from a multicultural background and enjoyed spending time with foreign students. The weekly folk dancing enabled Prosenjit Poddar to establish a relationship with Tatiana. They would dance together and talk to each other. During the fall semester of 1968, Prosenjit told Farrokhg Mistree, his friend from India, of his increasing romantic interest in Tatiana. Farrokhg advised Poddar to pursue educational goals, not romance, and described him as socially and sexually naive.

If one accepts that someone is both socially and sexually naive, we must then ask if the individual's naivete is born from problems with sexuality in general. Is it culturally related to the separation of the genders and prohibitions against associating with the opposite sex? Does it relate to difficulties perceiving others? Whatever the reason, a lack of maturity in this area can lead to the misinterpretation of behavior.

Tatiana and Poddar's social contact in the fall culminated in a New Year's Eve kiss. This kiss allegedly took place while they were alone in an elevator during a party. Prosenjit interpreted this New Year's Eve gesture as a sign of betrothal. One can imagine that, for someone from the untouchable caste, experiencing a kiss would carry with it the potential for excess meaning.

Tatiana, however, was not interested in having an intimate relationship, leaving Prosenjit confused. Prosenjit attempted to sort out what he wished to be true from what was actually true about the state of their relationship. He developed the belief that deep down she truly cared for him. His proof that she had those feelings was based on her willingness to dance with him, the phone contact they had, and the long talks with him in his room. These conversations occasionally concluded by her kissing him goodbye (Winslade & Ross, 1983).

At this juncture, a discontinuity existed between what Poddar wished for and what he perceived was the state of their relationship. Information was sought to resolve this dilemma. However, his objectivity became compromised by desire and need. Obsessive consideration did not resolve his confusion. Areas to explore in his assessment included the frequency and intrusiveness of his thoughts about this "special person" as well as the resolution he was seeking.

Poddar observed that Tatiana would often break their dates or fail to show up when he expected her. In addition, she would talk of other men in his presence. He also felt that, on occasion, she would ignore him for the entire evening. From a cross-cultural perspective, it is easy to imagine the significance of this behavior taking on different meanings. In cases of immigrant persons who stalk, there is the added dimension of misconstruing the meaning of the victim's behavior since it is based on different expectations of the meaning of interactions (Meyers & Meloy, 1994).

Poddar had audio recorded approximately 40 hours of his and Tatiana's conversations. During the winter months, he frequently replayed and listened to the recorded conversations in order to determine what her true feelings were. Beset by doubts and attempting to reconcile what he wished for with what was real, Poddar suffered a severe emotional crisis. Others observed his speech becoming disjointed, with periods of affective lability characterized by weeping. Eventually he needed to withdraw from his winter quarter classes.

His desire for a romantic relationship with Tatiana and his subsequent lack of success resulted in a defensive intellectual attempt to examine the details of their interactions with the hope that he would gain some perspective. Thought and consideration were used in an effort to contain and limit his stirred up feelings. Poddar became obsessed with the "real" meaning of Tatiana's actions.

His obsessive symptoms need to be examined on two levels: First, what is the central purpose of his symptom, and second, how effective were his ruminations in working through the impasse and related fears? Obsessive rumination can be used to stave off a psychotic decompensation or depression, or may merely be a temporary exacerbation of a character trait. Psychologists are often referred individuals for testing and asked to address the emotional problems masked by obsessive symptoms. For the higher functioning individual obsessive defenses can work to bind anxieties. More primitive personality dynamics are involved when the obsession with another is utilized to avoid the awareness of one's own problems.

The second area of inquiry regarding obsessions relates to the symptom's effectiveness in gaining perspective and resolution of the conflict that propelled the rumination. When obsession fails to move the person toward resolution, the loss of balance is noticeable. Poddar's withdrawal from his coursework illustrates the extent to which an obsession can grow and disrupt other aspects of one's life. This disruption is first seen in the individual's inability to stop thinking about the other individual or object. Finally, despite efforts to shift focus, to follow through on other goals, life becomes derailed, as he feels hopelessly swept into rumination or action.

Poddar was following the advice of his friend Mistree when he attempted to break clean from his desired and confusing relationship with Tatiana. Initially, his attempts to gain some distance and terminate the relationship were successful. Poddar appeared to be recovering his sense of balance. However, his obsessive concerns and desires were reactivated when Tatiana called during March and told him that she missed their talks. Toward the end of March 1969, Poddar proposed marriage to Tatiana. According to Windslade and Ross (1983), Tatiana did not say either yes or no to this proposal. Once again Poddar returned to study the tapes of their conversations, feeling an increasing sense of rejection.

Of course, love and rejection are a traumatic experience for most people. Identity, self-value, and the worth of the rejecting other person are brought into question when a hoped for relationship falls. Rejection, loss, and trauma present us with information that may be very discrepant from our view of the world, of others, and ourselves. For Horowitz (1974), pathology arises from our difficulty processing discrepant information, leading potentially to a new experience of ourselves.

The rejection of the marital proposal can be seen as the major traumatic incident in Poddar's case. His attempt to move beyond this trauma was not successful. By history, Poddar's obsessive rumination can be described as the search for information gone awry. Seeking information is a means of coping with trauma. Intrusive and obsessive rumination are often symptoms of trauma. The inconsistent behavior of Tatiana could be seen as information Poddar could not integrate, leading to a confused state. His feelings of rejection may have activated a prior negative sense of himself, and he felt anger being ridiculed. The "obsessive following" of stalking (Meloy & Gothard, 1995) can thus be conceptualized as an attempt to process the trauma that arises from unrequited love in a fragile individual.

An inability to relinquish the feelings of obsessional love has also been described in psychotherapists who sexually abuse their clients (Twemlow & Gabbard, 1989). These therapists are well-functioning professionals who nonetheless end up in unethical and highly pathological relationships that destroy their careers and damage their clients. They justify their behavior under the guise of having "true love" for their clients. Twemlow and Gabbard referred to these therapists as suffering "lovesickness," and conservatively estimate that one-half of therapist–patient sexual contact involves lovesickness (1989, p. 73). Poddar's claimed love for Tatiana was similarly ruminative and destructive. Lovesickness is not a concept that has been traditionally applied to stalkers, but the striking parallels suggest it can be useful. Romantically, obsession with another has been equated with true love. However, this is not the case in relationships where the victim experiences fear and intimidation. The pursuer's actions are not synonymous with truly caring for someone else. In the pathological obsessional relationship, the individual loses an appreciation of the actual person he is pursuing. There is a lack of reciprocity in the feelings the stalker has for his prey.

Poddar felt a special connection with Tatiana, as if she were the only one who could understand him. Similarly, lovesick therapists claim these same feelings toward their clients. The inability of the therapist to quiet the stirred affects or thoughts resembles that of a love-obsessed pursuer. For the therapist, the impact of the obsession follows a pattern. First, sessions with the client lose direction and focus. Second, they are unable to follow the advice of their supervisors and the caveats of their training. Poddar was unable to follow the advice of his friends and co-workers. Third, the hours between the sessions become occupied with the thoughts of this patient. These therapists are not merely seeking to have sex with their patients, but instead have lost the sense of themselves and their ethics in their pursuit of a "love." Lovesick individuals experience themselves as fused with another individual, experiencing ecstasy and passion (Twemlow & Gabbard, 1989). This state is characterized by the intrusive thinking of the other and the physical sensation of being in love such as "walking on air, having one's heart in one's throat" and finally a sense that "one is incomplete without the other" (p. 75). Those who are lovesick share with stalkers the underlying feeling that their imagined partner makes them complete and thus the union is right for both of them.

Clearly, lovesickness that is limerance (infatuation) gone awry sets the stage for actions that transgress societal and personal boundaries. When the sense of self is lost, as well as the recognition of another's needs, the ability to organize one's actions and make sense out of one's emotional life is lost. Based on the record, Poddar's obsession eroded his ability to function. The diagnostic implication of this concept of lovesickness and obsession in general is that psychopathology increases when there is a disruption in identity and a distortion in the perception of others. Thus, on a continuum of idealization, pathological attachment needs to be examined in terms of the ability of the person to maintain some stability in his view of himself and others. Further, other pursuits and interests are maintained in a healthy relationship. If there is normative romantic idealization, it occurs without selectively seeing someone as being all good or, conversely, all bad (splitting). There is also a presence of some mutual affection.

During early spring, Poddar began to believe that Tatiana's friends were smirking and laughing at him. He even felt that his friend, Farrokhg Mistree, was gaining some type of secret enjoyment at his disgrace. He openly began voicing threats to harm Tatiana. Poddar is quoted as saying to his friend Mistree, "even you, Mistree, laugh at my state, but I'm like an animal. I could do anything, I could kill her. If I killed her what would you do?" When Mistree told Poddar he would tell the truth, Poddar replied, "then I would have to kill you, too" (Winslade & Ross, 1983, p. 58).

How did Poddar reach this state of mind? We can speculate that he had a propensity for an affective, paranoid, or delusional disorder. The question that remains, however, is why the stalker experiences these thoughts and emotional swings, particularly in the context of a relationship with a certain individual or individuals. A theoretical explanation can be drawn from the work of Michael Balint (1965, 1968). Using a metaphor from geology, he indicated that some individuals have a condition analogous to geological faults. On the surface, these "faults" may not be visible, but with sufficient pressure, the destructive presence of these fissures makes itself known. For Balint, this fault could be triggered by a new relationship.

Something resonates in the internal experience of love-obsessed individuals that only becomes activated when they find the object of their desire. The dawning of infatuation shatters an equilibrium that results in emotional instability and an impairment in reality testing. The person who is pursued feels both angry and frightened and typically responds negatively to attention and the seeking of a relationship. This rejection evokes affective lability, rage, and feelings of shame in the stalker (Meloy, 1996).

Balint (1968) might have suggested that the psychopathology of the stalker stems from a profound disturbance in identity and in relationships with others. The "basic fault" is a disturbance in the capacity to be intimate with other people. For Balint, the search for a primary object of love was essential to an understanding of the majority of the psychopathology that we see. The person with whom one becomes obsessed is suffused with primitive longings. The stalker on some level could be seen as seeking to restore the "passive object of love" (p. 63), the first object sought by the infant (Balint, 1968). Hence, obsessional love is in actuality a masked effort to obtain total and unconditional primary love. Balint believed that the desire to obtain this primary love is the basis of all erotic strivings (Balint, 1965). He saw aggression and rage as a reaction to the lack of primary love. When the stalker becomes obsessed with the person who represents this primary love object, he experiences "both a benign and malignant regression" (Greenberg & Mitchell, 1983, p. 183). Balint believed that both psychopathology and aggression center on difficulties in object relations. These difficulties can result in a disintegration of relationship seeking, often progressing to rage and desires for revenge. In Poddar, we see the emergence of fantasies of revenge.

We can speculate that his relationship with Tatiana activated primitive experiences of himself and internal object longings. These feelings and thoughts propelled his desire to marry and possess her. As with an earthquake, before internal pressures activate the basic fault, the person can appear normal, as if standing on firm ground. As seen in Poddar, some stalkers can achieve a modicum of success. They may have relationships with others, with no overt signs of their interpersonal hunger and emotional weaknesses. It is evident that Poddar had performed well in school in his native India, and at times was able to perform with academic distinction. It was in the wake of his longed for relationship with Tatiana Tarasoff that these abilities in and of themselves became compromised.

Balint's view that some individuals are motivated by the desire to obtain a primitive and basic attachment ties in nicely with the preoccupied attachment patterns described by Bartholomew (1990). These relationships emphasize gaining approval, validation, and self-worth. There are also similarities with Dutton's (1995) description of "intimacy anger." It is axiomatic that most individuals do not seek validation from everyone they meet. We look for different kinds of interactions or support from different people. For the object of obsession, whether it is the abused, jealously controlled spouse or a loved person from afar, different needs are felt.

Poddar returned to school and work suffering from low morale and ruminating about Tatiana. On two occasions he told fellow co-workers that he would like to "blow up Tatiana's house" or perhaps the entire block (T. Goldman, *Tarasoff and implications for practice,* unpublished manuscript, p. 5). Despite these threats, he made no attempt to obtain explosives. His friends tried to convince him that actions such as these were foolish and something in which he should not engage.

Fantasies can discharge hostility for some individuals. The burning of someone in effigy can dissipate the anger that person feels. Other individuals become more emboldened by their thoughts of revenge, with fantasy fueling the final acts of violence. It is thus useful to inquire about the relationship between the stalker's thoughts and actions. Thinking can provide a more economical alternative to acting. Thought has been characterized as interposed somewhere between perception, impulse, and action. Thoughts are supposed to refine and adapt our impulses and desires and provide a substitute for potential actions. The world of thought, however, does not reproduce sensory feedback; in some ways it is both less and more than actual experience (Pruyser, 1979). Fantasy has the capacity to elaborate and build on our sensory input and provide us with ideas. At times, however, thoughts have no basis in reality.

Fantasy and reality become confused and, rather than discharge affects, these very thoughts kindle and create more rage, fueling the eventual explosion. The critical question becomes whether or not thinking and fantasy can discharge, corral, and metabolize a person's impulses, obsessions, and desires.

During the summer of 1969, Tatiana Tarasoff went on a trip to South America. Upon the suggestion of his friend, Mistree, Poddar sought outpatient psychiatric services at Berkeley's Cowell Memorial Hospital. This appointment took place in July and the treating psychiatrist, Stuart Gold, M.D., diagnosed Prosenjit as suffering from schizophrenia, paranoid type, and prescribed antipsychotic medication. Mistree did inform the evaluating psychiatrist of the death threats Poddar had made toward Tatiana Tarasoff. Following the evaluation by Dr. Gold, Poddar was referred to a psychologist, Lawrence Moore, Ph.D., who saw him for seven sessions. During this treatment, Dr. Moore noted that Prosenjit Poddar was rational at times, and on other occasions appeared to be psychotic. Given this description, Poddar's diagnosis would appear to be borderline personality disorder. Issues of trust and fears of betrayal surfaced frequently in the treatment. At one time, Poddar asked to return to Dr. Gold for treatment since he no longer trusted Dr. Moore. Dr. Gold sent Poddar back to Dr. Moore after their meeting.

During the summer months, Prosenjit established a relationship with Alex Tarasoff, Tatiana's brother, with whom he shared an academic interest in electronics. This was a way of maintaining a relationship with Tatiana. In September,

Prosenjit and Alex moved into an apartment together. It was Prosenjit Poddar's fantasy that Tatiana would eventually share that apartment with him. The plan that Prosenjit was working on was to rescue Tatiana from a life-threatening situation that he would orchestrate. As a result, she would see him as her savior and recognize the quality of his love and the extent to which she really needed him (Winslade & Ross, 1983).

The different narrative options individuals believe are possible speak to their level of adaptability and mental health. Healthy fictions have a degree of plausibility and are not juxtaposed with a tragic ending if everything does not turn out as planned. The Thematic Apperception Test is often used by psychologists to determine an individual's style of story telling and the types of themes that dominate and shape his experience. This can be a useful test to flush out narratives related to issues of loss and success. If an interview is relied upon, allowing the person to tell his story will often reveal these themes or life scripts.

The shifting between desires to embrace and to destroy speaks to the presence of a borderline level of personality (Kernberg, 1984; Hamilton, 1988; Chatham, 1985; Meloy, 1989). What becomes apparent is the shifting of the person's perception of the other from an idealized to a devalued object. Splitting, projection, and projective identification are often present in those individuals who are organized at a borderline level. These shifts make it difficult to sort out genuine experience from an internal world colored by affective swings and wishful fantasies.

As he worked his plan, Poddar informed his friend Mistree that he was going to purchase a handgun. He also decided to discontinue his treatment with Dr. Moore. Mistree called the psychotherapist to discuss Poddar's plans, including Poddar's decision to purchase a gun (Mills, 1984). During the final session, which took place August 18, 1969, Poddar discussed his need for getting even with his girlfriend who had betrayed him and violated his honor. Dr. Moore told Prosenjit Poddar that he may need to take steps to restrain him if he continued to discuss his wish to kill Ms. Tarasoff. Poddar angrily left the office (Winslade & Ross, 1983).

Dr. Moore talked to Dr. Yandell, the assistant director of psychiatry, and also to Dr. Gold about the threats. On August 20th, with their support, he called the campus police and wrote a letter to Chief Beall. In this letter Dr. Moore explained that Poddar's mental state, "varies considerably. At times he appears quite rational and at times quite psychotic." He also indicated that at this point he was a danger to the welfare of other people and himself, and that he had been "threatening to kill an unnamed girl who he feels has betrayed him and violated his honor" (T. Goldman, *Tarasoff and implications for practice,* unpublished manuscript, p. 106).

The purpose of this letter was to bring about a commitment using the 2-month-old Lanterman-Petris-Short Act. Chief Beall agreed, and it was recommended that Poddar be confined. When the campus police eventually spoke to Poddar, it was in the presence of Alex Tarasoff. In this conversation he denied possessing a weapon or having made any specific threats. He indicated that he and Tatiana had a troubled relationship. The officers concluded that Poddar appeared rational and not dangerous. They obtained a promise from him to stay away from Tatiana Tarasoff. Alex Tarasoff did not take the matter seriously himself and did not tell his sister or any other family member. Apparently, neither the therapists nor the campus police understood precisely how the civil commitment process worked (Mills, Sullivan & Eth, 1987). The city police should have been contacted instead of the campus police. The city police would have then transported Poddar to the county psychiatric facility for evaluation.

The campus police informed the clinic of their decision not to civilly commit Poddar for psychiatric treatment. Dr. Powelson, the psychiatric departmental chief, had returned from vacation and, after reviewing the matter, concluded that Dr. Moore had overreacted. Dr. Powelson requested that the correspondence to the police be returned and he ordered Dr. Moore to "falsify clinic records by expunging all references to the divulgence of confidential information and threats that promulgated its divulgence" (Myers, 1986, p. 241; *Tarasoff v. Regents of the University of California,* 1973, p. 894). All copies of Dr. Moore's communications were destroyed, although a copy of Dr. Moore's note to Police Chief Beall still exists (in brief for respondent, Moore, in *Tarasoff v. Regents of University of California,* on file with the clerk of the Supreme Court of California, 1 Civil No. 31, 168).

During the police department's interview to determine if Poddar should be committed, he appeared to be rational. It is not uncommon for individuals who have higher areas of attainment and functioning in their lives to at times have shifting experiences of themselves and others. Caught at a more functional moment, the so-called neurotic defenses are more visible among stalkers. These include minimization, rationalization, and the ability to generate a plausible explanation for their pursuit behavior (Meloy, 1996).

In September 1969, Tatiana returned from South America. She again resumed her folk dancing where Poddar watched her and, on occasion, had conversations with her. One time, Tatiana was laughing about a "summer affair with a dashing Argentinean" (Winslade & Ross, 1983, p. 64). Poddar perceived this behavior as a purposeful and cruel slight. He then began to occasionally carry a firearm that he had legally purchased.

On October 24, he requested that Alex Tarasoff intercede on his behalf. Alex responded that he should not bother with his sister and that the relationship between Poddar and his sister was "all over" and best forgotten. In the face of Poddar's insistence to see his sister, Alex Tarasoff shoved Poddar into a wall. He told Poddar that he better stay away from Tatiana altogether. He also indicated that Poddar would cause the wrath of his father if he continued to bother his sister (Winslade & Ross, 1983).

On October 27, 1969, after a sleepless night, Poddar decided that he needed to see Tatiana at her family home. He thought that if he could find out why she behaved so unkindly toward him, this information would free him from his obsession. He became increasingly more angry, and he became frightened that he might hurt her. He decided he needed to talk to her. He left his apartment at 8:00 a.m. in order to arrive at Tatiana's house after Mr. Tarasoff had left for work. At Tatiana's request, Mrs. Tarasoff answered the door and told the young man to leave, adding that he should "go back to India where he belonged" (Winslade, 1981, p. 143).

Poddar returned to his apartment apparently in a miserable state, and may have struggled with his urge to kill Tatiana. At one particular point during the day, he thought he heard voices. Later he resolved to go back to her family home and speak to her before anyone else came home. On this trip, he left with a kitchen knife and a pellet gun. Poddar said that the knife was taken for protection against Tatiana's father. After he rang the doorbell, Tatiana answered the door and indicated that she wanted him to leave, adding that her father would soon return home. He did not heed her advice. A struggle then followed during which Tatiana screamed and ran out of the house. He shot her with the pellet gun and stabbed her 14 times with the butcher knife. She died next to her front door from the knife wounds. Poddar phoned the Berkeley City police, stating he had just stabbed someone and wished to be taken into custody.

Object relations theory has been used to help explain the actions of a stalker who commits murder (Meloy, 1989, 1992, 1996). This theory is based on the premise that most people are relationship seeking. It is apparent that identity, our sense of the world, our view of others, our language, and our ability to identify what we are feeling develop through our connection with others. Meloy (1988, 1992) explained the relationship between narcissistic feelings and violence. Early disturbances and difficulties with primary relationships influence desires and the types of relationships that are sought. The failure to obtain adequate soothing and appropriate limit setting can lead to narcissistic defenses, including a grandiose view of oneself exquisitely sensitive to rejection. For Poddar, the issue of loss of honor became tantamount, and shame coalesced as a motivator to retaliate. In self-psychology language (Kohut, 1971), shame is an intersubjective reality that can fuel rage or dejection.

Whatever formulation one utilizes, there is clearly a disturbance in stalkers in their perceptions of both themselves and others. Unresolved anger from prior rejection, hostility used to block other feelings such as sadness, and the confusion between the bad parts of oneself and the need to devalue the rejecting party, can all lead to precipitous and dangerous actions. Just as the destroying of the love object can be related to the attempt to destroy unacceptable parts of oneself, the dynamics involved are complex and must be analyzed on an individual basis. The stalking of a celebrity rather than an acquaintance evidences different interpersonal, self, other, transferential, and narcissistic elements that may be more fantasy bound.

CRIMINAL PROCEEDINGS

Poddar pleaded not guilty by reason of insanity in his criminal trial. He did not testify. Three psychiatrists and a psychologist did testify that he suffered from paranoid schizophrenia and that he could not harbor malice and forethought to be held legally responsible for his actions. The court-appointed psychiatrist claimed that the defendant was schizoid and could possess the necessary mental states to be found guilty of first- or second-degree murder. A neurologist believed that there was a nonspecific pathological lesion, tumor, or scar that impacted his behavior (*People v. Poddar,* 1974).

The trial lasted approximately 17 days and Poddar was convicted of second-degree murder. In 1972, the court of appeals reduced the charge to manslaughter based on poor jury instructions. The California Supreme Court later overturned this decision with a five to two vote on February 7, 1974. The California Supreme Court declared that, without the error in the jury instructions, it was "reasonably probable" that a result more favorable to the defendant would have been reached (*People v. Poddar,* 1974, p. 350). Poddar's attorney ultimately got his client released after he had served approximately 5 years in prison. An informal agreement that sanitized Poddar's legal records was reached. He made the symbolic act of unofficial exile (Winslade, 1981) and immediately returned to India. Poddar was later married to an attorney (Winslade & Ross, 1983).

CIVIL PROCEEDINGS

It is the ramification of the civil suit for negligence against the Regents of the University of California that brought about the so-called duty to warn for mental health professionals. The Supreme Court ruling in *Tarasoff v. Regents of the University of California* (1974) came to the unprecedented finding that, owing to the patient–psychotherapist special relationship, a duty to warn existed:

> When a doctor or psychotherapist, in the exercise of his professional skill and knowledge, determines, or should determine, that a warning is essential to avert a danger rising from the medical or psychological condition of a patient, he incurs a legal obligation to give that warning. (p. 914)

The first Tarasoff ruling was quickly responded to by mental health organizations. Amicus curiae briefs were filed, supporting the defendant's request that the court rehear the case (Mills, 1984). The central theme in these briefs was that clinicians have no inherent ability to predict violence. The American Psychiatric Association brief suggested that imposing a duty to warn would lead to many false-positive predictions that would result in almost routine breaches in confidentiality. These violations of privilege would result in the loss of the therapist–client relationship, to the detriment of those needing treatment. Part of the fear was that alerted clients would not disclose their violent fantasies and thus compromise the success of treatment.

In a rare decision, the California Supreme Court agreed to rehear the case and issued a second opinion—four of the seven judges concurred—which is now referred to as Tarasoff II (Mills, 1984). The court did find again that therapists have a duty to potential victims. However, the duty was more broadly defined as a duty to protect. The court indicated that:

> When a therapist determines, or pursuant to the standard of his profession should determine, that his patient presents a serious danger of violence to another, he incurs an obligation to use reasonable care to protect the intended victim against such danger. The discharge of his duty may require the therapist to take one or more various steps depending on the nature of the case. Thus, it may call for him to warn the intended victim or others likely to apprise the intended victim of danger, to notify the police or take whatever steps are reasonably necessary under the circumstances. (p. 346)

The duty to protect goes beyond the expectation that those at risk need to be warned. A therapist may need to civilly commit or voluntarily hospitalize a patient in order to protect others.

The basis of this duty being imposed is the court's belief that a "special relationship" exists between the therapist and a client. In a recent review of the 20 years since the Tarasoff decision, Anfang and Appelbaum (1996) provided an excellent summary of the evolution of case law and statutes addressing the appropriate response that mental health practitioners can make when faced with a situation that may evoke the duty to protect.

Standards of care and who should be warned vary from state to state. It is important for the clinician to discuss her decisions with colleagues in order to firmly establish the reasonableness of her actions and how others would act, given the same or similar circumstances. Questions that deal with the difference between a violent fantasy and a plan to harm someone else, for instance, are sometimes difficult to sort through. Even after more than 20 years, the Tarasoff doctrine "continues to confuse and confound" (Anfang & Appelbaum, 1996, p. 67). Asking when it is appropriate to breach confidentiality in order to protect others continues to be one of the frequent subjects of consultation within the mental health community.

ASSESSMENT OF DANGEROUSNESS IN A TARASOFF SITUATION

When a therapist is required to judge a client's propensity to harm someone else, based on his statements or preoccupation with another party, it is important to remember the general factors involved in the assessment of violence risk (Monahan,

1993). These factors include the patient's past history of violent and dangerous acts, demographic characteristics, personality characteristics, cognitive style and functioning, social history, history of criminal acts, current perceived stress, the nature of the social environment, means to accomplish violence, access to a victim, substance abuse, presence of anger, psychodiagnosis, current level of functioning, and prior responses to treatment (Monahan & Steadman, 1994). Other variables that need attention in making a threat assessment include the risk of precipitating events. Often these events involve confrontation, rejection, or some type of loss. It is also helpful to look for escalation in the behavior toward the object of obsession, such as increased frequency of attempted contacts. The actual risk of violence to a victim of a stalker is relatively low (3–36%), making these events difficult to predict (Meloy, 1996).

SUMMARY

Prosenjit Poddar's obsession with and pursuit of a relationship with Tatiana Tarasoff is an example of stalking. However, this is clearer in retrospect then it was at the time. To use Poddar as a case study is difficult because of the "multiple layers of permanent ambiguity" (Winslade, 1981, p. 146). Based on the record we will never fully know his mental state or his intentions. Still, in light of object relations theory, the rediscovery of De Clérambault's syndrome, and the growing understanding of stalking, the story of Prosenjit Poddar and Tatiana Tarasoff takes on new meaning.

There have been several attempts to classify individuals who engage in obsessional pursuit and stalking behavior (Zona, Sharma, & Lane, 1993, Harmon, Rosner, & Owens, 1995; Mullen & Pathé, 1994). Poddar falls within Zona's "simple obsessional" group: those that were prior acquaintances of their victim. What was postulated in this chapter was that those who stalk suffer from *a basic fault* in their capacity to have relationships with others. These problems erupt in the presence of limerence and the activation of primitive wishes for unrequited love. These vulnerabilities may not be apparent until the person moves toward a longed for relationship, which unsettlingly stirs primitive wishes and stresses the foundation of the individual's personality.

It is the hallmark of failing obsessional defenses that the subject's additional activity does not contain and stave off underlying anxiety and fear. New information sought only confounds, confuses, and reignites the obsessional thoughts about the object. For Poddar the call from Tatiana Tarasoff expressing her wish to renew their friendship was enough to shatter the calm he had found in early spring. Again the metaphorical daisy picking of "she loves me, she loves me not" resumed. The obsessive lives with the fixed idea or delusion that additional information, communication, or contact will resolve his quandaries: to be driven by obsession is painful and consuming. This is evident in the reports of Poddar's friends.

When the linking fantasy of the hoped for union evaporates, the person beset by obsession can easily experience shame and humiliation. This unwanted experience of self is often defended against with rage (Meloy, 1996). The obsessional pursuer feels that the idealized relationship will liberate and benefit both parties concerned. In response to rejection, additional fantasies become generated in which the pursuer starts to imagine ways in which he can orchestrate matters in order to obtain the recognition and the results he desires. This was seen in Poddar's idea that if he were to rescue Tatiana Tarasoff, even if it were orchestrated, she would then be able to appreciate the depth of the love he had for her and she had for him. Obsession fuels narcissistic dependence and an inability to get distance and separate oneself from the object of one's desire.

In order to accomplish this separation it is easy to rely on defenses such as splitting. Seeing the other as all bad diminishes the longing for love at the cost of maintaining a disequilibrium of self. The protracted conflict that is experienced by an obsessional pursuer or follower can fuel what appears to be a senseless attack (Satten, Menninger, & Mayman, 1960). This stream of obsessive thought, coupled with strong affect, wishes, and ambivalence can also stir a catathymic reaction (Wertham, 1937; Meloy, 1992). Anticipated loss generates suicidal thoughts that result in rage oscillating between the self and the other person, fueling in turn homicidal fantasies (Revitch & Schlesinger, 1981). The situational and interactive elements of the relationship between the stalker and victim can, on occasion, result in homicide.

Poddar's last attempt at a conversation with Tatiana Tarasoff did not elicit the outcome he desired. It has, however, left us with a case history of erotomania, stalking, and homicide. The Tarasoff case will also continue to raise questions about the nature of confidentiality and how to predict violence. It leads us finally to question the pathological variants of relationships, and how longings and obsessions can lead to death.

REFERENCES

Anfang, S., & Appelbaum, P. (1996, July/August). Twenty years after Tarasoff: Reviewing the duty to protect. *Harvard Review of Psychiatry*, 67–75.

Atwood, G., & Stolorow, R. (1984). *Structures of subjectivity: Explorations in psychoanalytic phenomenology.* New Jersey: The Analytic Press.

Balint, M. (1965). *Primary love and psychoanalytic technique.* New York: Liveright.

Balint, M. (1968). *The basic fault.* London: Tavistock.

Bartholomew, K. (1990). Avoidance of intimacy: An attachment perspective. *Journal of Social and Personal Relationships, 7*, 147–178.

Chatham, P. (1985). *Treatment of the borderline personality.* New York: Jason Aronson.

Dutton, D. (1995). *The domestic assault of women.* Vancouver: University of British Columbia Press.

Greenberg, J., & Mitchell, S. (1983). *Object relations in psychoanalytic theory.* Cambridge: Harvard University Press.

Hamilton, G. (1988). *Self and others: Object relations theory in practice.* Northvale, NJ: Jason Aronson.

Harmon, R., Rosner, R., & Owens, H. (1995). Obsessional harassment and erotomania in a criminal court population. *Journal of Forensic Sciences, 40,* 188–196.

Horowitz, M. J. (1974). Stress response syndromes, character style and dynamic psychotherapy. *Archives of General Psychiatry, 31,* 768–781.

Jablonski v. United States, 712 F.2d 391 (9ᵗʰ Cir. 1983).

Kernberg, O. F. (1984). *Severe personality disorders: Psychotherapeutic strategies.* New Haven, CT: Yale University Press.

Kohut, H. (1971). *The analysis of the self.* New York: International Universities Press.

Kohut, H. (1977). *The restoration of the self.* New York: International Universities Press.

Kohut, H. (1982). Introspection, empathy and the semi-circle of mental health. *International Journal of Psychoanalysis, 63,* 395–407.

Leonard v. Iowa, 491 N.W.2d 508 (Iowa Sup. Ct. 1992).

Leonard v. Latrobe Area Hospital, 625 A.2d 1228 (Pa. Sup. Ct. 1993).

Lipari v. Sears Roebuck, 497 F. Supp. 185 (D. Neb. 1980).

Meloy, J. R. (1988). *The psychopathic mind: Origins, dynamics and treatment.* Northvale, NJ: Jason Aronson.

Meloy, J. R. (1989). Unrequited love and the wish to kill: Diagnosis and treatment of borderline erotomania. *Bulletin of the Menninger Clinic, 53,* 477–492.

Meloy, J. R. (1992). *Violent attachments.* Northvale, NJ: Jason Aronson.

Meloy, J. R. (1996). Stalking (obsessional following): A review of some preliminary studies. *Aggression and Violent Behavior, 1,* 147–162.

Meloy, J. R., & Gothard, S. (1995). Demographic and clinical comparison of obsessional followers and offenders with mental disorders. *American Journal of Psychiatry, 152,* 258–263.

Meyers, J., & Meloy, J. R. (1994). Discussion of "a comparative study of erotomanic and obsessional subjects in a forensic sample" [Letter to the editor]. *Journal of Forensic Sciences, 39,* 906–907.

Mills, M. (1984). The so-called duty to warn: The psychotherapeutic duty to protect third parties from patients' violent acts. *Behavioral Sciences and the Law, 2,* 237–258.

Mills, M. J., & Beck, J. C. (1985). The Tarasoff case. In J. C. Beck (Ed.), *The potentially violent patient and the Tarasoff decision in psychiatric practice* (pp. 2–7). Washington, DC: American Psychiatric Association Press.

Mills, M. J., Sullivan, G., & Eth, S. (1987). Protecting third parties: A decade after Tarasoff. *American Journal of Psychiatry, 144,* 68–74.

Monahan, J. (1993). Limiting therapist exposure to Tarasoff liability: Guidelines for risk containment. *American Psychologist, 48*(3), 242–250.

Monahan, J., & Steadman, H. J. (1994). *Violence and mental disorder: Developments in risk assessment.* Chicago: University of Chicago Press.

Mullen, P., & Pathé, M. (1994). Stalking and the pathologies of love. *Australian and New Zealand Journal of Psychiatry, 28,* 469–477.

Myers, C. J. (1986). The legal perils of psychotherapeutic practice: The farther reaches of the duty to warn. In L. Everstine & D. S. Everstine (Eds.), *Psychotherapy and the law* (pp. 223–247). New York: Grune and Stratton.

Peck v. Counseling Service of Addison County, 499 A.2d 422 (Vt. 1985).

People v. Poddar, 103 Cal. Rptr. 84 (1972).

People v. Poddar, 518 P.2d 350 (Cal. Sup. Ct. 1974).

Pruyser, P. W. (1979). *The psychological examination.* New York: International Universities Press.

Revitch, E., & Schlesinger, L. B. (1981). *The psychopathology of homicide.* Springfield, IL: Charles C. Thomas.

Satten, J., Menninger, K., & Mayman M. (1960). Murder without apparent motive: A study in personality disintegration. *American Journal of Psychiatry, 117,* 48–53.

Schuster v. Altenberg, 424 N.W.2d 159 (Wisc Ct. 1988).

Stone, A. A. (1984). *Law, psychiatry and morality.* Washington, DC: American Psychiatric Press.

Tarasoff v. Regents of the University of California, 108 Cal. Rptr. 878 (1973).

Tarasoff v. Regents of the University of California, 529 P.2d 553 (Cal. 1974).

Tarasoff v. Regents of the University of California, reargued 17 Cal.3d 425, 551 P.2d 334, 131 Cal.Rptr. 33 (1976).

Twemlow, S., & Gabbard, G. (1989). The lovesick therapist. In G. Gabbard (Ed.), *Sexual exploitation in professional relationships* (pp. 71–87). Washington, DC: American Psychiatric Press.

VandeCreek, L., & Knapp, S. (1993). *Tarasoff and beyond: Legal and clinical considerations in the treatment of life-endangering patients.* Florida: Professional Resource Exchange.

Wertham, F. (1937). The catathymic crises: A clinical entity. *Archives of Neurology and Psychiatry, 37,* 974–977.

Winslade, W. J. (1981). Psychotherapeutic discretion and judicial decision: A case of enigmatic justice. In S. F. Spicker, J. M. Healey, Jr., & H. T. Englehardt, Jr. (Eds.), *The law–medicine relation: A philosophical exploration* (pp. 139–157). Boston: D. Reidel.

Winslade, W. J., & Ross, J. W. (1983). *The insanity plea.* New York: Charles Scribner's Sons.

Zona, M., Sharma, K., & Lane, J. (1993). A comparative study of erotomanic and obsessional subjects in a forensic sample. *Journal of Forensic Sciences, 38,* 894–903.

CHAPTER 14

Applying Functional Analysis to Stalking Behavior

Darrah Westrup, M.A.

This chapter applies an assessment technology, functional analysis, to stalking behavior. This approach is suggested as a means to gather information that might be of service to law enforcement officials, mental health professionals, stalking victims, and others who contend with stalking. However, functional analysis is representative of, and indistinguishable from, the behavioral approach to understanding behavior in general. This chapter therefore indirectly reflects a broad behavioral perspective of stalking behavior, beginning with a proposed behavioral definition. A critical commentary of the literature on stalking is also provided, with emphasis on the practical utility of these efforts. Because functional analysis is an approach based on the principles of behavior analysis, a basic background in these principles from which to view the approach is furnished, along with a general guideline for conducting a functional analysis. In the final section, functional analysis is retrospectively applied to a real stalking situation in order to demonstrate this procedure.

DEFINITION OF STALKING

There is a conspicuous lack of agreement among definitions of "stalking" in the literature (Westrup & Fremouw, in press). Furthermore, many definitions are problematic for reasons explained below. This confusion obstructs meaningful interpretation of the literature and impedes practical communication efforts among academic, public, law enforcement, and legal communities. Scientific progress in

The Psychology of Stalking: Clinical and Forensic Perspectives

understanding stalking must begin with consensus on a description of what is meant by this term.

There are two general problems with definitions of stalking found in the literature. First, the term "stalking" does not differentiate between a general class of behaviors (that are limited only by the constraints of the stalker) and the specific act of following someone. For example, although the general public refers to several behaviors as stalking (e.g., telephoning, letter writing), stalking also properly refers to the act of stealthy pursuit, or tracking, that can occur in a stalking situation as well as in noncriminal situations (DeVinne et al., 1982; Neufeldt et al., 1988). Perhaps it is for this reason that researchers have introduced new terms, such as "obsessional following" (Meloy & Gothard, 1995), to denote the class of behaviors that are generally considered stalking. However, these alternative terms often suffer from the same problem of specificity. For example, obsessional following can refer to the general class of relevant behaviors (e.g., letter writing, telephoning, etc.), but can also be applied to a specific act (i.e., literally following) within this class. The second general problem with current stalking definitions concerns the use of the word "obsessional." Obsessions have been traditionally viewed as being unwanted or intrusive thoughts (American Psychiatric Association, 1994, *DSM-IV*). However, many authors either do not make this traditional distinction or they imply that obsessions are benign from the stalker's perspective. For example, Zona, Sharma, and Lane (1993) stated that an obsessional stalker is one who has ". . . persistent ideas, thoughts, impulses, or images that result inevitably in some act in relation to the victim" (p. 896), and Harmon, Rosner, and Owens (1995) and Meloy (1996) used the term in reference to the stalker's preoccupation with the target. In addition to the potential for idiosyncratic interpretation, this definition of stalking implies that obsessions *cause* stalking behavior, which teeters dangerously close to circular reasoning (i.e., someone stalks because of obsessions, which are evident because only an obsessed person would stalk). Although constructs must often be employed at the level of explanation, this is problematic at the level of definition. Abstract definitions run the risk of being interpreted differently depending on one's perspective. Consider the evolution of the *Diagnostic and Statistical Manual of Mental Disorders, Fourth Edition* (American Psychiatric Association, 1994). Beginning with publication of the third edition in 1980, the definitions of diagnoses included in the manual have become increasingly explicit. This occurred in response to the poor reliability and lack of interclinician agreement that resulted from imprecise diagnostic criteria (APA, 1994). The study of stalking behavior will similarly advance from a clear definition and precise inclusion criteria.

In response to the arguments raised above, the following definition is proposed: "Stalking behavior" is defined as one or more of a constellation of behaviors that (a) are directed repeatedly toward a specific individual (the "target"), (b) are experienced by the target as unwelcome and intrusive, and (c) are reported to trigger fear or concern in the target. The proposed definition retains the term "stalking" as a global descriptor of the behavior that is persistently used by the general public. The word "behavior" also helps underscore that the term refers to a class of behaviors. This definition leaves open-ended the potential behaviors involved (i.e., telephoning, following, letter writing), yet assists classification of stalking behaviors based on the criteria. A stalker is someone who engages in behaviors meeting these criteria (Westrup & Fremouw, in press).

RESEARCH COMMENTARY

Research on stalking behavior is actually at an early stage. The work done thus far is typical of that done in an emerging area: necessarily broad, descriptive, and hypothesis generating rather than hypothesis testing. It is appropriate that critical reviews of work done to date evaluate the general trends as well as specific findings. In other words, in a developing area of study, it is as important to evaluate the merit of the questions being asked as it is to examine the answers that are obtained. Valid questions are the hallmark of advanced understanding. The purpose of this section is to provide a brief critical commentary on the stalking behavior literature with emphasis on the basic utility of these studies (see Meloy [1996] and Westrup and Fremouw [in press] for more detailed reviews).

Much of the research conducted thus far has focused on examining particular characteristics of stalkers. This has typically been done by between-group comparisons (i.e., stalkers and other offenders) or by within-group comparisons (i.e., erotomanic vs. nonerotomanic) in order to determine types or categories of stalkers. Presumably (because most authors do not explicitly state this), the overall objective is to discern distinguishing features of stalkers (i.e., presence of a particular mental disorder, previous criminal history, education level), that might indicate (a) who stalks, (b) who is likely to stalk, (c) why someone stalks, (d) which stalkers are most dangerous, and (e) how to effectively intervene. Whether any or all of these practical objectives have been attained is one consideration, and another is whether these objectives are *possible* given the approaches taken.

To date, there are only seven empirical studies of stalking. Of these seven, four have been directed toward determining characteristics of people identified as stalkers (Harmon et al., 1995; Kienlen, Birmingham, Solberg, Regan, & Meloy, 1997; Meloy & Gothard, 1995; Zona et al., 1993). Although the information gathered from these efforts is substantial, it is important to first point out some consistent difficulties that restrict interpretation of the results generated. As previously noted, there is a lack of agreement in the literature regarding the terms and definitions used to refer to stalking. A second common problem occurred in studies that separated stalkers into groups based on some classification scheme (Harmon et al., 1995; Kienlen et al., 1997; Zona et al., 1993). In most cases, the criteria used to separate the groups were unclear or questionable, which makes interpretation of the findings difficult.

To demonstrate the problems that arise from problematic classification, consider the effort by Harmon et al. (1995). Forty-eight obsessional followers were separated according to the type of attachment (i.e., affectionate/amorous vs. angry/persecutory) between the stalker and target. However, as pointed out by the authors, the perceptions and emotions stalkers entertain toward their targets often change over time (Mullen & Pathé, 1994a; National Institute of Justice, 1993; De Becker, 1994). For example, a stalker who initially was infatuated with his target (placing him in the affectionate/amorous group) may become vindictive (placing him in the angry/persecutory group) as he is repeatedly rebuffed.

As another example, Zona et al. (1993) separated 74 stalkers into three groups, (a) erotomanic, (b) love obsessional, and (c) simple obsessional, based on their "quality of obsession" (p. 896). The authors rightly attempted to provide clear operational definitions of a vague and difficult to interpret construct (i.e., "quality of obsession"), but also engendered some difficulties as a result. For example, membership between the erotomanic and the love obsessional groups rested on whether the stalker believed an actual relationship existed with the target, but there has been ongoing controversy as to whether the belief in an actual relationship should be the cardinal criterion of erotomania (Mullen & Pathé, 1994a,b; Seeman, 1978; Segal, 1989). In addition, the criterion between simple obsessionals and other subjects was whether a prior relationship (as judged by the authors) had existed between the stalker and target, without distinguishing depth or type of relationship. The prior relationship group not only included former intimates, but also included cases where the stalker and target were mere acquaintances (i.e., neighbors). Someone stalking an ex-spouse could be in the same group as someone stalking an employer, for example, but their obsessions and behaviors could be quite dissimilar. Differences among the three groups are therefore difficult to interpret meaningfully.

Kienlen et al. (1997) separated stalkers into those with psychotic and nonpsychotic views of reality. This is a more useful distinction, as it avoids the necessity of making fine distinctions between diagnoses, and the presence of psychosis is more easily determined. However, because this was a retrospective archival study, the validity of this determination of psychosis is clouded. Also, it is not exactly clear from their report what criteria were used to arrive at this conclusion. A strength of this study is that it was (partially, at least) theory-driven. Specifically, information (i.e., psychosocial stressors prior to the stalking behavior, developmental difficulties) was gathered that appeared to support Meloy's theory of pathological attachment (1992). Unfortunately the absence of a control group or base rate information with which to cross-reference the results impedes their utility.

Meloy and Gothard (1995) sought to gain clinical information on "obsessional followers" (p. 258) by comparing a group of 20 obsessional followers with 30 other criminal offenders diagnosed with mental disorders. Although no differences were found in prevalence of Axis I disorders, a diagnosis of schizophrenia was significantly less common in the obsessional followers group. Obsessional followers were also significantly less likely to have a diagnosis of antisocial personality disorder. The fact that no one diagnosis was found to be particular to obsessional followers reflects, as they noted, the extreme heterogeneity of the stalking population. In line with the perspective taken in this critique, the question must be raised as to what is gained by ascertaining diagnoses of stalkers. Knowing that a stalker has bipolar disorder does not tell us *why* that individual is stalking; otherwise, all bipolar individuals would stalk.

These four studies sought to discern distinguishing features of stalkers by either (a) creating subsets of stalkers and comparing them, or (b) comparing stalkers with other populations. All four yielded information on stalkers that is detailed elsewhere (Meloy, 1996; Westrup & Fremouw, in press). The practical utility of the studies was obstructed by (a) the questions actually being asked, (b) the classification systems used, and/or (c) the diversity of the stalking population.

The final three of the seven studies focused more on stalking behavior per se than on determining characteristics of stalkers. Dietz et al. (1991a,b) conducted two correlational studies that explored the relationship between letter writing and subsequent approach behavior. An asset of these studies was that their goal, to ascertain whether certain letter characteristics could be associated with approaching the target, is of obvious benefit to those who deal with stalking behavior. In actuality the studies demonstrated the remarkable variety in both writers and their missives. It may be that the focus on topography (e.g., lined paper vs. plain, blue ink vs. red) is not a useful direction to take with a behavior that can manifest in literally limitless ways. The last study included in this review (Fremouw, Westrup, & Pennypacker, 1997) is an exploratory study that determined the prevalence of stalking behavior in a college population as well as its impact on stalking victims. This study demonstrated a surprising prevalence rate, but was limited in reliability by its source of data (victim self-report) and in generalizability by the fact that it dealt only with a college population. No information regarding why this behavior occurs was gained.

When considering the empirical work on stalking, two important and appropriate questions to ask are: "What have we learned overall?" and "Of what value is this information?" General descriptive information regarding those who engage in stalking behavior has been gathered, but *why* individuals stalk others has not been empirically examined. Efforts to predict, prevent, or treat this behavior have not been appreciably aided by these efforts. It is safe to say at this point that a different approach to the task is needed. Perhaps it is time to ask different questions. The remainder of this chapter is devoted to the functional analysis of stalking behavior, a method to determine the function of stalking behavior. This method, by asking a different question, gathers different data that may assist our efforts to understand stalking behavior.

FUNCTIONAL ANALYSIS

Functional analysis is derived from a behavior analytic approach to understanding behavior. It is a pragmatic approach to understanding behavior, as the focus is on predicting and controlling behavior by identifying variables that can (at least potentially) be manipulated to affect behavior (Baum & Heath, 1992; Skinner, 1953, 1977). Because functional analyses emphasize environmental variables and rely heavily on observable behavior when available, the conclusion has been drawn that unobservable responses (e.g., thoughts, feelings, physiological responses) are not of interest. This is an incorrect assumption. In fact, private events are viewed as real, physical events that may be included in a complete account of behavior (Baum & Heath, 1992; Skinner, 1953, 1977, 1981). Private events, however, are not viewed as causes of behavior. Instead, the goal of a functional analysis is to determine the *environmental* variables that are related to the private event. In other words, rather than assuming that a feeling (e.g., anger, jealousy) *caused* a subsequent behavior (e.g., vandalizing someone's home), a functional analysis would suggest that both the feeling and overt behavior were responses in a particular chain of events. The functional analysis would also indicate the environmental variables in this chain of events that were related to both the feeling and the subsequent behavior. Functional analyses do not attempt to completely explain behavior, rather, they simply assist the assessor to develop hypotheses as to what *controllable* factors are at work (Haynes & O'Brien, 1990).

Although the application of functional analysis has been explored extensively within some populations (e.g., people with developmental disabilities, chronic psychiatric populations), it has only recently been applied to more typically developed adults. It is therefore accurate to say that the clinical application of functional analyses is still under development (R. Hawkins, personal communication, October 27, 1997). Important questions remain to be answered, such as (a) how best to conduct a functional analysis, (b) how to implement treatment, and (c) how to validate empirically the clinical efficacy of the approach (Haynes & O'Brien, 1990; Sturmey, 1996). In its favor, functional analysis is based on general learning principles that have strong empirical support (Ferster, 1973; Haynes & O'Brien, 1990; Skinner, 1953, 1969, 1981; Sturmey, 1996).

Operant conditioning theory, first developed by Skinner (1953), forms the foundation of functional analysis. The three-term contingency—antecedent–behavior–consequence or "ABC" paradigm—used in functional analysis is credited to Skinner's work with operant conditioning. In essence, Skinner was able to demonstrate conclusively in a series of laboratory experiments that the frequency of a behavior could be controlled by manipulating environmental variables. He was further able to show that targeted behavior increased or decreased in a systematic and predictable fashion depending on the way reinforcement and punishment were arranged (the "reinforcement schedule"). Operant conditioning has subsequently been the subject of extensive examination, both in the laboratory (see any issue of *Journal of the Experimental Analysis of Behavior*) and in applied settings (see any issue of *Journal of Applied Behavior Analysis*).

PRINCIPLES OF FUNCTIONAL ANALYSIS

Functional analyses are used to (a) identify two sets of variables, those that precede a behavior (the "antecedents") and those that follow it (the "consequences"); and (b) identify the relation between antecedents, behaviors, and consequences. Antecedents are the events that "trigger" a particular behavior, but this trigger is only effective because of its relation to reinforcement. If a particular antecedent is associated with behavior that has been reinforced in the past, the behavior is more likely to occur again in the presence of that antecedent. This relation between a given behavior, antecedents, and consequences is called a functional relation. Therefore, the goal of a functional analysis is to identify functional relations at work with a given behavior.

A functional relation occurs when a contingent relation is observed between two or more variables, that is, when a change in one results in a change in the other (Haynes & O'Brien, 1990; Skinner, 1953). As an example, consider an employer who implements a new policy wherein employees are paid double for working overtime. If she subsequently notices an increase in overtime hours, she may be observing a functional relation between the extra pay and the hours worked. It cannot be said conclusively that the extra pay *causes* the employees to work longer, however. Rather, the change in work hours is contingent upon the pay increase. The fact is that many intervening variables (e.g., fear of losing one's job, wanting to stay out of the house, a history of being reinforced for working hard) might have influenced employees to work extra hours. This example illustrates two important features of functional relations: (a) They imply a contingent covariance as opposed to direct causality, and (b) the presence of one functional relation does not preclude the presence or impact of other functional relations potentially involved in a given behavior. For the purposes of this chapter the discussion that follows focuses only on these two aspects of functional relations. Many other important features of functional relations are nicely outlined in works such as Haynes and O'Brien (1990).

Reinforcement occurs when a stimulus (tangible or intangible) is delivered contingent upon a behavior that serves to maintain or increase that behavior. The stimulus can be something as concrete as an autographed photo from a stalker's victim, or as intangible as the fear in her voice at the other end of a telephone line. It should thus be apparent that a reinforcer is not defined structurally, but rather functionally—it must strengthen the behavior.

Reinforcement can be further broken down into two types, *positive* and *negative*. Positive reinforcement occurs when a stimulus, provided contingent to a behavior, serves to strengthen it, such as being paid a bonus to excel at work. Negative reinforcement strengthens a behavior by removing something aversive. The behavior of pushing a snooze button is negatively reinforced by removal of the incessant, annoying buzzing of the alarm. It may also be positively reinforced, if pushing snooze becomes more likely in the future because it gains a few more minutes of blessed sleep. Again, the distinguishing feature of reinforcement, positive or negative, is that it serves to strengthen a behavior, or makes its future occurrence more likely.

The manner in which reinforcement is related to a behavior, the "reinforcement schedule," has an important effect on the behavior. Beginning with Pavlov's work (1927), then Skinner's (1953, 1969) and countless subsequent studies, this phenomenon has been shown to be consistent and predictable. Behavior is further influenced by the rate at which the reinforcement occurs. The following example is often used to illustrate this phenomenon: Someone who has received a soda every time he inserts the correct change into a Coke machine will stop inserting money if he no longer receives a soda. However, that same individual may repeatedly insert money into a slot machine, even though he usually receives nothing in exchange. This precept, that behavior is more intractable when reinforcement is variable, is also a well-established behavioral principal and can be seen in many examples of human behavior. Variable reinforcement, for example, can explain why a woman might remain in an abusive relationship. The woman whose husband alternates between being tender and loving one day and abusive the next would be more compelled to remain in the relationship than would the woman who received only abusive treatment from her husband. Similarly, a stalker whose behavior is occasionally, even rarely, reinforced by the victim may stubbornly persist, even though his behavior is usually not reinforced (Meloy, 1996).

When a behavior is no longer reinforced, *extinction* occurs, that is, the behavior ceases. However, a phenomenon called an *extinction burst* can occur when behavior is initially no longer reinforced. Skinner first discovered in 1953 that when a behavior that has been reliably reinforced no longer results in a reinforcer, the behavior actually accelerates before ceasing altogether. For example, a child accustomed to getting a candy bar by pouting in the grocery store checkout line will escalate to a full-fledged tantrum when first told no. If the parent withstands the onslaught and refrains from rewarding this behavior, the pouting and the tantrums will no longer occur in that context.

Punishment occurs when a stimulus is delivered contingent to a behavior that subsequently weakens it or makes it less likely to occur in the future. Spanking a child for disobedience is an obvious example, as is arresting someone for committing a stalking crime. However, similar to a reinforcer, a punisher is defined solely upon its functional relation to the behavior. In other words, if arresting has no effect, or does not negatively correlate with a decrease in the criminal behavior, it is not a punisher of that behavior.

A functional analysis also considers those environmental setting events or cues prior to a behavior that are functionally related. Known as *antecedents,* these cues can be either proximal or distal, so long as they serve to evoke the behavior in question. The power of an antecedent to evoke a behavior depends on the historical relation between that antecedent and past consequences. That is to say, if an antecedent precedes a behavior that is reliably rewarded, the likelihood is increased that the behavior will be repeated in the presence of that antecedent. For example, if Bill typically "gives in" to a request when cajoled, and "Sam" does not, being in the presence of Bill is more likely to evoke cajoling than being in the presence of Sam. In this example, Bill is functioning as a "discriminant stimulus" for cajoling behavior.

CONDUCTING A FUNCTIONAL ANALYSIS

There is no gold standard functional analysis procedure. As pointed out by Haynes and O'Brien (1990), a standardized procedure can impose unnecessary constraints on determining functional relations. At the same time, an assessment protocol does help ensure that the complete range of important questions are asked. Because they share a common objective, most functional analysis procedures follow a similar protocol. The following has been drawn from O'Neil et al. (1990) and is intended only as a general guideline.

A logical place to begin is to select the targeted behavior. Factors to consider include: What behavior is most problematic, most amenable to change, and most dangerous? (See Hawkins [1986] for an excellent discussion on the selection of target behaviors.) An operational description of the behavior is needed so that it is described in specific, observable detail. Its topography must be assessed (i.e., what does the behavior look like, how is it enacted), as well as its course: for example, whether the behavior appears suddenly, or begins gradually and then escalates. The frequency and duration of the behavior must be determined. For example, does the stalker call nearly every day? Twice an hour? How long do the calls last? The intensity and severity of the behavior must be evaluated, such as determining when and if some calls are more obscene than others. Similarly, it is important to notice whether behaviors covary, or appear to be linked. For example, does the stalker typically phone the same day he or she was seen following the target?

Next, a functional analysis would consider the antecedents to the behavior. In what settings, or in response to what triggers, do they occur? At what time of day are they most likely? What time of day or night are they least likely? Where do the behaviors typically occur? At home? At work? At the grocery store? Where have they not occurred? O'Neil et al. (1990) pointed out the importance of looking at what they termed "social control," meaning that the behavior may be more or less likely to occur when the target is in the company of certain individuals (e.g., is there someone with whom the behaviors never occur?). Do there seem to be particular events that trigger the behavior, such as responding angrily or ignoring the stalker? The authors also suggest considering the following question: What would be the one thing you could do that would be most likely to make the undesirable behaviors occur? (p. 4).

Finally, consequences to the behavior must be assessed. How did people respond to the behavior? What usually happens when the behavior occurs? O'Neil et al. (1990) suggested examining what the individual, the stalker in this case, gains from the behavior and what he or she avoids by it. What is rewarding or aversive to one person might not be to another. For example, verbal disapproval from an authority figure is aversive to most people and they would work to avoid it. However, for some people (e.g., disgruntled employees) verbal disapproval from authority figures (e.g., supervisors, management) might actually be rewarding and increase stalking behavior. Aspects such as the amount of time between the stalking behavior and the consequence, how the target responds, are also important to consider.

APPLYING FUNCTIONAL ANALYSIS TO STALKING BEHAVIOR

A functional analysis of stalking behavior should generate hypotheses regarding effective intervention. "Intervention" refers to (a) efforts by stalking targets, law enforcers, consultants, etc., to diffuse a stalking situation, and (b) efforts by mental health professionals to treat those who engage in stalking behavior. Both objectives can be assisted by the information gained from this approach. Before a case is presented, two caveats are offered. First, the following is a real-life situation. It is presented because sufficient details are available to illustrate how a functional analysis might be done. In actuality a functional analysis was not formally conducted in this case and much important information was subsequently overlooked. Second, ways in which a stalking victim may reinforce stalking behavior are discussed. Inadvertently reinforcing a behavior is not the same as "causing" it, and it is certainly not the same as being responsible for it.

A woman ("Susan") who taught an undergraduate course found herself in a difficult situation with a female undergraduate. This student ("Jenny") had some difficulty in the course and began to visit Susan during office hours for individual assistance. Susan was friendly and supportive and did her best to allay Jenny's concerns about the course. This interaction continued for several weeks without incident, with the exception that when other students happened to also be present Jenny was noticeably quiet, almost sullen. Three lecture sessions before the semester was over, Jenny arrived early for class, and taking Susan aside, explained that she was having a "tough day." She told Susan that she had been banging her head against a wall in the bathroom. Further questioning by Susan revealed that Jenny occasionally did this when she was upset or nervous, and that she was currently receiving counseling for this behavior as well as for some other difficulties. Susan gently informed Jenny that head-banging was not appropriate behavior for her classroom, and that if Jenny felt she would be unable to refrain, she needed to leave the room. Susan then assured Jenny she would follow her as quickly as she could to make sure she was all right. At no surprise to the reader, Jenny did rush out of the classroom mid-lecture and began to run, head-down, into the walls of the hall just outside the classroom. Susan did follow her, managed to quiet her, and walked her outside to where Jenny's mother was waiting to drive her home.

This scene repeated itself next session, with Jenny again arriving before class to warn Susan of her impending actions. Susan reminded Jenny that head-banging was not appropriate classroom behavior, but added that if Jenny had to leave she would not follow her because she had a class to teach, it wasn't fair to the other students, and it seemed an inappropriate role for her. So, when Jenny abruptly left the classroom that day, Susan continued her lecture. Soon sounds of Jenny crashing against the other side of the classroom wall became audible, then more and more intense until they filled the classroom. Despite her fright, Susan continued her lecture, her students sitting silent and tense. Finally the banging ceased. Jenny stood sweating and clearly furious at the classroom door. Susan, however, simply continued her lecture and Jenny eventually left. The last and final class session, Jenny arrived for class on time, did not attempt to speak with Susan, and sat quietly throughout the final exam.

Soon after the semester's end, Susan received a letter from Jenny. The letter was friendly and upbeat, asking Susan whether she thought they could develop a friendship. Susan wrote an answering letter stating as carefully as she could that she did not feel she was the appropriate person for that role. She stated that Jenny seemed to be in a difficult and important place in her life, and that given Susan's hectic schedule, she could not in good conscience offer a friendship she was not able to support. She added that she wished Jenny well and hoped she would succeed in her personal and educational goals. Within days she received an angry, condemning letter from Jenny, to which she did not respond. She quickly received several more letters that she returned, unopened. After approximately 10 such letters, they stopped.

Susan then began to receive anonymous phone calls. She would answer the call only to hear quiet breathing, and would quickly hang up the phone in response. Eventually she noticed that the calls seemed to occur in the early evening hours, and she began to ignore the phone at those times. In fact, she unplugged her phone immediately after it began to ring. She later bought an answering machine and screened every call before answering it. After several weeks, the number of unidentified "hang-ups" on her machine decreased, finally stopping altogether. Although she never had any tangible evidence, Susan is certain her caller was Jenny.

The nadir occurred about 2 months after the semester had ended. On her way to answer a knock at her door, Susan glanced out a front window and saw Jenny standing on the front step. She froze. Jenny, who hadn't seen Susan inside, waited for a few minutes then eventually left. This was to occur four more times. Each time, Susan, now on her guard, saw her in advance and waited silently inside for her to leave. The fifth and final time Jenny came to her home, Susan's car was in the driveway rather than in the garage as usual, and the sound of her stereo floated out the open windows—in other words, she was clearly home. Jenny knocked and waited, knocked and waited, for approximately 20 minutes while Susan tensely waited. Eventually, a dejected Jenny walked away and Susan has not heard from her again.

This situation reveals many problem behaviors: Jenny's excessive seeking of Susan, her anxiety and methods of coping, her intrusive actions. The first task of a functional analysis is to determine the level of analysis to be conducted. For example, the analysis could focus on the repeated telephoning (telephoning being the behavior in the antecedent—behavior—consequence paradigm). In this case the analysis would be directed toward the antecedents and consequences of telephoning. Alternately, "intrusive behavior" could be the target behavior (with the functional analysis determining the antecedents and consequences of this behavioral repertoire). Technically, a functional analysis could be conducted on the *thought* to call, with the thought being the behavior, the antecedent being the stimulus that evoked the thought, and the consequence being the event subsequent to the thought that reinforced it (although a functional analysis of a thought is more difficult and may have less utility). Functional analyses can thus be conducted at a micro or macro level depending on the ultimate objective (Haynes & O'Brien, 1990; Hawkins, 1986). A law enforcer charged with ameliorating a stalking situation may be concerned with a particular stalking behavior, such as conducting surveillance, but a clinician may be concerned with the entire response class, or with one distorted thought process.

Susan's initial concern was the head banging, a salient and disturbing behavior that was both physically harmful to Jenny and quite disruptive. Even though it is not a stalking behavior per se, we begin our discussion with this behavior as it clearly illustrates the functional relations described in the previous section, and also is an important factor in the broader problem between Susan and Jenny. The steps of the functional analysis of Jenny's head-banging are numbered below.

1. *Identify the behavior:* In this instance, the target behavior is banging one's head against a wall by bending over and running into it headlong. Much information

is missing regarding the behavior's frequency, but we do know from her self-report that Jenny had done this several times in the past, some days more than others. Susan also reported that once started, Jenny would bang her head approximately 10–15 times per minute. Duration is difficult to determine, because the behavior was typically interrupted: Jenny told Susan that her therapist dealt with the behavior in therapy sessions by physically preventing her from hitting her head. However, when uninterrupted during the second incident, the behavior lasted approximately 5 minutes. We also know from Jenny's self-report and Susan's observation that the behavior varied in intensity. For example, the force used in the first incident was appreciably less than that in the second, and the second became more intense as it progressed. Further, Jenny had told Susan that she occasionally banged her head in the school bathroom "very softly" when feeling particularly anxious.

2. *Identify the antecedents to the behavior:* Here again, we are handicapped by the information inherently missing in this retrospective, indirect report. However, in Jenny's own words we know "tough days" signaled an occasion when she was more likely to bang her head. Tough days were apparently days that evoked feelings of anxiety and depression. We also know that she banged her head in Susan's presence, in her therapist's office, and in the school bathroom. Jenny had also told Susan that she had not banged her head in her other classes. It is important to note that despite Jenny's ongoing anxiety regarding Susan's class, this behavior appeared only near the semester's end.

3. *Identify the consequences to the behavior:* Both Susan and her therapist responded to Jenny's self-destructive behavior by attending to it and physically forcing her to stop. Jenny apparently had an ongoing tendency to bang her head during therapy sessions despite her therapist's response, and Jenny continued to disrupt Susan's class despite being told the behavior was inappropriate. The fact that the behavior continued is evidence that it was being reinforced in some manner. Susan also realized that the behavior occurred very soon after assuring Jenny she would attend to her. Determined that she would not encourage the behavior again (a hypothesis formed by a sort of natural functional analysis), Susan withheld her attention when the behavior next occurred. She then observed an escalation of the behavior (an extinction burst), and eventual cessation. The fact that the behavior decreased and did not occur during the final session supports the hypothesis that Jenny was engaging in the behavior to get positive attention from others.

4. *Consider several functions of the behavior:* That the function of Jenny's head-banging was to get attention from others is only one hypotheses of several. For example, the final exam may have served as a mediating variable. That is, it may have been more important to Jenny that she complete the exam than obtain attention for banging her head. Perhaps the final class did not occur on a "tough day." The omission of further data precludes having proof that the function of the behavior was attention-seeking. When Jenny banged her head in the bathroom,

she did so quietly in order that she not be discovered. By her own report, she found this alleviated tension, and she continued to engage in the behavior. This suggests that more than one function is being served by the behavior. That is, Jenny banged her head to relieve tension and anxiety, in which case the temporary relief she felt afterward served to negatively reinforce the behavior. She also engaged in the behavior to gain attention from other key figures, in which case the behavior was positively reinforced by Susan's and her therapist's solicitous attention. The premise that a behavior can serve more than one function has been well demonstrated (e.g., Carr, 1994; Day, Horner, & O'Neill, 1994; Iwata et al., 1982).

FUNCTIONAL ANALYSIS OF OTHER STALKING BEHAVIORS OF INTEREST

One of the most common stalking behaviors is that of repeatedly telephoning an unfortunate individual who does not welcome the calls (Fremouw et al., 1997; National Institute of Justice, 1993). The behavior's topography may look very similar across stalkers and situations, because there is one standard way of picking up and using a phone. However, the function of the behavior may vary significantly. For example, one individual may be calling to anger the target, another to seduce, another simply to relieve his or her own anxious feelings. A stalker may begin calling for one reason and as the situation progresses, end up calling for another.

A functional analysis of unwelcome telephoning might begin by assessing its frequency. Susan reported that she experienced two or three "episodes" of calls per week. An episode consisted of the initial call, and then several in quick succession after Susan would hang up. The duration of these calling episodes lasted up to 20 minutes, but this can't be fully determined as Susan would occasionally unplug the phone when such an episode began. They seemed to vary in intensity; that is, the first couple of times that Susan ignored the phone, it rang for quite awhile. However, as time went on and she continued to fail to respond, the caller would terminate the call more quickly. There were also fewer calls per episode over time, but again the exact course was obscured by the unplugging of the phone.

An examination of the antecedents to the behavior reveals the first anonymous call to Susan began approximately 3 weeks after the end of the semester, about 1 week after she responded to Jenny's letter. They also typically occurred in the early evening (between 6:00 and 8:00 p.m.), on office hour days. That is, Susan's office hours occurred on Tuesdays and Thursdays, from 2:00 to 4:00, and the calls would typically, but not always occur on Tuesday and Thursday evenings.

Susan responded to the calls fairly consistently. After her first "hello," she did not attempt to engage the caller in conversation. Nor did she speak to the caller. Rather, she simply hung up the phone. She also reported that she did not want the caller to know she was "getting to her," so she never slammed down the receiver in anger. Rather, she would quietly replace it in the cradle. Susan said that at times after a calling episode began, she would unplug the phone in order to assure herself that the caller was unable to intrude upon her. In other words, she felt that if she was only acting as though she was ignoring the phone, the caller was still succeeding in intruding upon her. Although she noticed receiving fewer calls, Susan acquired an answering machine and began to screen her calls as a matter of course. The unidentified "hang-ups" that she experienced may or may not have been her tormentor, but Susan stopped receiving them, and when she began to answer the phone again, there were no more silent callers.

An analysis of the calling behavior alone, though incomplete and based only on observations by the target, suggests some functional hypotheses. Answering the call appeared to have a functional relation to the calling behavior, because when Susan stopped responding the behavior "dropped out" (the calls eventually ceased). In addition, the caller did not continue to let the phone ring endlessly, most likely because this was never reinforced; once the episode began Susan never responded again, no matter how long the phone rang. The number of rings the unidentified caller allowed quickly decreased—Susan estimated that even though the phone rang more than 20 times after her very first hang-up, it rang perhaps five times each call thereafter.

Susan had formed her own hypotheses regarding the function of the calls: (a) the caller wanted some connection with her, and/or (b) the caller wanted to provoke her for some reason. In either case, she did not want the behavior to serve its purpose and so she ignored it as best she could. She never prolonged the encounters (i.e., she hung up immediately), did not leave the impression she was upset (did not slam down the receiver), and once she realized when the calls were likely to occur, she was careful not to answer the phone at those times. The fact that the frequency, intensity, and duration of the calls decreased indicated her hypotheses were correct.

The above example of telephoning behavior had at least one function: it gained Susan's attention. When the behavior did not serve its purpose it ceased, or was extinguished. Structurally similar behavior can have very different functions, and the triggers (antecedents) and maintaining factors (consequences) are unique to the situation and individual involved. The following example may help illustrate this point. A woman was tormented by incessant obscene calls from an anonymous caller. This woman responded to the calls somewhat erratically; that is, she would sometimes answer the phone, respond angrily to his obscenities, and slam down the receiver. He would then call again. In response the woman sometimes let the phone ring; at other times she eventually answered the call. As the calls progressed she became more fearful, and would plead with the caller to identify himself. Remembering that a target does not cause stalking behavior nor is she responsible for it, it can be hypothesized that this individual's responses were maintaining the calling behavior (by way of a variable response schedule) because it increased in frequency.

This latter case has an interesting conclusion. One evening, fed up with feeling victimized, the woman responded to the caller in similar fashion. She told him what she'd like to do to *him,* as crudely and lasciviously as she could manage. Her tormentor was silent and hung up the phone. Unfortunately, this was only a temporary victory, for he called again soon after. But the interaction had been informative. She now had a working hypothesis that the function of this caller's behavior was to discomfort or embarrass her, not to engage in a sexual conversation, or simply gain her attention, because he abandoned the call when her response no longer revealed embarrassment or discomfort. She then decided to respond in an antithetical manner and located a police whistle. The next time this man called she blew the whistle into the phone with all the strength she could muster. After months of torment, her whistle strategy vanquished the caller in two calls.

The power of an intermittent reinforcement schedule is seen by the fact that when this woman alternately responded to (reinforced) then ignored the calls, they increased in frequency. Her discomfort had a functional relation to the calling behavior. When she pleaded, or responded angrily, the caller remained on the line. When she responded in an assertive fashion, he abandoned the call. When she responded aggressively by blowing a whistle, not only was the function of the behavior unfulfilled, but the whistle functioned as a punisher (i.e., its loud shriek resulted in cessation of the calling). Both functional relations, that is, the relation between the behavior and reinforcer—her distressful response that was now with-held—and that between the whistle sound and decreased calling, resulted in the behavior's cessation.

Returning to our case of Susan, consistent ignoring or reinforcement of the telephone appeared to extinguish the calling behavior. In contrast, Susan reinforced Jenny's letter-writing by corresponding with her. Despite Susan's courteous yet direct request that Jenny not do so, Jenny continued to send letters. In fact, after Susan's first response, four or five letters arrived in quick succession, indicating that Susan's response reinforced the writer. However, when Susan no longer responded to the letters, that is, withheld reinforcement, they became less frequent, eventually ceasing altogether. A similar functional relation is seen vividly in Jenny's final attempt to engage Susan by visiting her at home. When Susan, clearly at home, did not answer her door, Jenny's visiting behavior was extinguished as well.

The discussion to this point has focused on problem behaviors using information gathered largely from the victim's own observations. A clinician treating a stalker, or a law enforcement officer interviewing a suspected stalker, has the added advantage of learning important details as to what triggers the stalking behavior. For example, a clinician treating the obscene caller described previously might determine that prior to calling, the individual felt angry and frustrated, and, that afterward, he experienced a reduction of tension. Although a good beginning, the analysis should not stop here because it is not possible to directly manipulate feelings. The functional analysis must identify the environmental variables that led to these feelings and to the calling behavior. Extending the analysis further, the clinician or officer might determine that the stalker was experiencing marital difficulties that were functionally related to his feelings of helplessness, rage, and frustration, all of which evoked the urge to call and distress a woman who could not defend herself. Each of these behaviors can be further broken down. For example, the behaviors known as "marital difficulties" are also composed of numerous "microlevel" variables (Haynes & O'Brien, 1990, p. 663). Regardless of the level of analysis, the resultant hypotheses would then direct intervention that, in turn, might address marital interactions, anger management, or stress reduction.

In the case of Susan and Jenny, Jenny's therapist could perform a functional analysis on each problem behavior. Or the behaviors could be viewed as being nested in a larger context that could also be functionally analyzed. In other words, the entire behavior constellation (i.e., the office visits, the head banging, letter writing, phone calling, and visiting) could be considered as the *B* in the ABC model. One might ask: What do these behaviors, as a whole, gain Jenny? From this perspective, the problem behaviors consist of Jenny inappropriately seeking Susan's attention. When Susan reinforced the behavior by attending to her, the course of the behavior appeared to escalate, both in intensity and in degree of intrusiveness. Jenny's seeking behavior began appropriately enough with the office visits, but when reinforced, soon escalated to disruptive behavior in class, unwelcome letters, anonymous phone calls, and home visits. Antecedents to the behavior appeared to be days that evoked anxious feelings. A thorough functional analysis would determine what it was about those days that evoked those feelings and would look for controllable variables, such as too much homework or interpersonal difficulties. Because her initial office visits were both negatively reinforced, via a reduction in anxiety, and positively reinforced, by gaining positive attention, they continued. In reinforcing Jenny, Susan became a *discriminant stimulus* for the attention-seeking behavior. That is, she increased the probability that it would occur in her presence. The seeking behavior then generalized to a *functionally equivalent behavior,* head-banging. This behavior was also negatively and positively reinforced, and served the same functions of anxiety reduction and gaining positive attention. Susan had become a discriminative stimulus, or signal, for two functionally equivalent behaviors; Jenny did not bang her head during her other classes. Similarly, office hour days functioned as discriminative stimuli, because Jenny would meet with Susan on those days. Office hour days then signaled days in which Jenny's seeking behavior would be reinforced, so that although the semester had ended, those days triggered behavior (telephoning) within the same response class.

Prior to the head-banging episode when Susan refused to attend to her, Jenny's behavior had been consistently reinforced. When her behavior was abruptly no longer reinforced, an extinction burst was the result (i.e., it dramatically increased in a burst before ceasing). A similar phenomenon occurred when Susan did not further respond to her letters; Jenny fired off several letters before stopping completely. Again, when Susan initially refused to answer the phone, the caller let the phone ring for an extreme number of times before finally terminating the call. The common denominator in the previous examples is that upon cessation of reinforcement, the behaviors escalated before ceasing completely.

The extinction burst phenomenon has interesting implications when the potential dangerousness of stalking behavior is considered. Even though it may be determined that a stalking target may be inadvertently reinforcing the behavior, removal of reinforcement may evoke an even more troubling response. It has been noted by several experts and stalking victims that a stalker "steps up" his or her intrusive behavior after the victim has made some move to foil the behavior (De Becker, 1994; National Institute of Justice, 1993). For example, it has been noted that the behavior of many stalkers seems to escalate after a restraining order has been obtained. Access to the victim or discriminative stimulus is denied, subsequently blocking the acquisition of reinforcement. The empirical data indicate that the continued absence of reinforcement would result in the behavior's cessation; however, the state of the current legal situation is such that a stalker's access to the victim is rarely blocked completely. Perhaps even more troubling are data that indicate the process of extinction can not only evoke a burst of responses, but may evoke *aggressive* responses. That is, the process of extinction itself is aversive, and can elicit aggressive behavior (Azrin, Hutchinson, & Hake, 1966). The disturbing implication of this research is that even if the previously reinforced behavior is not in itself aggressive, removal of reinforcement might evoke aggression. Perhaps extinction is not the best means to eliminate stalking behavior. Future amelioration of this behavior may depend on the mental health community providing effective treatment of stalkers and the legal community developing effective punishment of this behavior.

CONCLUSIONS

It is fairly easy to identify and examine the functional relations operating in the example of stalking behavior described in this chapter. Those who have contended with severely mentally disordered stalkers or who have endured protracted stalking may feel that functional analysis does not apply to their stalking situations. On the contrary, the influence of antecedent and consequence-contingent stimuli holds for all behavior, including that seen in psychiatric patients, those with developmental disabilities, and even in individuals without language. In fact, the bulk of the applied work in functional analysis is with psychiatric and developmentally disabled populations (Iwata et al., 1982; Nees, 1994; Scotti, McMorrow, & Trawitski, 1993; Scotti, Morris, McNeil, & Hawkins, 1996).

This chapter has introduced functional analysis as a way to examine stalking behavior. More than a method of gathering data, the approach assesses the *function* of behavior. The functional analysis of stalking behavior will thus help identify the factors that are evoking and maintaining the behavior, in turn guiding efforts to intervene.

This chapter, however, is incomplete. Incomplete because the reviews of stalking research and functional analysis were only cursory introductions to complex topics, to which many people have devoted much time and energy. Incomplete because so many questions remain to be answered. Incomplete also, because the application of functional analysis to stalking behavior seems promising, but not yet realized.

REFERENCES

American Psychiatric Association. (1994). *Diagnostic and statistical manual of mental disorders* (4th ed.). Washington, D.C.: Author.

Azrin, N., Hutchinson, R., & Hake, D. (1966). Extinction-induced aggression. *Journal of the Experimental Analysis of Behavior, 9,* 191–204.

Baum, W. M., & Heath, J. L. (1992). Behavioral explanations and intentional explanations in psychology [Special issue]. *American Psychologist, 47,* 1312–1317.

Carr, E. G. (1994). Emerging themes in the functional analysis of problem behavior. *Journal of Applied Behavior Analysis, 27,* 393–399.

Day, H. M., Horner, R. H., & O'Neill, R. E. (1994). Multiple functions of problem behaviors: Assessment and intervention. *Journal of Applied Behavior Analysis, 27,* 279–289.

De Becker, G. (1994, August). *Intervention decisions: The value of flexibility.* Paper presented at the CIA Threat Management Conference, Washington, D.C.

DeVinne, P. B., et al. (Eds). (1982). *The American heritage dictionary.* Boston: Houghton Mifflin Company.

Dietz, P. E., Matthews, D. B., Martell, D. A., Stewart, T. M., Hrouda, D. R. & Warren, J. (1991a). Threatening and otherwise inappropriate letters to members of the United States Congress. *Journal of Forensic Sciences, 36,* 1145–1468.

Dietz, P. E., Matthews, D. B., Van Duyne, C., Martell, D. A., Parry, C. D., Stewart, T., Warren, J., & Crowder, J. D. (1991b). Threatening and otherwise inappropriate letters to Hollywood celebrities. *Journal of Forensic Sciences, 36,* 185–209.

Ferster, C. B. (1973). A functional analysis of depression. *American Psychologist,* 857–870.

Fremouw, B., Westrup, D., & Pennypacker, J. (1997). Stalking on campus: The prevalence and strategies for coping with stalking. *J. Forensic Sciences, 42,* 664–667.

Goldfried, M. R., & Sprafkin, J. N. (1976). Behavioral personality assessment. In J. T. Spence, R. C. Carson, & J. W. Thibaut (Eds.), *Behavioral approaches to therapy.* Morristown, N.J.: General Learning Press.

Harmon, R. B., Rosner, R., & Owens, H. (1995). Obsessional harassment and erotomania in a criminal court population. *Journal of Forensic Sciences, 40,* 188–196.

Hawkins, R. P. (1986). Selection of target behaviors. In R. O. Nelson & S. C. Hayes (Eds.), *Conceptual foundations of behavioral assessment* (pp. 1–41). New York: Guilford Press.

Haynes, S. N., & O'Brien, W. H. (1990). Functional analysis in behavior therapy. *Clinical Psychology Review, 10,* 649–668.

Iwata, B. A., Dorsey, M. F., Slifer, K. J., Bauman, K. E., & Richman, G. S. (1982). Toward a functional analysis of self-injury. *Analysis and Intervention in Developmental Disabilities, 2,* 197–209.

Kienlen, K. K., Birmingham, D. L., Solberg, K. B., Regan, J. T., & Meloy, J. R. (1997). A comparative study of psychotic and nonpsychotic stalking. *Journal of the American Academy of Psychiatry and the Law, 25,* 317–334.

Meloy, J. R. (1989). Unrequited love and the wish to kill: The diagnosis and treatment of borderline erotomania. *Bulletin of the Menninger Clinic, 53,* 477–492.

Meloy, J. R. (1992). *Violent attachments.* Northvale, N.J.: Jason Aronson.

Meloy, J. R. (1996). Stalking (obsessional following): A review of some preliminary studies. *Aggression and Violent Behavior, 1,* 147–162.

Meloy, J. R., & Gothard, S. (1995). Demographic and clinical comparison of obsessional followers and offenders with mental disorders. *American Journal of Psychiatry, 152,* 258–263.

Mullen, P. E., & Pathé, M. (1994a). Stalking and the pathologies of love. *Australian and New Zealand Journal of Psychiatry, 28,* 469–477.

Mullen, P. E., & Pathé, M. (1994b). The pathological extensions of love. *British Journal of Psychiatry, 165,* 614–623.

National Institute of Justice. (1993). *Project to develop a model anti-stalking code for states.* Washington, D.C.: Author.

Nees, N. A. (Ed.). (1994). Functional analysis [Special issue]. *Journal of Applied Behavior Analysis, 22(2).*

Nelson, R. O., & Hayes, S. C. (1986). The nature of behavioral assessment. In R. O. Nelson & S. C. Hayes (Eds.), *Conceptual foundations of behavioral assessment* (pp. 1–41). New York: Guilford Press.

Neufeldt, V., et al. (Eds.). (1988). *Webster's new world dictionary.* New York: Simon & Schuster.

O'Neil, R. E., Horner, R. H., Albin, R. W., Storey, K., & Sprague, J. R. (1990). *Functional analysis of problem behavior: A practical assessment guide.* Sycamore, I.L.: Sycamore Publishing.

Pavlov, I. P. (1927). *Conditioned reflexes* (G. V. Anrep, Trans.). London: Oxford University Press.

Scotti, J. R., McMorrow, M. J., & Trawitski, A. L. (1993). Behavioral treatment of chronic psychiatric disorders: Publications, trends, and future directions. *Behavior Therapy, 24,* 527–550.

Scotti, J. R., Morris, T. L., McNeil, C. B., & Hawkins, R. P. (1996). DSM-IV and disorders of childhood: Can structural criteria be functional? *Journal of Consulting and Clinical Psychology, 64,* 1177–1191.

Seeman, M. V. (1978). Delusional loving. *Archives of General Psychiatry, 35,* 1265–1267.

Segal, J. H. (1989). Erotomania revisited: From Kraepelin to DSM-III-R. *American Journal of Psychiatry, 146,* 1261–1266.

Skinner, B. F. (1953). *Science and human behavior.* New York: The Free Press.

Skinner, B. F. (1969). *Contingencies of reinforcement.* New York: Appleton-Century-Crofts.

Skinner, B. F. (1977). Why I am not a cognitive psychologist. *Behaviorism, 5,* 1–10.

Skinner, B. F. (1981). Selection by consequences. *Science, 213,* 501–504.

Sturmey, P. (1996). *Functional analysis in clinical psychology.* New York: Wiley.

Westrup, D., & Fremouw, W. J. (in press). Stalking behavior: A literature review and suggested functional analytic assessment technology. *Aggression and Violent Behavior.*

Zona, M. A., Sharma, K. K., & Lane, J. (1993). A comparative study of erotomanic and obsessional subjects in a forensic sample. *Journal of Forensic Sciences, 38,* 894–903.

CHAPTER 15

Threat Management of Stalking Cases

Stephen G. White, Ph.D. and James S. Cawood, CPP

This chapter addresses the practical issues and methods of assessing and preventing violence in stalking cases. Our approach is that of a psychologist specializing in risk assessment and a security professional specializing in the use of investigative and security methods for preventing violence. We both consult on incident management strategies, particularly in corporate or work environments.

Other chapters in this volume have discussed psychodynamics, etiologies, and diagnostic issues. Our discussion of types or definitions of stalking, dynamics, or diagnoses pertains to risk assessment and violence management per se. We assume the readers are familiar with some of the considerable and growing literature on violence prediction research and actuarial predictors (e.g., Monahan, 1981; Wilson & Herrnstein, 1985; Monahan & Steadman, 1994) and important concepts such as base rates and true and false positives and negatives. Given the low base rates for violent behavior and the difficulty of prediction, the tasks in threat assessment and management are to sort out the large majority of cases that have a very low risk of violence and do not need intensive case management; identify the few cases that *pose* a high risk of violence and therefore justify the necessary, costly and/or disruptive measures to protect safety; and find appropriate and reasonable strategies for ongoing assessment and monitoring of the cases that fall in between these extremes, until the violent pathway of the subject is clear.

Various authors have pointed out that stalkers or obsessional followers are a diagnostically heterogeneous and complex group, more similar in what they do (Rudden, Sweeney, & Francis, 1990; Meloy, 1996). Relatively few obsessional

The Psychology of Stalking: Clinical and Forensic Perspectives

followers commit violence toward their targets or involved third parties; studies show homicide rates around 2%, but other forms of violence such as assault and battery vary from 3% to 36% (Meloy, 1996). Dietz reported that fewer than 5% of erotomanics are violent, based on studies of letters to celebrities and politicians (Dietz et al., 1991a,b). However, and bearing on the prediction of violence and threat management strategies, studies show that more than half of obsessional followers have criminal histories (Harmon, Rosner, & Owens, 1995; Mullen & Pathé, 1994; Meloy & Gothard, 1995) and as a group are more intelligent than other offenders, contributing to their resourcefulness and manipulativeness in their pursuit activities (Meloy & Gothard, 1995). Menzies, Fedoroff, Green, and Isaacson (1995) found that two factors predicting dangerousness in erotomanics were the presence of other antisocial behaviors and having more than one target victim. Kienlen, Birmingham, Solberg, O'Regan, and Meloy (1997), in a comparison of psychotic and nonpsychotic stalkers, found that psychotic subjects visited the victims' homes significantly more often than nonpsychotic subjects, yet nonpsychotic subjects made more verbal threats and acted out violently more often than psychotic subjects.

Violence potential needs to be considered in stalking cases, although the statistically much more likely scenario for the victims of these individuals is prolonged or recurring periods of stressful and fear-inducing harassment and intimidation.

Certain personality characteristics associated with obsessional following also overlap with those factors considered to be clinically relevant in assessing violence potential: borderline, histrionic, paranoid, psychopathic, and especially narcissistic disorders or traits. Meloy (1996) offered a psychodynamic formulation that attempts to explain the violent behavior of obsessional followers:

> The acting out of their obsession in pursuit, and in a few cases eventual violence, is likely due to a disturbance in their narcissistic economy. A real event, such as acute or chronic rejection, challenges the compensatory narcissistic fantasy that the obsessional follower is special, loved, idealized, admired, superior to, in some way linked, or destined to be with the object of pursuit. Disturbance of this narcissistic fantasy, imbued with both a sense of grandiosity and a feeling of pride, triggers feelings of shame or humiliation that are defended against with rage. (pp. 159–160)

Who then, from the threat management perspective, is likely to have this equilibrium sufficiently disturbed to act violently, and what is the evidence suggesting it in a given case?

The basic tools of threat management consist of assessment methods to determine the level of risk at certain times (e.g., interviews, background investigations, records reviews, evaluations, monitoring information sources) and interventions designed to prevent violence or minimize the likelihood of harm (e.g., target hardening or removal, protective orders, voluntary or involuntary treatments, law enforcement interviews or confrontations, arrest and detention, prosecution). In practice, appropriate security precautions are at times advisable before assessments or investigations are completed because of the need to ensure safety when the level of risk remains unknown. In addition, *not* intervening may also be the best decision choice to avoid a violent outcome in a given case (see, e.g., de Becker, 1994).

Thus a "cookbook" approach to cases is not advisable. Certain important case management issues should be recognized, however, by those presuming to predict and prevent stalking-related violence. These include:

1. The significance of individual subject and case context factors in predicting and/or preventing violence. Research-based actuarial predictors of violence are the starting point for any case, but must be looked at in the context of the unique descriptors and interacting factors in a given situation (see, e.g., Meloy, 1987; Dietz, 1989).

2. In the beginning of a case there is usually a considerable amount of pressure on the risk assessment specialist to predict how potentially and imminently dangerous a given situation is, most often with insufficient data to make such critical judgments (Limandri & Sheridan, 1995).

3. Responding to cases effectively means understanding the multiagency nature of managing violence potential in a social system with participants from different disciplines. Those involved include law enforcement agencies, the criminal justice system, mental health professionals, private attorneys and security specialists, victim advocacy resources, the victims themselves and their friends and allies, and certain vested third parties, such as employers of possible targets. Understanding the goals, perspectives, tools, and biases of these agencies or entities is important, as well as understanding how to communicate and collaborate on case issues and management. Teamwork is an ideal that the involved parties should strive for, to promote a shared view of a case, its level of seriousness, and timely communication regarding changes in behavior or actions.

4. Inherent in any question of predicting and/or preventing violence is what we refer to as "the intervention dilemma." Any active response (e.g., law enforcement "knock and talks," protective orders, involuntary hospitalization) intended to prevent violence can, in fact, have three possible outcomes: it may deter violence, have no effect on whether a given individual acts violently, or it can increase the possibility of violence. We are very concerned with whether an intervention may actually provoke a subject to feel humiliated or challenged and subsequently to act out. Law enforcement and the judicial system are obviously not able to control all potentially dangerous persons who are entitled, in their own right, to certain civil liberties.

Threat management is far from a science and far from perfect. Theories of intervention are debated among widely recognized practitioners (see for example, "Stalking in L.A.", *The New Yorker,* February 24 and March 3, 1997). The poles of the argument tend to be "come down hard and swift on them" (e.g., strictly enforced protective orders, arrest, imprisonment) versus "quietly disappear" (better to relocate since it is so hard to control a violence-inclined stalker). Not appreciating the very low base rates for violence and the high false positive rates, interveners can mistakenly judge their chosen interventions to have been successful because violence did not follow, when in fact, it would not have followed regardless of what was done (de Becker, 1994). For example, if we accept Meloy's (1996) data on the frequency of interpersonal violence (3–36 percent), then we can assume that 63–97 percent of cases will not evidence assault regardless of the intervention.

CASE STUDY

We offer a case description as a way to present the issues, methods, and strategic considerations that may present themselves in a workplace stalking case in which a concern for violence exists. The following information was initially presented to us by our client, the employer of the female victim of the subject described here, a stalker with a 10-year history of preoccupation and pursuit of this woman. Although we worked for the employer, we also assisted the primary target in various ways. We selected this particular case not because of its dramatic or sensational nature and outcome, but because it exemplifies the complexity of case material, system activities, and the need for assessors and case managers to recognize the point that the preferable response may be to *not* take direct action toward the subject. As the reader will note in this case, a great deal of activity and agency involvement had preceded our own participation.

An attractive 29-year-old female employee in a Southern California software development company approached her employer to notify them that she believed security should be increased at her worksite based on a series of contacts from a persistent, unwanted "admirer." Further data gathering by the employer's management revealed that the victim had known this individual from a period 10 years earlier when she had been the manager of a blues band. At first he had been a musician, and when he failed in that role, he was allowed by her to continue as a "roadie" to the group, helping with support tasks. This lasted until the band dissolved 4 years later, a period marked by his expressing his growing romantic interest in her, which she did not reciprocate. A pattern of unwelcome interest eventually emerged, the victim having now been pursued by this individual for more than 6 years through telephone calls, messages, letters, and direct contact at places she frequented, such as retail stores. He had allegedly made threats in the past to kill her and himself. There was no initial indication of his approaching her at her worksite, although he had called her there and also threatened to get her fired. He was unemployed and apparently receiving welfare payments.

The recent precipitating event leading to the victim's taking a more concerted action was that upon returning to her home one day after work, the subject was parked nearby. She drove away to avoid him and he followed. A "chase" ensued that lasted about 20 minutes. She eventually appeared to lose him and returned home. He then called her and stated, "Sorry to freak you out. I only wanted to talk to you." The next day the victim filed a temporary restraining order and hired a private investigator to serve it. The subject eluded being served several times until the investigator lured him to a restaurant, claiming to have a message from the victim. The investigator served the order to the subject in the restaurant parking lot, with the police standing by. The subject then threatened the investigator and the victim in the presence of the police, who searched his car and found no weapons. The subject did not appear for the hearing to make the order permanent. While attempting to avoid service of the permanent order, he was arrested on an outstanding warrant for a felony count for the cultivation and sale of marijuana. The victim, who had left town after the hearing, returned to find a stage prop from the old band on her front porch and two audio tapes of recently recorded long messages to her from the subject, apparently left there before his arrest. The subject was unable to make bail, but the private investigator learned he had made more threats while in jail. The victim then informed her employer of her situation. We were invited to assist with the case by the employer's legal counsel.

The first need in a case such as this is to obtain an initial impression as to whether an imminent risk requiring immediate security actions by the various parties exists. This goal must be accomplished in the context of becoming acquainted with and understanding the interests, priorities, resources, and emotional reactions of the various constituents affected by the case, that is, the victim and her employer representatives.

ENGAGEMENT AND INTAKE

This goal led us to conduct the following immediate steps:

1. Establish a working relationship with the employer–client management representatives. This allowed us to educate them and explain the nature of and steps in assessment, and the pros and cons of intervention options. It was important to define the boundaries between the employer's obligations to the victim and other employees and the victim's personal responsibility to manage her own plan for safety and/or prosecution of the subject.

2. Interview the victim for three purposes: (a) to collect data pertinent to the assessment of risk, such as the history of their relationship, a chronology of events, the presence of risk factors, and her own conscious or unwitting positive reinforcement of his pursuit or attack-related behaviors; (b) to assess her personal

response to her predicament vis à vis her motivation, capacity, and resourcefulness to engage in an informed strategy of response; and (c) to assess her understanding of the boundaries between her own and her employer's interests.

3. Conduct a security analysis with the following objectives: (a) to promptly assess the defensibility of the worksite and the victim's home; (b) to identify security system measures that could be introduced to enhance the protection of these areas; and (c) to address better protection of the victim during periods of travel or when visiting other various locations.

The employer understood the necessity of a multifaceted threat response plan and was willing to protect the victim's employment status and collaborate with her on a protection plan necessary for both parties at the worksite. They were significantly willing to review their own security measures and protocol as necessary. They also opted, at our recommendation, to have a complete background investigation conducted by us on the subject.

Although the major components of case management (interviews, background investigations, law enforcement liaison, and security measures) are discussed sequentially here, in practice they often are conducted simultaneously, resulting in a formulation of the risk posed by the case and a multifaceted response plan appropriate to the risk level and case context. A strategic issue in this case was being appropriately prepared for the release of the subject from jail when that occurred.

Evaluating whether someone poses a risk of violence involves attempting to answer specific questions that serve as guidelines in any inquiry. Various versions and discussions of the points to be covered in an inquiry or clinical evaluation of risk are available in the literature (see, e.g., Monahan, 1986; Meloy, 1987; Dietz, 1989; Campbell, 1995). Fein, Vossekuil, and Holden (1995) stressed the importance of seeking information about *attack-related* behaviors (e.g., expressed interest in, communication with or approaching potential targets, weapons practice, history of violence). The answers to these and other important assessment questions were the focus of our inquiry, and to some degree were provided by the victim in this case:

- What is the nature of the threat, the specific harm, or act?
- Where, when, by whom, and how would it be carried out?
- What does the subject want?
- What means does he have to act violently?
- How desperate does he appear?
- What is his motive(s)?: for example, jealousy, possessiveness, envy, revenge, sadism, pathologic need for attention, forgiveness, to be "understood" (or combinations of these)
- What consequences (if any) does the subject seem unwilling to pay or subject himself to in his quest?
- Is he moving toward or away from the target, or vacillating?

- What other life stressors are present for the subject and what evidence suggests how he copes with such stressors?
- What actuarial and clinical predictors of violence are present?

Additional information is provided by a background investigation, which we discuss below. Answering these questions leads to considering what responses and interventions would likely move the subject away from violence, or toward violence and against whom.

VICTIM INTERVIEWS

The victim agreed to interviews both by the security specialists, to ascertain the more obvious risk factors leading to decisions about immediate security steps to consider, and by the psychologist, to assess in more detail the history, individual psychodynamics and motivations, and interactional dynamics bearing on the question of risk prediction and management. Obviously there is considerable overlap in the areas of inquiry by these specialties, and the interviews are dependent as well on the individual experience and skills of the particular professionals. What we learned from the victim in our interviews was that she was at a point where she was clearly resolved to end this subject's interference with her life. She did not reveal any past affection for him nor feel sorry for him. However, she had tolerated a considerable amount of undesirable behavior intermittently over a period of years rather than attempting to definitively end any contact with him. The explanation for this seemed to be her own self-perception as "being tough" and not easily intimidated or likely to modify her lifestyle activities. The cyclical nature of the subject's stalking activities—there were long periods of no contact— also reinforced this attitude of hers. It was a long time before she believed she might be in danger.

We learned additional pertinent case facts from the victim:

- She had never dated nor had sexual relations with the subject, but had felt "sympathetic" toward him in the initial months of the band because of his isolated social life and apparent knack for evoking sympathy; he claimed to have had sex with only one woman, describing it as "traumatic" because he couldn't perform.
- A pattern emerged in his angering people for not performing his duties, apologizing profusely or appearing very hurt by her or others' reactions, and then being allowed to continue in his job. He was persistent in not taking "no" for an answer and was perceived to "wear people down" in this manner.
- A pertinent example of this was her discovery that he had, after being in the band for several months, tapped her phone. When she discovered this and confronted him he apologized profusely, leading her to relent and allow him to remain with the band.

- He was never observed to physically assault anyone, but had, while intoxicated, gotten angry and thrown things.
- He was known to trade handguns at local flea markets.
- After 3 years she finally terminated his employment. He expressed his desire to remain in contact and even to date, but she did not return this interest. Soon thereafter she began to spot him in stores she would frequent, and eventually realized he was following her.
- About 2 years later the victim was contacted by a female informant previously unknown to her. The informant told her that the subject's house contained a small sleeping area in one room with shackles nearby and pictures of the victim on the walls around the area.
- For approximately the next 3 years a pattern of contact emerged around holidays such as Thanksgiving, Christmas, Valentine's Day, and her birthday, consisting of increased phone calls, attempts to talk to her in public, or sightings of him by her. Then there would be no contact for several months. In the phone calls, sometimes as many as a dozen in one night, he would beg her to go out with him or see him. He would escalate to screaming, sometimes making threats, and then in the final calls apologize, but ask again if they could just meet and talk. Although she did not report any of this activity, she began to keep a journal and tapes of some of the messages.
- In what was the 7th year of knowing her he began to show up as a "badly dressed" woman and ask her how he looked.
- About the same time she consulted with a psychotherapist who advised her to stop all contact with him and not to react to him if he attempted contact.
- His apparently most serious threat occurred in the 10th year, approximately 8 months prior to the recent events. In a phone message he stated his "deep love" for her, but that he was also filled with "hurt, anger, and rage." He said, "I should be electronically monitored because I think it's a real danger I might come and track you down and fucking kill you in murder suicide. . . . A fucking restraining order ain't going to do jack shit. Because like I said, . . . if I'm going to do it I'm going to fucking do it. I've been so fucking miserable these last five years."
- Following another street encounter after this threat—he came up to her on the street wearing a dress, asked her how she was and stated he just wanted to talk—she screamed angrily. He stated, "I didn't mean to scare you and I would never hurt you. I only want to be friends." The victim went to the police who reviewed her journal and tapes and took the case to the district attorney for review.
- Several months later she noticed him sitting in his car in her neighborhood and somehow learned he was trying to move into her area. She located the potential landlord and persuaded him not to rent to the subject. The landlord then informed the subject that the apartment was already rented. The subject then left the victim a message stating that he believed she interfered, that he is being evicted from his current home, and that he knew that moving into her neighborhood would upset

her, "but maybe I should do it just to spite you." A few days later the chase incident occurred.

ASSESSMENT OF SUBJECT COMMUNICATIONS: THE TAPES

In the taped messages to the victim the subject revealed that this "will probably be my last and only opportunity to ever say anything to you ever again" because he expected to be served shortly with the restraining order. He stated she had a right to be upset about threats he had made, but that he was "venting my anger" out of frustration in not achieving "some kind of reconciliation . . . I would never hurt you . . . , It was always clear to me we were never going to be lovers . . . all I've wanted to all along here in my attempts to communicate with you is just to sit down and make peace with you and let you know that you didn't have anything to worry about and we could go on with our lives . . . Am I such a horrible person that you couldn't allow me some kind of closure with dignity?" He depicted the car chase incident as "just wanting to talk to you" and explained why he was looking for a dwelling in her neighborhood. "I wasn't chasing you . . . I was cutting over and you happened to take that side of the street to avoid me so you know like it just kind of pissed me off and I backed up and I was thinking about catching up with and saying, 'Look, relax. I'm not chasing you', but I know that would make things worse so I just took off. . . . I could have turned around and chased you . . . that's why I called later to tell you that I knew you must be totally freaked out that you thought I was chasing you. . . . Oh, God, I'm sorry . . ."

At the end of the first tape he states, "This is actually good-bye. This is my last communication with you. Good-bye." The second tape begins, "I'm sorry, I have a few more things to say." He then reveals that the process server was knocking on his door that morning but he didn't answer. "After I make this tape, and send it off to you I'll go ahead and let them serve me and then there won't be any more communications. I won't be able to." He then stated that she had exaggerated facts on the declaration attached to her restraining order, he really hadn't stalked her, and he hoped she would not have the order renewed. He expressed that someday, "even if it's five or ten years," she would call to say, "Let's get together for coffee, sit down and talk, and just for no other reason, just to cool the vibes."

The tone of the messages was somewhat plaintive and pleading, repetitively seeking forgiveness, not especially angry, and not explicitly threatening. Many of his points were repeated a number of times. As is characteristic of some of these individuals, they perceive and illogically explain their disturbing intrusions of others as attempts to reassure the victim they mean no harm and only want to be understood or forgiven: "I was chasing you to explain to you you have nothing to worry about." The conscious sentiment is to be friends. The unconscious psychodynamic is often retaliation for narcissistic wounding and (in the most serious cases) a wish to destroy the envied goodness in the victim and restore the idealized fantasy (Meloy, 1996). In the audiotape the subject offered his apparent reactions to being served with a protective order, which could then be compared to how he actually behaved as a measure of his psychopathology and risk.

The decision to obtain protective orders must take into account that there is little consistent evidence, but much anecdotal information and strong opinions, as to their effectiveness in preventing violence and under what circumstances. The majority of the domestic violence research studies do indicate a positive effect in protecting the victim and reducing violence risk (Meloy, Cowett, Parker, Hofland, & Friedland, 1997). In the individual case the best predictor of reaction to such an order is the subject's reaction to previous orders, if known. A presumed benefit to obtaining an order is that the case becomes official with law enforcement who now have the grounds for detention if the order is violated. An individual victim should be aware, however, of the importance of and commitment to reporting violations, as violations that have no aversive consequences for the subject serve only to increase his sense of empowerment and control. Again, as with other interventions, protection orders are not foolproof, and there are many cases of homicide, especially involving domestic violence, that show a history of multiple violations of protection orders prior to the violent conclusion.

BACKGROUND INVESTIGATION

Based on the established truth that the best predictor of future violence is past violence, a prompt and relevant background investigation is central to a credible assessment of violence risk. Investigative organizations specializing in this area should be able to provide the majority of their information, at least verbally, within 48 to 72 hours of the initial request. Relevant information is any that may provide insights into the individual's nature, his or her tendencies or patterns in dealing with life events, especially stressor situations, and reactions to those persons perceived as antagonists. Information of interest includes past violent behavior; the use or training in the use of weapons, including military service; criminal activity and civil judgments; substance use or abuse; past or current stressor events (divorce, death, births, poor finances, accidents or injuries, loss of employment, lawsuits, natural disasters, etc.) and the subject's reactions to these events.

For stalking cases, the scope of investigation should normally include a public records check of all states, counties, and municipalities of adult residence and employment. (See the Appendix for a list of the types of records that might be researched.) Juvenile records are normally sealed from public view. To facilitate such a public records search, the following information is helpful and available from interviewees or records:

- full name
- other names used (aliases)
- current or last known address
- social security number
- date of birth
- place of birth
- driver's license number
- name of spouse or significant other
- names of any past employers with dates of employment, locations, job descriptions and reasons for leaving, if known
- past addresses of residence and dates of residence

This information should be indexed against any newly acquired information to ascertain if there are conflicting dates of birth or social security numbers, and significant gaps in employment. The residence and work address information will be used to identify jurisdictions in which public records need to be checked. Should the investigators or assessment professionals have access to employment records, review of employment evaluations and records of disciplinary actions can provide insight into trends in the subject's work performance, attitude, and expectations, and reactions to authority figures, discipline, and limit setting. The subject's record of response to criticism may also reveal information about his psychological defenses, emotions, and thought patterns. Accelerated deterioration in work productivity could correlate with the preoccupation, mental and behavioral, that partially defines stalking.

Information concerning past or current treating mental health or other professionals, if legally obtainable, and access to these providers, is very beneficial in ascertaining the subject's mental status, physical condition, or use of medications. Victim safety must be weighed against the subject's privacy when considering initiating such contacts. In addition, some health professionals may feel obligated to notify their patients of any such contacts, risking incitement of the subject.

The background investigation of this subject revealed that he had no record of additional criminal convictions or civil actions against him other than the current activities discussed here, that is, the marijuana charges and the stalking-related violations. The police had revealed to the victim that there were no indications of weapons registration.

CASE AND RISK FORMULATION

Without a clinical evaluation, which we did not undertake in this case, there are limits to speculating about diagnostic formulations. But with the information we had, we felt that this subject, an obsessional follower (Meloy & Gothard, 1995), was organized at a borderline level of personality. Splitting was evident in his contrasting behaviors of love and idealization versus rage and devaluing. Since he never appeared to articulate that the victim loved him, he is not technically an erotomanic. However the masochism inherent in the erotomanic's pleasurable suffering of unrequited love seemed present in this case (Meloy, 1989). The subject had maintained his unrewarded affections for the victim over a decade, a very long period of time. His sense of suffering and misery permeated his communications. The evidence of the sleeping area with shackles and the victim's pictures posted close by suggested she held a place in the subject's infantile, dependent, and masturbatory fantasies. He seemed to fit Segal's (1989) description of the typical erotomanic as withdrawn, lonely, and underemployed. The preoccupation with an attractive, appealing target is the maladaptive, defensive response to this social condition, providing some solace to the subject.

We felt this subject posed a moderate to high risk of violence to the victim upon release from jail. This assessment was based on the presence of these identified initial risk factors:

- male
- direct verbal threats
- suicide threats
- anger and grandiosity
- likely personality disorder
- triangulation involving law enforcement and judicial system
- presence of depressive symptoms
- underemployment
- long-term preoccupation with the victim
- physical approaches toward the target in multiple locations
- stated sense of desperation to "resolve" his situation
- history of involvement with firearms: buying, selling, and carrying

Mitigating violence potential were:

- no violence in the 10 years of knowing the victim
- absence of known psychotic delusions or acute psychotic states
- no known abuse of alcohol or stimulants

We especially noted in this case the presence of specific threats, the capacity to carry them out, a history of proximity seeking by the subject, and little evidence of anything else important in his life. Interpreting whether threats of violence will lead to violence is a difficult and controversial area, with little definitive help available from research (Macdonald, 1968). The vast majority of threats are never acted on, and they must be interpreted in the context of all the other information available about a case, including the capacity, willingness, and readiness of an individual to be violent. Meloy (1996) found that approximately one-half of obsessional followers made threats to person or property, and one-fourth of this group acted on their threat. The best approach is to analyze a subject's history of threats and their relationship to his subsequent violence. "Threats may inhibit, disinhibit, or have no relationship to his actual violence in any one subject" (p. 158). In our case there was a continuing, but intermittent, pattern of threats over the years, peaking in angry outbursts, but no physical assaults or other violence toward the victim, or any known record of violence in the history of the subject. This was the most encouraging information in the case (although the absence of past violence does not at all mean someone could not be very dangerous). We also were aware that only recently had there been any serious legal consequences applied to the subject for his actions. He was now clearly involved with the judicial system and could directly experience the punishments it could deliver. His response to these "interventions" would be additional diagnostic and motivational information regarding his risk potential: Would he escalate or retreat?

INTERVENTION STRATEGY

Several areas of response can be undertaken, and they usually occur simultaneously. Besides the background investigation, these include law enforcement liaison and security measures.

Law Enforcement Liaison

Involving law enforcement agencies is necessary to assist in the assessment and resolution of many stalking cases, since they provide valuable resources to the victim. These include access to criminal history and weapons registration information and, of course, the ability to arrest and detain a subject.

The involvement of the victim with law enforcement, however, needs to be carefully managed for the safety of the victim and third parties. In an immediately violent or high-risk situation, the goals of law enforcement and the victim are very closely aligned around protecting the victim as a target. But in a nonurgent response situation, law enforcement's objectives and response may not be as closely allied with the goals or wishes of the victim. Although the reasons for this can be numerous, such as lack of special training for handling stalking cases, lack of resources, or different community or agency priorities or policies, one result to the victim can be increased endangerment due to the inaction or inappropriate action of public safety agencies. The most effective means for the victim to protect him- or herself from this result is to learn what policies and resources each law enforcement agency has to "risk manage" stalking cases and to develop close personal communications with specific law enforcement personnel—officers, detectives, and watch commanders—to discuss with them expectations for their assistance.

When we entered this case, the target had already engaged the services of a private investigator and contacted two law enforcement agencies, one in the county of the subject's residence, and the one responsible in her county of residence where she was pursuing stalking and phone harassment charges. She also had sought and obtained a restraining order. The victim had established considerable rapport with both law enforcement agencies and with the district attorney's office in the subject's county. This relationship had led these agencies to provide the victim with an apparently significant level of response (Orion, 1997).

If such is the case, a victim can establish a good working relationship with law enforcement and is more likely to be listened to, communicated with, and seen as a personal priority by individual officers. Given the case load of most law enforcement agencies, this is the most a victim can and should expect from them. It is important for victims to attempt to establish their contact at the command level, since these officers have the authority to instruct others as to case priorities and the response of different shifts.

Security Measures: The Victim

We learned from our security review that the victim had already taken a series of beneficial steps at her home. She had upgraded her security by adding deadbolts and other locking mechanisms, increased exterior lighting of her property, trimmed foliage around the residence to eliminate hiding places and increase the field of view from the house, and installed window coverings on all windows. She had established a second phone line allowing her answering machine to screen and record all calls from the subject to her original phone number. The chase incident had taught her the importance of being aware of all that was going on around her and who was close to her while in transit.

Security Measures: The Workplace

The worksite posed a number of security problems. It was a multitenant high-rise building with no systems designed for observing people in the immediate exterior areas or for tracking people inside the building. In addition, there were no panic buttons or devices to notify personnel of the presence of an unwanted intruder or danger. We consequently developed for the employer an incident response strategy for the workplace if the subject appeared there. This included increased observation of the city blocks surrounding the building and the ground floor lobby. Receptionists were trained in observation techniques and the use of an internal and law enforcement notification system and protocol for appearances by the subject. A plan was established to lock down the building and relocate and/ or evacuate the target and co-workers in extreme situations.

Any law enforcement response to the target's employer site, however, would average 8 to 10 minutes, more than enough time for a homicide to occur in these situations (see, e.g., Meloy, 1997a). Consequently, victims and their supporters need to be aware that they are solely responsible for their safety, particularly in the critical opening moments of a confrontation. This is why in more serious cases the target may consider a temporary or permanent relocation and change in her work location or employer.

The disruption to the victim by these measures should not be minimized. It is ultimately the victim's decision to balance his or her need for physical safety with the loss of familiar surroundings and relationships. This is an emotional issue and one that a mental health professional, appropriately knowledgable about stalking and risk factors, can help the victim work through her options (Meloy, 1997b).

Third parties such as employers, who must be concerned about everyone's safety, may face very serious dilemmas, strategically and legally, in trying to balance their various obligations to the targeted employee and the remainder of the work-force. A relatively new tool available to employers in California and being discussed in various other jurisdictions in the United States is a "corporate" restraining order (California Code of Civil Procedure Section 527.8). By providing employers with court orders prohibiting harassment of their employees *in general,* its advantage is not having the requirement of naming individual (target) complainants. However, as mentioned earlier, there are always pros and cons to the use of restraining orders. Before obtaining one, employers should consider the possibility of projecting themselves into a dyadic conflict that becomes triangulated. That is, they could now be perceived in the mind of the subject as protectors of a target or targets when they were not previously. This perception could stimulate the subject to attack employer representatives.

DISPOSITION OF SUBJECT

One month after being jailed the subject appeared in court and pled no contest to two felony counts for cultivating marijuana and possession for sale. He was sentenced to 90 days in the country jail and 2 years probation. Due to the victim's work with the district attorney, a "stay away" order was issued during sentencing protecting the victim from the subject, and the subject's compliance was made a mandatory requirement of probation. He was also ordered to obtain a mandatory psychological examination, enter a drug counseling program, register as a drug offender, and submit his person and property to search and seizure by any police officer or his probation officer (a Fourth Amendment waiver).

After his release from jail for drug charges, the law enforcement agency in the area of the victim's residence finally completed their case workup on a charge of terrorist threats (California Penal Code Section 422) and issued an arrest warrant. It took them 5 weeks to locate the subject and detain him. During this time the victim did not see or hear from the subject. He was convicted of the terrorist threats charge and placed on probation. The victim was kept informed of the case during the brief trial and was consulted concerning the terms and conditions of his probation. At the time of his release from jail she left town for a period of 3 days, but then chose to return.

DECISIONS ABOUT RECOMMENDING FURTHER INVOLVEMENT OR INTERVENTIONS

It was our decision not to recommend to the victim that she, or we on her behalf, advocate for a more vigorous prosecution of this subject, or attempt to increase his jail time. The district attorney had determined that the subject had done nothing to warrant more serious charges. If we had attempted to do so, we might have lost the cooperation we were getting from the criminal justice system. After our assessment work and the institution or support of the security precautions mentioned above, we only recommended that the situation be monitored for new information that would warrant concern.

Surveillance may be frequently contemplated by anxious targets and their professional resources, and it has a certain emotional appeal. However, it may create more risks than benefits in the vast majority of cases. Surveillance is costly, difficult to maintain, and more often detected than is generally understood. Once "made" by a subject, the pursuers are now perceived by him to be enmeshed in his life spaces and pursuits, paranoia is escalated, and reality-based concerns by a subject of aggression against him come to the fore (Meissner, 1978). A subject seriously considering violent action may be triggered to complete his goal upon discovering surveillance. It is perhaps most justified when the risk of violence appears imminent, yet situationally unpredictable, and there is a perceived lack of ability to otherwise control the subject's behavior through prompt law enforcement responses or target hardening. We did not recommend surveillance in this case.

In our follow-up with the victim 6 months later she indicated that she had had only one contact with the subject. They had encountered each other in a public place, she believed, by accident, and "both of us were scared" and immediately left the area in opposite directions. She was reminded to note the dates when the "stay away" order (resulting from the subject's criminal sentencing) and her civil restraining order would end in 3 years, and to be extra vigilant in the days and weeks following their expiration. She understood the need to take a long-term view of success regarding contacts by the subject, that his preoccupation existed for years although his contacts were intermittent, and that it would presumably take years to determine if he had lost interest in pursuing her.

RESPONDING TO THE MOST SERIOUS CASES

When the risk of violence appears high or imminent in a case, then it becomes necessary to pursue more serious options. These strategies are focused on creating physical barriers that prevent subject access to the target, as opposed to negative reinforcers for escalated risk behaviors, such as restraining orders. Examples are incarceration of the subject, relocation of the target, increasing security measures at the target's home or workplace, and armed personnel to protect the target. Also included are direct communication and coordination with prosecutors and law enforcement for additional support, including special units in municipal and state law enforcement agencies, and federal agencies such as the U.S. Postal Inspection Service, the FBI, or the Secret Service. The purpose here is to facilitate the apprehension of the subject and then to provide input that will influence his prosecution, sentencing, incarceration, and parole or release conditions. See Saunders (Chapter 2) for a more thorough discussion of the legal strategies in prosecuting stalking cases. In very serious cases target relocation, including a change of identity, may be the best safeguard if imprisonment or commitment cannot be effected or maintained.

The option of involuntary hospitalization, including mandatory pharmaco-therapy, should be considered for subjects with delusional, schizophrenic, or mood disorders (Roth, 1987; Monahan, 1993). Providing hospital admissions and treatment staff with all the data suggesting the subject is a "danger to others" may facilitate decisions to hold patients and should be assertively offered by outside professionals. The challenge with hospitalizations is to hold resistant patients long enough to effect a change in the course of their condition; if they do not continue to meet criteria for presenting an imminent risk to the community they will usually be released under most civil commitment laws. An ineffectual hospital stay can become another source of antagonism for a subject.

In summary, the focus of strategies for more serious cases is to physically control the subject to prevent harm to targets.

SUMMARY

Threat management is an imperfect art: costly, time-consuming, and necessary over extended periods of time in stalking cases. The task is to discern through assessment the less frequent high- or moderate-risk cases requiring intensive or ongoing case management from the large majority of low- or no-risk cases. Risk assessment tools are multidisciplinary and intended to provide corroborative and cross-validating sources of information: collateral interviews, background investigations, records reviews, clinical evaluations, and ongoing monitoring of information sources on a subject. Individual subject and context factors are combined with recognized actuarial predictors of violence to formulate case opinions of risk level and threat management strategies. Intervention tools include target removal, hardening, and security protection, protective and restraining orders, voluntary or involuntary treatments, law enforcement liaison, confrontations, arrest and detention, and prosecution. Threat management professionals should be aware of this intervention dilemma: any active response intended to prevent violence can have three possible outcomes: It may decrease, increase, or have no effect on whether or not a given individual acts violently.

Case management invariably involves a number of agencies with different perspectives, goals, and tools regarding violence prevention. These include law enforcement, the criminal justice system, mental health professionals, attorneys, private investigators and security professionals, and other victim-related resources. The interests of third parties, for example, employers or others who could become enmeshed in potential target pools, need to be considered. Teamwork and timely communication among the involved parties and professionals is a desirable case management goal. Cooperation should also reduce the likelihood of counterproductive inconsistencies in response strategies that subjects are prone to work to their advantage, whether their intention is to physically harm their victims or just to harass and manipulate them.

In conclusion, the threat management of stalking is a complex and potentially long-term endeavor. The tactics of each case are different but the strategy is the same: apply methods, derived from empirical data, that minimize or prevent violence.

APPENDIX[1]

SAMPLE LISTING OF INVESTIGATIVE RESOURCES FOR AN IN-DEPTH BACKGROUND ASSESSMENT INVESTIGATION

1. Criminal Court Records
   a. Municipal Court—Misdemeanors
   b. Superior Court—Felonies
   c. Federal District Court

[1]This appendix was originally prepared by author Cawood for use in the chapter titled, "A Plan for Threat Management," which has been published as Chapter 40-I, Appendix C, pp. C1–C2 in the *Protection of Assets Manual* by The Merritt Company, Santa Monica, CA (1-800-638-7597). Reprinted with permission.

2. Civil Court Records
   Civil court proceedings revolve around issues of commerce, damages, and family law.
   a. Small Claims
   b. Municipal Court
   c. Superior Court
   d. Federal District Court

3. County Clerk's Office
   This office maintains records of Fictitious Business Names (FBNs), birth, death, and marriage.

4. Correctional Records
   We have found that one of the quickest ways to ascertain if someone has been in prison is to contact the prison system and request information concerning the subject. The system is indexed by name and date of birth. The information provided will include date entered, jurisdiction sent from, correctional ID, prisons where housed, release date, and parole information. This information can be used to locate criminal history information in previously unknown jurisdictions.
   a. Department of Corrections (various states)
   b. Federal Bureau of Prisons

5. Law Enforcement Information
   Municipal, County, State, or Federal agencies or departments
   a. Incident Reports
   b. Police Contacts with Subject
   c. Outstanding Warrants
   d. Weapons Registration, if available

   Depending upon the state, this information may be found at the local, county, or state level.

6. Financial Records
   Each of these sources may hold various information concerning the subject's past and current financial transactions. Analysis of this information can provide insight into the subject's current financial status.
   a. Recorder's Office (or local equivalent)
      This county office holds records concerning grant deeds, deeds of trust, tax and other liens, abstract judgments, financial statements, consumer uniform commercial code filings (UCCs), and some death records.
   b. U.S. Bankruptcy Court
   c. State Board of Equalization
      Information can be obtained concerning business re-sale permits and reported sales figures at this agency.

d. Secretary of State

This office maintains records concerning officers and directors of corporations and their registered agents. Business Uniform Commercial Code (UCC) filings are also available here.

e. Department of Corporations (some states)

This department maintains detailed records concerning corporations, foreign corporations operating in the state, and registered limited partnerships.

f. Automated Credit Reports

These reports are available from three major nationwide services: Experian (formerly known as TRW), Equifax, and TransUnion. They are regulated by the Fair Credit Reporting Act (FCRA). Other than with the written permission of the consumer, there are a limited number of exemptions which can be used to obtain a credit report. The "employment" exemption normally used by business should *not* be used for workplace violence assessments because the credit reporting agencies will immediately notify the consumer of the request. This is not desirable.

7. Department of Motor Vehicles

a. Driver's Record Information

Information of value from this record includes verification of name, date of birth, and violations, which may include accidents and substance abuse charges. Residence address may be restricted, unless service of process is the intended use of the information.

b. Vehicle Registration

REFERENCES

Campbell, J. C. (Ed.). (1995). *Assessing dangerousness: Violence by sexual offenders, batterers, and child abusers.* Thousand Oaks, CA: Sage.

de Becker, G. (1994, June). *A white paper report—Intervention decisions—The value of flexibility.* Draft prepared for the attendees of the Threat Management Conference, Anaheim, CA.

Dietz, P. E. (1989). Defenses against dangerous people when arrest and commitment fail. In R. I. Simon (Ed.), *American Psychiatric Association review of clinical psychiatry and the law* (pp. 205–219). Washington, DC: American Psychiatric Press.

Dietz, P. E., Matthews, D., Van Duyne, C., Martell, D., Parry, C., Stewart, T., Warren, J., & Crowder, J. (1991a). Threatening and otherwise inappropriate letters to Hollywood celebrities. *Journal of Forensic Sciences, 36,* 185–209.

Dietz, P. E., Matthews, D., Martell, D., Stewart, T., Hrouda, D., & Warren, J. (1991b). Threatening and otherwise inappropriate letters to members of the United States Congress. *Journal of Forensic Sciences, 36,* 1445–1468.

Fein, R. A., Vossekuil, B., & Holden, G. A. (1995). Threat assessment: An approach to prevent targeted violence. In *National Institute of Justice: Research in action* (pp. 1–7). Washington, DC: U.S. Department of Justice.

Harmon, R., Rosner, R., & Owens, H. (1995). Obsessional harassment and erotomania in a criminal court population. *Journal of Forensic Sciences, 40,* 188–196.

Kienlen, K. K., Birmingham, D. L., Solberg, K. B., O'Regan, J. T., & Meloy, J. R. (1977). A comparative study of psychotic and nonpsychotic stalking. *Journal of the American Academy of Psychiatry and the Law. 25,* 317–334.

Limandri, B. J., & Sheridan, D. J. (1995). Prediction of intentional interpersonal violence: An introduction. In J. C. Campbell (Ed.), *Assessing dangerousness: Violence by sexual offenders, batterers, and child abusers* (pp. 1–19). Thousand Oaks, CA: Sage.

Macdonald, J. (1968). *Homicidal threats.* Springfield, IL: Charles C. Thomas.

Meissner, W. W. (1978). *The paranoid process.* New York: Jason Aronson.

Meloy, J. R. (1987). The prediction of violence in outpatient psychotherapy. *American Journal of Psychotherapy, 41,* 38–45.

Meloy, J. R. (1989). Unrequited love and the wish to kill: The diagnosis and treatment of borderline erotomania. *Bulletin of the Menninger Clinic, 53,* 477–492.

Meloy, J. R. (1996). Stalking (obsessional following): A review of some preliminary studies. *Aggression and Violent Behavior, 1,* 147–162.

Meloy, J. R. (1997a). Predatory violence during mass murder. *Journal of Forensic Sciences, 42,* 326–329.

Meloy, J. R. (1997b). The clinical risk management of stalking: "Someone is watching over me. . ." *American Journal of Psychotherapy, 51,* 174–184.

Meloy, J. R., & Gothard, S. (1995). Demographic and clinical comparison of obsessional followers and offenders with mental disorders. *American Journal of Psychiatry, 152,* 258–263.

Meloy, J. R., Cowett, P., Parker, S., Hofland, B., & Friedland, A. (1997). Do restraining orders restrain? *Proceedings of the American Academy of Forensic Sciences, 3,* 173.

Menzies, R., Fedoroff, J., Green, C., & Isaacson, K. (1995). Prediction of dangerous behavior in male erotomania. *British Journal of Psychiatry, 166,* 529–536.

Monahan, J. (1981). *The clinical prediction of violent behavior.* Washington, DC: U.S. Government Printing Office.

Monahan, J. (1986). Dangerous and violent behavior. *Occupational Medicine: State of the Art Reviews, 1,* 559–568.

Monahan, J. (1993). Limiting therapist exposure to Tarasoff liability: Guidelines for risk containment. *American Psychologist, 48,* 242–250.

Monahan, J., & Steadman, H. (Eds.) (1994). *Violence and mental disorder: Developments in risk assessment.* Chicago: University of Chicago Press.

Mullen, P., & Pathé, M. (1994). Stalking and the pathologies of love. *Australian and New Zealand Journal of Psychiatry, 28,* 469–477.

Orion, D. R. (1997). *I know you really love me.* New York: Macmillan.

Roth, L. H. (Ed.). (1987). *Clinical treatment of the violent person.* New York: Guilford Press.

Rudden, M., Sweeney, J., & Francis, A. (1990). Diagnosis and clinical course of erotomanic and other delusional patients. *American Journal of Psychiatry, 147,* 625–628.

Segal, J. (1989). Erotomania revisited: Kraepelin to DSM-IIIR. *American Journal of Psychiatry, 146,* 1261–1266.

Wilson, J., & Herrnstein, R. (1985). *Crime and human nature.* New York: Simon and Schuster.

INDEX

1890